Successful Societies
How Institutions and Culture Affect Health

Why are some types of societies more successful than others at promoting individual and collective well-being? Focusing on population health as an indicator of social success, this book opens up new perspectives on the ways in which social relations condition health and the public policies that address it. Based on four years of dialogue among scholars from diverse disciplines, it offers social epidemiologists broader views of the social determinants of health and social scientists a sense of the fascinating puzzles of population health. The chapters consider health inequalities in the developing, as well as developed, worlds. They locate their roots not only in economic resources, but in the social resources provided by the institutions and cultural repertoires constitutive of social relations. They examine the AIDS epidemic in Africa, the sources of the health gradient, the role of collective imaginaries, destigmatization strategies, and the historical basis for effective health policies.

Peter A. Hall is Krupp Foundation Professor of European Studies at Harvard University and Co-Director of the Successful Societies Program for the Canadian Institute for Advanced Research. He is the author of *Governing the Economy* (1986) and more than seventy articles in comparative political economy. He is an editor of many books, including *Changing France: The Politics that Markets Make* (2006), *Varieties of Capitalism: The Institutional Foundations of Comparative Advantage* (2001), and *The Political Power of Economic Ideas* (1989).

Michèle Lamont is Robert I. Goldman Professor of European Studies and Professor of Sociology and African and African American Studies at Harvard University and Co-Director of the Successful Societies Program. She is the author of *Money, Morals, and Manners* (1992); *The Dignity of Working Men* (2000); and *How Professors Think* (2009) and edited books such as *Cultivating Differences* (1992), *The Cultural Territories of Race* (1999), and *Rethinking Comparative Cultural Sociology* (2000). She served as Chair of the Council for European Studies from 2006 to 2009.

ary coop   ∽gy
to epidemiology, medical sociology, and political science and raises
fascinating questions about what makes societies work. By comparing countries, the volume forces us to challenge common modes of
reasoning. This book is a wonderful piece by a group of 'collaborative
public intellectuals.' It should be read all over the academia and by
the general public."

– Peter Gourevitch, University of California at San Diego

"Hall and Lamont have assembled an insightful, provocative, and
readable set of essays that challenge social scientists to consider the
puzzle of what makes a successful, healthy society. The answer is: there
is no one, universal answer; there are multiple models of well-being.
Together the volume builds a powerful argument for the significance
of culture. Economic resources and societal inequality are significant.
Yet so are those diverse cultural practices and structures that provide
meaning and a view of who am I, who are we, what is the good life,
what is possible, what is just, who counts, and who doesn't."

– Hazel Rose Markus, Stanford University

"With an exquisite sense of timing this remarkable collection of uni-
formly excellent essays by a dazzling array of social scientists, historians, and epidemiologists arrives after an almost 70-year-long wait for
a contemporary sequel to Karl Polanyi's paradigm-changing critique
of the 'standard of living' axiom that higher wages are enough to
improve the well-being of a society torn apart by unfettered laissez-
faire policies. Just as Polanyi demonstrated that the societal health of
a people depends on market-embedding institutional arrangements
and a cultural ethic of solidarity, so too *Successful Societies* represents
nothing less than a paradigm-shifting challenge to prevailing market
models of what counts as societal success and why some achieve this
more than others. Deploying an enormous range of empirical data,
the inspiration of thinkers from Amartya Sen to Pierre Bourdieu, and
a newly humanized understanding of societal success, the volume is
also an urgently needed normative manifesto for the indispensability
of egalitarian and inclusive 'social imaginaries' in tandem with institutional foundations for democratic participation."

– Margaret Somers, University of Michigan

Successful Societies

How Institutions and Culture Affect Health

Edited by

PETER A. HALL
Harvard University

MICHÈLE LAMONT
Harvard University

CAMBRIDGE
UNIVERSITY PRESS

CAMBRIDGE UNIVERSITY PRESS
Cambridge, New York, Melbourne, Madrid, Cape Town, Singapore,
São Paulo, Delhi, Dubai, Tokyo

Cambridge University Press
32 Avenue of the Americas, New York, NY 10013-2473, USA

www.cambridge.org
Information on this title: www.cambridge.org/9780521736305

First published 2009

Printed in the United States of America

A catalog record for this publication is available from the British Library.

Library of Congress Cataloging in Publication data
Successful societies : how institutions and culture affect health / edited by Peter A. Hall,
Michèle Lamont.
p. cm.
Includes bibliographical references and index.
ISBN 978-0-521-51660-0 (hardback) – ISBN 978-0-521-73630-5 (pbk.)
1. Social medicine. 2. Medical policy. I. Hall, Peter A., 1950–
II. Lamont, Michèle, 1957– III. Title.
RA418.S835 2009
362.1–dc22   2008044144

ISBN 978-0-521-51660-0 Hardback
ISBN 978-0-521-73630-5 Paperback

Contents

Contributors   *page* ix

Preface   xi

Introduction   1
Peter A. Hall and Michèle Lamont

1 Population Health and the Dynamics of Collective
   Development   23
   Clyde Hertzman and Arjumand Siddiqi

2 Social Interactions in Human Development: Pathways to
   Health and Capabilities   53
   Daniel P. Keating

3 Health, Social Relations, and Public Policy   82
   Peter A. Hall and Rosemary CR Taylor

4 Population Health and Development: An Institutional-
   Cultural Approach to Capability Expansion   104
   Peter Evans

5 Responding to AIDS in Sub-Saharan Africa: Culture,
   Institutions, and Health   128
   Ann Swidler

6 Responses to Racism, Health, and Social Inclusion as a
   Dimension of Successful Societies   151
   Michèle Lamont

7 Collective Imaginaries and Population Health: How
   Health Data Can Highlight Cultural History   169
   Gérard Bouchard

8 Making Sense of Contagion: Citizenship Regimes and
   Public Health in Victorian England   201
   Jane Jenson

9   The Multicultural Welfare State?   226
    Will Kymlicka

10 From State-Centrism to Neoliberalism: Macro-Historical
    Contexts of Population Health since World War II   254
    William H. Sewell, Jr.

    Bibliography   289
    Index   335

Contributors

Gérard Bouchard, member of the Royal Society of Canada and the Académie des lettres du Québec, is professor at the Université du Québec à Chicoutimi. Trained in sociology and history, he has spent more than twenty-five years conducting multidisciplinary research in various fields of population and social history. In 2007–8, he co-chaired with Charles Taylor a public consultation commission on inter-ethnic tensions in Québec.

Peter Evans is Professor of Sociology and Marjorie Meyer Eliaser Professor of International Studies at the University of California, Berkeley. His work on the comparative political economy of national development is exemplified by his 1995 book *Embedded Autonomy: States and Industrial Transformation*. He is now working on "counter-hegemonic globalization."

Peter A. Hall is Krupp Foundation Professor of European Studies at Harvard University and Co-Director of the Successful Societies Program for the Canadian Institute for Advanced Research. His books include *Varieties of Capitalism: The Institutional Foundations of Comparative Advantage* (2001).

Clyde Hertzman is a physician-epidemiologist, Director of the Human Early Learning Partnership (HELP), and Professor in the School of Population and Public Health at the University of British Columbia. He is a Fellow of the Canadian Institute for Advanced Research (CIFAR), a Canada Research Chair in Population Health and Human Development, and a Fellow of the Royal Society of Canada.

Jane Jenson holds the Canada Research Chair in Citizenship and Governance at the Université de Montréal, where she is professor of Political Science. Her research focuses on comparative social policy.

Daniel P. Keating is a developmental scientist working at the University of Michigan, as Professor of Psychology, Psychiatry, and Pediatrics; Research Professor at the Center for Human Growth and Development; and Faculty

Associate, Survey Research Center, Institute for Social Research. Most recently his work has focused on understanding the developmental mechanisms that are the causal underpinnings of social disparities in child health and development, including current planning and implementation of the U.S. National Children's Study.

Will Kymlicka is the Canada Research Chair in Political Philosophy at Queen's University and a visiting professor in the Nationalism Studies program at the Central European University in Budapest. His most recent book is *Multicultural Odysseys* (2008).

Michèle Lamont is Robert I. Goldman Professor of European Studies and Professor of Sociology and African and African American Studies at Harvard University and Co-Director of the Successful Societies Program. Her most recent book is *How Professors Think: Inside the Curious World of Academic Judgement* (2009).

William H. Sewell, Jr., is the Frank P. Hixon Distinguished Service Professor Emeritus of Political Science and History at the University of Chicago. His most recent book is *Logics of History: Social Theory and Social Transformation* (2005). He is currently working on the cultural consequences of early capitalist development in eighteenth-century France.

Arjumand Siddiqi is a social epidemiologist. She is Assistant Professor in the Gillings School of Global Public Health at the University of North Carolina, Chapel Hill; a Faculty Fellow at the Carolina Population Center; and a Junior Fellow of the Canadian Institute for Advanced Research. She is interested in societal determinants of inequities in health and human development.

Ann Swidler is Professor of Sociology at the University of California, Berkeley. Her most recent book is *Talk of Love: How Culture Matters* (2001). She is currently studying cultural and institutional responses to the AIDS epidemic in sub-Saharan Africa.

Rosemary CR Taylor is Associate Professor of Sociology and Community Health at Tufts University. Her current research explores the response of societies and their governments to health threats perceived to accompany people and products across increasingly open national borders.

Preface

This book is the result of an encounter between a heterogeneous group of social scientists and the Canadian Institute for Advanced Research (CIFAR). This innovative research organization has a well-established practice of supporting the work of researchers over several years so that they can engage in interdisciplinary exploration of new and important topics. Unlike other funding organizations, CIFAR gives its researchers carte blanche. It does not require a predefined plan with clear deliverables. It recognizes the open-ended nature of the research process and aims to facilitate and empower it. This highly original approach often leads to unexpected results.

In 2002, some of us were contacted by CIFAR and asked to come together to think about what defines successful societies and the social conditions that sustain them. After supporting research teams in the fields of population health and human development for a decade, CIFAR was turning its efforts in a new direction to consider a wider range of social factors affecting population health. It called upon us to bring to the table the analytical tools we had deployed in our respective research on a range of topics, including the impact of institutions and cultural frameworks on social relations. Thus an interdisciplinary team that included sociologists, political scientists, a historian, an epidemiologist, and a psychologist came together. We met several times a year in various locations to exchange papers, to learn from each others' work, and to interact with other scholars. From this experience emerged a common definition of the problems we wished to consider together.

Our joint effort began in January 2003 with a first meeting at the Center for Advanced Studies in the Behavioral Sciences in Palo Alto, California. We debated at length the meaning of "successful societies" and whether one could use the term while avoiding ethnocentrism. We agreed that health outcomes (low infant mortality, high life expectancy) are useful universal indicators of successful societies. We also agreed that our efforts should be concerned with "health plus," that is, with the wider correlates of positive health outcomes, such as greater equality, social inclusion, and democratic participation. We spent the following years analyzing how various aspects of social life might contribute to such outcomes. We developed empirical projects that build directly on a joint cognitive platform. This book is the product of the first four years of our collaboration, which is still ongoing.

At the outset, none of us claimed ownership of the term "successful societies." Yet, slowly, we made it ours and attached to it the questions that became our common agenda. Exchange was possible because we interacted pragmatically around the concept of a successful society, while maintaining purposefully a certain ambiguity about the terms of the collaboration, including the full meaning of "successful societies." We developed a complementary understanding of the contexts that sustain such societies. A complex picture emerges when the topics we study are considered in juxtaposition to one another.

Now the time has come to offer the product of our joint endeavors to the informed public and the critical eyes of our colleagues. We hope that the book will be read by a wide range of readers. Our goal is to generate new dialogues and to create new bridges between fields. *Alea jacta est* ...

We are most grateful to the Canadian Institute for Advanced Research for the generous support that made our collaboration possible. We express our great appreciation to Chaviva Hosek, president of CIFAR, for her intellectual vision and her continuing engagement with our work. We also thank Penny Codding for her wise guidance, Sue Schenk for her constant help as the project developed, and Susan Leclaire for the many ways in which she facilitated our work. The production of the book would not have been possible without the technical assistance of Heather Latham and Joe Cook, whom we gratefully acknowledge.

Within the Successful Societies Program, we have benefited enormously from continuous input from the members of our advisory committee, many of whom faithfully attended most of our meetings: Suzanne Berger, Natalie Zemon Davis, Danielle Juteau, Richard Simeon, and Wolfgang Streek, and in particular, Jonathan Arac, the chair of this committee. Our final formulations were improved by the comments of several new members joining the program: James Dunn, Ron Levi, and Leanne Son-Hing.

Finally, we thank the colleagues who took time to offer insightful comments on the book manuscript: Blair Wheaton, John Hagan, and the dedicated members of the program's review committee, Marcel Fournier, Peter Gourevitch, Kathy Newman, Claus Offe, Stephen Toope, and Leonard Syme, its chair. During the years when we were working with these ideas, dozens of scholars took the time and trouble to present their work at meetings of this program. Our conversations with them were deeply stimulating and are reflected in many ways in the pages of this book. We dedicate the book to these scholars and to the power of intensive interdisciplinary exchange.

Introduction

Peter A. Hall and Michèle Lamont

Across time and space, the social fabric is woven differently. How do differences among societies affect the well-being of those who live in them? Are some types of societies more successful than others at promoting individual lives and the collective development of the community? How might the character of a society have such effects, and how are such societies built? These are large questions of classic interest to the social theorists of modernity, such as Comte, Tocqueville, Durkheim, Weber, and Marx, with a pedigree that stretches back to the utopian writings of Bacon, More, and Saint-Simon.

In recent years, however, social science has been more reluctant to tackle such questions. There are good reasons for caution. Post-Enlightenment thought observes that the success of a society is difficult to define independently of complex normative issues, not least because trade-offs must often be struck between goals or groups. Assessing the multifaceted web of social relations connecting members of society also poses major empirical challenges. Even the most promising studies in contemporary social science usually fasten onto one or two dimensions of it to the exclusion of others. Their formulations reflect a balkanization among disciplines that has seen some scholars focus on strategic interaction, while others concentrate on symbolic representations or psychosocial processes, each construing institutions and human motivation in different terms.

There is something becoming in the modesty of contemporary social science. It has made focused empirical inquiry more practicable. But something has also been lost. There are good reasons for believing that well-being is conditioned by many dimensions of social relations, but we do not know enough about how those dimensions interact with one another, whether some are substitutes or complements for others, and by what standards some societies can be said to be more successful than others.

This book steps into that breach. We define societies as patterns of social relations structured by institutional practices and cultural repertoires. We are especially interested in understanding how institutions and cultural structures combine to advance (or limit) collective well-being. If this scope connects us to a classic literature, for conceptual tools we draw on contemporary arguments about social networks, identity, social hierarchies, collective action, boundaries, and social capital. Our objective is not to supersede such perspectives but to build on them. We are especially interested in understanding the effects of institutions, organizations, and available cultural repertoires and how they interact with one another.

Our premise is that some societies are more successful than others but, unlike some of the modernization theories of the 1960s, we do not claim there is a single path to success, and, precisely because institutions interact with local cultures, we are skeptical about proposals to identify "best practices" that can readily be transferred from one society to another. There may well be more than one way to solve similar problems. Nevertheless, the contributions the structures of society make to social welfare should be investigated.

A wide range of outcomes can be associated with successful societies, including nonviolent intergroup relations, open access to education, civic participation, cultural tolerance, and social inclusion. We see each as desiderata. However, the priority each should be assigned is open to debate, and engaging in that debate could easily absorb much of this volume, leaving little room to consider the issues that most concern us, namely, how institutional and cultural structures feed into such outcomes. Therefore, the empirical outcomes on which we have decided to focus the book are those of population health, taken as a proxy for social well-being. We concentrate on the health status of those living in a particular country, region, or community and what we sometimes describe as "health plus."[1]

This is an appropriate choice. On the one hand, a focus on population health fits well with our understanding of successful societies. A successful society is one that enhances the capabilities of people to pursue the goals important to their own lives, whether through individual or collective action, and, as we will argue later, population health can be seen as an indicator of such capabilities.[2] On the other hand, health is a relatively uncontroversial measure of well-being – longer life expectancies and lower rates of mortality can reasonably be associated with the success of a society – and it provides measurable outcomes to explain.

In these outcomes are many sets of puzzles for social scientists. Consider three examples. When the communist regimes of Eastern Europe fell after 1989 – in a set of developments some described as the "end of history" – one

---

[1] We owe this term to James Dunn who uses it to indicate that good health is usually accompanied by higher levels of self-esteem and associated with many other valued social outcomes, including fruitful employment and a satisfying family life.

[2] For an influential argument that associates development with the promotion of capabilities, see Sen (1999), although the meanings we associate with "capabilities" are more specific than his.

might have expected life to improve for those people who had been given new freedoms, and for some it did. After dipping amidst the transition, male life expectancy in the Czech Republic, for instance, began to improve more rapidly than under the previous regime, to reach 72 years by 2001. But male life expectancy in Russia dropped sharply during the transition and remained so low that it was barely 59 years in 2001. Why did a historic development improve collective well-being in one nation and erode it in another?

Recent gaps in the trend lines for life expectancy in the United States and Canada are equally puzzling. In the two decades after World War II, Canadians and Americans gained years of life at about the same pace. However, life expectancy has been increasing more slowly in the United States since the 1970s, such that the average Canadian now lives two years longer than his American neighbor. Moreover, women, who live longer than men, are losing their relative advantage at a faster pace in the United States than in Canada. These gaps translate into millions of years of productive life. Why are they occurring?

Some of these puzzles have policy implications. As sub-Saharan Africa copes with a devastating AIDS epidemic, some governments have had much more success than others. Uganda brought its rate of HIV infection down from about 20 percent of adults in 1992 to less than 8 percent a decade later, while Botswana has seen the rate of infection climb toward 38 percent. By most conventional measures, however, Botswana is much better governed than Uganda. How can one explain these differences in the success of AIDS prevention strategies? These are the types of puzzles this book tackles. For answers, we look to new ways of understanding the relationship between institutional frameworks, cultural repertoires, and population health.

From the Material to the Social in Population Health

What accounts for variation across countries and communities in the health of the population? Although they loom large in popular conceptions, variations in the quality and availability of medical care do not fully explain such differences. New vaccines, diagnostic procedures, and treatments have reduced the incidence and effects of many diseases, but comparisons over time and countries show that this type of innovation explains only a small portion of the variance in population health.[3] Much more can be attributed to the economic prosperity of a country or community and corresponding improvements in sanitation, housing or basic utilities.[4] But material factors alone do not provide complete explanations. Among the developed countries with annual per capita incomes greater than about US$11,000, there remain wide variations

---

[3] For a classic statement, see McKeown (1965) and the controversy published in the *American Journal of Public Health* (2002). Compare Cutler, Deaton, and Lleras-Muney (2006).

[4] Pritchet and Summers (1996).

in population health that bear no relationship to national income. The United States has the world's highest income per capita, for instance, and spends more on health care per person than any other country in the world, but it ranks only forty-first in terms of average life expectancy. Population health is clearly conditioned by factors that go well beyond the medical or material.

Much the same can be said about the distribution of health inside each society. The chapter in this book by Clyde Hertzman and Arjumand Siddiqi describes a familiar "health gradient." In all countries, people of lower socio-economic status tend to have worse health than those in higher socioeconomic positions – a relationship so pervasive that some describe social inequality as the "fundamental cause" behind disparities in population health.[5] But how is this gradient to be explained? Some of it turns on the distribution of material resources: people with higher incomes are likely to be able to purchase the housing, health care, and opportunities for relaxation that contribute to better health. Nothing in our analysis disputes this basic point. However, there is more to one's position in a social structure than the material resources associated with it, and some of these other dimensions are likely to be consequential for health. Even studies of baboons show that position within a social hierarchy engenders physiological effects that impinge on health.[6] One of the objectives of this book is to explore how such dimensions of social relations can affect the distribution of health across the population. We are looking for the social sources of the health gradient.

Of course, this is a problem central to social epidemiology, a field on whose findings we build. One of our objectives is to integrate work in social epidemiology with the concerns of a wider range of social sciences, and to that task we bring a distinctive perspective, which emphasizes the impact on health of institutional structures and cultural repertoires. Many social epidemiologists share these concerns, but they tend to focus on a limited range of social relations and to conceptualize explanations based on them in terms of relatively undifferentiated categories, such as the "psychosocial." We look at the impact of a broader range of institutional structures and cultural repertoires with special emphasis on how they relate to one another.[7] This perspective allows us to identify a number of dimensions of social relations consequential for population health that

---

[5] Link and Phelan (1995; 2000). For overviews of the large literature on this topic, see Adler and Newman (2002); Lynch et al. (2004); Wilkinson (2005); Leigh and Jencks (2006).

[6] Sapolsky, Alberts, and Altmann (1997).

[7] Social relations broadly construed are the day-to-day interactions, informal (left to the subject's agency) or formalized (into structures, institutions, traditions), between individuals and groups, along with their various correlates: symbolic, material and social *stricto sensu* (hierarchies, networks, solidarities, and so on). Our analysis focuses on cultural structures and institutions rather than other dimensions of social relations. Cultural structures are representations (identities, scripts, frames, myths, narratives, collective imaginaries) that feed into behaviors and social boundaries. Institutions are defined as a set of regularized practices, whether formal or informal, with a rule-like quality in the sense that the actors expect those practices to be observed. (See footnote 52, in this chapter.)

deserve more attention than they have received and to deepen our understanding of the ways in which the effects of institutional structures can operate through the cultural frameworks they sustain. Although grounded in on-going research projects, all the chapters in this book are exploratory. Our objective is to widen the lens through which issues of population health can be seen.

Pathways from Institutions and Culture to Health

The chapters in this book approach population health from multiple angles. Some consider the challenges to health posed by contemporary developments. Others address problems associated with policies to improve health. Some focus on the impact of collective representations or symbolic boundaries. However, all are concerned with the roles played in such processes by institutional and cultural structures, which affect health through many routes.[8]

Among these routes, this book accords special importance to the health effects that follow from what is sometimes called the "wear and tear of daily life."[9] Although less dramatic than a virus that decimates the population, the toll taken by the stresses of everyday life may be just as great, given the number of people they affect. Many studies show that the emotional and physiological responses generated by the challenges people encounter in daily life condition not only their risk behaviors but also their susceptibility to many of the chronic illnesses that have become the dominant causes of mortality in the developed world, including stroke and heart disease.[10]

Daniel Keating's chapter describes the biological pathways linking the anger, anxiety, or depression generated in daily life to a person's health. Chronic exposure to high levels of stress has been associated with cumulative developments in the neuroendocrine system that inspire hypertension and poor health. Negative emotions such as depression, resentment, and anxiety appear to raise all-cause mortality, as well as the risk of coronary heart disease, through their effects on the sympathetic-adrenal-medullary (SAM) system, hypothalamic-pituitary-adrenocortical (HPA) system and immune system.[11] In many cases, these effects seem to operate, much as aging does, to induce progressive increases in the physiological costs of meeting new challenges from the social environment, thereby reducing resilience to health threats over time.[12] Moreover, there can be interaction along these pathways. The

---

[8] In this and subsequent sections, our argument has been shaped by ongoing conversations with the members of the successful societies program and influenced by joint work and discussion with Rosemary CR Taylor. See Taylor (2004).

[9] On the impact of the "wear and tear of daily life," see Hawkley et al. (2005). Also relevant is research on the allostatic load (for example, Szanton, Gill, and Allen 2005).

[10] For overviews, see Brunner (1997; 2000); Hertzman and Frank (2006); and Keating (Chapter 2, in this volume).

[11] Chrousos et al. (1995); Brunner (1997); Lovallo (1997); Sapolsky, Alberts, and Altmann (1997); Taylor, Repetti, and Seeman (1999); and Keating (Chapter 2, in this volume).

[12] See also Schoon (2006).

development of reflective consciousness, widely associated with the growth of the prefrontal cortex during adolescence, for instance, can condition the levels of stress experienced later in life.[13]

To understand how institutional practices and cultural frames impinge on health, we develop a particular conception of how the wear and tear of daily life is generated.[14] We suggest that wear and tear depends crucially on the balance between the magnitude of the *life challenges* facing a person and his or her *capabilities* for responding to such challenges. We use the term "life challenges" to refer to the tasks a person regards as most important to life, ranging from basic efforts to secure a livelihood and raise a family to others whose importance will vary across individuals – such as securing material goods, companionship, or social prestige in specific arenas of activity.[15]

We conceptualize "capabilities" in terms that borrow from psychology as well as sociology.[16] To some extent, these are constituted by basic attributes of personality associated with reflective consciousness and emotional resilience, which are conditioned by the experiences of childhood and refined in the contexts of adulthood.[17] But a person's capabilities depend on much more than personality. They include the ability to secure cooperation from others, which invokes a person's capacities for meaning-making and self-representation and the recognition he receives from the community, as well as the institutional frameworks that allow for recognition and effective cooperation.[18] Ultimately, they depend on access to the range of resources that can be used to resolve life's problems. The import of this equation should be apparent. As the life challenges facing a person loom larger relative to his or her capabilities for coping with them, we expect that person to experience higher levels of wear and tear in daily life, feeding into feelings of stress, anger, anxiety, and depression that take a toll on health.

The impact of material circumstances on health is readily captured by this model. In general, people with higher incomes face fewer – and generally different – challenges than those with low incomes. Even more important, however, is the contribution economic resources make to a person's capabilities. In

[13] One implication is that there are significant life course effects, as adult health is affected by childhood circumstances. Keating and Hertzman (1999b); Hertzman and Power (2006; Wheaton and Clarke (2003) advocate combining temporal and contextual perspectives to mental health.

[14] A more complete exposition of this model can be found in Chapter 3 and various dimensions of it are described in other chapters.

[15] In some psychological models, these challenges are described as "stressors." See Kubzansky and Kawachi (2000).

[16] Our formulation should not be confused with that of Sen (1983), although we find his work highly suggestive, and Evans makes use of it in his chapter for this volume.

[17] This model is a very basic one that should suffice here, although others may be able to refine the list of personality attributes constitutive of fundamental capacities. On stress throughout the life course, see Gotlib and Wheaton (1997).

[18] See Bourdieu and Wacquant (1992).

most societies, income is a multipurpose instrument that can be deployed to meet many kinds of challenges, ranging from securing housing to finding a partner. In short, the balance between life challenges and capabilities is a function of material resources. We acknowledge the important impact economic inequality has on the distribution of health across populations and nations.

However, the advantage of our model is that it also illuminates the role played by institutional practices and cultural frameworks in the determination of population health. The core point is that a person's capabilities can be augmented (or attenuated) not only by his access to material resources but also by his access to social (including symbolic) resources. A number of scholars have suggested that the correlates of social class constitute such resources.[19] However, existing attempts to enumerate them remain limited. Our analysis can be read as an effort to specify in more detail how resources are constituted and how they work their way into health. We focus on the ways in which institutional structures and cultural frames are constitutive of such resources, and we explore the ways in which those resources affect peoples' health by conditioning their capabilities for coping with life challenges.

The results are informative for comparisons across communities. Some societies seem to have more symbolic and social resources than others. However, the analysis also illuminates the familiar relationship between socioeconomic status and health, revealing pathways through which social inequalities impinge on health. Moreover, instead of assuming that the distribution of resources corresponds exactly to the distribution of economic resources, we look into that relationship, allowing for the possibility that social and symbolic resources may not be as tightly coupled to income inequality as some studies imply.[20]

These points are at the center of the collective analytical framework that has emerged from our collaborative research over the past five years. Building on our conversations, Hall and Taylor develop some of these ideas in their chapter. They argue that people's health is affected by capacities for coping with life challenges that depend on the character of the institutional and cultural frames in which they live. They suggest these frameworks supply "social resources" crucial to many people's health. Among the factors that contribute to these resources are a number that have been of interest to social epidemiologists, as well as a number of others, including: the character and density of social networks, associational life, a person's position within social hierarchies with a certain shape and dimensionality, and the collective narratives that specify symbolic boundaries and give meaningfulness to certain kinds of lives. Hall and Taylor contend that the distribution of these social resources may be as important to the health of an individual as the economic resources she commands.

---

[19] Giddens (1975); Pearlin and Schooler (1978); Weber (1978); Bourdieu (1984); Link and Phelan (1995, 2000); Kristenson (2006); among others.

[20] For a theoretical model spelling out the determinant role of semiotic practices in relation to material resources, see Sewell (2005).

Bringing Culture Back In

Social epidemiologists have shown, in repeated studies, that social relations matter to people's health. Broadly speaking, the field has emphasized three types of relationships. The first is the set of social networks to which people belong. There is substantial evidence that people with close ties to others, through marriage, friendship, or social networks, tend to enjoy better health and to recover more effectively from illness than those who have relatively few such ties. Research shows that the level and intensity of contacts with others affect all-cause mortality, self-rated health, and rates of recovery from illnesses such as myocardial infarction. Membership in networks offers resilience against depression, illness, and addiction.[21]

A second body of work emphasizes the secondary associations and trust in others they are said to promote, arguing that such associations provide a community with multipurpose "social capital" that can be used to mobilize collective action, especially to press governments to address the needs of the community.[22] Studies show relatively strong correlations between the density of membership in secondary associations and average levels of health across communities. Those who belong to such associations also appear to be healthier, even when factors such as age, income, and social class are controlled.[23]

If the concept of social capital highlights symmetrical relations among people, a third set of studies stresses the asymmetrical relationships found in hierarchies. Pioneering studies of British civil servants, for instance, have found differences in their health, corresponding to their rank within the employment hierarchy, and others find a relationship between the level of autonomy people enjoy in their job and their health.[24] Others suggest that society-wide status hierarchies may have health effects based, in particular, on the feelings of relative deprivation that high levels of income inequality may engender.[25]

This book is inspired by these lines of research.[26] They blaze important paths. However, we think those paths are still too narrow, notably in the range of social relationships they consider and how they construe the causal linkages to population health. One of the objectives of this book is to broaden prevailing conceptions of how social relations impinge on health, and we think one of the principal ways to do so is to bring the cultural dimensions of such

---

[21] See the pioneering work of Berkman and Syme (1979); Berkman (1995); Berkman et al. (2000); Smith and Christakis (2008).

[22] Putnam (2000). "Bridging social capital" that connects people across subgroup lines is said to be especially important.

[23] Kawachi, Kennedy, and Wilkinson (1999: Chapters 22 and 23).

[24] Marmot (2004).

[25] There is controversy about some of these points. See Wilkinson (1996; 2005); Kawachi (2000).

[26] We would like especially to thank Mel Bartley, Lisa Berkman, Martin Bobak, Katherine Frohlich, Arthur Kleinman, Michael Marmot, James Nazroo, Nancy Ross, Ingrid Schoon, Gerrg Veenstra, and David Williams for discussing their research with the participants in this project.

relationships into fuller focus. Doing so reveals new causal logics and enriches understanding of the pathways to which social epidemiology has pointed.

Scholars who look at the impact of social networks on health have been the most expansive in their formulations. They argue that networks provide logistical support for important tasks, such as rearing children, securing employment, and managing illness; information about how to approach these tasks; and social influence useful for securing the cooperation of others. Close contacts provide the emotional support that wards off feelings of isolation or depression.[27] This is congruent with our model. In each of these ways, membership in social networks can improve a person's health by enhancing her capabilities for meeting life challenges.

However, these formulations stop short of capturing the full meanings people give to their relations with others. What is missing is a sense of the moral valence people attach to people around them. Long ago, sociologist Max Weber made the point that there is no action and social relationship without meaning. Building on this insight, recent network analysts have observed that the social connectedness of a society is not specified simply by the structural properties of networks, such as their density or even the instrumental functions they serve, but by the meanings those networks produce and convey.[28] For those who belong to a network, membership is often associated, not only with arrangements of mutual convenience, but with value-laden judgments about the self and others, defined at its limits by a sense of who belongs, who should be defended and respected, and who is only at the margins.[29] People use these meanings to derive purposes for their actions as well as a sense of what they can reasonably expect in moral terms from each other. Those meanings constitute social resources. The research of Sampson and his colleagues underlines this point. They find that variations in the level of violence present across Chicago neighborhoods are best explained, not by the presence of social networks per se but by whether people in each neighborhood believe it appropriate for them to admonish their neighbors' children.[30]

Studies of the relationship between health and social capital take an even more restricted view of social relations and how they condition behavior. By and large, they emphasize relationships built on a logic of mutual exchange, whereby face-to-face encounters in associations or networks create generalized trust and a diffused reciprocity that can be mobilized for collective action.[31] There is evidence that relations of this sort can improve the

[27] See, for instance, the nice formulations in Berkman et al. (2000).

[28] See especially Emirbayer and Goodwin (1994). It should be noted that social epidemiologists often acknowledge, explicitly or implicitly, these dimensions of networks without always drawing out the full implications. For a more detailed critique of the place of culture in the literature on health and disparities, see the chapter by Lamont.

[29] For a classic article from this perspective, see Thompson (1971).

[30] Sampson, Raudenbausch, and Earls (1997).

[31] Putnam (1993).

ability of communities to press governments to address local problems. But this perspective misses many of the contributions that organizations make to a community's capacities for collective mobilization through the cultural frames they promote.[32]

Social organizations do not simply foster a diffuse sense of reciprocity. In many cases, they contribute important moral visions, identities, symbols, and historical narratives to the collective representations of a community, thereby influencing how individuals or groups see themselves and their relationship to the community as a whole. They convey information about the relative status of groups within the community. They communicate boundaries, defining inclusion or exclusion, and visions of what it means to belong to the community as a whole, which can promote specific models for action. These visions can be more crucial to mobilization, whether individual or collective, than the diffuse reciprocity engendered by associational life.[33] Cornell and Kalt, for instance, show how influential images of the "good Apache," derived from traditional collective narratives, could improve the well-being of bands of native peoples, and Oyserman and Marcus suggests that the models of "possible selves" presented to adolescents may influence their circumstances for years to come.[34]

The literature linking health to social status is especially important for its attentiveness to the distributional implications of social structure. However, there is no consensus in this literature about how social position affects health. Much of it relies on a vague concept of status or links status to health through a concept of relative deprivation that implies status derives mainly from income. In some instances, of course, status inequalities can give rise to a sense of deprivation, which affects a person's health by inspiring feelings of anger and resentment.

However, we think there is room for more multifaceted approaches to the relationship between status and health. On the one hand, differences in status may be grounded in a variety of sources. People may secure status in their local community and in their own eyes, not only from their material possessions but also from their commitment to collective solidarity or from their role in raising a family.

On the other hand, the effects of status may not operate entirely through feelings of relative deprivation. Hall and Taylor argue that social status conditions the toll daily life takes on people's health by affecting their capacities to secure the cooperation of others. Social status can condition a person's self-image in ways that increase the anxiety or stress he feels – what Giddens calls "ontological security" – without necessarily engaging feelings of relative deprivation.[35] Psychologists have noted that the stereotypes embedded in

---

[32] For an illustration of this point, see Small (2004). For relevant critiques, see Hall (1999) and Offe (1999).
[33] See Ann Swidler (Chapter 5, in this volume).
[34] Oyserman and Marcus (1990); Cornell and Kalt (1992).
[35] Giddens (1991).

status systems can influence the self-confidence and competence people bring to particular tasks, even if they are not conscious of it doing so.[36] Recognition influences self-efficacy independently of access to material resources. Being defined as able to achieve or as a valuable member of the community has to be a component of how inequality penetrates under the skin. In short, we need a more expansive conception of the mechanisms through which status works its way into health, notably by affecting the capabilities people bring to life challenges.

We should also acknowledge that the status order is a cultural construct whose shape varies across societies. Status is not determined exclusively by material affluence or position within formal hierarchies. The extent to which status corresponds to income will depend on the available cultural frames. Michèle Lamont's comparison of the French and the American upper-middle class, for instance, shows how much these two societies vary with respect to the value or prestige attached to money, culture, and morality. In another study, she finds that French and American workers employ quite different matrices for assessing the value of various groups, such as blacks, immigrants or the poor, which means that blacks and the poor are regarded in more inclusive terms in the French than American context.[37] Because the status or social recognition accorded such groups varies across national contexts, the social opportunities available to them do so as well, with important implications for their health.

The study of population health can be enriched by taking into account the meaning-laden dimensions that permeate all social relations, even when the latter might seem solely interest-based. Those who belong to a society are tied together by ideas of who they are and what they can do that are as evaluative as they are factual. These ideas underpin the judgments we make about others and ourselves. They provide resources for our imagination and specify its limits.[38] In some respects, these "webs of meaning" constitute moral orders.[39] They are organized around group boundaries that have negative (exclusive) aspects as well as positive (identity-bearing) aspects and embodied in hierarchies that assign status or prestige. They find voice in collective narratives grounded in tales about the historic struggles of the tribe or nation, redolent with implications about what a member can or should do – providing definitions of "possible selves" for individuals and aspirations for the collectivity.

For the purposes of this book, we put special stress on three dimensions of culture, which are often embodied in institutional forms. The first is the set of *symbolic boundaries* that define who is at the center of the community and who is at its margins.[40] Boundaries of this sort construct ethnicity and

---

[36] Shih, Pittinsky, and Ambady (2002).
[37] Lamont (1992; 2000; 2006).
[38] See Swidler (1986) on strategies for action.
[39] The phrase is that of Geertz (1973).
[40] On the literature on boundaries, see Lamont and Molnár (2002).

the other social categories that structure the transactions of daily social life. They may be more or less permeable. Closely associated with them are sets of evaluative criteria, which attach more or less opprobrium to one side of a boundary and give rise to the stereotypes that influence views of ourselves as well as others.[41]

The second dimension consists in the *status hierarchies* of a society, understood as implicit sets of principles for distinguishing among social positions and a distribution that assigns varying amounts of social prestige to those positions. We are concerned with the steepness of the relevant status hierarchies, namely, the distance in status between positions at the top and bottom, and in the multidimensionality of status distribution.[42] As Max Weber argued, where status can be secured in several different ways, the social disadvantages experienced by those who lack status on one hierarchy may be offset by the status they gain through alternative means. Relevant to such processes are the terms on which a society assigns status, whether on the basis of citizenship, learning, income, or some other criteria.

Finally, we are attentive to the *collective imaginaries* that portray a society and its members in particular ways. If nations are "imagined communities," as Benedict Anderson has suggested, it matters how they imagine themselves.[43] Collective imaginaries are sets of representations composed of symbols, myths, and narratives that people use to portray their community or nation and their own relationship as well as that of others to it.[44] By virtue of their contributions to collective identity, these imaginaries condition the boundaries and status hierarchies to which we have just referred.[45] In addition, by presenting a community's past in a particular way, collective narratives influence the expectations of its members about the future, suggesting paths of collective development available to the community and "strategies of action" feasible for individuals within it.[46] The moral valence of such representations lends them influence, but they have cognitive and emotional impact as well, conjuring up templates for action from the past.

These cultural frameworks condition the health of individuals and its distribution across the population in multiple ways. As noted later, they provide blocks on which effective policies to promote healthy behaviors can be built and underpin the collective mobilization central to securing more healthy living

---

[41] See Steele (1988); Steele and Crocker (1998); Krieger (2000); Son Hing et al. (2002).

[42] This issue is complicated by the fact that the matrices used to measure worth can vary across groups. For instance, academics spontaneously privilege responsibility and authority as criteria of evaluation, whereas electricians privilege the usefulness of one's work. See Ollivier (2000).

[43] Anderson (1991).

[44] Note that our definition departs from that of Castoriadis (1987) who coined the term "social imaginaries." See also Gatens (2004). On this subject, our formulations are influenced by the work of Bouchard (2003b; 2005).

[45] On social identity, see Ashmore et al. (2004).

[46] Swidler (1986).

conditions in many societies. However, we want to emphasize the ways in which cultural frameworks affect health by conditioning peoples' capabilities for coping with life challenges and, hence, the amount of daily wear and tear they experience.

Social recognition can feed directly into capabilities.[47] As we have noted, it can affect a person's capacities for securing cooperation from others. Those who belong to low-status groups or occupy positions with low social respect may find it more difficult to secure such cooperation. Research on racial discrimination indicates that social recognition is also likely to affect self-confidence and the effectiveness with which tasks are performed.[48] Here, there are important life course effects: the recognition one achieves in childhood has durable importance for the self-concept and health.[49] Even with the most auspicious upbringing, however, in the absence of cultural templates that sustain a sense of social recognition, adults can rarely sustain the self-esteem that feeds directly into health.[50]

The predominant models of cultural citizenship, social boundaries, and status hierarchies of a society will influence whether social recognition is available and who will receive it. Where the status hierarchy is relatively flat or there are diverse paths toward status, those in the lower rungs of the social ladder should be healthier on average than their counterparts facing steeper or dominant hierarchies. Much may depend on whether status is driven by income. American workers have a greater sense of personal distress, for instance, than their counterpart in countries such as Poland and Japan, and Lamont argues that a quasi-consensus on income and success as sources of worth (epitomized in the collective myth of the American dream) may contribute to that.[51]

However, the process whereby people cope with issues of social recognition is double-sided. Michèle Lamont's chapter for this book suggests that social recognition emerges from an active process in which individuals work toward shaping the symbolic representations of their group. They also engage in boundary work to influence how members of their own group understand their collective identity (for example, by competing to define what it means to be African American in the contemporary United States). She charts the ways in which minority groups have used "destigmatization strategies" to bridge group boundaries and challenge the symbolic representations on which discrimination is based (such as the view that blacks are lazy or less able). In this respect, the widely available social representations of groups must be seen as a set of collective resources, multidimensional in nature, that contribute to well-being, and Lamont argues that the impact of discrimination

---

[47] On social recognition, see Taylor (1993) and Lamont and Bail (2005).

[48] Steele (1999). Also Steele and Aronson (1998).

[49] Keating (2004); Steinberg et al. (2006).

[50] Steele (1988); Pyszczynski et al. (2004). For a cultural-psychological theory of self-esteem, see Miller, Fung, and Mintz (1996).

[51] Kohn (1987); Lamont (2000: 247).

on a person's health is likely to depend on how low-status group members understand and respond to discrimination. The extent to which they are able to exercise control over self-representation is likely to influence mastery and self-efficacy – psychosocial "coping" and "buffering" factors that have been linked to depression and health more generally.

The connections between collective narratives and population health are similarly complex. As Gérard Bouchard's chapter indicates, we cannot always expect a one-to-one correspondence between the collective imaginary of a society and the health status of its population. His work on the role of myths in modern society is a pioneering effort. In the Québec case, he finds competing myths concerning the trajectory of Quebec society (one "modernist," the other "defeatist") and uses the trajectory of population health to assess their empirical verisimilitude. Even though the health of the Quebec population has increased dramatically throughout the twentieth century, the infant mortality curve (to mention only one example) does not correspond to either of the two widely available narratives about macro changes in Quebec society and its collective imaginary during this period. Bouchard's work reminds us that collective narratives often gain autonomy from lived experience to influence the meanings groups give to their collective identity.

Institutions, Public Policy Making, and Health

This book has much to say about the roles that institutions play in population health and the contributions governments can make to it. Here, our emphasis is on expanding the range of institutions considered relevant to health and on illuminating the ways in which cultural frameworks condition the policies of governments and effectiveness of institutions.[52]

Peter Evans's study of population health in the developing world feeds into exciting new lines of research that see institutions as crucial to international development. However, he questions conventional accounts that associate improvements in health in the developing world primarily with increases in per capita income and the latter primarily with the development of property rights regimes. Building on the contention that population health depends significantly on the wear and tear experienced by people in their daily lives, he argues that population health should be better where higher levels of education and a shallower socioeconomic hierarchy provide the mass of people with more capabilities. The implication is that population health depends not only on acquiring a certain kind of state, with effective administrative capacities and

---

[52] We conceptualize institutions as sets of regularized practices with a rule-like quality in the sense that actors expect those practices to be observed. They vary, according to how those expectations are established, from formal institutions backed by sanctions, as are many policy regimes, to informal institutions grounded in perceptions that they serve mutual interests or embody patterns of behavior widely seen as appropriate. See March and Olsen (1989); Hall and Taylor (1996); Hall and Thelen (2009).

secure property rights, but on the development of a wider range of institutions at the societal level that broaden the capabilities of ordinary people. Evans devises an indicator of "societal success" to represent such institutions and finds that it explains a good deal of cross-country variance in life expectancy across the developing world.

Our emphasis on enhancing peoples' capabilities to cope with life challenges parallels Amartya Sen's insistence that development should be construed, not simply as a matter of increasing national income but as a problem of enhancing peoples' capabilities understood in more general terms.[53] But Sen says little about how such capabilities are to be defined or enhanced, other than to argue for collective deliberation.[54] The next step, as Evans notes, is to join the "capabilities" approach to development to the "institutional turn" taken by development economics to ask: what sorts of institutions are required if the capabilities of people in the developing world are to grow?

Our answer, articulated by Evans, suggests that the deliberative processes fostered by democratic institutions have a role to play but are insufficient to generate large improvements in health. Population health has been advanced most effectively in places where deliberative institutions are accompanied by high levels of social mobilization that enable communities to press governments into action on a sustained basis over time. The problem is thus one of explaining how populations are mobilized – a topic on which there is a large literature, little of which is pointed directly at issues of population health.[55] Evans and Swidler (in her chapter) show that this is where cultural frameworks are an indispensible supplement to institutional structures. Even though rights-based institutions are often a precondition for such moblization, it is most effective at securing enduring reforms in settings, such as that of Kerala, where political organizations have promulgated collective imaginaries that challenge traditional hierarchies and provide ordinary people with new understandings of themselves that are inclusive and politically empowering.

In sum, for the purposes of advancing population health in the developing world, a well-configured state is not a substitute for an organized civil society. And the development of secure property rights provides, at best, an indirect route toward gradual improvements in health, many of which can be accelerated if effective social mobilization can be achieved.

Ann Swidler takes this a step further to consider how cultural frameworks condition the effectiveness of policy regimes. Her comparison of AIDS-prevention programs in Botswana and Uganda has important implications for the role of institutions in socioeconomic development. Most of those who assign importance to institutions as a tool for development favor the types of administrative structures that Botswana has established, built on Weberian

---

[53] As noted, Sen's use of the term is more general than ours. Compare Sen (1983; 1999).
[54] See Polletta's (2002) important contribution to this topic.
[55] For a notable exception, see Tendler (1997) and for reviews, see Polletta and Jasper (2001) and Snow, Soule, and Kriesi (2004).

bureaucracies that are relatively efficient and relatively uncorrupt.[56] By African standards, Botswana ranks high on most measures of good governance. But Swidler finds that those institutions were ineffective at reducing rates of HIV infection, while the government of Uganda, whose state lacks many of the features associated with good governance, was able to secure dramatic reductions in the incidence of HIV infection.

Swidler compares the public campaigns mounted to shift people away from behaviors that put them at risk of HIV infection. She finds those efforts were effective only when they mobilized the systems of meaning implicit in the everyday relations of local communities. To some extent, this was a matter of social organization. In Uganda, prominent clan structures, if less democratic than the local governments of Botswana, provided effective vehicles for reaching local communities. The implication is that indigenous organizations may provide a more effective base for reaching and motivating ordinary people than the organizations with more social distance operated by national bureaucracies or transnational organizations.

The core lesson for population health is that campaigns designed to alter behavior, so as to improve public health or reduce other threats, must do more than convey information. They will be more effective where they tap into the social imagery of the local community, invoking the obligations ordinary people feel to their friends and neighbors. To do so, they must resonate with the taken-for-granted frameworks through which people understand their lives.[57] Conceptions of everyday justice, of courtesy, and of communal responsibility are the foundation on which the response to new social risks can be built.

This means that governments interested in promoting more healthy behavior must work with existing cultural resources. Swidler conjectures that local culture in Uganda may have provided more fertile ground for moral appeals for AIDS testing and safe sex than the context in Botswana, which attaches high value to respect for privacy and a formal civic courtesy. However, she notes that effective cultural matches are not simply "found" but actively created, by appeals that can change, as well as leverage, available cultural frames.[58]

The overarching point is that those interested in improving population health or advancing its development should not assume that a common institutional form will work well in all cultural settings. International development agencies tend to look for institutional templates that reflect a "best practice" they can urge on all countries. Swidler's research reminds us that effective institutional design must take into account the cultural context in which institutions will be deployed because it is often only by tapping into that context that institutions become effective.

At the most general level, this means that policy makers should think of themselves as operating within a certain structure of social and cultural

---

[56] See also Evans (1995).
[57] On resonance, see Schudson (1989).
[58] See also Cornell and Kalt (1992).

relations. For some decades, it has been customary for policy makers to think of the economy in structural terms. Few officials would propose a new economic policy without considering not only the likelihood of meeting its immediate objectives but also its ancillary effects on the structure of market competition. But because governments rarely think of society in such terms, policy makers often miss the opportunity to leverage local social resources.

Hall and Taylor pursue this point. They note that governments can sometimes enhance the impact of a policy – securing a social multiplier effect – by considering how the delivery of a policy affects networks of social relations. Unemployment benefits can be delivered, for instance, in ways that strengthen the social ties between unemployed people and those who can provide leads to new jobs. Day care can be used to build the wider social relationships on which parents depend for support. The cultural frames governments deploy when making policy that bears on minority groups can feed back into the capacities of members of those groups to secure the cooperation of others.[59] In each of these cases, new social resources are being created that can amplify the effects of policy.

Conversely, if inattentive to the structure of social relations, governments can inadvertently erode the social resources available to the community, embodied in the networks to which people belong, the associational life available to them, the character of the social hierarchy, and the collective narratives that give meaningfulness to individual lives. Housing policies or zoning ordinances that inadvertently eliminate sites at which the elderly congregate can leave them socially isolated. Nationalist narratives that disparage some groups, even obliquely, can make local cooperation more difficult.

In sum, although we often think of public policy making as an endeavor that allocates material resources or devises sanctions and incentives to secure particular behaviors, it should also be seen as a process of social resource creation. And, as we have argued, social resources are consequential for population health. Therefore, governments can improve the health of the population not only with policies directly aimed at it but by configuring a much wider range of policies to promote or redistribute social resources.

Jane Jenson reverses this optic to consider how the broader ambit in which policy is made conditions the types of policies that governments will adopt to promote health. Her chapter shows how key elements of the collective imaginary – encapsulated in the prevailing "citizenship regime" – affect the reception given to alternative medical paradigms. Using the case of the sanitarian movement in nineteenth century Britain, she argues that the enthusiasm governments develop for particular medical paradigms and the interventions they undertake to implement them are deeply affected by prevailing ideas about the responsibilities of governments and the rights of different groups of citizens.

---

[59] Soss (2008). Also see Steensland (2006).

In contrast to classic explanations for the history of health policy, which emphasize the impact of the political regime, Jenson develops a more subtle explanation built on conceptions of citizenship.

The concept of a citizenship regime nicely illustrates how closely institutional practices and cultural repertoires are bound up with each other. Collective representations are an important part of such regimes, providing collective narratives of exclusion and inclusion. But those representations gain force from the ways in which they are institutionalized. The division of responsibility for health care – among the state, the market, civil society, and family – is reflected, for instance, both in existing practices and in the moral schemas implicit in contemporary discourse. Practices that might otherwise fall into desuetude are made lively by the moral discourses associated with them. Institutional change entails shifts in both discourse and practice, which are ultimately accomplished through politics.

Will Kymlicka takes up one of the most prominent issues in contemporary political practice: do higher levels of immigration and the multicultural policies that accommodate it erode social solidarity and corresponding public support for generous social policies? Many argue that there is a trade-off between the "recognition" that multiculturalism accords minorities and the support for "redistribution" that underpins contemporary welfare states.

From the perspective of this volume, this trade-off poses a dilemma for population health. Because the respect accorded to members of minority groups affects the daily toll on their health, multicultural policies designed to build such respect should advance their well-being.[60] But social transfers enhancing security often improve the health of those at low incomes. If multicultural policies erode support for social services, governments face a difficult choice. Movement in either direction is likely to have adverse consequences for population health. In this context, Kymlicka's findings are important. After considering the arguments and evidence on both sides, he concludes that immigration and the multicultural policies that sometimes accompany it do not necessarily lower support for redistributive social spending.

In more general terms, Kymlicka observes that collective imaginaries are often more supple than some accounts imply. Concepts of the nation-state have long been among the most powerful of such imaginaries, responsible for the feelings of national belonging important to social solidarity. Some suggest that, as those images thin out in the context of more diverse societies and more cosmopolitan citizens, the nation-state will inevitably lose resonance as a factor of social cohesion. But, in the Canadian case, Kymlicka finds that multicultural policies have successfully modified the collective narrative of nationhood without eroding its role as a vehicle of solidarity. His analysis reminds us that collective imaginaries are not static frameworks but malleable representations susceptible to the creative power of politics, and that the political effects of social divisions are mediated by the collective narratives devised to describe them.

[60] Krieger (1999); Williams (1999).

Social Processes and Causal Structures

The perspective developed in this book draws attention to a range of determinants substantially wider than those often associated with population health. We identify a number of dimensions of social relations constitutive of social resources on which people draw to cope with life challenges and emphasize the ways in which cultural contexts mediate the impact of institutions and policies. Adopting such a perspective has implications not only for the variables on which studies might focus but for how they understand the causal structures through which population health is generated.

An instructive comparison might be to accounts that see population health as a function primarily of physiological processes. In such cases, the determinants of health should be observable in virtually any sample of human beings, provided an appropriate experimental or quasi-experimental technique is used. The suggestion that social factors also condition health complicates matters, requiring a focus on countries or communities, but, if the relevant social factors are construed in highly abstract terms and said to operate exactly the same way in all contexts, as some versions of "social capital" are, then their effects can be studied in virtually any social setting, whether of American states or Finnish cities. We think some of the factors we have adduced might fit this model.

However, we have argued that the effects of variables that might otherwise be seen as universal, such as membership in social networks, are often mediated by associated cultural frameworks that are highly specific to particular times and places. The effects of membership in such networks, for instance, can flow not only from the basic level of interhuman contact they support but also from the culturally specific messages a network conveys about the meaningfulness of life or the moral obligations owed others. Thus, studying the impact on health of membership in an American network may not tell us much about the impact of belonging to a Finnish network whose messages could be different.

One implication, of course, is that treating social factors as variables of the sort that can be entered into regression estimations, as if they operate like physical causes independent of cultural context, will capture at best only some of their effects. There is value in such efforts but also an urgent need to supplement them with comparative case studies of countries or communities and in-depth examination of small samples of subjects where the operation of cultural context can be discerned. If the social determinants of population health operate as we suggest, small-n comparisons that are carefully done can offer results equally, if not more, valid than those secured in large-n statistical studies.[61]

We are not suggesting that one cannot generalize about the impact of cultural frameworks but that this should be done on the basis of empirical investigations showing how they interact with other features of the social or institutional context. For this purpose, there is special value in comparative studies that look across countries. Even statistical research in social

---

[61] See Brady and Collier (2002); Hall (2003); and George and Bennett (2004).

epidemiology can gain from such comparisons. Studies of how position in a social hierarchy affects health, for instance, are likely to produce more robust results if they can examine its effects across cases in which the shape of the hierarchy differs. Many important features of social relations are structural attributes of society, whose effects cannot be ascertained without comparison across societies. To date, such research has been limited by the availability of good cross-national data – about health, cultural frameworks, and social relations. There is a strong case here for the collection of such data.

The perspective advanced in this book has similar import for how the causal processes that connect social relations to health are construed. In some instances, those may be relatively direct: higher levels of social status or membership in a denser set of social networks may provide individuals with social resources that enhance their health status. Even here, we need to be attentive to the time lags that may be associated with cause and effect. In other instances, however, the causal structures may not be so straightforward. As Clyde Hertzman observes, a set of social relations developed long ago or gradually over time, via a set of path-dependent processes in which subsequent developments depend on the character of previous ones, may affect population health only at a later point in time or in the presence of a specific kind of challenge. The resilience of population health in the Czech Republic in the wake of the collapse of communism may be attributable to this kind of causal process. The collective imaginary and social networks of the Czech Republic, for instance, may have provided the population with sources of resilience in the face of this shock, even though they may have had no discernible effects on health during the communist period. We do not know this for sure because research often focuses on effects that operate consistently across time and space rather than on those that may become important only in the context of specific junctures.

A useful analogy is to studies of well-being over the life course, which find that a person's resilience in adulthood, encompassing both physiological and mental responses, can depend on the experiences of childhood. The latter may operate in a number of ways – by engendering effects that lower one's subsequent resistance to health threats, by inducing a sequence of experiences or behaviors that cumulatively threaten health, or by producing latent effects triggered only in the presence of later experiences. There is some reason to think that social developments may operate on societies in analogous ways, drawing them into cumulative spirals that gradually enhance or erode population health or equipping them with characteristics that condition collective resilience in the face of subsequent challenges.[62] Although one must be cautious about drawing parallels between organic entities and social ones, there is a case for more research into the sources of social resilience.

Therefore, when considering the relationship between health and social relations, it is important to look for what Pierson calls "large, slow-moving processes" – the incremental shifts in tectonic plates that precede the

---

[62] Compare Schoon (2006).

earthquake – rather than seeking the causes for a health outcome entirely in that last set of events that precipitate it.[63] We do not need to go back to the Battle of Hastings to explain the English Civil War of the 1640s, but no adequate account of the causes of that war would stop with the king's effort to dissolve Parliament.[64] These injunctions apply with special force to studies focused on the social determinants of population health. Because many of those determinants are the product of historical processes, without looking into those processes, we can have at best incomplete explanations for health. Our perspective suggests that social factors should always be seen as the artifacts of historical processes. To study the latter can be revealing not only about the causal dynamics that lie behind population health but also about the wider implications of socioeconomic development.

William Sewell's chapter for this volume is a contribution to this kind of inquiry. He observes that many of the conditions associated with population health, including income inequalities, the level of provision of public goods, and the intensity of market insecurity, are deeply affected by developments on a transnational scale. To understand population health, he suggests, we need to look, not only at its immediate determinants, but at long-term shifts in the cultural and institutional frameworks governing global capitalism. In a highly suggestive essay, he traces the decline of a state-centric paradigm for economic governance and the rise of a neoliberal paradigm with attendant cultural as well as economic implications. His inquiry draws attention to factors impinging on population health that narrower studies miss, suggesting that health depends on some basic elements in the constitution of societies that are malleable over time. He reveals that population health is as much historically, as biologically, determined.

This perspective calls for more longitudinal analysis of the social determinants of health. Social epidemiology tends to concentrate on cross-sectional comparisons of cases observed at a single point in time. This emphasis is eminently understandable, given the available data, and we have called for more such comparisons. However, our perspective suggests that some of the most important causal processes associated with the social determinants of population health may be ones that operate dynamically over time, in ways that will be illuminated only by longitudinal studies of how they develop.

Conclusion

This book is addressed to social scientists, social epidemiologists, and the informed public. It is designed to promote several sets of dialogues. We have tried to show how fascinating the puzzles of population health are for many disciplines and how much social science can gain from turning more of its attention to them. By example as well as precept, we encourage analysis of

---

[63] Pierson (2004).
[64] See Stone (1972).

the large issues associated with how "successful societies" are constituted and more interchange between those interested in the role of institutions and those interested in the role of culture in social life. Both sides can benefit from that conversation.

Social epidemiologists long interested in the social determinants of health will find here new perspectives that broaden the range of determinants considered relevant to health and deepen our understanding of the role cultural frameworks play in them. Investigating some of the social processes identified here may be challenging, but we think there is room for empirical progress and no point in looking only at the lighted side of the street, if what must be found lies on the other side.

There are clear implications for policy in many of the chapters that follow. We suggest that governments can improve population health through a range of measures that extend well beyond conventional efforts at health promotion. Governments enhance population health by conserving social resources, much as the conservation of natural resources improves the environment. Against the view that population health is best advanced in developing countries by increasing gross domestic product, we argue that measures to improve skill levels and redistribute resources can have significant effects. We suggest that prevention policies will be more effective when they tap into the moral solidarities animating local networks.

This book is an exercise in interdisciplinary exploration. The objective of the chapters is not to resolve issues but to open up new ways of thinking about them. However, all advance an approach to population health that emphasizes the contributions cultural frameworks interacting with institutional structures make to the wear and tear people experience in daily life and to the effectiveness of public policy making. In this perspective, we see exciting agendas for further research.

1

Population Health and the Dynamics of Collective Development

Clyde Hertzman and Arjumand Siddiqi

INTRODUCTION

The level of health of people living in a society is an indicator of success of that society. Population health is determined by the circumstances and contexts of life, from the most intimate to the broadest socioeconomic element. These conditions, in turn, are strongly influenced by institutions and policies of a society. In this chapter, we argue that there are four main implications for the relationship between society and health. The first implication is that material and psychosocial conditions express themselves in the form of health inequalities or "gradients." The second is that public provision is critical to population health because it has the capacity to reduce the level of socioeconomic inequality generated by market forces and to buffer its effects. The third is that, since socioeconomic, institutional, and policy shifts often unfold over decades, population health must attend to these big, slow-moving processes. The fourth implication is that, in turn, a longitudinal perspective on population health trends can reveal large, slow-moving processes that might otherwise remain undetected.

From cross-sectional and life course studies, the mechanisms connecting society and health can be framed at three levels of societal aggregation. At the macro level are such society-wide influences as levels and fluctuations of national income, and particularly patterns of distribution, and policies intended to affect these (for example, income support, education, health care or employment policies). At an intermediate, or meso level, are the characteristics of one's immediate community or workplace. Influences here include, inter alia, how people interact with each other and the levels of local trust and civility, in the community and the workplace. These will be reflected, in part, in the nature and availability of schools, libraries, newspapers, policing and parks, and also in the nature of work characteristics and environments.[1] At the most micro level, there are the influences on health associated with

[1] Putnam (1993).

private life, such as the ability to purchase goods and services, the nature and quality of personal social support: intimate relationships, friendships, and the availability of personal help when needed.[2] Not all relevant influences fit neatly into one level of social aggregation. For example, job insecurity and sense of control are perhaps best understood as resulting from the interaction between macro, meso, and micro influences on the individual at a particular stage in the life course.[3]

We have many insights about the relationships between macro, meso, and micro determinants and population health from cross-sectional and life course perspectives. But we have few insights about the association between macro determinants and population health from an historical perspective that can capture big, slow-moving processes. This chapter attempts to fill this gap by focusing on a longitudinal perspective of macro determinants and population health trajectories using a comparative case study approach. A brief comparison between Finland and the Baltic countries demonstrates how long it can take between the time of onset of institutional and policy differences between societies (in this case, the dramatic difference between Soviet and capitalist systems) and the emergence of significant population health differences. The more detailed Canada/United States comparison illustrates how both institutional/policy regimes and population health trends can change slowly over time, yet result in large differences between societies. Further, this case study helps to specify which features of institutions and policies (for example education, employment, redistribution, public spending) have the greatest returns to population health. Finally, the Czech Republic/Russia comparison shows how a common, stressful societal transition may lead to bad health in bad times in one society, but good health in bad times in another. This difference can only be understood by comprehending processes that have unfolded the past.

POPULATION HEALTH: OVERVIEW AND CURRENT EVIDENCE

At the level of the individual, a large body of research has confirmed the intuitive notion that with health comes happiness.[4] This is not only due to the feeling of vitality one gets from the absence of disease or injury but also from the life opportunities that arise from physical and mental well-being, including the ability to work and earn money and to be unencumbered in the process of living. At the level of society, there are also many beneficial returns to a healthy population. Population health contributes to economic productivity and growth directly, as well as through its indirect effects on removing a significant barrier to human capital formation during the early life period of

---

[2] Berkman (1995); Rose (1995); Kaplan et al. (1996); Kawachi et al. (1997).
[3] Hertzman (2001).
[4] Diener (1984); Cummins (2000).

skills acquisition.[5] Although the relationship between socioeconomic position and health status is due mostly to the effects of the former on the latter,[6] health also contributes to socioeconomic status (SES) through the phenomenon of "social drift" in which ill-health can lead to deterioration of one's economic and social position and ability to contribute to society.[7]

Compared to other indicators of societal success, population health can be measured with a high degree of credibility. To be sure, health is a complex construct and can be measured in a variety of elaborate ways. Luckily however, simple indexes of health, such as mortality and life expectancy (itself a function of mortality rates), happen to correlate well with multidimensional health indexes.[8] The outcome of interest, death, is easily observable and countable and is not subject to legitimate controversy as to what it is and when it occurs. Compared with gross domestic product (GDP), literacy rates, and other indexes of societal progress, mortality statistics do not lead to endless discussions about whether they are a valid measure of the underlying construct. Death, after all, is death. Finally, societies have been recording vital statistics on life and death for decades in some places, and centuries in others; long enough to allow us to track societal progress over historical time. This last fact has permitted the rise of the study of "population health," which is the study of the determinants of systematic differences in health status among defined populations. We now have sufficient data to observe how health varies by nation, geographic region, SES, gender, and the like, permitting us to complement historical and social scientific studies with a population health approach to the dynamics of collective development.

Population health differs from traditional health studies in that it deals with "sick populations" rather than "sick individuals." Of course, the examination of the health of populations cannot be entirely separated from the study of individual health. Many investigators regard the determinants of population health as simply a mathematical function of the aggregated determinants of individual health – their means, mode, and the like; an approach that dominates thinking in public health. Population health goes further to add an ecological perspective that focuses on the *patterns* that arise among populations and their subgroups. Population health begins with the proposition that, at the societal level, observed patterns of health outcomes are more than just the sum of individual outcomes and, also, that determinants of health in populations are not just the sum of the risk and protective factors that affect individuals.[9] In other words, the determinants of health in populations are an example of Durkheim's[10] "social facts" while the determinants of health in individuals are "individual facts." Here we are primarily interested in the social facts.

[5] Weil (2005).
[6] Power et al. (1991).
[7] Blane (1999).
[8] Idler et al. (1997).
[9] Rose (1992).
[10] Durkheim (1951).

Several observations help to illustrate this point. In every society where it has been measured, smokers die of the same or a similar variety of predictable causes at higher rates than nonsmokers. However, smokers in some countries (notably Japan) still live as long, if not longer, than non-smokers in other wealthy countries.[11] The British Whitehall study,[12] as well as countless similar studies of health and social class, smoking, blood pressure control, and other traditional cardiovascular risk factors, help to explain the difference in mortality between individuals but do little to explain the systematic differences in heart disease mortality between those in higher and lower occupational grades of the civil service. To this latter observation we will return shortly.

Persuasive evidence of the significance of societal determinants comes from an historical observation made by Thomas McKeown,[13] who demonstrated that the precipitous decline in mortality from the major infectious diseases of antiquity, such as tuberculosis, during the past century and a half was not due to clinically effective vaccinations and antibiotic treatments. Rather, it had more to do with societal investments in basic infrastructure such as improved housing, clean drinking water and sanitation, and social changes such as increased child spacing. These diseases had been the major causes of mortality for centuries, yet effective clinical prevention and treatment interventions were developed and implemented after the death rates from these conditions had declined by approximately 90 percent from their levels at the onset of reliable data gathering in early nineteenth-century Britain. Thus, in direct contradiction to common belief, the vaccine and antibiotic revolution played a relatively minor role in lengthening human life expectancy in the modern world's wealthy societies. Instead, the explanation is to be found outside the realm of health care services in broader social processes.

What was true in the past is still true today. The average life expectancy difference between the healthiest of the world's wealthy countries and the least healthy is approximately five years. This five-year life expectancy difference (between approximately 74 and 79 years) is not accounted for by mortality early or late in the life course, but by an approximate doubling of age-specific mortality during the adult years (age 25–64).[14] Most important, the evidence is conclusive that national differences in spending on health care services do not explain the five-year life expectancy gap.[15] Scatter plots of health care spending versus life expectancy among wealthy countries consistently show no association whatsoever. We will discuss further what might account for this cross-national variation in mortality.

---

[11] Keys (1980).
[12] Marmot et al. (1991).
[13] McKeown (1976).
[14] Based on World Bank World Development Indicators data (World Bank 1993).
[15] Anderson et al. (2001).

THE PHENOMENON OF SOCIOECONOMIC GRADIENTS IN HEALTH

Finally, perhaps the most compelling support for turning to an investigative lens of societies comes from the evidence on socioeconomic gradients in health, as illustrated by the aforementioned Whitehall study. The "gradient effect" refers to the *standard-form* relationship that characterizes health status as one ascends from the bottom of the social hierarchy (defined, in various studies, by income, education, or occupation) to the top. It is standard form because it applies to a remarkably broad range of outcomes, and has been replicated in all wealthy societies where this relationship has been measured (we know far less about this relationship among developing nations).

There are four main characteristics of SES gradients in health:

1. Within a population, the effect of SES is continuous, or stepwise, such that each additional increment of SES results in additional gains to one's health status. In other words, there are successive increases in health status from lower to higher socioeconomic levels in society. The evidence for this is overwhelming for the wealthier nations and a burgeoning literature is suggesting that it holds true in resource-poor nations as well. The gradient effect, then, can be conceptualized as a linear relationship for the purposes of this discussion (see Figure 1.1). Gradients are contrasted with threshold effects, which implies that the effects of SES are continuous up to a given point, but that, after this point, changes in SES do not result in changes in health status. The most common threshold effect is the dichotomous relationship, wherein it is assumed that there is one level of health associated with being "rich" and another with

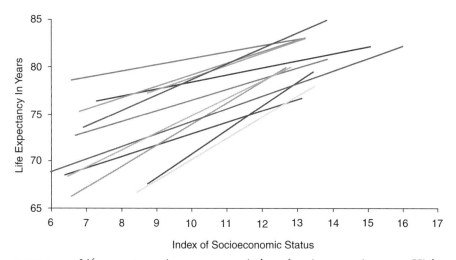

FIGURE 1.1. Life expectancy in years versus index of socioeconomic status. Higher values indicate higher socioeconomic status.

being "poor." In sum, the gradient effect instead suggests that there are degrees of change in health associated with degrees of change in SES.

2. The gradient cannot be explained away by reverse causation or differential mobility. In other words, the overwhelming portion of the relationship represents a "causal" link from socioeconomic status to health over the life course.[16] Those societies that produce the least inequality in health and human development across the socioeconomic spectrum also have the highest average levels of health and development. International comparisons have shown this for the development of literacy and numeracy skills across OECD countries[17] and for health status across the European community.[18] Further, as the major diseases have changed over time, the gradient effect has replicated itself on new diseases as they have emerged. Data from the beginning of the twentieth century for countries such as England and Wales show the gradient effect for the major causes of disease and death of the time (infectious diseases).[19] Over the next three to five decades those diseases declined and were replaced by chronic diseases such as heart disease. At first, heart disease displayed a different epidemiological pattern, disproportionately affecting those who were privileged enough to live long enough to get it. But over time the socioeconomic gradient re-asserted itself. In the case of heart disease, this occurred by the 1950s.[20]

3. Across populations or societies, the "steepness" of the gradient (in other words, the strength of the linear association) is not uniform. That is, if one plots on a graph the SES gradients in health in different societies (as depicted in Figure 1.1), the lines do not fall on top of one another, suggesting that the additional gains to health from increased SES are larger in some societies than in others. In fact, the pattern that emerges suggests that, across nations, differences in health outcome at high levels of SES are far smaller than at lower levels. In other words, those societies with a "shallow" SES gradient do not get that way by "pulling down" the health of the high SES groups, but rather by "pulling up" the health of the lower groups. Therefore, the average health of "shallow gradient" societies tends to be better than "steep gradient" societies.[21] This pattern is sometimes referred to as the "flattening-up" of the SES gradient.

4. The arrangement or ordering of nations in terms of the steepness of their gradients is not random. That is, although they have been poorly

[16] Adler et al. (1999).
[17] Statistics Canada and Organization for Economic Cooperation and Development (OECD) (1995).
[18] Wagstaff et al. (1991).
[19] Evans et al. (1994).
[20] Ibid.
[21] Hertzman (2001).

studied to date, there seem to be systematic differences in institutional arrangements between those societies in which the SES gradient in health is steep, versus those in which it is shallow.

These observations about socioeconomic gradients in health point to a series of propositions that implicate the role of societal institutions as fundamental determinants of population health and health inequalities. They are mainly propositions because, to date, very little empirical work has been done to test these relationships. The propositions are explicated in the following section.

SES Gradients Suggest the Fundamental Influence of Societal Determinants of Health

The observation that SES gradients in health are ubiquitous suggests that societal determinants are fundamental for population health. Here, there are two main lines of reasoning. First, if socioeconomic inequalities are critical for health, then so too are the societal conditions that create the inequalities themselves. The extent of socioeconomic stratification that exists in society is not innate. Rather, it is strongly influenced by actions and inactions taken by societies that, cumulated over time, become embedded in institutions. This notion is powerfully illustrated by contrasting poverty rates before and after taxes and transfers are accounted for. Data from the Luxembourg Income Study show that based on market income (that is, income prior to taxes and transfers) at 31 percent, poverty rates[22] in the United States were up to 5–6 percent lower than in several OECD nations, including France and Sweden, and on par with others such as Australia, Canada, Spain, and Germany. However, after taxes and transfers, the United States had the highest poverty rate among the OECD nations at 18 percent, between 6 and 11 percent higher than all other OECD nations with the exception of Australia, which has a post tax and transfer poverty rate of 16 percent.[23]

The difference in poverty rates is even more marked with respect to children. Prior to transfers, poverty rates across OECD nations for lone parents are consistently high, with a range of 32 percent in Italy, to a whopping 80 percent in the Netherlands. However, after redistributive measures were applied by governments, the rate for lone mothers was reduced to approximately 10 percent in many OECD nations, with a low of 4 percent in Germany. By contrast, the poverty rate for lone mothers in the United States remains at 60 percent.[24] In epidemiological speak, the function of societal policies can be

---

[22] For the sake of drawing comparisons, poverty was measured using the European Union's relative standard (50 percent of median income), and the relative standard equivalent of the United States poverty line (40 percent of median income).
[23] Smeeding and Ross (1999).
[24] Beaujot et al. (2002).

thought of as necessarily causally prior to the effects of socioeconomic status on health outcomes.

The second line of reasoning stems from the aforementioned observation that SES gradients vary in their "steepness" across societies, such that there is no necessary, or predictable, level of health associated with any given position on the socioeconomic spectrum. Instead, health status at any given position is highly dependent on the extent to which different societies tie SES to one's ability to procure health-promoting resources and, conversely, the extent to which SES serves as a sorting mechanism for "exposures" that are harmful to health. Institutional arrangements, then, play a role in distributing health-promoting resources and buffering individuals from adverse exposures to their health more successfully than others. It can be argued that successful societies are those whose institutions work to break these ties. In other words, in some societies, factors fundamental to health are provided as rights of citizenship, rather than according to socioeconomic privilege.

These two types of roles of institutional arrangements are difficult to separate, since they may function in a reciprocal manner. That is, reductions in income inequality provide public support for increases in systems that distribute resources in an egalitarian manner, and the egalitarian distribution of resources in turn may reduce levels of socioeconomic inequality.[25] From the perspective of successful societies, an imperative of future research is to understand which institutional features promote socioeconomic equalities in population health (and by extension, as aforementioned, improving average population health), and which detract from it.

Income inequality as a benchmark of society's institutional orientation has been investigated at length. Early cross-national research showing a significant association between income inequality and average health status seemed consistent.[26] Soon, however, the results of these studies were contested, with charges of poor quality data, lack of control for potential "confounders" (such as transfer payments and social spending), and, perhaps most notably, the suggestion that results were driven primarily by the United States, which would thus mean that the finding of high income inequality leading to poor health was based on exception and could not be considered a general rule.[27]

The characterization of transfers and spending as confounders is highly debatable, since these may instead be part of the causal mechanism linking inequality to health.[28] The suggestion that the United States is an outlier has gained momentum with recent null results found for within-nation studies conducted in Japan,[29] Denmark,[30] and New Zealand.[31] In addition,

[25] Kawachi (2000).
[26] Wilkinson (1996).
[27] Judge (1995); Mackenbach (2002); Lynch et al. (2003).
[28] Wilkinson (1998); Kawachi (2000).
[29] Shibuya et al. (2002).
[30] Osler et al. (2002).
[31] Blakely et al. (2003).

Dunn, Ross, and colleagues have examined this association at several levels of geographic aggregation, including metropolitan area and state/province. Their findings suggest that, in Canada (and several European nations), regional differences in income inequality are not significantly associated with differences in population health. However, in the United States (and Britain) significant associations do exist.[32]

Though collectively, these results lend themselves to an outlier interpretation, there are also other compelling explanations. First, the United States and Britain have the highest levels of income inequality among the wealthy nations and much wider ranges in inequality among regions, which may be one explanation for an association within those countries and not others.[33] But that is not the whole story. The difference in the strength of the association does not appear to be solely related to the degree of income inequality. Accompanying social policies also seem to matter.

A study of U.S. metropolitan areas found that the level of public expenditure partially accounted for the effect of income inequality on mortality.[34] Since these analyses are cross-sectional in nature, it is difficult to assess reciprocity between distribution of income and public provision; however, the results do suggest that these factors operate in tandem. This would explain null results in countries that, in addition to (and likely due to) low levels of income inequality, also have more generous welfare states, offering more to a greater percentage of their populations.

In the end, notwithstanding the controversy over the relationship between income inequality and average health status across regions and societies, the fact remains that socioeconomic gradients drive population health status and deserve explanation.

Historically and internationally, increasing wealth has been a strong correlate of improved health status. This is much less the case among the world's wealthiest countries today.

Differences in wealth (measured as gross domestic product per capita) amongst the world's wealthiest countries are only weakly associated with health status differences among them.[35] In the early part of the twentieth century, there was a strong correlation between increasing GDP/capita and increased life expectancy for all countries in the world. As the century progressed and wealthy countries became wealthier, a "flat of the curve" gradually developed wherein this association weakened considerably. By 1990, the flat of the curve included those countries with GDPs per capita greater than US$11,000.[36] Nonetheless, it is among this group of countries that we find the five-year life expectancy difference already described. The implication here is that substantial health differences exist among the wealthiest

[32] Ross et al. (2000; 2005).
[33] Ibid.
[34] Dunn, Burgess, and Ross (2005).
[35] Wilkinson (1986).
[36] Rodgers (1979).

countries of the world, but these differences are not explained away by differences in wealth.

A complex interplay exists between societal factors, including those that influence material living conditions and the psychosocial environment, and acts to support or undermine health status. These determinants of health act at various levels of societal aggregation.

From the time of conception and throughout the life course, population health is influenced by factors operating at three primary levels of societal aggregation. At the macro level is the national socioeconomic environment: how wealthy a society is and how that wealth is distributed. At the meso level is civil society. To what extent do the institutions of civil society, as they are encountered on a daily basis, buffer or exacerbate the stresses of daily living, and promote or undermine living conditions that, over the long-term, are compatible with health and well-being? This includes a range of factors: social trust, participation, psychosocial working conditions, responsiveness of institutions to changing population needs, and neighborhood cohesion and safety, to name a few. Finally, at the micro level, relations in the private realm are fundamental; that is, the quality of stimulation, support, and nurturance that individuals experience, especially in the earliest stages of life.

To understand what makes some societies healthier than others, it is necessary to consider these various levels of social aggregation simultaneously. A strong argument suggests that income inequality appears to affect health by undermining civil society and eroding social cohesion and political participation.[37] Another suggests that, in wealthy societies, anxiety is one of the most important pathways linking health to social and economic circumstances because relatively equal societies are less stressful, less hostile, and less violent than more unequal societies.[38] Moreover, there is a strong tendency for social relationships and levels of social trust to weaken as the social structure becomes more hierarchical. Wilkinson makes an analogy to primate research on social hierarchy and well-being to draw a clear distinction between the direct effects of social status, on the one hand, and the indirect effects of material circumstances that are closely associated with social status, on the other.

The physiological effects of low social rank were observed in monkeys even in the complete absence of the plethora of differences in socioeconomic circumstances found among humans. The effects cannot therefore be attributed to jobs, housing, smoking, diet, debt, unemployment or whatever. So rather than being linked to social status only indirectly, through such socioeconomic factors, the effects appear to be due to the direct, or "pure," effects of social status.[39]

Many investigators doubt the validity of considering the direct effects of social status and the indirect effects of material circumstances as mutually

---

[37] Daniels, Kennedy, and Kawachi (1999).
[38] Wilkinson (2001).
[39] Wilkinson (2001: 35–6).

exclusive. Rather, evidence suggests that there is a range of factors at work, from the material to the psychosocial, and that it is difficult to assign ultimate primacy to any one. For instance, living in an environment of tightly constrained choices has both a material and a psychosocial component, as does living day to day with low income. Loss of control in relation to the material conditions of daily life may contribute to psychosocial stress; on the other hand, strong social support may mitigate it. Finally, it is clear that resiliencies and vulnerabilities can accumulate over the life course. Because of this complexity, there have been calls for a shift in emphasis from the search for ultimate primacy to the "epidemiology of daily life."[40]

Thus, from existing population health research, it is possible to construct a simple narrative about the social facts of health in wealthy societies. The narrative goes something like this: the principal factors responsible for increasing life expectancy from less than fifty years to more than seventy years in wealthy countries are to be found outside the health care system as it is traditionally defined and, instead, in the broader social and economic environment. Socioeconomic factors that could be related to improved health include improvements in housing, water supply, pollution control, nutrition, child spacing, working conditions, education, and a wide range of psychosocial factors. These latter tend to be more compatible with human health in prosperous, tolerant, democratic societies with strong civic communities. Some of the conditions just mentioned have improved through conscious efforts to address health and well-being. But others have been by-products of societal development per se and not subject to conscious human agency in the name of health. In sum, the history, wealth, and social and institutional arrangements within any human society, whether consciously intended to do so or not, powerfully influence all aspects of living conditions in that society, and thus the life chances of its population. Population health then reminds us, first and foremost, that we are a social species, and our health and development depend upon the quality of the environments where we grow up, live, and work.

Reconnecting Populations to the Individuals That Comprise Them

The ecological lens employed by population health has highlighted the importance of social facts as determinants of health. However, eventually social facts must somehow "penetrate the skin" and become biological facts for individuals. The term "biological embedding" has been used to describe this process,[41] and a search for better understanding of the underlying processes

---

[40] Attributable to George Kaplan, University of Michigan. Quoted in Link and Phelan (1996).

[41] Other scholars have forwarded alternative but similar concepts to biological embedding. Notable are the terms "habitus" (Bourdieu 1984) and "embodiment" (Krieger 2005). Habitus refers to one's propensities, dispositions, or tastes that are acquired socially, or from cultural conditioning. Embodiment is the physical expression through the physical being of the ecological, material, and social conditions or environments in which humans exist. Embodiment

has motivated the new interdisciplinary study of experience-based brain and biological development.[42]

Over the life course, experience penetrates the skin in three distinct ways. First, there is a latent (or programming) effect, wherein very early life experiences *permanently* shape brain architecture and human biology, such that human development and health is affected later in life *irrespective of intervening experiences*. Second, there is a pathway effect, wherein developmental trajectories are, in part, determined by living conditions that are associated with well-traveled socioeconomic careers that unfold over the life course. Growing up in a strong, affluent family in a safe and cohesive neighborhood leads to successful early child development, which leads to readiness for school, which leads to school success, which leads to broad career choices and socioeconomic success in adult life, which, in turn, supports high levels of health, well-being, and coping skills for the balance of life. Third, there is a cumulative effect, wherein personal resources/resiliencies and injuries/vulnerabilities influence development and health through an accumulation of effects over the individual's life course in a dose-response fashion. For example, development and health are more threatened by several years of poverty in childhood than by several months of poverty. Poverty associated with an unstable family environment is more damaging than either factor alone.[43]

HOW DO WE KNOW WHAT WE KNOW ABOUT POPULATION HEALTH, AND WHAT ARE WE MISSING?

The Value of Comparative Perspectives

In the field of social epidemiology, a key discipline in the study of population health, there is a strong tendency to look for universals. When it comes to the study of society and health, this approach leads to a search for "one big gradient" that relates SES and health in a single, overarching manner in all wealthy societies, obscuring the differentiation among societies and, thus, the flattening-up of socioeconomic gradients (discussed earlier). Only by comparing whole distributions in *each* society to one another can we see that the link between SES and population health is modifiable, and thus worth talking about.

(which arises in the epidemiological literature), in contrast to habitus, is less oriented to explaining human behaviors and more concerned with health outcomes. Habitus (which arises from the sociological literature) is an attempt to understand how structural aspects of society are incorporated (in largely nonhealth terms) into individuals. Neither of these concepts explicitly links social circumstances to specific biological processes that influence health status.

[42] Davey Smith et al. (1997); Kuh et al. (1997); Lynch et al. (1997); Marmot et al. (1997); Power et al. (1997).

[43] Hertzman et al. (2004).

When Should We Care about and Measure Societal Determinants and Health Outcomes? Opening Up Time Horizons

To date, the preponderance of evidence regarding societal influences on population health has been acquired across relatively short scales of time. In terms of both determinants and health outcomes of interest, research has been confined to processes that unfold within an individual lifetime. This creates a problem that goes beyond the relative scientific merit of cross-sectional versus longitudinal research. Prospective studies are of course preferable to cross-sectional studies, since they provide a more robust means for establishing causality. However, there is a broader issue that the methodologies of cross-sectional versus prospective research do not address. The issue here is the *time frame of interest in which causal influences and their resultant health outcomes unfold at the level of society*. The timescale over which a society develops (or destroys) health-enhancing infrastructure and social safety net functions may be quite long. Also the timescale over which these changes influence population health is probably long, unfolding over more than a single lifetime.

Processes Unfolding over Time

Consider the comparison of history and health status between Finland and the Baltic countries (Latvia, Lithuania, and Estonia). These four countries shared a common history within the Czarist Empire from the beginning of the nineteenth century until World War I and the revolution of 1917. During the interwar period, all four countries were independent, and each exited the Czarist Empire with similar health status, as measured by life expectancy, at the end of the war. Between 1921 and the late 1930s, the life expectancies of these four countries were very similar and continued to track each other closely. After World War II, however, the Baltic countries were incorporated into the Soviet Union, while Finland remained independent. This created an important "experiment of nature" wherein societies with 140 years of common political and economic experience (and similar health status) found themselves in different political, social, and economic regimes. What happened to health status following these changes?

Although the male trends are more dramatic than the female, the general pattern is the same and may be broken into three phases. During the first phase, stretching from 1950 (the beginning of regularly collected, reliable life expectancy data in the postwar era) to the early 1970s, life expectancy among the four countries tracked closely, as it had during the interwar period. However, starting in the early 1970s, Finland gradually began to diverge from the Baltic countries. Finnish life expectancy continued to rise through the 1970s and 1980s whereas, in the Baltic countries, it stopped rising (females) or even declined (males) during this period. The third phase began with the collapse of the Soviet Union in 1989, wherein dramatic short-term declines in health status, for both males and females, were seen in the Baltic countries, whereas health status continued to rise in Finland (despite the fact that the impact of Soviet economic collapse was widespread unemployment in Finland, due to loss of export markets there).

In the paper "Big, Slow-Moving, and ... Invisible" Paul Pierson[44] makes the claim that

Especially in economics and political science, the time horizons of most analysts have become increasingly restricted. In choosing what we seek to explain and in searching for explanations, we focus on the immediate; we look for causes and outcomes that are both temporally contiguous and rapidly unfolding. In the process, we miss a lot. There are important things that we do not see at all and what we do see we often misunderstand.

In support of this claim, Peter Hall writes:

Social science tends to look for causes that are immediate antecedents to an outcome (à la Hume). So if there is a big outcome, it looks for a "big" cause, thereby potentially missing a set of developments that are highly consequential but that build up only gradually over time so that they are not much noticed at the moment the outcome appears. Similarly, large or small events may have effects that are long lasting and/or show up only over time that those searching for immediate effects may miss.[45]

To get beyond this problem, Pierson has proposed a simple 2×2 table, in which "cause" and "effect" can each be divided into "short-term" and "long-term," producing four combinations: short-short, long-short, short-long, and long-long.[46] From the perspective of population health, the use of the 2×2 table is very appealing because it provides a concise organization of the potential explanatory range of relationships between determinants and outcomes. In particular it opens our minds to long-term social processes (the cause) that may have either long-term or short-term impacts on health (the effect).

For the comparison of Finland versus the Baltic republics, this approach becomes important in understanding the distinction between the second and third phase just described. Whereas the third phase relates to causal mechanisms that unfold over the short term, phase two is an example of the "long time horizon of cause/long time horizon of outcome" contingency. Somehow, the health status influences of Finnish independence versus Baltic incorporation into the Soviet Union after World War II took more than twenty-five years to emerge, and, when they did, they emerged so gradually that the divergent trend in health status was not entirely evident, and not commented upon, until near the end of the Soviet period.

The Finland versus the Baltic countries comparison is then a clear-cut example showing that Pierson's long-long contingency *can* apply in the field

---

[44] Pierson (2003): 178.
[45] Peter Hall, in conversation.
[46] Pierson (2003): 179.

of population health. This is not to claim that a deeper analysis of the events of the postwar period would necessarily show that it *was* an example of the fourth contingency. Rather, it establishes the *plausibility* of the claim that social processes, evolving over decades, *can* have impacts on population health that, similarly, unfold gradually over years and decades. Analyzing population health in this comparative, historical perspective is consistent with the suggestion that analyses of the big structures and large processes that shape our era should be both concrete (having real times, places, and people as their referents) and historical (in recognizing that time matters).[47] However, this line of thinking also argues that for historical analyses to be useful, they must involve comparisons of *eras*, themselves bounded by well-defined processes or events. In the field of population health, we are not yet clear enough on the processes that influence health outcomes (nor the mechanisms through which societal factors manifest into health outcomes) to be able to define relevant eras with much precision.

Perhaps it is because of the intuitively appealing notion of boundedness (of both independent and dependent variables) in scientific study that the short-short contingency has been the dominant paradigm for research on population health. Short-term changes in health status, following dramatic social change (for example, the end of the Soviet era in Central and Eastern Europe) attract much more attention than gradual social change and its impact. This has meant that some very important phenomena have been ignored, and understandings about how slow-moving social change might influence human health and well-being have not been adequately explored.

We address these issues through a case study of population health in Canada versus the United States. Specifically, we examine health trends in these two nations over the past fifty years, and provide evidence of large and slow-moving structural changes in these societies that may account for both convergences and divergences in health status. We provide speculative accounts of the mechanisms through which these macro phenomena may lead to changes in population health. In particular, we focus not only on the manner in which structural changes in society are tantamount to the building up (or tearing down) of health-enhancing infrastructure but also on the fact that because these changes occur in a gradual manner, their effects on more meso-level and micro-level determinants of health culminate in population health shifts that are discernable only from an historical, longitudinal perspective.

Of note, despite the fact that we are dealing with two societies that have high-quality statistics-gathering capabilities, it was not easy to find comparable data covering the entire postwar period. Notwithstanding this shortcoming, the comparison of societal evolution in these two nations provides insights regarding institutional arrangements that are positive and those that are insufficient for supporting population health.

---

[47] Tilly (1984).

POPULATION HEALTH AND THE DYNAMICS OF COLLECTIVE
DEVELOPMENT: A COMPARATIVE, MULTIPLE-TIME HORIZON
PERSPECTIVE ON CANADA VERSUS THE UNITED STATES

The contrast of Canada versus the United States is particularly instructive.
The longitudinal approach that we have taken allows us to see dynamics
between societal structures and societal health status that would not otherwise be revealed. During the analysis that follows, we are able to establish
that (1) more wealth and spending on health care does not yield better health
outcomes, (2) public provision and income redistribution have greater effects
on population health, and (3) the gradual development of public provision
represents the buildup of social infrastructure that has long-lasting effects
on health status. We proceed by comparing Canada and the United States on
basic health outcomes and presenting an analysis of health differences using a
range of determinants of health for which routine data have been collected for
all or most of the period between 1950 and the present.

Health Outcomes

Figure 1.2 compares American and Canadian life expectancy, in five-year
averages, from 1950 to 2000. As of 1950, the life expectancy of Canadians
and Americans was similar, with a slight American advantage for women
and a small Canadian advantage for men. During the 1950s and 1960s, a
gap opened up such that both male and female life expectancy in Canada
increased faster than that in the United States. In the late 1970s, the gap
narrowed considerably, but starting around 1980, it opened again and continued to widen until it reached approximately two years by the end of the
twentieth century. Although differences in infant mortality contribute to
the gap, it is driven, primarily, by differences in adult mortality. A two-year
life expectancy gap may not sound like a lot, but during ages 25 to 64 it
translates into mortality rates 30 to 50 percent per year higher in the United
States compared to Canada. Socioeconomic analyses show that the poorest
20 percent of Canadians enjoy the same life expectancy as Americans of average income.[48] Thus, the Canada-United States difference is considerable and
deserves explanation.

The patterns of relative change in male and female life expectancy are
included here because they may reflect changing social roles. In both countries, female life expectancy exceeded male by approximately 5 years in the
early 1950s and reached its maximum (7.5 years in the United States, 7 years
in Canada) between 1975 and 1980. Then, the gap began to close as quickly
as it opened such that, by 2000, it was down to 5.5 years in both Canada and
the United States. We will expand upon this trend later.

---

[48] Singh et al. (2002); Wilkins et al. (2002).

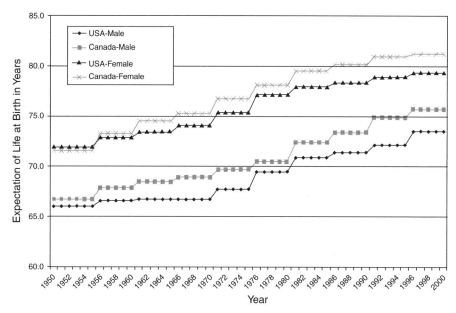

FIGURE 1.2. Male and female life expectancy in Canada versus the United States. *Source:* Organization for Economic Co-operation and Development Web site: http://www. oecd.org, accessed June 2008.

Analysis

Over time, more economic prosperity and more health care spending did not yield better health. We begin with the insufficient conditions, which we consider to be significant because their insufficiency is entirely counterintuitive. As mentioned earlier, research on other social processes in relation to population health came about only after cross-sectional studies showed little association between GDP per capita, health care expenditures, and measures of population health. Our data demonstrate that, even when a long view on measures of economic prosperity, spending on health care, and health are taken, the association is nonexistent.

Figure 1.3 shows that from 1975 to 1988, purchasing power parity (PPP) adjusted GDP/capita grew in Canada and the United States and tracked closely. From 1988 to 1993, however, PPP adjusted GDP/capita continued to grow in the United States, but did not grow at all in Canada. From 1994 to 2002, growth rates in Canada and the United States were once again in parallel, but because of the five-year period of stagnation in Canada, its PPP adjusted GDP/capita remained approximately 20 percent lower than that in the United States. A similar pattern emerged for unemployment rates (Figure 1.3), which show that from the end of the Second World War until 1982, unemployment rates in the two nations mirrored each other; however, from 1982 to 2000,

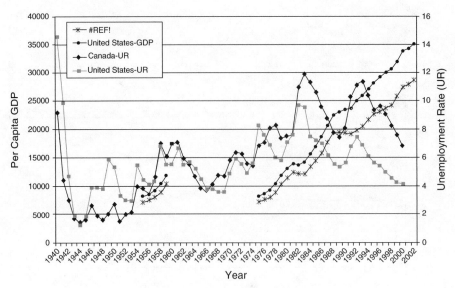

FIGURE 1.3. Per capita GDP and unemployment rates, 1940–2002.
Source: Organization for Economic Co-operation and Development Web site: http://www.
oecd.org, accessed June 2008.

unemployment rates in Canada were consistently 2 to 4 percent higher than those in the United States. These data demonstrate that Canadian health status increasingly surpassed that of the United States in a period in which economic growth in the United States moved increasingly ahead of Canada.

Moreover, spending on health care (Figure 1.4) in the United States increasingly surpassed Canada during a time in which Canada had a national Medicare scheme and the United States did not. From the 1960s to 1973, health care spending in the two countries tracked closely, reaching approximately 7 percent in 1973, at which point the spending trajectories of these two nations diverged considerably. Canada stayed under 10 percent until 2002; however, the United States rose to 14 percent by the same year. This occurred despite the implementation of a universal, single-payer Medicare plan in Canada, and a plan that is universal only for seniors in the United States. (It should also be noted that total government spending per capita on health care is greater in the United States than it is in Canada, despite the fact that coverage is not universal in the former.)

Having detailed social factors (growth and health care spending) that intuitively would foster health, but turn out to be insufficient for doing so, the health-promoting institutional features are also significant because of the contrast they create. The period during which Canadian life expectancy increasingly surpassed the United States was a time when Canada's levels of public spending on social programs, the redistributive work of its social safety net,

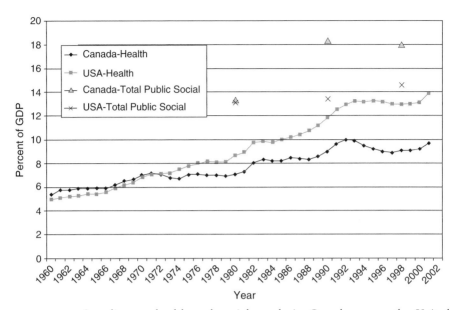

FIGURE 1.4. Spending on health and social goods in Canada versus the United States.
Source: Organization for Economic Co-operation and Development Web site: http://www.oecd.org, accessed June 2008. Data courtesy of Dr. Will Kymlicka.

levels of maintained income equity, and levels of access to education were all surpassing that in the United States (see Figures 1.4 and 1.5).

In 1980, public social expenditures consumed approximately 13 percent of GDP in both Canada and the United States (Figure 1.4). By 1990, a large and persistent gap had opened, such that Canada was spending more than 4 percent of GDP more than the United States (approximately 18 and 14 percent, respectively). Similar trends are also apparent when distributions of income are compared.

During the 1970s, the Gini coefficients of income inequality (Figure 1.5), post tax and transfer, were very similar in Canada and the United States (high 20s and low 30s, respectively), indicating a small difference in inequality, with Canada slightly more egalitarian. From then until the late 1990s, the Gini stayed in the same range in Canada but increased (became more unequal) in the United States, such that there was a five-point gap by the late 1980s and a gap of approximately seven points by the late 1990s. In other words, over this time, the United States became increasingly more income unequal than Canada.

This seems largely attributable to the differences in the redistributive policies in the countries. From the early 1980s to the early 1990s, the net impact of the Canadian tax and transfer programs was to reduce the level of inequality based on market income by up to 31 percent. By contrast, in the United

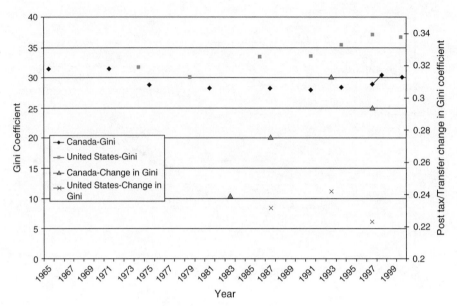

FIGURE 1.5. Income inequality in Canada versus the United States – the influences of taxes and transfers, 1965–2000.
Source: Organization for Economic Co-operation and Development Web site: http://www. oecd.org, accessed June 2008.

States, the redistributive mechanisms reduced inequality by between 22.5 and 24.5 percent during this period. The relative differences between the countries were particularly marked in their success at poverty reduction.[49] In 1974–5, taxes and transfers reduced poverty by approximately 11 percent in both countries. By 1994, poverty reduction had risen to 24 percent in Canada but only to 13 percent in the United States.

Thus, where the labor market intersects with the social safety net, Canada differs from the United States. In particular, Canada scores higher on the indexes of unemployment protection, labor relations, and corporate governance,[50] constructed during the 1990s, that are designed to distinguish "liberal" from "coordinated" market economies.

The Canada-United States comparison is one of public provision and redistribution trumping traditional economic growth and direct health spending in producing population health. This conclusion is reinforced by the observation that, from the early 1970s to the late 1990s, socioeconomic gradients in health status did not get steeper in Canada. Over the twenty-five-year period from 1971 to 1996, each of the income quintile groups in Canada gained equitably in terms of rising life expectancy.[51] The same was not true in the United States,

[49] Zuberi (2001).
[50] Estevez-Abe et al. (2001).
[51] Wilkins et al. (2002).

where the highest income quintiles gained life expectancy at a faster pace than the lowest quintile.[52]

WHY RELATIVE INCOME AND PUBLIC PROVISION MATTER FOR POPULATION HEALTH: A LOOK AT POTENTIAL MECHANISMS LINKING SOCIAL INEQUALITY TO POPULATION HEALTH

Earlier in the chapter, we touched on the issue of biological pathways through which societal factors could affect health. However, the manner and degree to which different factors actually "get under the skin" and trigger biology to an extent that would change the health of populations, remain vastly under-investigated. For now, what we have are plausible hypotheses. An important note before we present each of them. In the literature, often times each hypothesis has been presented as mutually exclusive of (and, in fact, in competition with) the others. For the sake of clarity, we will present each separately; however, it is our belief that these pathways operate together in different combinations and permutations in different contexts.

"The material well-being and its political support" hypothesis: This hypothesis suggests that inequality and public provision influence health through their effect on "the differential accumulation of exposures and experiences that have their sources in the material world."[53] It also asserts that lowering inequality leads to more political support for the availability of public goods and services, such as investments in education, health care, transportation, quality housing, and other health-related resources.[54] Income inequality is thought to be inversely associated with social spending due to the increasingly diverging interests of the rich and the poor, as the gap between them widens.

The psychosocial hypothesis: This hypothesis suggests that widening inequalities result in stress induced by the shame and frustration that accompanies feelings of material and status related inadequacies and the phenomena of "keeping up with the Jones."[55] It is buttressed by evidence showing that psychosocial stresses increase with decreasing SES, and that biological pathways that respond to psychosocial stresses also have the capacity to "age" human organ systems.

The social networks and social capital hypothesis: Another major hypothesis relates to the health impact of inequality through its effects on the ability of people to feel socially connected to others. Here, population health draws on Durkheim's seminal work on the association between social integration and suicide. Research on social networks and health has demonstrated that individuals with fewer ties to friends, families, and social groups have a much higher mortality risk than those who are more socially connected.[56] In fact,

---

[52] Singh et al. (2002).
[53] Lynch et al. (1997).
[54] Kawachi (2000).
[55] Wilkinson (1999).
[56] Berkman et al. (1979).

research in this area has been able to apply the gold standard methodology for establishing causality, the randomized controlled trial. By randomizing individuals to receive cold virus experimental evidence was able to show that those individuals with stronger social networks were less likely to contract cold symptoms than those with weaker networks.[57] This is attributed to the effects on the immune system of feeling connected to others. The more macro approach of looking at connected societies has also been explored. Using data from the United States, Kawachi and colleagues have used both ecological and multilevel studies to examine the relationships between income inequality, social trust, and measures of population health, finding strong associations between all three.[58]

The security hypothesis: So far, we have presented the hypotheses that have emerged from the field of social epidemiology, but these do not exhaust the possibilities. The big elements in the Canada-United States comparison focus on inequality and public provision suggesting that, from a population health perspective, the key differences between market economies are the returns to income and the extent/quality of public provision. Since these factors trump economic growth and health care spending, the question arises, can we disentangle the influences of public provision from income distribution? It may be that public provision acts as a mechanism to provide a measure of "security as a right of citizenship." In other words, the effect of public provision is to improve the security of individuals by reducing their exposure to market competition and other social risks. Clearly, some aspects of public provision improve the income of the less affluent but, in the Canada-United States context, most public provisions go to programs that improve security through mechanisms other than direct income redistribution.

The security hypothesis then suggests that reductions in inequality and improvements in public provision collectively work to provide individuals and societies many of the main health-promoting resources (such as income and education, but also quality transportation systems and clean, safe neighborhoods). Further, that there is some sense in which the government recognizes the "entitlement" of all citizens to these goods and thus works to provide them, thus decreasing the stress-inducing burden of individuals to find ways of procuring these resources themselves.

BIG, SLOW-MOVING PROCESSES

Understanding the Evolution of Population Health over Time

The Canada–United States comparison is a story of gradual change in population health status due to a combination of concurrent processes, long-term

---

[57] Cohen et al. (1997).
[58] Subramanian et al. (2002).

processes preceding the population health trend, and some combination of the two. The social processes tracked in this case study are concurrent with the divergence in health status between Canada and the United States, focusing our attention on the former. However, if it is true that the Canada-United States comparison is one of public provision and redistribution trumping traditional economic well-being and direct health spending from the perspective of population health, then long-term institutional evolution must be considered as well. In the United States, account needs to be taken of the New Deal, the postwar GI bills, the Great Society programs, and the Reagan-era rollbacks that followed. In Canada, the history is one of a more muted response to the Great Depression, but a gradual phasing in of national hospital and unemployment insurance, old age pensions, physician coverage, federal-provincial social assistance transfers, increasing secondary and tertiary education subsidies, and increasingly "progressive" labor legislation after World War II that caught up with, then surpassed, the American programs by the 1970s and were not eroded, at least to the same degree, thereafter.

THE MALE–FEMALE LIFE EXPECTANCY GAP

Many of these insights are also illuminated through a well-documented phenomenon that has been observed over the past thirty years. The trend in question is that of general worldwide convergence in life expectancies between males and females, such that from 1978 to 2003, males have experienced "catch up" with females, resulting in a narrower gap than previously documented. However, within the wealthier nations, the amount by which this gap has been reduced has differed and, it appears, systematically so. Here we pursue the hypothesis that, among the resource-rich countries, a pattern emerges such that the extent of the gender gap in life expectancy correlates highly with differences in social welfare institutions, as measured by the typology of welfare states created by Esping-Anderson.[59] Though indeed speculative, this question opens important avenues for further investigation of the effects of societal institutions on population health.

Remarkably, the ordering of nations fits his classification scheme perfectly, such that Liberal Welfare States (such as Canada and the United States and characterized by high use of market mechanisms to distribute social goods) exhibited the greatest narrowing of the gap (2.7 years on average between 1978 and 2003), Social Democratic States (such as Sweden, Denmark, and Norway, which provide the greatest extent of social goods without regard to gender or family status) experienced mid-level narrowing (1.8 years on average), and the Corporatist Welfare States (such as Belgium, Italy, and Germany, which favor distribution of benefits to families, rather than individuals) with the smallest narrowing (0.9 years on average). There were no overlaps between the three

[59] Esping-Anderson (1990).

groups of countries; all the Liberal Welfare States narrowed more than all the Social Democratic that, in turn, all narrowed faster than the Corporatist. Examination of the trends shows that the differences were primarily related to how women's life expectancy fared. It fared best in the Corporatist countries, worst in the Liberal, with the Social Democratic countries falling somewhere in between.

This strength of the association between reduction in the male–female life expectancy gap and the type of welfare state provides a strong indication that institutional features about societies have contributed in some important way. Due in large part to the women's movement, beginning in the mid 1960s, the proportion of women in the workforce increased substantially from the period immediately after to present day. If it is the case that, during this time, they did not experience reductions in their home task, then the second-shift phenomenon[60] and the increased "wear and tear" for women but not men, may help to explain, at the micro level, the convergence of life expectancies. It may also be the case that an increased presence of women in workplace environments (independent of the second-shift) resulted in health-harming exposures that had previously been limited to men. In either of these scenarios, it is clear that more attention needs to be paid to the epidemiology of daily life and the institutions that influence it.

Returning to the ranking of nations, it also seems that these micro phenomena may be entrenched in more macro features of society. For instance, the availability of affordable child care seems likely to be an important contributor to reductions in "wear and tear"; a factor that varies systematically among the different types of welfare states. The Liberal welfare states have generally been weak in family support programs and the provision of quality child care has largely been left to the market. Those that have the resources to procure it do; those that do not find makeshift alternatives. By contrast, the Social Democratic welfare states are far more generous, providing child care through subsidized or universal programs, as well as family support, but with a focus on encouraging female labor force participation. Finally, the Corporatist welfare states have generally focused more on family support programs than on child care. These institutional differences between the three groups of welfare states emerged gradually over time, as did the striking differences in the narrowing of the male–female life expectancy gap. This is another example where a careful study of big, slow-moving processes may provide a deeper level of understanding of the impact of society's institutions on health.

RECONNECTING THE MECHANISMS: DRILLING DOWN FROM
MACRO TO MICRO IN CANADA VERSUS UNITED STATES

Our discussion thus far primarily conveys the importance of societal institutions and policies in determining population health status. After all, most of

---

[60] Greenstein (2000).

the available data allow us to compare macro-level phenomena, though some of the indicators go to meso or micro levels, such as schools. This emphasis on the macro is salutary because, compared with individual-level factors such as health behaviors and genetic predispositions, the impact of society on our health has been sorely neglected. However, we believe that it is equally misleading to suggest (however implicitly), that the understanding of the effects of institutional features should be divorced from the understanding of the effects of more localized environments and individual determinants. For example, the security hypothesis underlies the interlinkage between macro, meso, and micro.

Without understanding how institutions are manifest in the social reality of "ground zero" (in the moment and at the local level) analysis at this high level is, at best, decontextualized and may be misleading.[61] Here, we need to add the term "local biologies" to the lexicon of biological embedding, habitus and embodiment. Local biologies refers "to the way in which physical sensations, well-being, health, illness and so on are experienced differently depending on evolutionary, historical, lifespan, social, and individual factors that vary from place to place."[62] The work of Collins and Lock remind us that "drilling down from macro to micro" is not an exercise in accumulating universal laws at the macro level that apply to all locales in a deterministic manner.

A qualitative study of low-income hotel workers' lives in Seattle and Vancouver provides evidence of the interdependence of the macro, meso, and micro levels of society in their contribution to supporting or undermining human well-being.[63] The study is important because it deals with an economically vulnerable group that includes many immigrants and visible minorities whose life experiences are exquisitely sensitive to societal institutions. The results clearly indicate that, in multiple domains, well-being in this population amongst those residing in Canada is superior to those residing in the United States. One major contribution was the higher rate of unionization found in Canada compared to the United States. The ability of unionized hotel workers to secure collective agreements in Canada provided them with higher wages, improved benefits, better working conditions, and increased job security than their U.S. counterparts. Further, there was a spillover effect even for non-unionized service sector workers, through the prevailing wage standards set by unions, and the ability of unions to advocate for workers at multiple levels of political organization.

Differences in medical insurance are also salient to this analysis. Lack of universal medical coverage among the Seattle workers led, in several cases, to severe economic hardship following illness, which none of the Canadian respondents reported.

---

[61] Collins (2004).
[62] Lock et al. (2006).
[63] Zuberi (2006).

Canada also maintains more generous social welfare policies than the United States. The study found that more hotel workers from Seattle reported having to rely on the financial support of their social networks during hard times, compared to respondents from Vancouver. Further, more respondents in Seattle worked multiple jobs to make ends meet. Those in Vancouver were more positive about their neighborhoods than those in Seattle. This "has to do with the higher levels of government support for the institutions and infrastructure in the neighborhoods where the ... 'working poor' live in Vancouver as compared to Seattle. In Vancouver, these neighborhoods often more closely resembled middle-class neighborhoods in terms of quality of life and density of community institutions."[64] This observation reflects the fact that Canada invests far more than the United States in "bread and butter" infrastructure such as high-quality public transit, public education, community centers, child care facilities, public recreational facilities, medical facilities, and well-maintained parks. This, in turn, leads to a greater opportunity to avoid marginalization and to join the middle class in Canada compared to the United States.

Overall, this example points to how Canada–United States societal differences at each level of aggregation lead to systematic differences in individuals' life experiences: material well-being, psychosocial supports and stressors, security and connection to community. In other words, Canadian societal institutions, compared to those found in the United States, are vastly more supportive of local biologies that are health promoting.

GOOD HEALTH IN BAD TIMES: RUSSIA VERSUS CZECH REPUBLIC

The mechanisms through which institutions influence population health are also well illustrated by comparing nations that experience different health impacts during difficult times. Here we examine Russia and the Czech Republic during the difficult postcommunist transition period of the late 1980s to mid 1990s. Russia experienced a massive decline in population health status during this period, such that by the mid 1990s male expectation of life had fallen to 57 years, compared to approximately 70 years in the Czech Republic. For females, life expectancy declined markedly in Russia from 74 to approximately 71 years, whereas in the Czech Republic, life expectancy for women was largely unaffected. Contrary to general expectations, mortality increases were greatest in the working age population (25 to 64) not in the young or the old.

Macro-level social disruption was widespread in Russia during the transition, but was muted in the Czech Republic, as underscored by several indicators described in this paragraph. A cardinal indicator of poverty, the percentage of births to women under the age of 20 years, declined by 40 percent in the Czech

[64] Ibid.

Republic, but increased by 32 percent in Russia from the late 1980s to the early 1990s. This resulted in an increase of children in infant homes[65] in Russia of 64 percent, with no change in the Czech Republic. As well, Russia witnessed a massive increase in adoption rates, where the rate doubled, compared with only a 54 percent rise in the Czech Republic.[66] At kindergarten, though both nations experienced a decrease in enrollment, it was far more modest in the Czech Republic (7.5 percent) than in Russia (19 percent).[67] In the Czech Republic, GDP per capita was largely unaffected by the transition (where it decreased by 3 percent), while Russia experienced large declines, in the order of 44.3 percent.[68] Real wages in Russia decreased by over half (55.4 percent), while the Czech Republic made modest gains of about 2 percent.[69] Another divergent factor at the macro level was income distribution. The Czech Republic was able to stabilize income distribution during this period (with a rise in the Gini coefficient of only .06 – from .20 to .26), whereas in Russia, the Gini coefficient surged from .27 to .48.[70] This suggests that the Czech Republic's economy was more resilient to the transition than that of Russia. However, unemployment rates were high in both countries during that time, which implies that there were also institutional differences that buffered the Czech Republic from health and economic losses but contributed to the shocks in these areas felt by Russia. This is further evidenced by the modest increase in annual internal migration rates[71] (often correlated with high unemployment) in the Czech Republic (0.98 percent) compared with Russia (5.5 percent).[72]

In 1996, the health of a random sample of 1,599 Russian adults was studied under the auspices of the New Russia Barometer. This work was important because it allowed researchers to drill down from macro to micro for understandings of the health crisis in Russia. The Barometer included information on the individual's life course, informal social networks, reliance on "civil society" institutions, socioeconomic circumstances, and perception of life chances.[73] Each of these dimensions helped explain Russians' health status: life course (represented by education), informal social network (marriage and capacity to rely on informal networks for food and other necessities), civil society (reliance and trust of formal institutions), socioeconomic environment (material deprivation), and perception of life chances (life control). Increased education, stronger informal social networks, lower levels of material deprivation, and high levels of life control were all associated with

---

[65] Figures represent rates per 1,000 population of children aged 0 to 3 years.
[66] UNICEF (1999).
[67] Ibid.
[68] Ibid.
[69] Ibid.
[70] Ibid.
[71] Figures represent the difference from 1989 to 1995 in the rate per 1,000 population.
[72] Arnold (1964); Addison et al. (2001).
[73] Hertzman et al. (2002).

better health. *Most important here, however, was the finding that high levels of reliance upon formal institutions in Russian society were associated with the worst health.* In other words, those whose informal networks for obtaining food and other necessities were too weak to provide for them had to fall back on traditional Soviet-style institutions. The fact that these people ended up with the worst health is evidence of the weakness of the meso-level institutions they were forced to rely upon during bad times.

In Russia the image that best described the institutional environment at the time of transition was an "hourglass."[74] This suggests a society with an elite that controls the available economic and political structures, a population whose capacity to buffer the stresses of daily living is limited, and individuals who have an overwhelming need to rely on the intimate realm of family and informal social supports to compensate for a lack of institutional supports. Before the political transition, the relationship between the top and bottom of the hourglass was stable, with a modicum of mutual obligation between the state and the individual. Afterwards, mutual obligation was abandoned. Those in early and middle adulthood, who were most reliant on formal institutions to earn a living and support families, were more vulnerable for increased mortality than the very young and the very old, whose well-being depended, to a greater extent, on the intimate realm of the family.

In summary, the transition from communism to a market-based economy disrupted population health in Russia far more than Czech Republic. It would appear that the manner in which the Czech Republic's institutions were organized buffered the impact of the transition on population health. Maintenance or improvement in national income and distribution of income, protection from the effects of soaring unemployment, and protection of those most reliant on formal institutions were features of the Czech transition, but not the Russian.

One additional factor is of note for this case study. The population health trends described for Russia and the Czech Republic and the institutional features used to explain their divergence occurred concurrently. However, to understand how societal institutions in Russia failed to respond in a manner similar to those of the Czech Republic, one must go further back in time. We suggest here that, when a dramatic, common current time change in macro determinants occurs (such as the postcommunist transition), that understanding population health similarities and differences across societies requires an historical perspective of institutional evolution; one that accounts for the gradual change of institutional features of society preceding sudden change.

Whether or not population health declines with a decline in prosperity will depend on the presence of institutions that fulfill several functions. First, it will depend on the existence of systems that redistribute income across the population (proxied perhaps by a measure of income inequality). There are

---

[74] Rose (1995).

two sides to those systems, one rooted in the structure of market mechanisms (some economies have institutions, such as strong trade unions, that resist increases in income inequality) and the other rooted in public policy (some polities have institutions for delivering services to the poor and for offsetting declines in market income with tax-based transfer programs). The evidence presented lends support to the hypothesis that, where these systems are strong (and they can be measured directly or they can be measured indirectly by the change in income inequality), collectively, they have the capacity to offset the effects of a decline in the rate of growth of GDP on population health.

Second, it will depend on a set of institutions that perform several health-related functions. These include, first, offering personal or family-based support that is, broadly speaking, material to those who lose access to work-related resources or public resources previously provided (including health care, child care, and loans) and, second, offering sources of personal meaning and the type of validation that enhances self-respect and hope to those who have lost employment or income. The hypothesis is that where social structures capable of providing this support are strong (and that is hard to measure but may be proxied by several social capital variables), a decline in the rate of growth of GDP will be accompanied by a smaller decline in health outcomes.

This formulation is germane not only to the question of good health in bad times but also to a focus on long-term causal processes because both of the sets of circumstances that have been described, which are capable of offsetting the effects of a decline in prosperity, are built up only over long periods of time. This includes: the institutions of the market economy, systems of public provision, and the relevant social structures. Furthermore, this formulation is based upon an implied notion that health-endangering stresses in the broad socioeconomic environment will be buffered by other social and institutional arrangements. Some of these latter are state programs, but others depend upon regional and local actors, family members, and the quality of informal social relations. In other words, understanding how societies maintain good health in bad times depends upon understanding how to think from macro to micro in terms of social processes that support or undermine health.

CONCLUSION

Our story began with the proposition that, among the wealthiest nations of the world, neither further increases in economic well-being nor increased spending on health care is a sufficient (or even necessary) condition for improving population health. Prior research has viewed health through the lens of socioeconomic inequalities and has provided remarkable insights. With the support of cross-national evidence, and in particular the phenomenon of flattening-up socioeconomic gradients across countries, we have come to understand that the association between SES and health, though resilient, is nonetheless modifiable. What then are the systematic differences across societies that account for this pattern? One strong candidate explanation is the

institutional differences between societies that create differences in the degree
of socioeconomic inequality, and the extent to which socioeconomic inequality affects the procurement of "resources" essential for health. Studies of population health have begun to address these institutional differences. However,
the methods and frameworks brought to bear on this issue so far are limited
in terms of the types of causal factors investigated and the ability to understand trends in population health over long periods of time. Our contention
is that research on population health to date has focused on point-in-time
understandings of health, particularly causal associations that occur concurrently to the health outcomes they affect. What is neglected is significant:
slow-moving processes of institutional evolution and resultant incremental
changes in population health.

Using the example of Canada versus the United States, we show what can
be gleaned from a comparative perspective and a long-term view. The long
view allows us to detect the gradual divergence in health status between these
two societies and to trace potential institutional causes that would otherwise
go unnoticed. We saw that, over a twenty-year period of economic stagnation and unemployment in Canada versus sustained economic growth in the
United States, health in Canada still prevailed. The dominant role played by
institutional factors such as mechanisms for income distribution and redistribution as well as the public provision of other health-related resources seems
to account for this most counterintuitive of trends. Public provision could be
seen as something that is established at one or two points in time and thus
not, strictly speaking, a large slow-moving process. However, it could act as
a buffer, offering better/good health in bad times and, therefore, reflect a factor whose effects are best seen perhaps over time. Moreover, if it is true that
once some substantial public provision is established, it tends to grow over
time, either because supply creates its own political demand or via some other
political mechanism, then it would qualify as a slow-moving process.

In summary, the perspective introduced here, and in particular the comparison of Canada and the United States, provides strong support for the use of
cross-national comparative work, and a long-term view on the investigation of
societies that successfully support population health.

2

Social Interactions in Human Development

Pathways to Health and Capabilities

Daniel P. Keating

The starting point for this chapter is the well-established finding relating social position to a wide range of health outcomes, described in numerous recent reviews of contemporary research and summarized in Chapter 1.[1] This has sometimes been described as the "health/wealth" effect because health outcomes, including mortality, are reliably associated with both household income and accumulated wealth. But aspects of social position beyond wealth or income are also reliably related to these health outcomes, sometimes even more strongly, as is often the case with educational level. Other features of social patterning, such as race, ethnicity, neighborhood of residence, or the degree of community segregation by income, education, and minority status, are also related to a wide range of health outcomes.[2]

A common finding on the pattern of effects of income, wealth, education, occupation, and social status on health outcomes is that it is almost invariably *monotonic*: The effects can be observed throughout the distribution, and tend to show the same trend across the entire population. In other words, having more of any of these social "goods" is associated with better health outcomes

---

[1] Recent reviews have examined numerous aspects of the social patterning of health, from a variety of perspectives (Keating and Hertzman 1999b; Hertzman 2001; Smedley, Syme, and Committee on Capitalizing on Social Science and Behavioral Research to Improve the Public's Health, 2001; Adler and Newman 2002; Rodgers 2002; Boyce and Keating 2004; Lynch et al. 2004:; Marmot 2004; Schnittker 2004; Hatch 2005; Link and Phelan 2005; Williams 2005). A general note to the reader: because this chapter draws upon large research literatures across a number of disciplines, the primary citations will be, where possible, to recent comprehensive reviews that are accessible to a wider audience. The primary research literature for various topics can be found in the bibliographies of those research reviews.

[2] It is also important to note that these various features of social patterning of health often interact with each other, yielding complex findings that health researchers continue to try to disentangle (Deaton 2002; Williams, Neighbors, and Jackson 2003; Marmot 2004; Stolley, LaViest, and Krieger 2004; Dunn, Burgess, and Ross 2005; Williams 2005; Dunn et al. 2006).

across the whole population distribution.[3] Threshold effects are generally not found; it seems that there is generally no level beyond some threshold of income, education, and so on, that, having been reached, no longer matters for health. These characteristics of the findings – monotonic throughout the population and without clear thresholds – have often been captured in the notion of a *gradient*, which can be graphed as a slope that depicts this relationship: having more social goods or a more advantaged social position (horizontal axis) is associated with having better health (vertical axis), at least at the population level (see Figure 1.1).

This gradient has been thought of in a number of ways, depending in part on the research discipline in which it is being studied, and in part on the theoretical orientation of the researchers. It can be thought of as an *income gradient* if the specific interest is on the distribution of health across levels of income. It can be seen as a *health gradient* if one focuses on the outcomes without committing to any particular input to the gradient. Given the observed pervasiveness of the relationship between social position (measured in a variety of ways) and health outcomes (broadly defined), it can perhaps be most generally described as a "social gradient of health," or for our purposes, simply as a *social gradient*.

The widespread acceptance of the reality of this social gradient does not imply widespread agreement as to its underlying causes, which remain in considerable dispute. The picture becomes more complex with the recognition that numerous social categories beyond income or education are implicated in the pattern of the social gradient, for example, race and ethnicity, where, unsurprisingly, minority populations are at a health disadvantage.[4]

Understanding the mechanisms and pathways that give rise to this social gradient is an essential task for an agenda focused on successful societies, on the reasonable, even indisputable presumption that good population health is a desirable outcome for any society. The range of possible mechanisms is lengthy, and most of the work within social epidemiology and economics, the disciplines that have given the most attention to this topic, has focused on broad social trends such as income inequality, access to health care, or differential health behaviors. Some portion of the gradient can be accounted for by each of these contributing factors, at least in some circumstances, but taken together, they do not appear to account for the majority of the differences among health outcomes that are cumulatively described as the social gradient.[5] Identifying the underlying mechanisms of the social gradient through studies of social partitioning have been only moderately successful, owing in part to the large amounts of variation in health outcomes that remain unexplained

[3] Marmot et al. (1997); Deaton (2002); Kristenson et al. (2004: 1512); Marmot (2004); Ross et al. (2006).
[4] Deaton and Lubotsky (2003); Williams, Neighbors, and Jackson (2003); Farmer and Ferraro (2005); Williams (2005); Borrell et al. (2006).
[5] Marmot (2004); Link and Phelan (2005); Ross et al. (2006); Hertzman and Siddiqi (Chapter 1, this volume).

and in part to the absence of knowledge about the specific pathways through which these social-level influences may operate.[6]

Bruce Link and Jo Phelan have argued that the search for explanatory mechanisms of the social gradient in health faces an even more significant challenge. In their argument for viewing socioeconomic status (SES) as a fundamental cause of differences in health, they observe that, historically, as various intervening mechanisms are addressed, the social gradient reappears though the operation of new intervening mechanisms.[7] In previous eras, the ability to live in areas with adequate sewage and clean water would have been a protective factor for those with an SES-advantage, but as these became more widespread (at least in the advantaged parts of the world), new mechanisms, such as differential material and personal resources, or differential access to social status, came to the forefront to reassert the social gradient. They argue that this persistence of the social gradient despite shifts in the intervening mechanisms supports a claim that social disparities are in themselves a fundamental cause of differences in health outcomes.

Even if we grant that the social gradient of health is fundamental and universal, it is also clear that the strength of the gradient differs dramatically across populations, and that there are dramatic population differences in overall health and longevity. We can describe these graphically as the slope and the mean of the gradient, respectively. The slope of the gradient indicates how strongly social position is associated with any given health outcome within a specific society or population. Steep slopes mean that, for that society, having an advantaged social position is a strong predictor of better health, whereas flatter slopes indicate that, in that society, social advantage confers only a modest health advantage. The mean of the gradient, for any particular society or population, simply indicates its average performance on the health indicator. Although there is no mathematical constraint on how slopes and means will relate to each other – any pattern is possible in theory – the repeated empirical finding is that societies with steep social gradients in health, where the health disparity between individuals in high status positions and those in middling or lower positions is starker, tend also to have poorer health on average compared to societies with weaker associations between social position and health.[8] In graphic terms, across different societies, steeper gradients (slopes) tend to be associated with lower average health (means), whereas flatter gradients are associated with better average health.

The implications of this pattern for social policy, and for a successful societies agenda, are profound. Although it may be impossible to eliminate the social gradient in health, as the fundamental cause argument would contend,

[6] Hertzman (2001); Adler and Newman (2002); Williams et al. (2003); Lynch et al. (2004); Williams (2005).

[7] Link and Phelan (2005).

[8] Vagero and Lundberg (1989); Kunst and Mackenbach (1994); Vagero and Erikson (1997); Willms (1999); Hertzman and Siddiqi (Chapter 1, this volume).

it is possible, in principle, to identify the mechanisms underlying the social gradient, precisely because it does vary across societies. If it were possible to intervene effectively on these mechanisms, this would have the benefit of not only ameliorating the effects on those in more disadvantaged social positions, but also of improving the overall population health of the society.[9] It is likely that such prevention and intervention efforts would need to be multifaceted and multilevel.[10]

Studies of the social gradient effect have yielded some strong clues about its origins and characteristics.[11] In this first section of this chapter, a brief summary of the main features of the social gradient highlights important and potentially valuable lines of inquiry for understanding those origins and characteristics, and provides a précis of the major mechanisms for "unpacking" the social gradient. The range of explanations that have been advanced is quite broad, including differences in the distribution of wealth or income, differences in health behaviors, differences in social expenditures that bear on population health directly or indirectly, differences in social cohesion or social capital, and direct psychosocial consequences of differences in status per se. Unpacking this social gradient in health is an essential step toward identifying its central dynamics, and is thus a key to effective prevention or intervention efforts.

The second section of this chapter addresses the conceptual understanding of these dynamics and research issues that are central to empirically unpacking the social gradient. The range and diversity of possible accounts that link social disparities in status or position with differences in health outcomes presents a daunting challenge. Explanations based on single variables seem implausible on their face, given the complexity of factors that are known to affect health. But a lengthy "laundry list" of possible accounts offers little guidance for either a research or a policy agenda.

Given that the robustness of the social gradient despite substantial variation across contexts, history, and even species,[12] a more coherent set of mechanisms may be at play. Resolving this core tension between complexity and coherence is difficult, and most likely impossible without an understanding of the underlying system.[13]

---

[9] "Flattening-up" is the term used by Hertzman and Siddiqi (Chapter 1, this volume).

[10] Smedley et al. (2001).

[11] Some of the prominent likely mechanisms have been identified in recent reviews (Keating and Hertzman 1999b; Hertzman 2001; Boyce and Keating 2004; Kristenson, et al. 2004; Marmot 2004; McEwen 2005; Sapolsky 2005; Williams 2005).

[12] An interesting convergence of observations in this regard can be seen by contrasting the work of Link and Phelan (2005), who start from the top down and find evidence for social position as a fundamental cause of health outcomes, and of Robert Sapolsky (2005), who starts from the bottom up in terms of primate stress biology, and finds, across various species and various ecological contexts, that there is always a social patterning of who suffers most from stress-related problems – although, depending on context, it may be either dominant or submissive members of the social group who are the worst off.

[13] "System" is among the terms most fraught with confusion and conflict in the interdisciplinary arena. For many social scientists, it invokes a history of functional determinism, in which the

System-level explanations offer the promise – although not the guarantee – of a coherent and integrated model that is productive in both the research and policy arena. Put another way, despite the enormously complex and interacting forces at work both at the societal and organismic level, we continue to find robust regularities in the pattern of health outcomes within and between countries. Understanding the sources of this regularity requires us to look beyond individual variables, or contests between two variables, and instead to focus on how the various inputs may be systematically coordinated such that the complexity of processes yields the observed regularity of outcomes.

In this context, it is productive to ask what characteristics of any proposed systemic explanation would be required to provide a sufficiently coherent account for research or policy agendas. In other words, it is necessary to specify what types and levels of mechanisms are necessary to understand how the social gradient is produced across widely varying geographic and historical contexts, and to identify the major dynamic processes that may be amenable to prevention or intervention.

The overall goals of this chapter are to describe the characteristics that a system capable of explaining the social gradient would need to have, to identify potential mechanisms through which social circumstances come to be expressed as social gradients in health, to sketch a research agenda to further illuminate these mechanisms, and to reflect on the nature of a policy agenda that could be influenced by this emerging knowledge.

Carol Worthman and Jennifer Kuzara recently proposed that such an enterprise needs to be both systemic in form and fundamentally interdisciplinary in its method.[14] Certainly, such a system would need to account for the strong reproducibility of the gradient effect across many different types of societies. In addition, it should be capable of specifying in a testable fashion which aspects of social organization are responsible for generating the social

---

actual, contextualized experiences of people and groups are subjugated to an overarching system-level account. For many scientists in physics and engineering, it is an inescapable construct through which the overwhelmingly complex interactions and state transitions of the physical world can be grasped. For many behavioral and especially developmental scientists, it is, in the sense of self-organizing dynamic systems, a promising metaphor or model that could accommodate and render coherent the complexity of multiple biobehavioral systems of the organism as it moves through time and space (Keating and Miller, 2000). It is used here in this last sense, as a way of organizing our understanding of the multiple interacting aspects of human development, by searching for more fundamental relationships among social, behavioral, psychological, and biological elements as they become organized, or self-organized, across time.

[14] Worthman and Kuzara (2005) focus on the intersection of epidemiology (specifically, the characteristics of the social gradient); life history (that is, the species-specific adaptations that set the limits for energy expenditure trade-offs among growth, reproduction, and maintenance); and individual developmental experiences (in the form of experience-expectant rearing conditions, or EERs). This notion of trade-offs, or regulatory balances among competing demands on the organism, are also central to the work of Robert Sapolsky (2005) and to the notion of allostasis and allostatic overload developed by Bruce McEwen (2005), which will be described in greater detail later.

gradient, for the variability among societies in the strength of the gradient effect, and for the apparently consistent association between steep gradients and overall lower performance on average health outcomes when societies are compared with each other.[15]

Because health outcomes are, in the final analysis, biological realities, any proposed system also needs to identify the mechanisms through which social disparities "get under the skin" such that they can exert the observed impact on health. As we shall see, the durability of the gradient effect across the life course needs to be included in any explanatory system capable of meeting empirical challenges. In other words, potential explanatory systems need to address (1) how disparities in social circumstances are actually experienced by the individual during the course of development, since it is these social interactions that actually have an effect on the developing organism. The systems also must address (2) how those differential social interactions are capable of getting under the skin so as to (3) alter health outcomes strongly enough to yield the robustly observed social gradient effect.

The social, biological, and developmental mechanisms that translate disparities in circumstances to disparities in outcomes are thus the focus of the third section of this chapter. Recent research offers direction in terms of key underlying mechanisms, and points toward the aspects of social interactions that are likely to be important at different points in development.[16] Three areas of intense interest in contemporary developmental research link closely with key social dynamics explored elsewhere in this volume.

First is the stress-response system, a biological system with a lengthy evolutionary history. It is activated under conditions that require the organism to take action in response to threat or to biological necessity, and is thus an essential facet of our biology. On the other hand, dysregulation of the stress-response system represents a long-term risk to health, because too much, too frequent, or too unrelenting release of cortisol – the circulating hormone central to this system – is toxic to internal organs at sufficiently high concentrations.[17] How this system is shaped early in development, in both humans and other mammals, plays a significant role in how it will function throughout the life of the organism.[18] In humans, the functioning of this system is closely linked to a psychological sense of *control*, especially in circumstances where uncertainty about the adequacy of one's performance in the face of some challenge is linked with social comparison or social evaluation.[19]

A second core biological and developmental system is related to the sense of social *connection*. The serotonergic system plays a key role in generating

---

[15] In Chapter 1 of this volume, Hertzman and Siddiqi illustrate the value of such a comparative approach in several country-level case studies.

[16] Keating and Hertzman (1999b); Boyce and Keating (2004); Worthman and Kuzara (2005).

[17] McEwen (2005); Sapolsky (2005); Worthman and Kuzara (2005).

[18] Meaney (2001); Gunnar and Donzella (2002).

[19] Dickerson and Kemeny (2004).

positive emotions associated with social relationships and is the target of a major class of antidepressant pharmaceuticals, SSRIs (selective serotonin re-uptake inhibitors, such as fluoxetine [Prozac] and related formulations). Dysregulation of this system, arising as an interaction between genetic factors and negative early developmental experiences, has been associated with substance abuse and with heightened aggression in both humans and nonhuman primates, as well as contributing to persistent vulnerability to depressive disorders.[20]

A third, later-developing system includes aspects of perceived purpose, hope, meaning, and identity. This system is uniquely human, evolving as a level of *reflective consciousness* that represents a coevolution of culture and mind.[21] The biodevelopmental focus of this activity is largely the prefrontal cortex of the brain (PFC), which undergoes substantial development during adolescence, including increased speed of transmission as well as amount and complexity of connections to other brain systems.[22] The implication of this is that the achievement of the specifically human level of consciousness involves an increased role of the PFC in the governance of brain and biologic systems.

Taken together, these core biologically based developmental systems can be viewed as forming the substrate of fundamental human capabilities, in the sense of that term as used by Amartya Sen.[23] Added to these subsystems, which support an increasingly conscious regulation of interaction with the world, would be the set of competencies and expertise that are contextually and culturally specific.[24] The evolutionary transition to fully modern humans

---

[20] Suomi (1999; 2000); Caspi et al. (2003).

[21] An interesting recent intersection of paleoanthropology and neuroscience has vastly increased our understanding of human speciation with respect to this coevolution of culture and mind, described in highly readable summaries by Merlin Donald (2001) and Robin Dunbar (1996; 2004). In short, the core idea is that the primary competitive advantage in the speciation of modern humans (*Homo sapiens*) was improved social coordination within larger groups, and eventually between groups. Based on a long buildup of various proto-components, language, culture, and mind coevolved rapidly to support such social coordination. In fact, there is a strong argument that the evolution of fully modern humans (us) from early modern humans occurred in the context of a millennia-long competition with archaic humans (Neanderthals) in the Levant, a competition that we lost for the first 30,000 years or so, but returned to win around 40,000 to 50,000 years before the present (BP) because of new adaptations that employed "flexible, symbolically reinforced alliance networks with wide situational variability in group size" (Shea 2003: 183) – in other words, a reworked interface of mind, culture, and social structure. A similar conclusion based on distinct patterns between Neanderthals and modern humans emphasized the similarities in material extraction but dissimilarities in social networks: "[I]t is the development and maintenance of larger social networks, rather than technological innovations or increased hunting prowess, that distinguish modern humans from Neanderthals in the southern Caucusus" (Adler et al. 2006: 105). A newly emerging field of neuroecology focuses on the evolutionary mechanisms of human cognition (Sherry 2006).

[22] Keating (2004); Giedd (2008).

[23] Sen (1999).

[24] Determining which of these competencies are key ones for effective participation in modern societies and economies is a complex and often controversial task (Keating 2001).

appears to have required a substantially refined brain architecture that leveraged existing mental capacity in a way that specifically afforded the ability to efficiently manage multiple complex cultural, social, and cognitive demands.[25]

Understanding the social gradient as being rooted in a system that links social circumstances and interactions with biological and developmental mechanisms is of more than merely scientific interest. It potentially grounds social policy formation and evaluation in a new and firmer interdisciplinary terrain. The implications of this new conceptual framework for societal decision making are potentially profound and are briefly noted at the conclusion of this chapter.

THE SOCIAL GRADIENT IN HEALTH

Chapter 1 and the preceding outline reflect the rapidly growing interest in understanding the social gradient in health, a research interest that involves an expanding number of disciplines beyond social epidemiology, including anthropology, developmental science, economics, ethology, and evolutionary psychology. Although there are great benefits to our understanding from this expanded interest, there are also numerous opportunities for researchers from different disciplinary traditions to "talk past" each other rather than to "talk to" each other.

A brief summary of what we currently understand about the social gradient in health sets the stage for an examination of the mechanisms that produce it. They are listed here as six specific propositions: (1) social and economic disparities are universally associated with differences in health outcomes, that is,

---

[25] This change in neural architecture seems to have arisen via a new set of connections between neocortical areas and the cerebellum (Weaver 2005), at about the same time that fully modern humans display functional adaptations that gave them a selective advantage over archaic humans (Adler et al. 2006; Shea 2003 – consult note 21 in this chapter). The functional significance of the changes observed in the human fossil record is that the complexity of mental demands in social coordination, culture-based intra- and intergroup interactions, and cognitively based new technologies appears to have reached something of a neocortical limit among early modern humans (Weaver 2005: 3579). Expanded cerebellar capacity did not eliminate neocortical processing limitations, but rather permitted much expanded and efficient procedural knowledge ("know-how") that in turn afforded much more rapid access to deployable semantic knowledge ("knowing-that"). There is a strong suggestion in this account, if supported by future research, that the hallmark of fully modern humans is the ability to rapidly access, use, and integrate information and knowledge across the multiple domains of social interaction, culture, and cognitive problem solving – not a bad definition of human capabilities. Supporting this speculation is the recent finding from neuroimaging that the cerebellum, like the prefrontal cortex, shows a pattern of later maturation during adolescent development (Giedd, Schmitt, and Neale 2007). Similar findings arise from comparative analyses of brain specializations among human and nonhuman primates, with the specifically human features being a larger neocortex (particularly the PFC), increased cerebellar connections with the cortical areas involved in cognition, and augmentation of the connectivity within the PFC (Rilling 2006).

they are pervasive; (2) the relationship between these disparities and health are generally linear, such that they can be described as the slope of a gradient;[26] (3) there are multiple sources of disparities in social circumstances that make a difference in health, including income, wealth, race/ethnicity, gender, and neighborhood/community of residence, among others; (4) the gradient effect is observed not only for morbidity and mortality but also for a wide range of developmental outcomes, including educational achievement, social competence, and behavior and emotional problems; (5) the effects of disparities are associated with life course patterns, such that the SES of the family of origin is implicated in the broad range of health and developmental outcomes;[27] and (6) societies differ in the steepness (slope) of the gradient and in the average performance on health indicators (mean), and the population slope and mean are usually correlated, such that steeper gradients are associated with lower mean outcomes.[28]

The import of these patterns is brought into sharper focus when one considers the magnitude of the effects. The effect of income differences, for example, is quite strong, in the range of 6.5 to 7 years of life expectancy when averaging across race and gender. Similar income effects in national samples are found for morbidity, self-reported health, and depressive symptoms.[29] Although most of the research attention has focused on the roles of income (and of income inequality) and education as they impact on health, it is clear that there are a substantial number of other sources of social disparities that similarly have an impact on health outcomes. Race and ethnicity clearly have a strong relationship with health outcomes, independent of income and education, but also as they interact with them. In terms of years of life expectancy beyond age 25 in the United States, for example, the average income differentials tend to be larger, at a little over 8 years, and black/white differentials at a bit more than half of that, around 4.4 years. Gender is another source of disparity in health outcomes, with women having about a 6.5 year life expectancy advantage over men. The extreme values, as these multiple sources are considered together, are even larger. From age 25, the average life expectancy for low-income black males is 66.6; for higher income white females, the figure is 82.8, a cumulative difference of 16.2 years.[30] As a comparison, this is the difference between the average life expectancy in Indonesia versus Japan.[31]

The implications of these provisional but key findings are profound, in that they suggest that the SES gradient is *pervasive* (occurring across many

[26] Hertzman and Siddiqi review some key evidence for these two points in the preceding chapter.

[27] Keating and Hertzman (1999a, 1999b); Boyce and Keating (2004); Worthman and Kuzara (2005); Hertzman and Power (2006); Keating (in press a).

[28] Hertzman and Siddiqi (Chapter 1, this volume).

[29] Fiscella and Franks (2000).

[30] Calculated from Williams (2005: Table 8.3).

[31] From the World Development Indicators (2006), available interactively at www.gapminder.org.

health and development outcomes), *portable* (as individuals, on average, carry that legacy into their adult lives), and *enduring* (as life course health effects). W. Thomas Boyce and I described the consequences in this way: "failure to attend to childhood circumstances may create, at the population level, a range of societal burdens that are hard to subsequently shift. Conversely, investments in early development may generate enduring societal opportunities."[32] Drawing on a range of work,[33] we proceeded to describe several hypothetical patterns of influence through which childhood circumstances may affect health outcomes over the life course, and for both scientific and policy purposes, it is helpful to attempt a conceptual disaggregation of such patterns.[34]

One pattern progresses through stability of socioeconomic circumstances from childhood to later life, with an accumulation of risk from a range of sources. In other words, individuals who grow up in more stressful circumstances tend to experience those same circumstances throughout their development. The implication of this *cumulative* pattern is that broad societal differences in the quality of the social and physical environment play a major role in developmental health outcomes, through the overall degree of social partitioning and the SES-related patterns that emerge in early life.[35]

A second set of childhood influences may be thought of as *pathway* effects, constituted by chains of risk or protection, which focuses our attention on the ways in which early circumstances constrain or enable trajectories of health and development. For example, educational attainment plays a substantial role in both subsequent health and social status. Beyond simple continuity, the early acquisition of competencies, skills, and dispositions likely affects directly the pathways leading toward future health, well-being, and developmental attainments. Such associations are likely attributable to sequences of linked exposures, in which early risk factors increase the likelihood of subsequent exposures, which in turn augment the probability of encountering others.[36] Another indicator of such pathway or linked effects is the phenomenon of resilience, in which significant early disadvantage is surmounted. The developmental trajectories of many children growing up in adverse or suboptimal circumstances belie the expected declines in physical and/or mental health that are known to be associated with such circumstances. Observations of anomalously good outcomes emerging from impoverished or unsupportive social settings are nonnormative, but far from rare. In such accounts, resilience appears

---

[32] Boyce and Keating (2004: 419).
[33] Hertzman (1999); Kuh and Ben-Shlomo (2004); see also Hertzman and Power (2006).
[34] Hertzman and Siddiqi (Chapter 1, this volume) also note the differences among cumulative, pathway, and latent influences.
[35] Hatch (2005); Luecken and Lemery (2004).
[36] In a review of the literature on the health effects of human development investments, we found that the evidence for direct effects was less than that for indirect effects operating through subsequent education and employment (Keating and Simonton 2008). This is perhaps attributable in part to the duration so far of the most relevant intervention/prevention studies, but it emphasizes the importance of understanding the full set of effects arising from differential experiences throughout the life course.

often derived from the establishment of chains of *protection* – individual characteristics and forms of individual support that predispose toward the pursuit of health-protective developmental trajectories.

A third type of influence can be thought of as critical period, sensitive period, or latent effects. Even after removing the effects from other, later sources – adult SES, differential developmental pathways, and so on – there is often a nontrivial impact of childhood circumstances on life course health outcomes. For example, the early instantiation of a dysregulated stress-response system (as already noted and described in more detail later) may affect developmental trajectories through success in selected environments (pathway effects), but in addition, may create a health risk that will become manifest only at a later stage in the life course as stressors accumulate and/or grow more intense. Note, in this example, that the early experiential calibration of stress-responsive neural circuitry might alternately affect later health via *risk accumulation* (cumulative, long-term costs of repeated activation of biological circuits), *pathway effects* (dysregulated reactivity biasing developmental trajectories toward risk induction or away from risk protection), or *critical period effects* (early exposure in, for example, infancy alone results in biological response profiles that jeopardize adult health and adaptation) – and it may also reflect the simultaneous operation of all three types of effects.

Thus, consideration of the characteristics of the social gradient effect (pervasive, portable, and enduring) and patterns of transmission (cumulative, pathway, and critical period) points toward a hypothesis of "biological embedding," a process "whereby systematic differences in psychosocial/material circumstances, from conception onward, embed themselves in human biology such that the characteristics of gradients in developmental health can be accounted for."[37] Entertaining the biological embedding hypothesis therefore entails a detailed consideration of the biological and behavioral mechanisms linking child development and later developmental health gradients.

Nancy Adler and Katherine Newman note in their review of the health inequalities literature, and how that body of work has been addressed, that "one needs to look even further upstream to consider their 'actual determinants.'"[38]

---

[37] Keating and Hertzman (1999b: 11). Hertzman and Frank (2006) systematically reviewed the construct and recent evidence regarding biological embedding.

[38] Adler and Newman (2002: 60). Disciplinary terminology in this area, as in many others, can hinder understanding. In the population health and social epidemiology literatures, "determinants" is a standard term to identify factors that have an independent influence on some outcomes. This language can be a red flag for developmental scientists, who associate the term with the notion of determinism, which, in a variety of flavors (genetic determinism, environmental determinism, infant determinism), is anathema in that it is taken to imply fixed factors whose expression is not contingent on other inputs or subsequent events – the core interests of developmentalists. They are more likely to use terms seen as more neutral, such as predictors, mediators, and moderators. If a strong theoretical claim is intended, then terms like mechanisms or developmental origins are employed, with a concomitant elevation of the evidentiary requirement. Most users of determinants do not intend this kind of determinism, but it is a common source of misunderstanding.

Understanding the mechanisms that generate the social gradient, and the pathways through which those mechanisms operate, is a theme that has been echoed often enough to have now become commonplace.

Much of the work looking beyond material resources and distribution to explain the social gradient in health has focused on psychosocial factors, at the interface of the social and the individual. At the broadest level, exposures to problematic social environments can be examined in the same way that exposures to harmful physical environments have been. A wide range of working and living conditions has been explored, and important relationships have been found in nearly all domains considered.[39] A particular aspect of the broader social environment, conceptualized as generalized social capital, social cohesion, or social trust, has also been studied as a significant contributor to the social gradient.[40] Relatively straightforward assessments of this construct, derived from general surveys, have shown strong associations with health outcomes. The degree to which these associations are primary or are instead driven by other (thus far unobserved) variables remains a controversial matter under continuing investigation. Finally, as noted earlier, the psychosocial consequences of differential status within social hierarchies have been studied as a central cause of health outcomes.[41] One particular feature of the status issue has warranted special attention: the role of discrimination and stigma associated with racial, ethnic, or minority status. A substantial research literature, especially in the United States, has focused on the general effect on health of patterns of discrimination and on the underlying processes through which they operate.[42]

An interesting but unresolved issue in considering these broad social contributions to the social gradient in health is how they relate to each other.[43] How do social policies that address the functioning of social institutions (income, employment, health care, housing, and so on) arise from and interact with social capital and social polity? For example, are differential expenditures across societies or jurisdictions on social domains (such as health or education), which have been shown to affect mortality outcomes,[44] independent of, reducible to, or interactive with the overall level of social capital in those societies? Are the psychosocial consequences of status in social hierarchies or of discrimination and stigma uniform across societies, or are they conditioned on other characteristics of those societies, such as the strength of collective identity, the availability of alternate avenues for coping with identity threats, or the material consequences of differential status? Understanding how these

---

[39] Adler and Newman (2002); House et al. (2008).

[40] Kawachi and Kennedy (2002).

[41] Marmot (2004).

[42] Deaton and Lubotsky (2003); Sidanius et al. (2004); Major and O'Brien (2005); Williams (2005); Borrell et al. (2006).

[43] This analysis is the focus of Hertzman and Siddiqi (Chapter 1, this volume).

[44] Dunn, Burgess, and Ross (2005).

core characteristics of societies interact with each other in a systemic fashion is one goal of the successful societies' agenda and is a central focus of this volume. The absence of a resolution to these questions makes it difficult to parse analytically the relative contributions of different aspects of societies, because the number of potential interactions among them is exponentially large. A clearer understanding of the causal links among social circumstances, social interactions throughout development, the biological and developmental consequences of those interactions and their impact on health and development outcomes, would seem to require a coherent conceptual framework through which to unravel the workings of this complex system.

A second fundamental issue, also unresolved, is how these psychosocial factors get under the skin. Many accounts make reference to a general stress model, on the reasonable assumption that problematic social circumstances are likely to be associated with higher stress, and that consistently higher experiences of stress are associated with negative health outcomes.[45] As we will see later, this remains a viable hypothesis, with three important qualifications. The first is that a much more refined understanding of stress reactivity has emerged from recent research, replacing a simple linear model (worse circumstances lead to higher stress leads to worse health) with a more complex regulatory model, in which there are a number of trade-offs and balances among location in the status hierarchy, patterns of social interaction within the social group, behavioral versus physiological expressions of stress, and other factors. These trade-offs have been identified in both human and nonhuman primates.[46] The second qualification arises from the findings that the stress-response system has set points that are established early in development and are directly influenced by the nature of the developmental experiences. These likely reflect differential strategies of the organism to cope with the average expected environment based on its first encounters.[47] The third qualification is that the stress-response system does not operate in a vacuum; other important regulatory systems, both biological and behavioral, interact with it to dampen or amplify its effects. Moreover, other such systems have developmental histories and health consequences of their own, to be explored in more detail later.

SOCIETY, BIOLOGY, AND HUMAN DEVELOPMENT: ESCAPING DETERMINISM

In order to cope with the emergent complexity about the social gradient in health, based on the analyses to this point, it is clear that a coherent conceptual framework is needed. A proposed model is depicted in Figure 2.1, and

[45] The social nexus of this general model is thoughtfully laid out by Hall and Taylor (Chapter 3, this volume).

[46] Fox et al. (2004); Sapolsky (2005).

[47] Meaney (2001); Gunnar and Donzella (2002); Boyce and Ellis (2005); Worthman and Kuzara (2005).

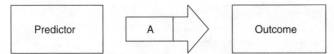

FIGURE 2.1A. Simplified mediator model: predictors to outcomes.

described in greater detail later. It serves multiple goals: to organize our current understanding, to serve as a research agenda for further investigation of
the social gradient, and to function as a provisional framework for revisiting
a range of issues in policy and practice. Conceptually, it is best described as
a mediator model. Mediators are constructs, measured in a range of possible
ways, that explain the observed association between an independent (or predictor) variable and a dependent (or outcome) variable.[48] In this case, the predictor variables are disparities in social circumstances or demographics. The
outcome variables are the full range of indicators of developmental health.
These outcome inequalities are the patterns we seek to explain.[49]

Before turning to the more detailed mediator model in Figure 2.1, it may be
helpful to consider a simplified mediator model. Begin with the relationship
we want to explain, between a predictor and an outcome, as represented in
Figure 2.1a.

A mediator hypothesis proposes that there are more fundamental processes
and mechanisms that explain the link captured in arrow A, and these are
called mediators. For such a model to be tested, we first need to find out
whether there is a link between the predictor and the mediators (shown as
arrow B in Figure 2.1b), and then whether the mediators are linked to the outcome of interest (shown as arrow C in Figure 2.1b).

The test of whether or not the mediators (statistically) explain the relationship between the predictor and the outcome is that the combined B and
C effects accounts for all (or some) of the A effect.[50] In that case, and if the
mediators are more fundamental variables in the system, we are in a position

---

[48] Based on the influential paper by Baron and Kenny (1986), MacKinnon et al. (2002) conducted a randomized simulation (Monte Carlo) study of different statistical methods to identify mediators, also known as indirect effects, surrogates, or intermediate endpoint effects.
They provide a comparison among various methods for testing the validity of hypothesized
mediators.

[49] The term "outcome inequalities" is helpful for maintaining the distinction between the
inequalities in health and development per se, as distinct from one explanation (of a potentially large set) that has been extensively considered by both economists and epidemiologists,
namely income inequality. As Hertzman and Siddiqi note in Chapter 1 of this volume, income
inequality likely plays some role in outcome inequalities, but it does not account for the
majority of them, and is typically found to be contingent on a range of other factors of social
structure.

[50] Kraemer et al. (2001) provided a straightforward conceptual model for distinguishing among
the relationships that variables have to each other under differing analytic approaches. They
also offer an important caution about the high bar that is set when claims of causal mediation

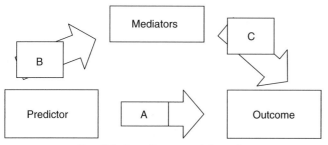

FIGURE 2.1B. Simplified mediator model: mediators.

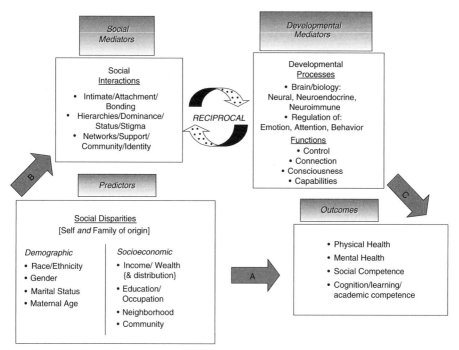

FIGURE 2.1C. Conceptual model of social and developmental mediators of the social gradient in developmental health.

to explain why this predictor is linked to this outcome. There are multiple ways to test such a claim, but the focus here is primarily on the model as a conceptual framework to discern the underlying systemic coherence. After describing the major elements of the model shown in Figure 2.1c (an elaborated

are made: "all causal chains consist of mediators, but not all mediators will eventually prove to be links of some causal chain" (Kraemer et al. 2001: 852).

mediator model, with specific content, but similar in structure to the preceding simplified model), we turn to the emerging evidence that provides initial support for the claim that social and developmental mediators explain the social gradient in health, and to the research directions needed to establish that claim more fully.

CONCEPTUAL MODEL OF SOCIAL AND DEVELOPMENTAL MEDIATORS OF THE SOCIAL GRADIENT IN DEVELOPMENTAL HEALTH

Two classes of mediators, which reciprocally influence each other, are shown in the model. Social mediators account for how structural and demographic differences translate into everyday experiences across the course of individual development in a way that matters to the organism. Developmental mediators account for the ways in which developmental experiences are translated into biological and behavioral changes in the organism.

Together, they serve as mediators of the relationship between social disparities and health and development inequalities, insofar as they explain (fully or partially) that relationship.

One of the key features of this proposed account is captured in the concept of biological embedding. Drawing on the rapidly emerging work in developmental neuroscience, we used this term to indicate that developmental experiences alter not only behavior, but also biology, and most particularly the brain and the systems it coordinates and governs.[51]

The introduction of biological factors into a prospective causal chain is a source of concern for many social scientists, understandably so given the historical use of biological arguments in ideologically motivated social arguments

---

[51] Keating and Hertzman (1999a). As always, it is helpful to make as explicit as possible the terminology that is used. In this context, "biologically embedded" means specifically the incorporation of developmental experiences into neural, neuroendocrine, and neuroimmune structure and function (including the bodily systems they operate on). It does not embrace any connotation of being developmentally "fixed"; how enduring or reversible any particular neural pattern is, once established, or how amenable to compensatory functions, remains an empirical question. It does imply that the brain/biology organization that has become embedded serves as a foundation for future functioning. For clarity, it is distinct from "embodiment," a philosophical position arising from cognitive science and linguistics, which emphasizes the material bases of mental activity, against Cartesian dualism (Rohrer 2001). It overlaps to some extent with Bourdieu's construct of habitus, the inculcation (and thus reproduction) of social structure into fundamental perception and cognition at a deep enough level that it is unrecognized as a social construction, and seems instead to be universal, natural, and obvious (Bourdieu 1992). The concept of biological embedding includes these cognitive and behavioral sequellae of the incorporation of developmental experiences into the organism at a fundamental level, but includes also the ways in which neural sculpting and shaping affect other aspects such as the stress-response system, the immune system, the cognition-emotion interface, and other bodily systems (Hertzman and Frank 2006; Keating and Hertzman 1999a).

(the case of social Darwinism leaps readily to mind). Experience in this arena does dictate prudence. It is important, therefore, to distinguish the notions of biological embedding, social mediation, and developmental mediation from connotations of biological determinism. At the same time, the comprehensive nature of the conceptual framework shown in Figure 2.1c may invite unintended conflation with two other sources of deterministic thinking: environmental determinism and infant determinism. Before proceeding to the details of the model, then, a brief digression to deal with these potential confusions is in order.

Genetic determinism: Genetic determinism in its simplest form holds that the observed variability in health outcomes is of entirely genetic origin, and the association with social status represents mechanisms such as asssortative mating or competitive fitness. Not only does the population evidence fail to support this stance – reverse causality has not fared well empirically, as noted in Chapter 1 – but strong experimental evidence also goes against it. In both human and nonhuman primate studies, the genetic evidence clearly supports the centrality of gene-environment *interactions* rather than direct effects of either – that is, not nature *versus* nurture but rather nature *and* nurture.[52] This is an important point that is often lost in journalistic coverage of medical science, in which the shorthand formulation is typically stated as "gene X found to cause condition Y." What this usually means, of course, is that the presence of gene X increases the organism's susceptibility, but the actual expression of condition Y is most often contingent on a range of conditional factors, both known and unknown. For most conditions, a one-to-one correspondence between a specific gene and an observed (phenotypic) condition is the exception rather than the rule.

Environmental determinism: By the same token, it is clear that genetic variability is significantly implicated in a wide range of behaviors and health. Developmental experiences do not write themselves on a blank slate. Genetic variability is a nontrivial contributor, although as noted, this variability is nearly always expressed through gene-environment interactions. Stephen Pinker has described one version of the history of the environmental determinism associated with the legacy of behaviorism, and its continuing cultural (and occasionally scientific) influence, although whether his treatment should be read more as polemic than history has been sharply debated.[53]

Infant determinism: Infant determinism is in many ways a more recent variant of the determinist coin, in that it is open to gene-environment interactions as a primary method by which early experiences become fixed in the organism. Its distinguishing claim is that subsequent developments are predestined by

[52] Suomi (2000); Champoux et al. (2002); Barr et al. (2003); Caspi et al. (2003); Ellis, Essex, and Boyce (2005). A collection of theoretical and empirical syntheses of current work in a number of domains of early child development on the integration of nature and nurture is available in Keating (in press a).

[53] Bateson (2002); Pinker (2002); Schlinger (2002).

those early patterns. Weighing against this claim is the evidence for cumulative and pathway effects, and not only critical or sensitive period effects, in health and development outcomes. In an excess of zeal to support investments in early child development and education, some advocates have embraced a form of infant determinism by seeming to claim that development from birth to 3 years (or 5 years) sets a fixed pattern for the life course. Clearly, the early years establish a strong foundation for subsequent development, but the evidence does not support a belief in fixed or immutable patterns formed in early development.

Evolution, development, and epigenesis: The evidence unequivocally requires that we abandon arguments exclusively from nature or nurture, as most working scientists have already done, and instead focus our research efforts on the formidable task of understanding the underlying mechanisms of nature-nurture, gene-environment, and gene-gene interactions over the course of development. The broader context of this discussion is the major shift in our understanding of the nature of evolution itself in the last decade or so.

Two threads of this work set the stage for the next wave of research in this area. A new perspective on evolution, combining the classic neo-Darwinian mode of mutation/variation/selection with a more refined understanding of how genetic activity interacts with its local environment (including other genes) from the embryonic phase onward, has resolved a number of problematic issues such as, why do we humans have far fewer genes than expected, and how could evolution have proceeded more rapidly than expected? Under the rubric of "evo/devo," the new approach emphasizes the complexity of interactive processes combined with a preservation of simple forms.[54] A related construct that has been elaborated within developmental science is the notion of epigenesis.[55] The core idea is quite similar, in that understanding the emergence and stabilization of any developmental feature requires a synthesis of interacting genetic and environmental factors as they impinge on the organism across time.

---

[54] Ziff and Rosenfield (2006) reviewed several recent books that update our understanding of the mechanics of evolution, in dramatic ways. Perhaps most significant is that gene-gene interactions and the role of regulatory genes (especially Hox genes) replace the more limited and slower route of individual genetic mutation and selection as the sole, or perhaps even primary route for evolutionary change. This responsiveness of the genetic code to local contextual circumstances, in the embryo and in the newborn, puts the final nail in the coffin of the classic nature-nurture debate, if one were needed. They note: "The new field of study in which these breakthroughs have been made is called Evo Devo, short for evolution and development, 'development' referring to both how an embryo grows and how the newborn infant matures into an adult." This perspective has already made its way into the study of early child development, with specific reference to the shaping of the stress response system (Boyce and Ellis 2005).

[55] Gottlieb and Willoughby have recently reviewed the current status and future prospects of the epigenetic approach for guiding research programs (2006).

The demise of deterministic approaches is of course only part of the task, and it is likely to be seen retrospectively as the easy part. What is required at this point is an integrated conceptual framework capable of guiding research at the intersection of society and human development. Abandoning the archaic nature-nurture debate in this pursuit is only the first step, but it is an important step in clearing the field for the complex task ahead.

SOCIAL AND DEVELOPMENTAL MEDIATORS OF THE SOCIAL GRADIENT IN HEALTH

As noted previously, the complexity of the social gradient in health expands rapidly as we include a wider range of types of disparities and outcomes and simultaneously probe for underlying mechanisms. But the complexity itself can swamp our efforts to understand the system as a whole. At the same time, however, key empirical patterns of the gradient recur despite the complexity: its pervasiveness across multiple health and development indicators; its reemergence even as intervening mechanisms shift; and its durability across the life course. These replicated observations place significant constraints on the nature of the mechanisms that are proposed to explain the gradient.[56]

Figure 2.1 depicts the key components and relationships of a working model. Drawing on the preceding analyses, this figure illustrates a mediator model for the social gradient effect, including both social and developmental mediators, which are reciprocally related to each other. As previously noted, a mediator model is one in which an established empirical relationship is hypothesized to be explained (fully or partially) by a mediating construct or set of constructs (represented by measurable variables) that is hypothesized to be the causal mechanism underlying that relationship.

Social disparities predict health outcomes (Arrow A): This restates the starting observation of this chapter, that disparities in social circumstances predict observed outcome inequalities in developmental health. In Figure 2.1, a number of the refinements discussed earlier have been incorporated.

First, the social disparities known to matter as predictors (in the box labeled *Predictors*) is expanded beyond income and status (socioeconomic status [SES] or position [SEP]).[57] Education, race/ethnicity, gender, neighborhood or community of residence, and marital status all make contributions, as do additional characteristics of the environment of early child development, including parental education, parental SES/SEP, and maternal age. Moreover,

---

[56] An additional constraint, of course, is that it must be testable at least in its component parts, or ultimately through consilience of evidence (Wilson 1998) across the full system. In this model, a developmental system is proposed (compare note 13 in this chapter; Gottlieb and Willoughby 2006).

[57] In another theoretical disagreement reflected in academic jargon, some researchers prefer SEP because they regard SES as identifying in advance a contested theoretical claim that it is status per se that matters.

these factors interact with each other in both amplifying and compensating fashions. The model proposes that it is through the way in which these variables translate into experienced social interactions that the effects on subsequent health and development will occur. Devising ways to link population indicators with underlying social interactions represents a significant methodological challenge.

Second, the outcomes (in the box labeled *Outcomes*) are the full range that we have expanded to encompass a broad notion of developmental health. One area of special interest is the degree to which different developmental health outcomes share *common developmental pathways*. The considerable overlap among developmental health outcomes suggests such a possibility, although this is not sufficient evidence for common mechanisms or pathways.[58] But if there are common mechanisms and pathways linking social disparities with multiple outcomes, the potential implications for societal approaches are substantial. For example, do countries with steep gradients and poorer health outcomes also have steep gradients and worse mathematics achievement, for example? If there is a generalized country effect of steeper/worse and flatter/better across a number of indicators, the search for underlying mechanisms would be different than if the findings revealed substantial trade-offs among different outcomes. A systematic exploration of common versus distinct pathways will be both informative and necessary.

Social disparities predict variability in social interactions (Arrow B): This link is important, because it is the interactions that are experienced by the organism, not the social addresses of demographic location or SES/SEP. The specific categories of social interactions (shown in the box labeled *Social Mediators*) are intended to reflect a dimension from more micro level and immediate (close, regular, face-to-face), through meso level (representing the nature of one's interactions in groups, from kindergarten to the workplace), to more macro level (representing the broad range of social networks and community membership, including their collective identity aspects, taken up by Michèle Lamont in greater detail in Chapter 6). These categories also align with key themes of, respectively, control, connection, and consciousness in the developmental functions, which are described in more detail later.

This is a central link for the major thrust of this volume. Social disparities are generated through institutional arrangements, cultural patterns, and generalized social capital. These social disparities are constituted differently across societies, through the interface of historically conditioned institutional and cultural structures and processes (not represented explicitly in Figure 2.1). Social disparities then impact on subsequent health and capabilities via the social interactions to which they give rise – in conjunction with how those social interactions are embedded in and responded to by individuals, both behaviorally and biologically.

---

[58] Essex et al. (2002).

Social mediators and developmental mediators reciprocally affect each other over the course of development. This reciprocal relationship (shown in Figure 2.1 as the pair of arrows labeled *Reciprocal*) is the core of the proposed mediator model. How developmental processes and functions are formed and expressed is the central question of developmental science. Recent research in developmental neuroscience has enabled a unique new look into this particular "black box." We are only beginning to grasp the important processes here, such as the sensitivity of neural systems to early developmental experiences, the iterative relationship between brain and behavior over the course of development, and the life course impact of early development.[59] But our current understanding and evidence are sufficient to propose with some confidence what the broad themes of this reciprocal relationship will be, particularly in light of the constraint imposed by the theoretical model that the downstream consequences for developmental health must be a key part of the story. The major features of this emerging story are presented later, along with evidence and examples that support and illustrate them.

The set of developmental mediators (shown in the box labeled *Developmental Mediators*) includes categories of developmental processes and developmental functions. The functional significance for the organism is the focus of the second category, and these serve as organizing principles for understanding the focal aspects of development. The category of developmental processes addresses how the systems that subserve these functions are formed, and how they operate.

Developmental processes and functions affect downstream outcomes of developmental health (Arrow C): This completes the causal chain of the model depicted in Figure 2.1. Specifically, the contention is that developmental processes and functions are expressed in a wide range of outcomes, contingent of course on subsequent life course circumstances (see the preceding section against infant determinism). This relationship places further constraints on the nature of possible explanations of the social gradient in health.

To summarize, the test of mediation is that the causal chain shown as Arrows B and C (encompassing as well the reciprocal relationship between social and developmental mediators) reduces or eliminates the observed direct effect of social disparities on developmental health outcomes shown as Arrow A.[60] Four leading potential mediator systems that appear to meet

[59] Keating and Hertzman (1999a); Boyce and Keating (2004); Boyce and Ellis (2005); Worthman and Kuzara (2005); Gottlieb and Willoughby (2006).

[60] For empirical research, specific pathways require testing through covariance structure modeling (such as structural equation modeling [SEM] or multilevel/ hierarchical linear modeling [MLM/HLM]); quasi-experimental intervention and prevention studies; and/or investigations using formal experimental designs. The comprehensive model here serves as a conceptual framework to describe the hypothetical connections, within which specific investigations can be generated. The strongest tests of the causal chain will require a convergence of evidence across multiple studies based on different methodologies (Kraemer et al. 2001).

all the constraints implied by the research reviewed to this point and fit the conceptual model are described in the remainder of this section: a sense of control, a sense of connection, the emergence of consciousness, and the integration of collective and individual capabilities. A comprehensive review of each of these literatures is beyond the scope of this chapter, but the broad outlines of current research convey how they may function as mediators of the social gradient in health.

A SENSE OF CONTROL: SOCIAL HIERARCHIES AND THE STRESS RESPONSE SYSTEM

The first of the proposed mediator systems focuses on the notion of psychosocial control that figures prominently in contemporary theories of social disparities and health.[61] The functioning of the stress response system (principally based in the limbic hypothalamic-pituitary-adrenal [L-HPA] axis) is a prime candidate for understanding the origins and impact of this psychosocial variable. The now commonplace methodology of the collection of cortisol (a central part of the L-HPA axis function) nonintrusively from saliva samples has greatly expanded the information about how the human stress response system reacts to challenges, and about its diurnal rhythms, both of which vary across individuals and can thus be related to behavioral and health characteristics.

The central story line on this psychosocial dimension is by now familiar. Threats to status or dominance in social hierarchies activate a stress response, which can become dysregulated (in this case, up-regulated or overactive). In studies of nonhuman primates, initially baboons, Robert Sapolsky found these patterns of dysregulation in response to a variety of status threats.[62] Bruce McEwen developed the notions of allostasis and allostatic overload to capture the long-term consequence of continuing dysregulation of the stress response system:

The term "allostasis" has been coined to clarify ambiguities associated with the word "stress." Allostasis refers to the adaptive processes that maintain homeostasis through the production of mediators such as adrenaline, cortisol, and other chemical messengers. These mediators of the stress response promote adaptation in the aftermath of acute stress, but they also contribute to allostatic overload, the wear and tear on the body and brain that result from being "stressed out" ... result[ing] in many of the common diseases of modern life.[63]

The precise physiological mechanisms through which these effects occur are a source of intense current investigation, including the study of other features of the biological stress response system, and our understanding of how the L-HPA system develops and functions has increased rapidly in the last

---

[61] Marmot (2004).
[62] Sapolsky (2005).
[63] McEwen (2005: 315).

decade or so.[64] A brief summary of current scientific work provides evidence for key features of the mediator model, using the model in Figure 2.1 as the reference point.

Social interactions, especially around status issues, matter to L-HPA functioning across a broad range of circumstances in which social disparities are experienced. One typical pattern is for lower-SES individuals to have higher baseline cortisol, a blunted response of the L-HPA axis to challenge, and then a slower return to a higher baseline.[65] Workplace interactions have been frequently studied with respect to the stress response system, especially in circumstances where demands are high but the ability to control one's response to the demands is low. Another common trigger for the stress response system is the experience of discrimination and stigma, particularly where there exists a threat to identity.[66] Experimental evidence confirms that the most elevated cortisol reactivity occurs in response to uncertainty about one's ability to cope with a challenge in combination with the perception that one's success will be subject to social evaluation.[67] The evidence is quite strong to support the links around issues of control, from social disparities to variations in social interactions to the functioning of key physiological systems.

These links, however, operate in the context of a complex, highly regulated system, rather than as a one-to-one correspondence from circumstances to stressors to physiological response.[68] In a recent review of the effects of

---

[64] Gunnar and Donzella (2002); Boyce and Ellis (2005); Hertzman and Frank (2006); McEwen (2005); Sapolsky (2005). Cortisol is one of the glucocorticoids (GC), a class of adrenal steroid hormones secreted during stress that also includes hydrocortisone in primates and corticosterone in rodents. They are "double-edged" as they "help mediate adaptation to short-term physical stressors yet are pathogenic [disease-producing] when secreted chronically" (Sapolsky 2005: 651). It should also be noted that the L-HPA axis is not the only physiological system involved in stress response. Rather, it is a complexly regulated system involving the sympatho-adrenal-medullary (SAM) axis, which produces the catecholamines epinephrine and norepinephrine, and the neuroimmune system, which produces the key agents in host defense against infection and injury and has been shown to be affected by psychosocial factors (in the field of psychoneuroimmunology, PNI [Coe 1999]). In addition to the primary agents (HPA, SAM, and PNI), there are a number of other physiological systems that serve as antagonists and regulators, including serotonin and oxytocin, discussed in the section that follows (Suomi 2000; Carter 2003). GC's, and cortisol in particular, have proven more amenable to behavioral and health investigations, because of their relatively longer time course and because they can be measured in the saliva of human and nonhuman primates. See also Boyce (in press) and Gunnar and Loman (in press).

[65] Kristenson et al. (2004); Hatch (2005); Hertzman and Frank (2006).

[66] Major and O'Brien (2005). Lamont's discussion (Chapter 6, this volume) of everyday destigmatizing strategies suggests both the range of approaches by different non-mainstream groups, and how they are rooted in specific cultural milieux. Also, Borrell et al. (2006) found that skin color was not related to self-reported health in a large national sample, but perceptions of racial discrimination were strongly related.

[67] Dickerson and Kemeny (2004).

[68] Dowd and Goldman (2006) did not find significant relationships between basal biomarkers of stress and the SES/health relationship, although the older age of the population studied and the pattern of attrition make it harder to gauge how generally the findings will apply.

social hierarchy on primate health, Robert Sapolsky identified seven different dimensions that have been shown to affect stress response across a range of species, including how dominance is established and maintained, the stability of ranks, the availability of coping styles for those lower in the hierarchy (including avoidance of higher-ranking individuals), and personality factors. Systematic reviews of the empirical literature support the view that such factors interact with each other, with subordinate animals showing elevated stress hormones when they are subjected to high rates of stressors, when they have low availability of social support, and when they have few kin around as protectors.[69] Similarly, Bruce McEwen and colleagues elaborated on the construct of allostatic load among humans in the context of trade-offs experienced by individuals with different personality characteristics and coping styles. They describe these types as "Hawks" (showing a tendency to high aggression) and "Doves" (showing a tendency to low aggression). They contend that these trade-offs in stress management lead the former to experience lower (down-regulated) HPA reactivity, higher (up-regulated) SAM activity that is connected with preparation for fight or flight, and lowered serotonin uptake, which in combination may have long-term consequences for (among others) increased impulse control problems, hypertension, and cardiac arrythmias. In contrast, Doves show the reverse pattern on these regulatory systems, with a greater propensity to anxiety disorders, metabolic syndromes (including obesity, perhaps owing in part to the fact that food interrupts the HPA cycle), and depression.[70] At a more general level, these patterns reflect distinctly different modes of response, survival, and resource allocation at the species and individual levels. It is also clear that elevated risks and vulnerabilities in both directions are socially patterned, resulting in regularities of their relationships with social position.[71]

There is also good evidence that L-HPA function is shaped by early social experience in both animal and human models, as indicated in this summary:

[R]odent, nonhuman primate, and human research all point to a common conclusion: that both genetic and environmental factors contribute to the calibration of biological stress response systems over the course of early development. ... Stress reactivity ... appears to become "canalized" over time, revealing progressively greater resistance to change and diminishing plasticity ... [F]indings suggest ... that social contextual effects over the first 3–5 years of life may have particular potency in the calibration of stress responsive biological systems.[72]

---

[69] Sapolsky (2005: 650).

[70] Korte et al. (2005). These categories are akin to the distinction in developmental psychopathology between "externalizing" and "internalizing" disorders. A similar distinction is captured in the description of behavioral stress response styles of "fight or flight" (more combative, aggressive) versus "tend and befriend" (more affiliative, less aggressive), which represent different modes of allocating resources among the biological demands on the organism (Worthman and Kuzara 2005).

[71] Fox et al. (2004); Boyce and Ellis (2005); Ellis, Essex, and Boyce (2005); Korte et al. (2005); Sapolsky (2005); Worthman and Kuzara (2005).

[72] Boyce and Ellis (2005): 278.

This calibration is affected both by normative variation in early developmental experiences, as in elevated cortisol levels among children in low-quality day care settings compared with those in higher quality settings or at home,[73] and also dramatically by extreme variations of abuse and neglect.[74] In terms of Figure 2.1, the early developmental experiences in close relationships prepare the organism for the challenges it is likely to face in the average expected environment predicated on the conditions of that early environment.[75]

Taken together, the cumulative evidence on the stress response system, including the psychosocial impacts on its expression, the impacts of early development on its calibration, the social distribution of those impacts, and the health consequences of dysregulation in this system, supports the plausibility of this as a route for social and developmental mediation of the social gradient in developmental health.

A SENSE OF CONNECTION: SOCIAL RELATIONSHIPS AND THE SOCIAL REWARD SYSTEM

A second candidate mediator system focuses primarily on the notion of social participation, belonging, and connection. The major focus of research on the underlying physiology has been on the functioning of the serotonergic system (measured as the metabolite 5-hydroxyindoleacetic acid [5-HIAA]), which is the target of the pharmaceutical fluoxetine (the class that includes Prozac).[76]

In this instance, we can begin with social variations that disrupt the development of the serotonergic system, and both animal and human evidence point toward disruptions in the attachment relationship between (typically) mother and infant as one primary source of variation. It is also important to note that there is genetic variation in the serotonergic system (in the serotonin transporter gene, 5-HTTLPR). In both animal and human studies this plays out as a *gene-environment interaction* such that genetic risk is activated *only* in circumstances of disrupted parent-child relationships.[77]

The observed consequences of a disrupted serotonergic system are manifold, including elevated risks for depression, aggression, and substance

---

[73] Geoffroy et al. (2006).

[74] Gunnar and Donzella (2002); Boyce and Ellis (2005); Hertzman and Frank (2006).

[75] It is important to avoid teleology in this formulation, since neither the organism nor its parents consciously predict what the future will hold. But there appears to be an evolutionarily preserved variability in the stress response system that responds to the likely environment, based on current experience. There is also a contribution, however, from the nongenomic legacy transmission of early adversity, through the mechanism of rendering inoperable the regulator portion of the relevant gene (a process known as methylation, from the chemical activity responsible for "turning off" that gene segment).

[76] Suomi (2000).

[77] Studied experimentally through peer-rearing manipulations in rhesus macaques (Suomi 2000) and through longitudinal investigations that describe a developmental history of abuse/neglect in humans (Caspi et al. 2003).

abuse.[78] Each of these is linked in turn with adult morbidity and early mortality. In addition, effective functioning of this system seems to act as an antagonist and/or compensator for disruptions to the stress response system, and thus disruptions in its function make it less likely that otherwise valuable coping strategies will be available or effective, such as the protective factors found in human and nonhuman primate studies of having kin and/or social support networks.

This system involving social connection may well be significantly influenced by a related neuroendocrine system involving oxytocin and vasopressin.[79] This system has received considerable recent attention as a potential basis for basic trust and social bonding among individuals in social situations, particularly in intimate relations (especially in maternal nursing and in pair-bonded sexual relations). This system provides a valuable illustration of research directions in the investigation of prospective candidate systems linking social disparities in circumstances to important outcomes in developmental health, through the operation of fundamental developmental mechanisms. In contrast with the HPA-axis and the serotonergic systems, we are just beginning to learn how this system develops in humans, and what its consequences are for developmental health, although the prospects are that it may play a key protective role.

Once again, there is evidence for the full set of linkages across the mediator model shown in Figure 2.1: social interactions influence core developments in brain/behavior processes, the developmental functions influence future interactions and reflect the impact of the early developmental history, and there are downstream consequences for a number of areas of developmental health, including social competence and substance abuse. It is important to recall that these mediator systems do not function in isolation, as noted earlier. An intriguing speculation by James Jackson suggests how some of these trade-offs among mediating mechanisms may account for epidemiological patterns, specifically the apparent disjunction between African American versus white disadvantage in physical health and seeming advantage in mental health indicators. He suggests that to buffer the effects of stress, African Americans are more likely to employ direct coping strategies like eating (which disrupts the HPA axis cycle), smoking, and drinking (which substitutes chemical messengers for disrupted serotonergic functions), which help to buffer negative effects on mental health but at a heavy cost in terms of physical health.[80] Whether that particular mediating account proves to be true or not in future investigations, it does illustrate the potential advantage in moving toward a developmental mediator account in terms of focusing efforts on prevention and intervention. Including the early developmental history, and parental and family stressors in such an account would likely be additionally informative.

[78] Suomi (2000); Bennett et al. (2002); Champoux et al. (2002); Barr et al. (2004); Pihl and Benkelfat (2005).
[79] Carter (2003); Febo, Numan, and Ferris (2005).
[80] Summarized in Carpenter (2002).

THE EMERGENCE OF CONSCIOUSNESS: IDENTITY AND MEANING

A third candidate mediator system focuses on developments in the second decade of life. This system is uniquely human, evolving as a level of reflective *consciousness* that represents a coevolution of culture and mind. The biological focus of this activity is largely the prefrontal cortex of the brain (PFC), which is disproportionately larger (relative to body-size-corrected brain volume) in humans, both archaeologically and by comparison to contemporary nonhuman primates. The PFC achieves this differential size largely during the adolescent transition, and is connected in developmental time with increased speed and amount of connections to other brain systems.[81] The implication of this is that the achievement of the specifically human level of consciousness involves an increased role of PFC governance of brain and biologic systems and is deeply connected to functions such as perceived purpose, hope, meaning, and identity. A second implication from the nature of PFC growth (proliferation of new synapses in early adolescence, and pruning of those during later adolescence) is that this growth is sensitive to developmental experience, in much the same way that early experience shapes brain and biologic systems (like the L-HPA and serotonergic systems).

The specific nature of developmental shaping is less well known in this case, at least in part because research cannot be clearly guided by animal models. But we do know that this is a period of increasing behavioral self-regulation, including advanced cognitive facilities of logic and emotion/attention regulation and the development of self-aware identity, during a period when greater autonomy of action increases the risks from behavioral misadventure.[82] Similarly, precise connections from these acquisitions and outcomes in developmental health are more difficult to specify, given the complexity of the system, but there is an established link from related aspects such as hopelessness or lack of meaning to a range of negative health outcomes.

Another reason to incorporate this candidate mediator system into the model is that it is likely to be a mediator of the functioning of the stress response system during adulthood. As noted previously, the two elements that stand out as the most influential in producing the stress response are cognitive uncertainty and the prospect of negative social evaluation. Both of these are significant functions of the self system, and thus the experience of stress, both psychosocially and physiologically, is substantially affected by the way in which prefrontal (conscious) functions have been shaped by developmental experiences. Given the multiplicity of ways in which individuals can cope with stressors, the ability to navigate alternate responses in a conscious fashion, utilizing available capabilities, may prove to be a powerfully organizing protective factor. Within identity, for example, the relative roles of the private

---

[81] Keating (2004); Giedd (2008). For the more general background on the neural evolution of this system, see note 21 in this chapter.
[82] Steinberg et al. (2006).

self, presented self, collective identity, and their potential conscious integration into an authentic self create multiple routes to developmental health.[83] The decreased prevalence of youth suicide in Canadian First Nations' tribes that have achieved greater collective autonomy is an example of collective identity as both a protective factor (in the positive case of communities with more firmly established collective identities) and a risk factor (in the negative case of communities that had not done so).[84] The potential responses to identity threat arising from stigma are numerous; awareness of them, and of their risks and benefits, may well be important mediators of the link between social disparities and developmental health. Future research will be needed to more firmly establish this mediator pathway, and its central mechanisms.

AN INTEGRATED SYSTEM: COLLECTIVE AND INDIVIDUAL CAPABILITIES

To understand and to investigate the way in which specific social and developmental mediator pathways function, it is necessary to disaggregate them into components. It requires moving back and forth between highly specific investigations of particular neural functions and related features of the local environment, and broader levels of developmental function that organize larger patterns, such as control, connection, and consciousness.

Another level of integration should be borne in mind, although our ability to empirically describe it is some time off. According to the proposed model, social interactions and developmental processes and functions are reciprocally related across the course of development. It is compatible with a view that at the individual level, the functions of control, connection, and consciousness become linked with specific competencies and expertise as those are required by particular cultural and historical demands – in a word, capabilities – and to the extent that society provides affordances for the expression of those capabilities. The development of competence rests on a complicated neural substrate that incorporates basic processes with the acquisition of expertise over very long periods of time.[85] This implies another on-going systemic relationship between the capabilities that exist throughout the population and the ways in which collective capabilities structure the opportunities for them to develop.[86]

A major implication of this model of the social gradient is that looking through the lens of human development processes and outcomes may focus attention on core social facts that may be otherwise overlooked. Productively sustaining this attention through practical action in the arena of social policy development and evaluation could potentially make a significant contribution

---

[83] I appreciate the discussions with Gerard Bouchard that helped me to clarify this formulation.
[84] Chandler et al. (2003).
[85] Keating (1990; 2004).
[86] Keating (1998; 2001).

to an agenda for successful societies.[87] The major claims are that enhancing collective and individual capabilities throughout all sectors of society is likely to have the greatest return for health improvement (by "flattening the gradient higher"); that such enhancement will need to go beyond direct health and/ or income policies and focus instead on a full range of human development policies;[88] and that such a focus requires a deeper understanding of the links between social institutions and their cultural character, including how these societal processes produce the social interactions that shape the development of human capabilities – the specific societal processes that are explored in depth throughout this volume.

[87] These topics are explored in more detail in Keating (in press b).
[88] Keating and Simonton (2008).

3

Health, Social Relations, and Public Policy

Peter A. Hall and Rosemary CR Taylor

Governments are often urged to take steps to improve the health of their citizens. But there is controversy about how best to achieve that goal.[1] Popular opinion calls for more investment in medical care and the promotion of behaviors associated with good health. However, across the developed countries on which we focus here, variations in the health of the population do not correspond closely to national levels of spending on medical care, and there remain many uncertainties about how governments can best promote healthy behavior.[2] Expanding access to health care offers greater promise, but, as many chapters in this book note, health care is only the tip of the iceberg of population health.

The objective of this chapter is to extend our understanding of how governments affect population health. We develop a distinctive perspective on this topic that suggests governments do so by creating or eroding social resources when they make public policy. Our analysis turns on a contention at the heart of this volume, namely, that the structure of social relations in which people are embedded conditions their health. In social epidemiology, there is substantial evidence to support this claim but continuing controversy about which aspects of social relations impinge on health and through which causal mechanisms this occurs.[3] We shed light on these issues by proposing a model linking social

---

[1] For synoptic statements, see Acheson (1998); Adler and Newman (2002).

[2] Variations in population health over time may be more closely related to spending on nutrition and sanitation, medical technology or health care. Compare Cutler et al. (2006) and McKeown (1965). For discussion of how governments do or do not promote healthy behavior, see Swidler (Chapter 5, in this volume) as well as Taylor (1982).

[3] For recent overviews of these controversies, see Berkman and Kawachi (2000); Wilkinson (2005); Carpiano et al. (2008).

An earlier version of this chapter was presented *at the annual meeting of the American Sociological Association, Montreal, Quebec, Canada,* August 10, 2006. For insightful comments on various drafts we are grateful to the members of CIFAR's Successful Societies Program, its advisory committee, Susan Bell, Michèle Lamont and Bo Rothstein. For research assistance, we thank Marius Busemeyer and, for logistical assistance, Emily Putnam.

relations to health and then use that model to identify the dimensions of social relations most likely to impinge on health. Our approach goes beyond many current formulations to incorporate a fuller appreciation for the ways in which cultural frameworks matter to variations in population health.

The wider significance of our argument lies in the portrait it draws of public policy making. Policy is often said to affect collective well-being by redistributing economic resources. Many policies work this way. However, we argue that public policies also affect collective well-being through their impact on the structure of social relations because those relations are social resources on which individuals draw to advance their own welfare. In short, we see public policy making as a process of social resource creation and social resources as central to population health.

A BASIC MODEL LINKING POPULATION HEALTH TO ECONOMIC AND SOCIAL RELATIONS

We begin by developing a general model designed to capture some of the important ways in which economic and social relations feed into health. It has special relevance for the gradient that links health to socioeconomic status, measured by income, occupation, or educational level. As the opening chapters in this book indicate, in all developed and most developing countries, people with lower levels of socioeconomic status tend to have poorer levels of health. The problem is to explain both the existence of this gradient and variations in its shape, indicating that disparities in health across socioeconomic groups are greater in some communities or countries than in others.[4] Such variations are large enough to represent millions of years of healthy lives foregone.

Although well documented in epidemiology, the health gradient is not well explained. Many analysts attribute the gradient to differences in the material resources available to people at different income levels. Some attribute it to social factors, such as variation in the presence of social networks among different segments of the population.[5] However, the literature is not always clear about precisely how social factors impinge on population health. One of the objectives of this chapter is to explore how they do so.

Moreover, epidemiology has had difficulty disentangling social from economic factors. Link and Phelan argue that the "fundamental cause" of the gradient lies in "socioeconomic status," but whether there is an operative social force of such generality captured by that term remains an open question.[6] Many

---

[4] For discussion of these gradients, see Hertzman (Chapter 1, in this volume) and Keating (Chapter 2, in this volume). For an especially powerful illustration of gradients, see Banks et al. (2006).

[5] For recent overviews, see Kawachi, Kennedy, and Wilkinson (1999); Berkman and Kawachi (2000); and Heymann et al. (2006).

[6] Link and Phelan (1995; 2000). For a recent effort to identify some of the mechanisms through which socioeconomic status might work, see Carpiano et al. (2008). Within wider literatures, this engages issues of how social classes are constituted.

studies treat cross-national differences in social factors as if they are rooted in material factors.[7] Of course, social factors often have economic roots. But we try to delineate the dimensions of social relations relevant to population health in terms that separate them from economic relations, so that their own impact can be appreciated and subsequent work can investigate, rather than assume, how much they depend on economic relations. One advantage of this approach is that it reveals that governments affect the provision of social resources in ways that do not depend entirely on how they distribute material resources.

Our focus is on the affluent democracies, where population health is not closely correlated with political stability or gross domestic product per capita, and our objective is not to review every way in which social relations impinge on health but to concentrate on a specific set of causal chains. We attribute particular importance to the toll taken on health by the "wear and tear of daily life."[8] This is appropriate for the OECD countries where chronic diseases that have been linked to such wear and tear make a large contribution to life expectancy, and national differences in rates of mortality turn primarily on differences in mortality in the working age population, namely, among people exposed to the pressures of working lives.[9]

This perspective emphasizes the impact of experiences of stress and the emotional states associated with them, such as anxiety, resentment, and frustration.[10] Although these are not the only causes of illness, a substantial body of research shows they are closely associated with a person's health. In Chapter 2 of this volume, Daniel Keating traces the biological pathways whereby such experiences produce negative physiological effects.[11]

We deploy a simple but relatively general model to identify how much stress and accompanying emotional pressure a person is likely to experience in daily life. At its heart are two main components. On one side is the magnitude of the *life challenges* facing individuals, namely the tasks associated with reaching goals they consider important, such as finding a companion, raising a family, or securing a livelihood. We assume that life satisfaction depends heavily on the effectiveness with which people accomplish these tasks, and we identify two ways of doing so, through individual and collective action, defining

---

[7] Compare Link and Phelan (1995) and Wilkinson (2005).

[8] This model influences many of the chapters in this book. See McEwen (1998, 2005) and Taylor et al. (1999).

[9] See Chapter 1 in this volume by Clyde Hertzman and Arjumand Siddiqi.

[10] We follow a substantial literature in conceptualizing stress as an experience associated with systematic physiological responses. Its level depends on the magnitude of the stressors one encounters and on attributes of personality that affect how much stress one feels in the face of such experiences. A person's physiology, conditioned by past experience, also affects his physiological reactions to subsequent stressors. See Haslam et al. (2005). As we construe them here, a person's capabilities condition both the degree to which any particular task constitutes a stressor and the degree to which a stressor of given magnitude results in feelings of stress.

[11] See also Chrousos et al. (1995); Brunner (1997); Lovallo (1997); Sapolsky et al. (1997); Taylor et al. (1999); Brunner (2000).

the latter as group-based endeavor to secure changes in public policy or to improve the community.

On the other side of the model are a person's *capabilities* for taking effective action to cope with these life challenges.[12] These are constituted, first, by key attributes of personality, including emotional resilience, reflective consciousness, and self-esteem. These attributes are established in childhood but refined in later life. Evidence shows they condition a person's ability to complete many kinds of tasks successfully and to control behaviors associated with poor health, such as those involving smoking, exercise, and diet.[13] The second constitutive element of a person's capabilities lies in her capacity to elicit the cooperation of others. Performing many of the tasks of daily life, associated with finding child care, work, or housing, requires the cooperation of other people. Where cooperation is difficult to secure, accomplishing such tasks becomes more onerous. Finally, some challenges can be addressed best by collective action. In such cases, people need the capability to act in concert, whether to pressure governments to provide better health care and a safer environment or simply to clean up the neighborhood.

Our core contention is that the amount of wear and tear a person suffers in daily life turns on the *balance* between these life challenges and capabilities. Those who experience more difficult life challenges or do so with fewer capabilities will consistently experience higher levels of stress and feelings of anxiety, anger, and frustration that lead to poorer levels of physical and mental health. Everyone experiences some challenging moments, but we are referring to life challenges and capabilities that tend to be durable over time. It is the consistent quality of such experiences that works its way most perniciously "under the skin."[14]

Social and economic relations enter this model as factors that condition the balance between challenges and capabilities found at typical positions in a given society. Of course, life challenges and capabilities vary across individuals. However, we are interested in systematic variations in population health across social groups and societies. In the following sections, we use this model to derive propositions about the dimensions of economic and social relations likely to affect population health and review the evidence for whether they do so, before turning to the effects governments can have on social relations.

THE IMPACT OF ECONOMIC RELATIONS

One of the advantages of this model is that it captures the effects of economic as well as social relations on population health. As many analysts have noted, the economy can be seen as a set of individual and collective actors endowed

---

[12] Our concept of capabilities is narrower than the influential formulation of Sen (1999). For analogous formulations inspired by his, see also Bartley (2006).

[13] Grembowski et al. (1993); Berkman et al. (2000).

[14] Taylor et al. (1999).

with particular levels of material resources (in the form of wealth, income, or skills) and politically established rights (notably property rights) linked together in relations structured by markets, hierarchies, and other institutions supporting cooperation.[15] From the perspective of our model, the economy is important to the health of the population because the distribution of material resources conditions the magnitude of the life challenges facing people and their capabilities for meeting challenges. Access to material resources makes it easier for people to find a good job, secure a decent residence, take care of children, and the like. In short, our model incorporates the contention that the distribution of material resources provides part of the explanation for the familiar health gradient.

The implication is that governments can mitigate the health effects of material inequality by redistributing income, providing public services such as day care, social insurance, and health care, or promoting education to enhance marketable skills.[16] Considerable evidence supports these propositions. Up to some point of diminishing marginal returns, income certainly conditions the health of individuals. Disagreement exists as to whether a more equal income distribution improves the health of the population as a whole, but some evidence supports that claim.[17] The public provision of services is associated with better population health and may sometimes be a substitute for income redistribution.[18] A number of analysts have argued that wider access to education can improve the health of the population.[19]

However, our model suggests that the structure of economic relations may affect the health of the population in other ways as well, notably through the intensity of labor market competition it promotes and corresponding insecurities in the employment relationship.[20] Relatively little is known about how the intensity of market competition affects population health. On the one hand, it may improve the opportunities available to some people.[21] On the other hand, by increasing insecurity, it may generate more stressful experiences that can lead to

---

[15] Williamson (1985); Hall and Soskice (2001); Greif (2006). In these models, both political and economic relations are often construed in market terms. For alternative views of the economy, see Smelser and Swedberg (1994).

[16] The public provision of day care has special importance. If it is not merely custodial but stimulating and supportive, day care can have durable effects on children's health that last through adulthood, as well as relieving parents. See Keating and Hertzman (1999b).

[17] For recent overviews, see Lynch et al. (2004); Wilkinson (2005: Chapter 4). Compare Beckfield (2004). At issue in this debate is not only whether income distribution conditions population health but why it does so.

[18] Ross et al. (2006).

[19] See Keating and Hertzman (1999b); Cutler et al. (2008); Evans (Chapter 4, in this volume).

[20] Bartley et al. (forthcoming).

[21] Increasing market competition might also lead to higher levels of GDP per capita but, across the developed democracies, population health is not closely related to those levels. Some perspectives suggest that economies with high levels of strategic coordination as well as those with high levels of market competition can perform well in economic terms; see Hall and Soskice (2001).

poorer health, especially for segments of the population endowed with few marketable assets. The precipitous declines in health in some states following the transition to capitalism in Eastern Europe, to which Clyde Hertzman draws attention, suggest that such risks are real. But the impact on health of increasing market competition may be mediated by other factors, such as overall levels of unemployment and the character of social benefits, raising issues that deserve more study.

SOCIAL RELATIONS AS SOCIAL RESOURCES

Since Adam Smith, it has been customary to construe the economy in structural terms. One of our core contentions is that societies should be seen in analogous terms, namely, as structured sets of social relations that impinge on population health. To establish this point, we pursue three lines of analysis. First, we try to identify the principal dimensions of social relations likely to condition population health, with an emphasis on those comparable across societies. Using the model we have just described, we then outline a set of causal paths whereby these dimensions affect the health of the population.[22] Finally, we adduce some evidence drawn from the literature suggesting that each of these dimensions impinges on health.

Most views of the social relationships important to health follow two traditions in the study of society.[23] The first has roots in the conceptions of Emile Durkheim, who saw societies as interconnected wholes joined by personal relations and a collective consciousness. This perspective emphasizes the importance of social connectedness. From their connections with others, people are said to derive not only logistical support but emotional sustenance and a sense of self.

A second approach to society is reflected in the formulations of Max Weber and Karl Marx, who put more emphasis on relations of domination. On this view, individuals are deeply affected by asymmetries in their relations with others, construed in terms of class, status, or power. Weber directs our attention to the importance of separating the impact of status from the impact of material inequality because differences of social class rooted in economic relations are closely aligned with distinctions of status rooted in cultural frameworks in some societies but not in all. Accordingly, we explore the impact on population health of *social connectedness* and *social hierarchy*, taken as constitutive features of social structure.

At the foundation of our analysis is the contention that many dimensions of social relations constitute *social resources*, analogous to economic resources, on which people can draw to cope with life challenges.[24] When required to

---

[22] As noted, we are not claiming these are the only paths through which social relations condition health.

[23] See Berkman (1995); Berkman et al. (2000).

[24] For analogous formulations that use the term "social resources" slightly differently, see Pearlin and Schooler (1978); Link and Phelan (2000); Kristenson (2006).

care for children or aging parents, for instance, people call upon the social networks in which they are embedded and the concepts of moral obligation fostered by particular communities. To secure the cooperation of others, they draw on their social status and levels of generalized trust in local networks or society as a whole. To mobilize support for action on behalf of the community, they tap the collective purposes defined by prevailing social imaginaries. Like economic resources, social resources can often be put to multiple uses. What individuals attempt to do and the confidence brought to those tasks can also be conditioned by the templates for action present in predominant cultural narratives.[25]

Rather than seeing a person's capabilities as a set of attributes or endowments possessed by the individual, we see social resources as intrinsically relational, that is, constituted by the quality of a person's relations with others.[26] Whereas some of these relationships can be understood in the rationalist terms of strategic interaction, others are given by institutional practices and cultural frameworks that are collective features of a society.[27] Let us consider the relevant dimensions in more detail.

The Impact of Social Connectedness

We use the term "social connectedness" to refer to the character of the ties that individuals have to others in society. It is reflected in people's contacts with others, whether frequent and familiar or more distant, and in the images people have of the community to which they belong, regardless of their personal contacts. The social cohesion of a society turns on the quality of such attachments. Existing analyses emphasize some dimensions of social connectedness more than others.

Social Capital

One of the most prominent perspectives construes social connectedness in terms of "social capital," seen in Robert Putnam's influential formulation as generalized capacities for cooperation that are said to arise from repeated face-to-face interaction in social encounters or secondary associations. These capacities for cooperation turn on relations of mutual reciprocity that are built on relatively rationalist exchanges and the social trust that is said to

---

[25] These characteristics are sometimes described as a person's self-efficacy; see Steele (1988; 1999); Grembowski et al. (1993); Steele and Arsonson (1998). See also Swidler (1986); Oyserman and Markus (1990); Oyserman et al. (2006).

[26] This formulation parallels contemporary understandings of the firm. At one point, a firm's competencies were thought to depend on its assets, namely, on the capital, technology, and skills it possessed. But recent analyses suggest that the competencies (and success) of a firm depend even more heavily on the quality of the relationships it is able to form with other actors, including its clients, employees, and suppliers of goods or finance. See Dosi and Teece (1998).

[27] See also Hall and Taylor (1996).

accompany them.[28] This account views social capital as a multipurpose social resource of such singular generality that even those who do not participate in associational life are said to benefit from it.

From the perspective of our model, social capital contributes to population health through two pathways. Higher levels of social trust make it easier for everyone to secure the cooperation of others, thereby enhancing their capabilities for coping with life challenges. The networks of reciprocity encouraged by personal contact in civic associations or social networks also facilitate collective action – to address the challenges facing the community directly or to pressure governments to do so – especially when these networks run across racial or ethnic boundaries that might otherwise limit social trust. There is some evidence for these propositions. On a variety of measures, average levels of health across communities are correlated with the levels of social trust and numbers of secondary associations found in them.[29] The concept of social capital provides one way of understanding how the structure of social relations generates resources that underpin population health.

Social Networks

As many analysts have observed, however, the effects of social networks on population health may not flow entirely through the generalized mechanisms of social capital. There are a number of more direct ways in which membership in social networks enhances people's capabilities for coping with life challenges, thereby contributing to their health.[30] Networks can provide *logistical support* for important life tasks, such as rearing children, securing employment, and managing illness, as well as *information* about how to cope with such challenges and *social influence* useful for securing the cooperation of others in life tasks or collective action. As sources of *emotional support*, some kinds of networks condition the psychological resilience of individuals in the face of challenges.

Of course, the contribution a network makes to the resolution of particular kinds of challenges depends on its character.[31] Social networks may be dense, linking people to many others, or relatively thin. They can be based

---

[28] Putnam (1993; 2000). Social trust refers to the general willingness of people to trust others in the community. For a critical discussion, see Cook et al. (2005).

[29] Kawachi et al. (1997); Kawachi, Kennedy, and Glass (1998); Kawachi, Kennedy, and Wilkinson (1999: Chapters 22 and 23). Of course, these correlations may reflect mechanisms other than those posited by this general conception of social capital, including the support provided directly to individuals by social networks, as noted in subsequent paragraphs; and levels of social trust are not always closely correlated with the density of associational membership.

[30] We use the term "social networks" to refer to the contacts people have with other people. These formulations are influenced by the analysis of Berkman et al. (2000), which covers such pathways in more detail. There is a large literature based on various psychological models about how social networks impinge on physical and mental health. For a review regarding mental health, see Almedom (2005).

[31] See Erickson (1996; 2002).

on frequent or infrequent contact, on face-to-face, or more distant, relations. They can embody strong ties that reflect intimacy or weak ties based on passing acquaintance. Networks may be deeply intertwined or segmented by social group. These dimensions are consequential. People seeking work, for instance, may benefit more from weak ties to many others, whereas people recovering from illnesses may benefit more from deep attachments to a few individuals.[32]

More research is needed to establish the value of networks with specific kinds of dimensions for meeting particular kinds of challenges.[33] However, convincing evidence now links a person's health to the overall density of the social networks in which he is embedded. Studies show that the level and intensity of a person's contacts with others are related to all-cause mortality, self-rated health, and rates of recovery from a variety of illnesses such as myocardial infarction. The emotional attachments provided by close relationships seem to improve resilience against depression, illness, and addiction.[34]

Membership in associations underpins people's capabilities in analogous ways, thereby reducing the stress associated with important challenges. Day care cooperatives help parents cope with the demands of a family. Sports clubs provide companionship and opportunities for exercise. Self-help groups oriented to the control of risky behaviors constitute one of the fastest-growing segments of the nonprofit sector. Not surprisingly, studies find that those who belong to such associations are likely to be healthier, even when factors such as age, income, and social class are controlled.[35]

There is a distributive side to social connectedness. As Putnam posits, the benefits of social trust may be available to all in relatively equal amounts.[36] However, people with less income and lower-status occupations tend to belong to fewer associations and smaller social networks that are based on closer attachments to fewer friends.[37] Therefore, discrepancies in social connections may be one of the factors contributing to the gradient observed between social class and health, and, if the relationship between income (or occupational status) and membership in social networks (or associations) varies systematically across countries, that may help to explain cross-national variation in the shape of the health gradient.

Collective Imaginaries

The social connectedness of a society is specified not simply by the density or character of its social networks, but by the content of the messages about

---

[32] Granovetter (1974); Case et al. (1992).

[33] However, see Lin et al. (2001).

[34] Syme and Berkman (1979). For broad reviews, see Berkman (1995); Berkman et al. (2000).

[35] Kawachi et al. (1999: Chapters 22 and 23).

[36] If so, the health of most of the populace should be better in societies with higher levels of social trust.

[37] For the British case, see Goldthorpe (1987); Allan (1990); Oakley and Rajan (1991). See also Carpiano et al. (2008).

meaning and morality those networks convey.[38] Social relations are structured by a set of collective representations that contribute to the social cohesion of a society by specifying a set of purposes individuals can use to guide their actions, a vision of what it means to belong to the community as a whole, and a sense of what can reasonably be expected in moral terms from others. As a short form, we refer to these dimensions of social relations as features of a society's collective imaginary.[39] The concept of social trust is too thin to capture such dimensions fully.

The key point here is one anthropologists have advanced for some time.[40] Social relations are central to the meanings individuals assign to their lives and actions, and that meaningfulness can often be important to their health. People have more psychological resilience – against depression, anxiety, and other adverse emotional states – when their lives appear to them as purposeful; and within the collective imaginary people find representations of the community and their place in it that are constitutive of feelings of belonging and allow them to define larger purposes for themselves.

Moreover, the social order is also a moral order – marked by customary attitudes with normative force that specify what individuals can expect of one another. As factors of social cohesion, these go beyond the relations of reciprocal exchange emphasized in conceptions of social capital to approach what Thompson called the "moral economy" of a community.[41] They define the informal obligations people feel toward each other and the standards of behavior to which they can hold other people.[42]

There are a variety of ways in which these dimensions of the collective imaginary feed into people's capabilities and hence into their health. They affect an individual's willingness to turn to others for help and the likelihood it will be supplied. To motivate others to join in collective action, people also call upon collective representations of the purposes and standards of the community, making moral as well as material appeals.

As Durkheim noted, collective representations of society condition the emotional resilience of individuals in the face of challenges. By virtue of how they define the community, these visions can enhance or erode people's feelings of social isolation, as well as their levels of optimism about their own fate and that of their community – feelings generally seen as important to health.

Collective imaginaries also specify a range of behaviors seen as appropriate for particular contexts or types of people. They usually identify a set of

---

[38] Emirbayer and Goodwin (1994).

[39] For related formulations, see Bouchard (2000; 2003b) and Castoriadis (1987) whose concept of the social imaginary differs in some ways from ours.

[40] See Geertz (1973); Kleinman (1981). Although this perspective is appreciated by social epidemiology it is less well-represented there because it references variables that are difficult to measure systematically across communities.

[41] Thompson (1971).

[42] See Swidler (Chapter 5, in this volume); see also Taylor (2004).

gender roles and help define what Swidler calls the "strategies for action" on which individuals in various social positions draw to cope with life challenges.[43] When confronted with a challenge, a person tends to ask "what can someone like me do about that?" The answer will be influenced by personal experience, but also by the conceptions of "someone like me" available in the prevailing collective imaginary.[44] In such respects, collective imaginaries are both enabling and constraining. They encourage or discourage a range of behaviors relevant to health, and they are ultimately constitutive of people's capabilities.

Evidence about the impact of social imaginaries on population health is difficult to gather. However, a number of cases establish some of these causal links. Attitudes toward risky behaviors vary systematically with social position in ways that suggest those attitudes do not simply reflect the general skills conferred by education but also the dispositions associated with a particular "habitus."[45] At the communal level, Erikson's investigation of the traumatic symptoms following a flood in Buffalo Creek found that many of those symptoms were a reaction, not to the physical disaster itself, but to a loss of the sense of communality once fostered by the tight-knit community swept away by the flood.[46] Eberstadt associates part of the decline in population health in the Soviet Union prior to perestroika with the demoralization that set in, as the values once promoted by the Soviet leadership lost resonance for ordinary people, leaving them uncertain about what their nation promised or what the future would hold.[47]

However, there are limits to the effect of a collective imaginary. In Chapter 7 of this volume, Gérard Bouchard reminds us that a society's imaginary is made up of many different images, myths, and collective representations on which diverse individuals draw differently. It constitutes a repertoire that can enable various types of action, even if its overall contours are constraining. Some groups create countercultures that take them in different directions, albeit conditioned by mainstream imaginary, and, as Michèle Lamont suggests, individuals can develop strategies to offset some of the effects of a dominant imagery.[48]

[43] Gatens (2004).

[44] Swidler (1986); see also Oyserman et al. (2006).

[45] Bourdieu uses the concept of the "habitus" to indicate the sets of norms and practices embodying views about appropriate behavior that are associated with particular positions in the structure of social relations. See Frohlich et al. (2001); Veenstra (2005); Cockerham (2007). Compare Cutler and Lleras-Muney (2008).

[46] Erikson (1976).

[47] Eberstadt (1981). This is a controversial claim since there is debate about the timing and sources of declining health in the former Soviet Union, but it highlights the contribution a collective imaginary makes to community capabilities and individual resilience. See also Field (1986); Garrett (2000).

[48] See Lamont (Chapter 6, in this volume). Also Willis (1977) and Crocker and Major (1989).

Social Hierarchy

As Weber has emphasized, the structure of social relations is also characterized by the asymmetries of social hierarchy. Some arise from formal hierarchies that assign a delimited range of power and autonomy to each position inside them. Others stem from informal hierarchies allocating levels of prestige or social status – a concept that figures prominently in studies of population health.[49] How do the shapes of social hierarchies and relative positions within them impinge on health?

There is substantial evidence that the formal hierarchies associated with employment affect health by restricting a person's autonomy at work. Those with less control available to meet the demands of the workplace experience more stress and daily anxiety, with corresponding effects on their health.[50] Some argue that steeper social hierarchies engender more intense feelings of relative deprivation.[51] However, our model suggests two other pathways from social hierarchy to health, operating through the effects of status on capabilities for coping with life challenges. One turns on the problem of securing cooperation. To meet life challenges, a person requires the cooperation of others, and people of lower social status are likely to have more difficulty securing such cooperation. Status is an all-purpose social lubricant conditioning the cooperation one receives from others. As a result, people with low status should experience more wear and tear as they attempt to meet the challenges of daily life.[52]

The other pathway turns on problems of recognition. The levels of stress or anxiety a person experiences depend not only on the magnitude of the tasks confronting him but also on the confidence he brings to them. People with low levels of self-esteem are less likely to attempt challenging tasks, less likely to succeed at them, and more likely to find such tasks stressful.[53] Self-esteem is established initially in childhood, but it is influenced by subsequent experiences, during which our images of ourselves are affected by those reflected in the mirror society holds up to us.[54] Where those images are more negative, self-esteem is likely to suffer. In short, social recognition is crucial to self-recognition, and higher social status confers more favorable social recognition. As a result, higher status individuals should have greater levels of self-efficacy that reduce the amount of stress they experience in daily life, promoting better health.

[49] For synoptic works, see Marmot (2004); Wilkinson (2005). We use the terms "status hierarchies" and "social hierarchies" as synonyms to denote these informal hierarchies. By social status, we mean the level of general social prestige a person enjoys.

[50] See Karasek (1979); Marmot et al. (1997); Collins et al. (2005); Bartley (2005).

[51] Wilkinson (1996).

[52] For more general discussion of this point, see Marmot (2004).

[53] MacLeod (1987); Steele (1988).

[54] A similar analysis applies to self-efficacy, a concept associated with the confidence an individual brings to a specific set of tasks, rather than self-esteem understood as a variable with more general application. See Grembowski et al. (1993).

These observations have important implications for cross-national analysis. Although some analysts think social hierarchies are biologically embedded, the *shape* of such hierarchies is manifestly different across societies and ultimately an artifact of cultural and institutional frameworks.[55] If we are correct, these differences condition, in turn, the distribution of health across populations. Societies that deprive large numbers of people of social status should have lower overall levels of health than those that assign status more evenly. National variations in population health should follow variations in the social hierarchy.

However, we need ways of characterizing that variation. Many analysts assume a person's status simply corresponds to his occupation, generating a similar status curve in advanced industrial societies. But sociological research reveals more diverse sources of status and wider variation in the shape of such curves.[56] With this in mind, we suggest three dimensions of social hierarchy likely to be consequential for population health.

The first is the steepness of the status hierarchy associated with income or occupational position in any given country, understood as the size of the status differentials between typical positions along it, reflected, for instance, in the levels of social prestige enjoyed by those at each decile in the income distribution. This relationship may not be linear, and the shape of the curve is important. If, as Runciman notes, feelings of relative deprivation are usually based on comparisons made with others in proximate social positions, the poor may be more affected by the shape of the curve at the bottom half of the income distribution than at its top.[57]

Equally important is the multidimensionality of status attribution, reflected in the number and variety of social roles that confer prestige in any given society. People live in social settings defined by overlapping circles of family, workplace, neighborhood, and nation, each associated with distinctive components of the collective imaginary. In principle, a person may secure status from his role in any of them. In societies where people typically derive status, not only from their family origins or occupation but also from their roles as fathers, consumers, or citizens, the overall distribution of status may be more even, to the advantage of those in lower-status occupations.[58] Of special significance here is the degree to which status depends on income. Where it does, the distribution of social resources parallels the distribution of economic resources, and the status hierarchy will reinforce the health effects of income inequality. In some societies, however, income and status may not be so closely coupled.

Social hierarchies can also be characterized by the status they assign to readily identifiable groups in society, such as gender and ethnic groups.

---

[55] Bourdieu (1983).
[56] Boltanski and Thévenot (1991); Lamont (2000); Sing-Manoux et al. (2005).
[57] Runciman (1964).
[58] See Sieber (1974); Thoits (1983); Steele (1988).

Status differences of this sort may be as large as those rooted in income or occupation.[59] Typically, they are reflected in the stereotypes that are familiar features of collective imaginaries and constitutive of the social boundaries discussed by Michèle Lamont in Chapter 6 of this volume.[60] Evidence from psychology suggests that such stereotypes can have powerful effects on the efficacy with which people perform certain tasks. They can affect self-esteem and a person's capacity to secure the cooperation of others.[61]

Empirically, it is difficult to separate the effects of status from those of income, and there are few studies that allow one to assess the health effects of cross-national differences in status hierarchies. However, three streams of evidence converge to suggest that status affects health. The studies of British civil servants conducted by Marmot and others found that, even when other risk factors were controlled, those in lower status positions in this occupational hierarchy suffered from more health problems than officials of higher status.[62] Studies of primates other than human beings show that those with low status display a range of physiological effects associated with poor health, such as atherosclerosis, obesity, worse cholesterol profiles, and behavioral depression.[63] And, although the interpretation is hotly contested, the finding that average levels of health are worse in countries where the income distribution is more unequal may indicate the adverse health effects of a steeper status hierarchy.[64] Taken together, these studies offer tentative support for the contention that social hierarchies condition population health.

The Capabilities of Communities

Of course, the structure of social relations affects, not only the capabilities of individuals, but what might be called the capabilities of communities. Some of these reside in the capacities of members of the community to cooperate to advance everyone's health, through efforts to reduce rates of violence, improve local housing, clean up the environment, and the like.[65] Others reside in the capabilities of governments to address community health issues, reflected in policies to cope with infectious as well as chronic diseases, to improve sanitation, regulate food or occupational safety, and otherwise to provide a healthy environment.[66]

---

[59] Williams (1999, 2005); Krieger (2000).

[60] See also Lamont (2000). As she points out, members of identifiable groups can use various strategies to offset the effects the status order might otherwise have on their endeavors.

[61] Steele (1988); Steele and Aronson (1998). Compare Elmer (2001); Pyszczynski et al. (2004).

[62] Marmot (2004).

[63] See Shively and Clarkson (1994); Sapolsky and Share (1994); Brunner (1997); Sapolsky et al. (1997); Shively, Laer-Laird, and Anton (1997); Keating (Chapter 2, in this volume).

[64] For overviews, see Wilkinson (1997, 2005: Chapter 4); Berkman and Kawachi (2000); Lynch et al. (2004).

[65] Other examples could be given. See Sampson et al. (1997; 2002).

[66] For overviews, see McKeown (1965); Acheson (1998); Adler and Newman (2002).

Many factors condition the capabilities of communities and their governments, but among these are various features of the structure of social relations.[67] As Peter Evans observes, an effective civil society requires more than
civil rights and the existence of town meetings.[68] It depends on sustained
mobilization, and capacities for collective mobilization turn on the density
of existing social networks and the quality of the local solidarities animating
them.[69] Such capacities are also conditioned by the collective imaginaries of
a community, which specify what people owe one another, why they should
band together, and just how to improve their lives.[70]

The capacities of governments to implement various kinds of policies also
depend on how society is organized and the cultural frameworks that impinge
on that. Studies have shown that the effective implementation of industrial or
agricultural policies turns on how the relevant segments of society are organized.[71] However, measures to protect the health of citizens and to shift people
away from behaviors that put their health at risk can also depend on the character of local arrangements. Eric Klinenberg considers why existing social
protection systems failed to shield elderly residents from the effects of a devastating heat wave in Chicago. He found, for example, that many refused offers
of support because, in the context of a culture that idealizes self-sufficiency,
they were reluctant to admit dependency.[72] In cases such as these, cultural as
well as institutional frameworks at the local level make some types of policies
more or less effective.

As Ann Swidler indicates in Chapter 5 of this volume, this is an important part of the story underlying the AIDS epidemic in various African countries, and others confirm this point. Helen Epstein argues that differences in
HIV infection rates in South Africa and Uganda can be explained in large
part by a destabilization of the family in South Africa that was engendered
by apartheid and a migrant labor system that eroded a sense of trust and
community. Ugandans, on the other hand, are more likely to live in enduring
rural communities that confer on them greater capacities to take care of one
another, allowing for a more open response to AIDS.[73] Philip Setel shows how

---

[67] These factors include the structure of the state and the rules of the political system. The factors most important to mobilizational capacities in particular may also be different at the
national level than they are at the local level. Compare Wilkinson (2005: 227ff.).

[68] There is a large literature on the conditions that allow for effective mobilization citing factors
we do not cover here, including different views of the resources required for mobilization. For
examples, see McAdam et al. (1996; 2001).

[69] Putnam (2000); Warren (2001); Swidler (Chapter 5, in this volume).

[70] Recent declines in the capacities of socialist or Catholic organizations to mobilize their
European constituencies reflect this point. In many cases, the relevant organizations continue
to exist but collective imaginaries have changed in ways that deprive the left and political
Catholicism of much of their mobilizing power. See Valle (2003).

[71] For examples, see Keeler (1987); Atkinson and Coleman (1989); Golden (1993).

[72] Klinenberg (2002).

[73] Epstein (2007).

the transformation of the Chagga in Tanzania into a migrant group whose regulated domestic life was undermined created new aspirations and a loosened control over sexuality – in effect, a "reordering of desire" that set the stage for transmission of HIV.[74] Catherine Campbell, Paul Farmer, and others have argued that governments and donor agencies that do not understand these changing ways of life and patterns of belief cannot speak to them in their prevention strategies.[75]

PUBLIC POLICY MAKING AS SOCIAL RESOURCE CREATION

We have argued that, over the course of a lifetime, a person's health depends on the balance between his life challenges and capabilities, which feed into the amount of wear and tear experienced in daily life. We suggest that a person's position within the structure of social relations provides social resources that condition those capabilities. Like economic resources, many of these social resources can be put to multiple uses. Moreover, like some kinds of economic resources, if investments are made in them, social resources can grow over time. The more some networks are used, for instance, the stronger they become. By increasing the effectiveness of individual and collective endeavors, these social resources also enhance the well-being of societies.[76]

This approach to population health has important implications for public policy making. It invites the question: what are governments doing when they make policy? It is conventional to say that governments redistribute material resources and deploy legal sanctions or fiscal incentives to induce prescribed patterns of behavior.[77] Many policy makers see their actions in these terms. However, our analysis suggests that public policy making can also be seen in another light – as a process of social resource creation or erosion – with important consequences for the well-being of the community.

In many cases, governments are inattentive to this dimension of policy making, and social resources are eroded as an unintended consequence of policies adopted for other purposes.[78] Why might this be so? Consider the case of economic policy making. Because officials think about the economy as a structured set of market relations, when formulating a tax or industrial policy, they consider not only whether the policy will secure its intended goals but also the side effects of that policy on the overall structure of market competition. By contrast, policy makers rarely consider the ancillary effects their policies might have on social relations because they are less accustomed to thinking about society as a structure of social relations.

---

[74] Setel (1999).

[75] See in particular Campbell (2003); Farmer (2005).

[76] This point follows, for instance, from Putnam's (2000) formulations about social capital.

[77] The most famous definition in political science is that public policy is the authoritative allocation of resources. Currently, social transfer programs now consume close to half of public budgets.

[78] Phillipson et al. (2004).

This was not always the case. In nineteenth-century Europe, where social classes were a prominent feature of politics, officials often considered the impact of policies on class relations.[79] But such perspectives shifted over time. The prosperity of the second half of the twentieth century reduced class conflict and, as William Sewell notes in Chapter 10 of this volume, the end of the century brought to the fore a neoliberal paradigm that made market relations much more central to policy making and relegated social relations to its sidelines.[80]

Of course, there is also something counterintuitive about the proposition that public policy can influence the structure of social relations. Social structure is often seen as the immutable product of long-term socioeconomic processes independent of the actions of government.[81] However, to say that social structure is not putty in the hands of government does not mean policy is without effect on it. Over the long run, the impact of actions seemingly inconsequential at the time can cumulate into major changes in social relations.[82] The shifts in class structure after World War II, for instance, owe much to the gradual expansion of public employment in that period.[83]

Whether public policy can affect the dimensions of social relations we have identified as pertinent to health is an open question. The available evidence is limited but, in the following sections, we review it and consider what types of policies might sustain or erode social resources.

Social Connectedness

Although it is only one of several dimensions of social connectedness, social capital has been the subject of more cross-national empirical work than most other dimensions of social relations. As Putnam defines it, "social capital" entails participation in voluntary associations and high levels of social trust. Although early accounts saw social capital as a resource created by long-term socioeconomic developments largely independent of public policy, recent studies suggest that public policies can have important effects on it.[84]

Comparisons between the United States where levels of social capital have declined and Britain, which retains more substantial civic networks, indicate that social capital was sustained in Britain by postwar policies that expanded access to higher education and deployed voluntary associations to deliver social services. At the individual level, higher levels of education encourage more intense civic engagement, and governmental support for the volunteer work of

[79] See Chevalier (1973).
[80] See Graubard (1964); Goldthorpe et al. (1969); Dalton et al. (1984).
[81] Compare Putnam (1993); Tarrow (1996); Skocpol and Fiorina (1999).
[82] See Pierson (2004); Hertzman (Chapter 1, in this volume).
[83] Goldthorpe (1987).
[84] Compare Coleman (1990); Putnam (1993); Mettler (2002); Field (2003: Chapter 5).

charitable associations seems to sustain a country's associational life.[85] Similar effects have been found in the Nordic nations, where moves to professionalize the delivery of social services seem to have eroded social capital, while efforts to support the organizations of civil society have preserved it. Some argue that social capital can be sustained by a "social investment state."[86]

These findings are consistent with the history of public policy. For more than a century, the development of trade unions, religious organizations, and agricultural associations in Europe has been tied to governmental support for their endeavors. Skocpol finds that the growth of associational activity in the United States was also linked to the structural development of government.[87]

Governments also seem to be able to influence the levels of generalized trust associated with social capital. Although the presence of a democratic regime does not guarantee social trust, repression almost certainly erodes it. Booth and Richard find a significant correlation between the repressiveness of Central American regimes and levels of trust among their citizenry, as Inglehart also argues, not because democracy creates trust but because repression undermines it.[88] Political corruption seems to affect social trust adversely. Wuthnow argues that social trust declined in the United States as a result of a drop in political trust linked to the Watergate scandal of the 1970s, and even petty corruption encourages distrust among the citizenry.[89] Thus, policies that reinforce the even-handedness of public administration may enhance levels of social capital.

Kumlin and Rothstein argue that specific features of the design of policies can also affect levels of social capital. They find that the recipients of benefits distributed via a means test are less likely to be trusting of others than the recipients of universal benefits going to all citizens. Since those eligible for means-tested benefits may be less trusting in the first place, it is tempting to ascribe such findings to selection bias, but they show up even when income, class, and other attributes associated with the propensity to trust are controlled.[90] The implication is that, if the design of a policy implies benefit recipients cannot be trusted, they may become less trusting.

Moreover, there are distributive dimensions to such policies that deserve attention. Although Putnam views social capital as a resource enhancing the well-being of everyone in society, the networks that underpin it offer even more

---

[85] Hall (1999); Glatzer (2008). For overviews of social capital, see Warren (1999); Edwards et al. (2001); Stolle and Hooghe (2003).

[86] Selle (1999); Torpe (2003); Jenson and Saint-Martin (2003).

[87] Skocpol and Fiorina (1999).

[88] The proportion of people expressing trust in others varies from about 25 percent to 65 percent across democracies. Inglehart (1999); Booth and Richard (2001); Howard (2003); Uslaner (2003).

[89] Wuthnow (2002). See also Sztompka (1999); Freitag (2003); Rothstein (2003; 2005).

[90] Kumlin and Rothstein (2005). See also Murray (2000); Svensson and Von Otter (2002); Wallis and Dollery (2002).

direct benefits to those within them. Therefore, it matters whose networks are sustained by public policy. Although associational life remains relatively vibrant in Britain, for instance, it has become an increasingly middle-class phenomenon – as the trade unions, cooperatives and religious organizations that were once pillars of working class life have declined. Movement away from traditional working-class communities by people seeking work in the wake of deindustrialization has eroded the informal social networks to which many workers once belonged.[91] As a result, although levels of social capital remain substantial in Britain, as a social resource it is being redistributed in ways that reinforce, rather than offset, the unequal distribution of economic resources.

At issue here is not only the creation of social resources but also the success of public policy. Many policies have network effects that can be leveraged to enhance the impact of policy. Unemployment policy provides a classic example. As we have noted, a person seeking work benefits most from a large network of weak ties to others who already have jobs in order to secure references and information about openings.[92] But policies that require the recipients of unemployment benefits to gather at manpower centers tend to give the unemployed precisely the wrong sort of ties, namely to other people who are also unemployed, whereas policies that provide temporary work or training in firms put them in touch with people with jobs.[93]

In much the same way, day care centers can be designed to enhance the social networks among parents that serve as further sources of support for child rearing, and care for the aged can be designed to embed the elderly in support networks rather than separating them from such networks.[94] In short, by designing policies with an eye to their network dimensions, governments can sometimes achieve a social multiplier effect that improves the impact of policy and augments social resources more generally.[95]

Social Hierarchy

Can public policy have analogous effects on social hierarchies? There is plenty of historical evidence that it can. The process whereby governments expanded the conception of citizenship to encompass civil, political, and social rights was, as Marshall observed, a form of "class abatement".[96] Measures to encourage collective bargaining and support trade union organization improve job security and the control ordinary people have over their working conditions – factors closely associated with their health. In countries where status is closely linked to income, policies to reduce income inequalities may also reduce status inequalities.

---

[91] Hall (1999).
[92] Erickson (2001).
[93] 6 (1997).
[94] Jacobstone and Jenson (2005); Keating et al. (2005).
[95] Policy Research Institute (2005).
[96] Marshall (1965 [1949]).

Whether governments will take such steps is, of course, another question. In many historical cases, the redistribution of status was contingent on a redistribution of power that emerged only from political struggles conducted over long periods of time. However, it is worth noting that gaining rights of citizenship improved the status as well as the economic situation of those on the lower rungs of the economic ladder. Rights-based regimes often shift the status order, as well as the distribution of economic and political resources.

In this realm, political rhetoric also matters. The status order is defined by collective imaginaries and the symbolism governments deploy is a constitutive element of those imaginaries.[97] By celebrating the sacrifices ordinary people make in their daily lives, governments can valorize a wide range of endeavors and accord recognition to those who might otherwise have little, thereby undercutting the monotonicity of a status order that might otherwise be based exclusively on wealth.

The recognition governments afford to identifiable racial and ethnic minorities is especially important. By articulating national narratives that are inclusive, politicians enhance the status of groups that might otherwise feel marginalized. Kymlicka argues that the multicultural policies adopted by some governments effectively shifted the social imaginary, affording a new status to ethnic minorities.[98] There is similar evidence that the rights-based policies adopted in the wake of the Civil Rights movement in the United States improved both the status and health of African Americans.[99]

In each of these cases, however, the results turned not simply on what politicians said but on what governments did. These are instances in which cultural frameworks and institutional procedures are closely intertwined. If recognition is to shift social hierarchies, the ideals and idioms promoted by leaders must also be institutionalized at multiple levels of governance.[100] The social recognition accorded people turns not only on what politicians say but also on what "street-level" bureaucrats do.[101] This is why racial profiling, for instance, or practices that allow the police to treat members of minorities differently from other people has an importance that extends beyond crime.[102] The behavior of public officials sends important signals. If the public authorities treat individuals even-handedly, others in society are more likely to do so as well, thereby enhancing their social resources. When a person is shown respect, that experience also feeds into his self-respect, conditioning his capabilities for coping with life challenges.

---

[97] Lukes (1975); Kertzer (1989).

[98] See Kymlicka (Chapter 9, in this volume) and the references therein.

[99] Kaplan et al. (2008).

[100] On institutionalization, see Jepperson (1991).

[101] Lipsky (1980); Bartley (2006: Chapter 10); Canvin et al. (2006).

[102] Tyler and Blader (2000). See also Soss (1999).

Communal Capabilities

In similar ways, governments can influence the capabilities of communities. Public policies that support civic associations and social networks enhance the capacities of communities to mobilize. By evoking particular sets of ideals and social boundaries, the collective narratives politicians deploy to define the nation also affect the ease with which groups will band together. Comparing closely matched communities in Tanzania and Kenya, for instance, Edward Miguel found that the Tanzanian communities were more effective than the Kenyan at cooperating across ethnic lines to promote local education, and he traces the origins of this cooperation to the ideology of national unity promoted in Tanzania, without an analog in Kenya.[103]

In Chapter 5, Ann Swidler also shows that public policies can be more effective when they exploit local social solidarities. She argues that AIDS prevention policies in Uganda were more successful than those in Botswana because they spoke directly to the types of obligations characteristic of the moral imagery of social networks in Uganda.

However, efforts to shape the collective imaginary are not costless, and there are trade-offs to the adoption of any particular imaginary. The ideology of national unity pursued in Tanzania during the 1960s, for example, was achieved at the cost of repressing many local cultures, much like antecedent attempts to turn "peasants into Frenchmen."[104] The efforts of successive governments to promote a view of Sweden as "the people's home" encouraged egalitarian attitudes, but this conception has not equipped the nation to cope with the ethnic diversity that accompanies recent waves of immigration.[105] Even different versions of republicanism of the sort found in France and the United States, for instance, foster distinctive types of social recognition with corresponding advantages and disadvantages for particular groups.[106]

CONCLUSION

We have argued that the overall health of a population and its distribution across social groups are dependent on the wear and tear ordinary people experience in daily life, which is conditioned, in turn, by the balance between the life challenges facing those people and their capabilities for coping with them. We contend that this balance is determined, not only by economic resources, but by the social resources available to individuals and communities, and we have identified several dimensions of social relations constitutive of those resources. Nothing in this argument suggests that income is unimportant. But we believe that the distribution of social resources is also important to

---

[103] Miguel (2004). See also Wallerstein (2002).
[104] Weber (1976).
[105] Berman (1998).
[106] Higonnet (1988); Lamont (2000).

the health of the population, and, in keeping with the themes of this volume, our conception of social resources includes the cultural frameworks bound up with social connectedness and hierarchy. In short, we argue that population health is determined as much by the structure of social relations as by the structure of economic relations.

Against the view that social relations are determined entirely by long-term socioeconomic developments, we have argued they can be conditioned as well by public policy. Public policy making should be seen as a process of social resource creation. This is not to say that it is easy for governments to create social resources, and in some cases efforts to do so entail costs or complex trade-offs. Like policies that create market opportunities, however, policies that create social resources have deep and diffuse effects because people use those resources for many purposes. The clear implication is that governments should pay as much attention to the conservation of social resources as they do to the protection of natural resources. By designing policies to leverage existing social resources, governments can secure social multiplier effects that enhance the effectiveness of policy.

Although our analysis draws on a wide literature, it is obviously suggestive, rather than dispositive, about many of these issues. Our objective has been to show that there is real value in pursuing research that asks how the structure of social relations impinges on health and what governments can do to enhance social resources. Because social relations vary at the national level, this calls, in particular, for more intensive cross-national empirical inquiry and the development of new data sets to make such inquiries possible. Our review of the issues and evidence indicates there is genuine promise in such research and there are issues at stake that should be of concern to all governments and their citizens.

4

Population Health and Development

An Institutional-Cultural Approach to Capability Expansion

Peter Evans

Health and well-being vary most dramatically across the countries of the Global South. The quest to alleviate misery and deprivation in these countries is both most urgent and most frustrating. Consequently, any effort to analyze the social roots of improvements in population health must consider the dynamics of population health and development in the regions where more than four-fifths of the world's people live: Asia, Africa, and Latin America.

Exploring the social roots of improved population health in the Global South inevitably involves a dialogue with development theory. Two apparently unconnected paradigmatic shifts have recently captured the attention of development scholars and are making inroads into policy debates. The institutional turn in growth theory has shifted attention from levels of investment and getting prices right to the historical processes that generate enduring rules, norms, and organizational structures.[1] The capability approach has provided new analytical foundations for both expanding the definition of development goals and defining the political processes that can legitimately prioritize this expanded set of goals.[2]

This chapter focuses on the intersection of development theory and population health. First, it explores the institutional and cultural roots of improvements in population health. This effort will be undertaken using the broad institutional-cultural approach to population health that characterizes the chapters that make up this volume. Cross-national comparisons of life expectancy and a

[1] See especially Acemoglu et al. (2001); Rodrik (2002); Acemoglu et al. (2005).
[2] See especially Sen (1999).

I would like to thank the members of the Successful Societies Program, especially co–program directors Peter Hall and Michèle Lamont, as well as the members of the Successful Societies Advisory Committee for their unflagging provision of close readings and constructive suggestions through the several drafts of this chapter. I would also like to thank Sarah Staveteig, who has been a close collaborator in the thinking and analysis that went into this chapter from the beginning, and Anna Wetterberg, who provided invaluable feedback in the final stages.

set of case studies will be the empirical springboard. Second, I hope to make a contribution to development theory. More specifically, I will advance the claim that an expanded institutional-cultural approach points us toward the possibility of integrating the institutional turn and the capability approach.

ARGUMENTS ABOUT POPULATION HEALTH AND DEVELOPMENT

In work on the Global South, theories of improved health and well-being have traditionally been seen as part of the general quest for improved material circumstances of living. This makes common sense. A large proportion of the roughly five billion people who live in the Global South cannot take the material necessities of life for granted. Given the harsh realities of material deprivation, it is natural to assume that improved well-being of all kinds is primarily a function of increased real incomes. Nonetheless, neglecting institutional changes whose role is distinct from the effects of increased incomes is a mistake. The evolution of population health debates in the North makes this clear.

In the North, the McKeown thesis, put forward in a series of pioneering articles and in two very influential books,[3] argued that changes in living standards rather than improvements in health care were responsible for the historical improvement of longevity in Europe (see discussion in Jenson chapter in this volume). According to Colgrove, "sophisticated analyses in the field of historical demography effectively overturned the McKeown thesis in the early 1980s," as new data analysis indicated that McKeown underestimated the importance of public health measures.[4] Yet, McKeown continued to influence policy and, perhaps even more important, continued to influence it in a direction that McKeown may not have intended. Critics like Szreter argue that McKeown's failure to "foreground the importance of politics, ideologies, states, and institutions in producing the kind of societies that distribute their material wealth, food, and living standards in a health-enhancing way for all concerned" is implicated in the "dismantlement" of redistributive public health policies.[5] As Jenson makes clear, the political dynamics are more complicated than McKeown's critics acknowledge.[6] Nonetheless, Szreter's point remains well taken. Income-based models lend themselves to the interpretation that invisible economic forces are responsible for improving welfare rather than health-directed human agency.

The problem is not just the proclivity of policy makers (in both North and South) to conflate an emphasis on income growth with an endorsement of reliance on invisible economic forces. Posing the choice as one of living standards versus health-directed human agency, also leads to conflating human agency

[3] McKeown and Brown (1955); McKeown et al. (1972; 1975), McKeown (1976); McKeown (1988).

[4] Colgrove (2002).

[5] Szreter (2002).

[6] Jensen (Chapter 8, in this volume).

with deliberate modifications of policies, organizations, and resource alloca-
tions directly related to the delivery of health care.[7] Together, these two effects
lead to neglect of precisely the kind of changes that I will argue are central:
changes in institutions, culture, and social relations not normally considered
part of health policy, but likely to have profound long-term effects on population health.

When applied to the Global South, these arguments about the determinants
of population health become arguments about development theory. Over the
latter half of the twentieth century, development theory has been profoundly
transformed. The early statist version of the development project in the immediate post–World War II period floundered in the 1970s and 1980s, at least in
Africa and Latin America.[8] A more strictly market-focused version of development policies gained ascendance in the 1980s and remained dominant
through the end of the century.[9] The new version, known as "the Washington
consensus" or (by its detractors) as "neoliberalism," relied on civil society to
constrain the state politically and "getting prices right" to produce growth
and improve well-being.[10]

Unfortunately, neither the original development project nor its neoliberal
successor managed to combine increased standards of living with increased
inclusion in a way that came close to replicating the experience of the industrialized North during the post–World War II "Golden Age of Capitalism." The
vast majority of the citizens of Africa and Latin America, as well as most Asian
agriculturalists (outside of China), experienced little "catch-up" in the sense
of a diminished gap between their living standards and those of the North.[11]
Consequently, it is not surprising that the vision of increased capital accumulation in the presence of functioning markets as sufficient to deliver well-being
no longer has the political or intellectual charisma that it did fifty years ago.
Antidevelopment has become a powerful position among critical intellectuals
in both North and South. They see the very concept of development as an
example of Foucauldian discursive domination.[12] Antidevelopmentalists like
Gustavo Esteva or Arturo Escobar[13] argue that growth of real incomes only

---

[7] This second conflation is obviously not intended by McKeown critics like Colgrove and
Szreter, who are trying to focus attention on public health in a broad sense rather than health
delivery per se.

[8] Failure should not be overstated. Where the earlier versions of the development project were
successful – most obviously in East Asia, but to a lesser extent in Latin America – they did
indeed raise living standards. See Evans (1992; 1995); Kohli (2004).

[9] McMichael (2005).

[10] See Sewell (Chapter 10, in this volume).

[11] Again, some countries – most notably China and India – have grown impressively during the
period of neoliberalism's global hegemony. Nonetheless, the gap between initial postcolonial
expectations and subsequent lived experience in the Global South is disheartening for the
impoverished majority of the population, even within success stories like India and China.

[12] Ferguson (1994).

[13] Esteva (1992); Escobar (1995).

"expands the reign of scarcity" by inculcating new needs faster than they can be satisfied.[14]

The nostalgic romance of antidevelopment provides no policy strategy. Yet, even though most governments in the Global South (and to some degree multilateral institutions like the World Bank) understand the need for a broader set of policies focused more directly on well-being, they remain mired in the intellectual and organizational legacies of prior paradigms. Disillusionment is easily hijacked by a fundamentalist political agenda, which threatens to fill the vacuum created by contemporary development theory's failing charisma. A growing gamut of movements reject the priority of building a material base for the expansion of human capabilities in favor of a ruthless return to "traditional values" that are presumed to somehow compensate for the absence of a secure and promising material future. Insofar as they focus on destroying existing public institutions to make way for the new order they envision, such movements represent what might be called "the dark side of the Polanyian movement for social protection" – rejections of the social trauma created by the expansion of the self-regulated market turned into a political project of reaction.[15]

Fortunately, promising new perspectives that could serve to revitalize development theory are emerging and provide the basis for more efficacious development policy. On the one hand, even when development is defined in terms of economic growth, it is increasingly conceived of as the product of institutions rather than the accumulation of capital.[16] On the other hand, Amartya Sen's capability approach has provided new analytical foundations for a broad and flexible definition of development in which income growth is only one component. If these two approaches could be integrated, the result could have a significant impact on both policy and theory.

Institutional approaches now dominate the mainstream of development economics.[17] In their contribution to the *Handbook of Economic Growth*, Acemoglu, Johnson, and Robinson argue unambiguously for the thesis that institutions are the "fundamental determinants of long-run growth."[18] Dani Rodrik, in a coauthored paper called "Institutions Rule" is equally straightforward: "the quality of institutions 'trumps' everything else."[19] Easterly and Levine and Bardhan, among many others, offer further support for the primacy of institutions.[20] No one denies the role of traditional determinants of growth, such as investment or technological progress, but institutional

[14] For a very different kind of intellectual disillusionment with development policy see Easterly, which is based on participating for twenty-five years in the formation and evaluation of development policy, especially at the World Bank. Easterly (2001b).

[15] Doran (2002).

[16] It should be noted that the members of the CIAR program on "Institutions, Organizations, and Growth" have played a central role in this transformation of development theory.

[17] Evans (2004; 2005; forthcoming).

[18] Acemoglu et al. (2005).

[19] Rodrik et al. (2004).

[20] Easterly and Levin (2003); Bardhan (2005).

analysis is considered fundamental to understanding the levels and effects of these variables. The extent to which a given level of investment or a particular innovation actually results in a sustained increase in output is viewed as depending on the institutional context.

Institutional approaches are attractive because they allow consideration, in principle, of a wide variety of norms, networks, and organizations.[21] In practice, however, they are likely to follow the "Northian" tradition and focus more narrowly on the set of institutions that define and enforce property rights.[22] Recognizing that markets don't arise automatically, but must be politically, socially, and culturally constructed and sustained is the important advance, but when employed by less sophisticated analysts or policy makers, this version of the institutional turn runs the risk of devolving into a new way of saying that markets plus capital is sufficient for growth.

Currently dominant institutional approaches have also failed to contribute to a reconceptualization of the goals of development that would allow broader concepts of well-being to take a legitimate place alongside income growth. Here, the capability approach offers an ideal complement. The capability approach has three main virtues. First, it is grounded, through Amartya Sen's own work as a theorist of the analytical underpinnings of conventional economics, on a thorough and convincing critique of reductionist definitions of utility as a basis for development goals. Second, its focus on public deliberation as the only analytically defensible way of ordering capabilities provides an analytical foundation for the role of civil society in setting developmental goals. Third, it has a strong foothold in the policy world. Mahbub Ul Haq, along with his collaborators and successors working in the orbit of the United Nations (UN) *Human Development Reports,* have made the capability approach the centerpiece of the UN's intellectual vision of development.

If its potential were fully realized, the capability approach could facilitate the emergence of alternative models of societal success. Its role could even end up analogous to that of classical and neoclassical economic theory in the emergence of conventional models of development from the end of the eighteenth century to the middle of the twentieth. To play this role, however, the capability approach needs to undertake an intellectual project similar to the one in which the proponents of the institutional turn are already engaged, constructing an analytically elaborated vision of the institutional foundations of capability expansion. The gap between Sen's analytical and philosophical formulations and the disembodied statistics of the Human Development Index (HDI)[23] must

---

[21] The definition of institutions offered by Douglass North in his Nobel Prize lecture is a good example of the generality with which they are defined – "the rules of the game: the humanly devised constraints that structure human interaction" (1997 [1993]). For an equally broad variant definition see Chang and Evans (2005).

[22] North (1981; 1990).

[23] See UNDP (United Nations Development Program) (2004). HDR's have included the HDI for fifteen years. By 2004 it was calculated for 177 countries.

be bridged by an analysis of the cultural and institutional foundations of capability expansion.

As a prudent analytical philosopher, Sen has made only the most modest and general set of claims as to how the goal of expanding human capabilities might be reflected in specific organizational structures or policies. Since the potential range of capabilities is almost limitless, development aimed at expanding capabilities could be many different things. Sen allocates the job of constraining the possibilities to informed, democratic, public deliberation, but even on the political side his main contribution is to argue compellingly that such deliberation can, in principle, order collective preferences.[24] As Stewart and Deneulin[25] have pointed out, specification of the appropriate scale and mechanisms for informed, democratic, public deliberation is left for others to figure out.[26]

The apparent lack of dialogue between the capability approach and institutional theories of growth is curious given obvious possibilities for convergence. Growth theorists increasingly emphasize the role of intangible assets (knowledge and ideas of various kinds) and human capital as key inputs to growth, suggesting that capability enhancement is a principal input to growth.[27] At the same time, advocates of the institutional turn are increasingly focused on the causes and consequences of the kind of collective goal-setting that Sen puts at the center of the capability approach. Democracy is seen as a meta-institution, promoting growth while the leaders of the institutional turn advance sophisticated institutional models of the "economic origins of democracy."[28] In short, development theory seems ripe for an institutional theory of development as capability expansion. Such a synthesis has the potential to produce an approach to development theory that is more analytically satisfying and more useful as a basis for formulating policy.

Analyzing the determinants of population health in the Global South focused on cultural and institutional determinants is a way to broach the task of integration. Life expectancy is one of the most generally accepted operationalizations of core capabilities.[29] As the previous discussion of population health debates in the North indicates, it is an outcome for which the potential gains from a more sophisticated institutional approach are obvious.

In the discussion that follows, I will first take a broad statistical look at apparent determinants of general variations in population health, using life expectancy as a proxy. The point of this exercise is to argue that there are

---

[24] Contra Arrow (1963 [1951]).

[25] Stewart and Deneulin (2002).

[26] See also Evans (2002).

[27] Such as Boozer et al. (2003).

[28] Rodrik (1999); Acemoglu and Robinson (2006).

[29] Life expectancy is one of the three components of the HDR's Human Development Index. Nussbaum, who is the most prominent capability theorist besides Sen, puts "being able to live to the end of a human life of normal length: not dying prematurely, or before one's life is so reduced as to be not worth living" first on her list of central human functional capabilities. Nussbaum (2000: 78–80).

good empirical reasons to believe that cultural and institutional factors must be analyzed along with material circumstances to understand these variations. At the same time, I will put forward the idea of societal support, which suggests that improvements in population health are likely to flow from a combination of two things: effective social provision of relevant collective goods (including rules and norms) by public institutions and mobilized engagement on behalf of improved health outcomes on the part of civil society.

These general ideas will be fleshed out through a set of case studies derived from the health and development literature: Sen's classic analysis of the sociopolitical dynamics of famines, the iconic case of social welfare improvements in the Indian state of Kerala, Tendler's analysis of health care delivery in Northeast Brazil, the fight against AIDS in Southern Africa, and O'Rourke's analysis of environmental issues in urban Vietnam. From these specifics I will synthesize a set of propositions as to how the interaction between public institutions and civil society engagement works (or fails to work) to provide improved population health. These propositions will point, in turn, toward possibilities for the fruitful integration of the capability approach and the institutional turn.

RECONCEPTUALIZING POPULATION HEALTH VARIATIONS IN POOR COUNTRIES

"Wealthier is healthier" is an attractive proposition.[30] If income growth fully dominated all other determinants of population health, then discussions of improving health-plus in poor countries could be transformed into discussions of economic growth. The impact of population health analyses on reconstructing the institutional turn would be correspondingly minimal. But, this is not the case.

For better or worse, no one, including Pritchett and Summers who coined the phrase, believes that "wealthier is healthier" offers a sufficient framework. Pritchett and Summers acknowledge at the beginning of their article that "other country characteristics besides income clearly play a large role in determining health."[31] They go on to note the existence of cases in which there are large discrepancies between income rankings and infant mortality rankings, such as Sri Lanka with exceptionally low infant mortality and Gabon, where infant mortality rates are exceptionally high.[32]

Such outliers are a potential source of insights regarding the cultural and institutional factors that modify the effects of income. Even a quick glance at the *Human Development Report* shows a number of positive and negative deviant cases. The countries that still claim to be "socialist" – Cuba and Vietnam – are positive outliers. Early work by Cereseto and Waitzkin suggests that the capitalist/socialist divide once held true more systematically.[33] Lena

[30] Pritchett and Summers (1996).
[31] Ibid: 845.
[32] Ibid: 846.
[33] Cereseto and Waitzkin (1986).

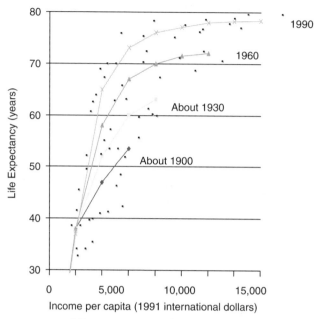

FIGURE 4.1. Life expectancy and income per capita for selected countries and periods. *Source:* World Development Report, 1993.

and London's follow-up suggests that, among poor countries at least, left/right differences among governments had systematic effects on health outcomes.[34] Among negative outliers, countries such as Gabon and Equatorial Guinea, where natural resource endowments inflate income in the absence of governance institutions with the capacity to translate wealth into well-being, are archetypical cases. Gabon has almost triple the purchasing power parity gross domestic product (PPP GDP) per capita of Vietnam, yet Vietnamese citizens have a life expectancy of 69 whereas Gabon's nationals can expect to live less that 57 years.[35]

If we return to focusing on systematic differences rather than outliers, then the well-known family of curves relating the changing relationship between income and life expectancy over time (Figure 4.1) is a useful starting point. Over the course of the twentieth century, the relationship between increased income and increased longevity has disappeared for an increasing number of countries at the top of national income distributions. In other words, the number of countries among which there is no systematic association between income and health has grown steadily over the course of the twentieth century.

[34] Lena and London (1993).
[35] UNDP (2004: Table 1, 139–42).

When we focus instead on life expectancy and income among contemporary poor countries, as in Figure 4.2, there is still a strong relationship. Income explains over a third of the variance. With a handful of exceptions (all of which are in Southern Africa), having more than US$5,000 PPP GDP per capita income guarantees what would have been considered a spectacularly long average life expectancy a century ago – 65 years or more. Yet, when we look at the scattergram, it is clear that there is a great deal going on here besides variation in income. If we look at countries with very low incomes – less than US$3,000 PPP GDP per capita – they cover almost the full range of life expectancy from around 33 in Zambia to 74 for Georgia. If we look at countries in which life spans are relatively long – longer than 65 – they cover almost the full range of incomes from about US$1,000 PPP GDP in Tajikistan to over US$12,000 in Saudi Arabia. In short, even though there is a strong correlation between longevity and GDP per capita, there is also a great deal of variation in longevity that is not explained by differences in national income.

What else besides income might give us leverage on life expectancy? The most obvious possibility is education. Although strongly correlated with income, education can support an independent set of explanatory claims. Conceived as "access to knowledge" (as in the UN's Human Development Index), education is a prime component of any multidimensional, capability-centered vision of well-being. One can think of societies that have high adult literacy and high school enrollment rates as providing a broader range

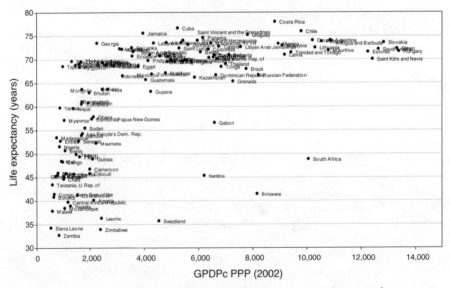

FIGURE 4.2. Pattern of relationship between life expectancy and income for countries with less than $15,000 GDP per capita (PPP).
Data Source: UNDP 2004.

of their citizens with access to knowledge. The spread of education can be taken as a proxy for the general commitment to social provision of capability enhancing resources. Adult literacy and gross school enrollments may be a better measure of widespread public provision than general public expenditure measures, since other social expenditures are often skewed toward providing services for more privileged groups.[36] Insofar as societies are expanding general access to knowledge, it is plausible that they are also more likely to support other forms of capability expansion, even if these other forms of support are not easily captured by available international statistics.

Education can also be interpreted in political terms, in relation to the deliberative goal setting and accountability that are important to both the capability approach and institutional theories of growth. Education should help in enabling citizens to engage in the informed public interchange, which is central to goal setting in the capability approach. It is also likely to facilitate the capacity of civil society to mobilize, making demands on the state and holding public officials accountable. In short, education represents the potential for political empowerment as well as being a proxy for the commitment of public institutions to social provision.

Measures of inequality are the other obvious candidate for a broadly available statistical measure likely to reflect fundamental institutional and cultural characteristic of societies related to health outcomes. Even though the relationship between income inequality and longevity in the developed countries of the North remains controversial and the data from the South are sparse, income inequality conceived of as a proxy for a set of deeply ingrained, inegalitarian, hierarchical institutions and social relations remains a promising candidate for explaining longevity in the South.

In the North, there is continuing controversy over whether income inequality is robustly associated with poorer health outcomes in rich countries. The review of the literature by Wilkinson and Pickett, for example, summarizes results from 155 papers, mainly on the industrial North, and concludes that the overwhelming majority of studies at the national level support an association.[37] Mackenbach concludes to the contrary that "evidence for a correlation between income inequality and the health of the population is slowly dissipating."[38]

This controversy is likely to continue, but Wilkinson and Pickett's basic position that "what matters is the extent of social class differentiation" still makes sense.[39] If higher levels of income inequality are associated with negative effects on health, it is likely to be because they are the most easily measured aspect of a set of historically robust institutions and social relations that disprivilege a large proportion of the citizenry. As Hall and Taylor point out

---

[36] For example, pension plans which only serve the minority regularly employed in the formal sector.
[37] Wilkinson and Pickett (forthcoming).
[38] Mackenbach (2002: 1–2).
[39] Wilkinson and Picket (forthcoming: 11).

in the previous chapter, the pathways connecting these institutions and social relations to negative health outcomes are likely to be multiple; not just material and psychosocial, but also cultural.

Like education levels, inequality levels should be thought of as a summary result that reflects a broad set of social, structural, cultural, and political dynamics. As suggested by Wilkinson, lower Gini indices reflect a larger complex of cultural and institutional structures – those that reduce social hierarchy.[40] The social forces that reduce hierarchy may take many forms, from the policies and institutions that shape the operation of job markets to those that make social boundaries more permeable (as in Lamont's discussion in Chapter 6 in this volume). They may result directly from mobilization by less privileged groups in civil society (most classically the labor movement), or they may result from policies instituted by governments.

What can we say empirically about income inequality and negative health outcomes in poor countries as opposed to rich countries? The data on inequality in poor countries are sparser and less reliable and so there are fewer studies to reference. The greater predictive power of overall income differences among poor countries reduces the incentive to work with inequality data. Even Beckfield, who includes poor countries in his sample and reports separate results for rich countries,[41] does not do a separate analysis for poor countries (probably because of missing data problems).[42] Nonetheless, if one is content with rudimentary analysis, it is possible to look at the relation between inequality and longevity in poor countries as well as the relation between education and longevity in these countries.

The dual possibilities for thinking about the social roots of lower inequality levels mirror those already discussed for education. Just as higher levels of education can be seen either as the consequence of commitment by those who control public institutions to social provision or as a key indicator that the citizenry is able to organize collectively and demand support for capability expansion, so lower rates of inequality can be seen either as a result of the policies and actions of established institutions or as the result of the collective efforts of the citizenry. Putting these two conceptualizations together, we might then consider the combination of education and the Gini coefficient as a proxy for societal support for capability expansion, with the source of the support rooted in public institutions, in civil society, or, more likely, some combination of the two. Finding aggregate statistical effects of societal support will not allow us to distinguish among the various ways in which more education and less inequality might lead to longer lives. Nonetheless, insofar as aggregate analysis reveals robust effects, we should be encouraged to look for case studies that might illuminate how societal support – either via the state or

---

[40] Wilkinson (1996).
[41] Beckfield (2004: 239).
[42] See appendix in Beckfield (2004: 242–4).

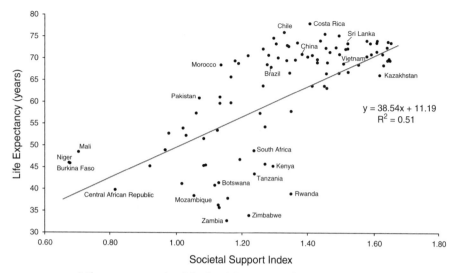

FIGURE 4.3. Life expectancy by "Societal Support Index" in poor countries, 2002. Poor countries are defined as countries with lower than $13,000 GDP per capita (PPP) in 2002. The "Societal Support Index" is the sum of a proxy for social provision of access to knowledge (education index, which ranges from 0 to 1) and a proxy for reductions in social hierarchy (1 – gini index/100, which ranges from 0 to 1). See Appendix A for more detail on these variables.

Data Source: United Nations Development Program (2004) and author's calculations.

via mobilization – might increase life expectancy and, by extension, improve health-plus outcomes more generally. The results that follow here are based on the data provided in the 2004 Human Development Report and are simply cross-sectional.[43]

Before embarking on any interpretation, the first question is whether there is a general statistical relation. Does combining education and inequality produce predictions of longevity in poor countries of a power comparable to those of GDP per capita? Whatever one thinks of the conceptual challenges of interpreting these statistics, the results are interesting. They are presented graphically in Figure 4.3 and in a summary table in Appendix A. Figure 4.3 shows a cross-national relationship among poor countries between the societal support index and our proxy for population health (life expectancy) whose strength is of the same order of magnitude as the relationship between income and life expectancy.[44]

[43] This is in contrast to Beckfield's change-score model in which, "the coefficients reflect the impact of within-country changes in income inequality on within-country changes in population health." Beckfield (2004: 236).

[44] The societal support index is the sum of a proxy for social provision of access to knowledge (education index, which ranges from 0 to 1) and a proxy for reductions in social hierarchy

A quick perusal of the regression results shown in Appendix A confirms the idea that our societal support index is a plausible statistical competitor with income as a way of thinking about the roots of population health. Societal support explains about the same level of variance as income (R^2 = 0.51 for the societal support index versus 0.47 for income). And, when income is included in the regression along with the societal support index, societal support remains as significant as income.

None of this suggests abandoning income as a statistical (or conceptual) predictor of population health, but it does suggest that complementary conceptual frames for thinking about the foundations of population health may be equally plausible, even when the contest is played out on the (far from level) playing field of cross-national regressions. In short, these results encourage us to examine case studies in the hope of further illuminating the ways in which supportive social policy might combine with mobilization to improve health-plus outcomes.

INSTITUTIONS, CULTURE, AND IMPROVED HEALTH OUTCOMES IN POOR COUNTRIES

Having made an excursion into the world of cross-national statistical variation it is time to return to cases. My five cases have already been introduced: (1) the sociopolitical causes of famines as interpreted by Sen, (2) the poor but healthy state of Kerala, (3) health delivery in Ceará, (4) the fight against AIDS in Southern Africa, and (5) the fight against pollution in contemporary, communist-ruled Vietnam. As the cases unfold, so does a complex, but coherent story of how the cultural, institutional, and political character of governance interacts with civil society's evolving capacity for effective collective action to produce (or fail to produce) possibilities for improved population health.

Famines offer a simple, but telling set of initial lessons. Sen (working with Dreze) has summarized them in a succinct and compelling way. My analysis follows his. The context of famines may involve declining or inadequate capacity to produce food, but reductions in productive capacity do not directly cause famines. During what may be the most famous historical case of famine in Europe – the Irish potato famine of the 1840s – Ireland continued to export food to England.[45] The 1974 famine in Bangladesh occurred in the context of peak national availability of food grains.[46] Even in contemporary African famines, starvation in the countryside may be accompanied by normal food prices in provincial capitals.[47]

(1 – Gini index/100, which ranges from 0 to 1). See Appendix A for more detail on these variables.

[45] Mokyr (1983); Ó Gráda (1988).

[46] Sen (1981).

[47] Sen (1999: 167).

The direct cause of famines is the failure of public institutions to respond to traumatic dislocations in the economic ability of the poorest segments of the population in a given area to purchase food. Minimal public capacity – as represented, for example, by the temporary provision of large-scale public works employment – is sufficient to avoid famines.[48] Almost all modern states have the bureaucratic capacity necessary to create temporary public jobs. Most have the capacity to at least temporarily supply food directly to potential victims. This is why famines do not happen in modern democratic societies (rich or poor).

The key missing capacity in famines is more political than administrative. Effective political institutions ensure that public authorities will be aware that traumatic, potentially tragic dislocations of the economic processes that normally allow citizens to obtain food have taken place. Even more important, political institutions motivate authorities to respond. Once the governing apparatus is informed and motivated, the administrative capacity required to ensure the delivery of temporary food supplies is within reach of even the most primitive contemporary government.

In an even modestly effective democratic system, failure to respond to exceptional distress is damning. Consequently, the transition from colonial rule to local rule is perhaps the single most important historical factor leading to the diminished prevalence of famine. Sen[49] makes this point by contrasting the Bengal famine of 1943 when the colonial administration allowed at least two million people to starve to death with postindependence periods of crop failure in which famine was consistently avoided.[50] Of course, independent governments can also lack the political institutions necessary for responsiveness and accountability. The famine in China during 1958–61, as well as contemporary African famines, provides tragic evidence.

Looking at famines provides us then with an institutional formula for the most rudimentary level of support for population health. There are two components: simple administrative capacity and minimally responsive and accountable political mechanisms. Even in the Global South, most states have the necessary administrative capacity. Standard, semicompetitive electoral democracy combined with baseline civil rights (freedom of expression and relatively uncontrolled media) suffice on the political side. There is a positive interaction between the political openness and administrative capacity since gross, unrestrained corruption is likely to be the biggest administrative barrier and democratic accountability is probably the best way to keep corruption from invading short-term humanitarian operations.

---

[48] Sen uses the example of the state of Maharastra in India where the creation of five million temporary public jobs prevented a famine during the severe drought of 1973, which resulted in a 70 percent decline in food production in some areas of the state. Sen (1999: 169–70).

[49] Sen (1999): 180.

[50] For a complementary analysis of the connection between famines and imperial rule, see also Davis (2001).

Moving from averting famines to promoting long-term positive changes in population health raises the bar. Yet, the underlying structural equation may take a similar form. At least this is what is suggested by examining the roots of success of the Indian state of Kerala in raising its population health indicators to levels far greater than those that would be predicted on the basis of its income.

Kerala's health successes are well known.[51] Infant mortality runs less than half the level of Brazil, one-third the levels of the rest of India, and almost at the same level as South Korea. Life expectancy is likewise closer to Korea than Brazil or the rest of India. Birth rates are low; literacy is high, especially among women. In the late 1990s, despite the fact that Kerala's income per capita was still slightly lower than that of India overall, life expectancy in Kerala was nine years longer, a difference in life expectancy almost identical to that which currently separates the United States and Mexico.[52] Likewise, infant mortality in Kerala was one-third of that in Brazil, even though Brazil's income level measured in real GNP was more than ten times that of Kerala. The Kerala model has its detractors,[53] but its population health accomplishments are impressive.

Social mobilization is most commonly identified as the key factor in Kerala's social transformation from a state characterized by some of the most degrading forms of caste stigmatization and one of the most oppressive and inegalitarian systems of agrarian production to one of the most egalitarian states in India and one of the best at delivering services. Throughout the middle third of the twentieth century, Communist Party organizers galvanized landless agricultural workers and tenant farmers to battle against Brahmin landlords in order to redistribute land and reduce rents. These struggles made an indelible mark, not just on the economy, but also on culture and social relations.

Kerala's welfare performance must also be understood in terms of the institutional and administrative infrastructure that underlies it. Lower infant mortality and longer life expectancy depend on high levels of state expenditure on health care, which is in turn reflected in a much more effective network of local health care facilities than most countries in the Global South enjoy. Kerala has more health centers per capita than the rest of India and about eight times the hospital beds per capita in its rural areas.[54]

Kerala's early communist-led regimes made full use of the competence built into the Indian civil service. When they first gained office in Malabar in the early 1950s, they received several distinctions from Nehru for good administration

[51] Among others Franke and Chasin (1989); Heller (1999; 2005).
[52] Heller (1999: 8); UNDP (2004: 168).
[53] Tharmangalam (1998).
[54] Franke and Chasin (1989: 42).

of local government.[55] At the same time, mobilized constituencies, whose relation to the state was institutionalized through the various communist parties (and eventually their competitors on the left and right, who were forced to recognize the advantage of having an organized base), enforced new standards of performance on the state apparatus.

Kerala suggests a virtuous interaction between mobilization and administrative capacity. Those who run Kerala's social services are rapidly made aware when their systems are not delivering. According to one researcher, "[I]f a PHC [Primary Health Centre] was unmanned for a few days, there would be a massive demonstration at the nearest collectorate [regional government office] led by local leftists, who would demand to be given what they knew they were entitled to."[56] Likewise, officials in the agency in charge of dealing with land reform openly affirmed to Herring that "without mass pressure and exposures of fraud and bureaucratic misbehavior, implementation might well have moved in the sluggish and corrupt manner typical of subcontinental [Indian] reforms."[57] Just as a system with clear market signals may be important in allocating resources to produce growth, an effective system of political signals from less privileged constituents is one key to the efficient delivery of health-related services.

Seeing Kerala's population health as arising from a combination of mobilization and the support of a committed and capable state apparatus is now the standard interpretation. In light of the focus on social imaginaries and collective narratives proposed in Chapters 3, 5, 6, and 7 by Hall and Taylor, Swidler, Lamont, and Bouchard, respectively, the Kerala case suggests an additional dimension to the story. Decades of social battles changed people's cultural images of themselves and their society. Humiliated lower-caste peons were given scripts in which they were heroic rather than despised, in which they were supposed to exercise agency rather than hoping for charity, and in which their neighbors were comrades in a collective endeavor rather than competitors for scarce resources. Everything we know about the psychosocial correlates of improved health suggests that this would make a difference.

Finally, another relatively unexplored dimension of the Kerala case is the microcharacter of the state apparatus itself. Most of the incumbents in the Kerala bureaucracy are Indian civil service types indistinguishable from those in other Indian states; however, at least some of them are themselves products of the very process of mobilization and social transformation that they are supporting. Do their own identities and collective narratives make a difference to the interaction of the state and civil society? One suspects that they

[55] Herring (1991: 1–15).
[56] Mencher (1980).
[57] Herring (1991: V–4).

must, and a very disparate case from the other side of the world reinforces this suspicion.

Northeast Brazil is not renowned for its effective public institutions, or its developmental successes. Yet, in the late 1980s, the government of the state of Ceará instituted a public health program (Programa de Agentes de Saúde, PAS) that eventually managed to reach 850,000 families and played a role in tripling the coverage of vaccinations and reducing infant mortality by 36 percent. The program was incredibly cost effective, requiring an investment of only US$2.00 per capita.[58]

The backbone of the program was comprised of roughly 7,000 unskilled health agents who were paid only the minimum wage. A good part of the secret of this program's success lay in its careful attention to the intangible aspects of building an effective public service. Creating esprit de corps and a sense of "calling" among the health agents played a key role in eliciting high levels of performance. They were made to feel that they were valued professionals, whose vital contribution to the welfare of their communities was recognized both by elite officials and the public at large. The state government aggressively disseminated a positive image of the program in the popular media. Selection of the health agents involved trips to small communities and the honor of being selected was insistently stressed. Those chosen responded accordingly. As one health agent put it, "I was ready to look for a job in São Paulo. Now I love my job and I would never leave and abandon my community."[59] Their commitment translated into superior job performance and effective service delivery. Their communities' appreciation of their high level of performance further enhanced their status and increased their intangible compensation.

Ceará's Programa de Agentes de Saúde brings to the fore two important, closely intertwined propositions. First, the changes in social relations that matter are not simply changes within civil society. They are also changes in the concrete social relations that connect civil society to public institutions. Second, social imaginaries and collective narratives are as important to the functioning of public institutions as they are to the transformation of civil society.

If Kerala and Ceará generate insight because they are sites of exceptional success, Southern Africa is a potential source of insight because it is the site of the most dramatic population health failure of the late twentieth century, which threatens to pervade the first half of the twenty-first century as well. Surprisingly, the lessons of failure support some of the same propositions that are generated by the analysis of success. Moving from Ann Swidler's discussion of the failure of Botswana to stem its AIDS epidemic to the effects of

[58] The classic original accounts of this case are Tendler and Freedheim (1994) and Tendler (1997). The version presented here is drawn from the interpretation of those in Evans (1997b; 2003).

[59] Tendler and Freedheim (1994): 1776.

social mobilization on behalf of AIDS victims in South Africa provides an illuminating set of illustrations.

Acknowledging the same public competence that institutional turn analyses of Botswana's economic success emphasize,[60] Swidler (Chapter 5, in this volume) asks why this apparently effective government proved not only no more successful than its neighbors in stemming the tide of AIDS, but was arguably less so. Her answer focuses on informal structures and sociocultural motivations. To cope with this sort of health crisis, successful public institutions must go beyond responsible, judicious performance of official duties. It is the state's mobilizational rather than its regulatory capacity that counts. An effective state must create new definitions of desirable, culturally valued behavior while helping create political and social space in which nongovernmental organizations (NGOs) and community groups can flourish. In short, Swidler postulates a relation between state and civil society similar to the one that produced mobilizational success in Kerala.

Extending examination of the struggle against AIDS from Botswana to South Africa again highlights the interaction of state and civil society but shifts the focus to civil society. The postapartheid African National Congress (ANC) regime in South Africa, despite its mobilizational origins, resisted responding to the AIDS crisis by trying to change values, behavior, or social relations. It even went so far as to deny the relevance of antiretroviral (ARV) drugs. If it had not been for a strong countermovement emerging out of civil society (building in part on organizational experience and social imaginaries produced by the same history of mobilization that produced the ANC), there might have been no movement in the direction of a more effective response.

The now-famous Treatment Action Campaign (TAC) represented not just the mobilization of urban youth against government denials and neglect, but also the construction of new self-identities and social connections for AIDS victims.[61] Spurred on by a victory in the courts, TAC was also instrumental in motivating the government to fight pharmaceutical companies for reduced ARV drug prices and is now taking its fight to local authorities who currently lack the capacity to effectively deliver the drugs.[62]

In their analysis of this case, Baccaro and Papadakis sharpen the emphasis on the mobilization of civil society by contrasting TAC to the National Association of People Living with AIDS (NAPWA), which is in turn part of the official South African National AIDS Council (SANAC).[63] While TAC was aggressively combining mobilization in the streets with litigation in the courts and forcing the government to move forward in the provision of ARV treatment, SANAC and NAPWA, despite their ostensible role of representing civil society, continued to passively legitimate the government's recalcitrance.

[60] Such as Acemoglu, Johnson, and Robinson (2001).
[61] This discussion of TAC is drawn from Jones (2005).
[62] See Klug (2002).
[63] Baccaro and Papadakis (2005: 36–45).

Baccaro and Papadakis conclude that the effectiveness of civil society in this case depends on adopting a communicative strategy that builds pressure on the state by accumulating power in the informal public sphere rather than simply engaging in deliberation with state officials.[64] Communicative strategies depend on "persuading as many citizens as possible of the moral appropriateness" of policies, not only through rational argument but also through "dramatic forms of social action ... from marching to engaging in hunger strikes and civil disobedience." Communicative actions sounds like what Swidler is advocating, except that Baccaro and Papadakis assume a refractory state that must be moved in a direction it does not want to go, rather than a well-intentioned state that simply does not understand the cultural and mobilizational requirements of the task at hand.

In the TAC case, mobilization against the state is the sine qua non of success, but the intransigence of the South African state should not obscure the fact that the capacity of public institutions remains key to success. Without a competent judiciary capable of standing up against other parts of the state apparatus, TAC would have been stymied. Nor could TAC have bargained directly with international drug companies itself; it needed the state. To build on its victories, TAC now needs increased capacity on the part of local public authorities to transform its campaign into widespread, tangible public health effects.

The TAC case shows how a *virtuous circle* interaction between the capacity of public institutions and civil society mobilization in pursuit of improved health outcomes must sometimes start with oppositional conflict rather than synergy. The story is particularly interesting because it parallels the dynamics of pursuit of a different set of improved health outcomes – the control of environmental pollution.

Trying to understand the possibilities for controlling the proliferation of environmentally dangerous toxic wastes in communist Vietnam during the transition to a market economy, Dara O'Rourke came up with the idea of community-driven regulation (CDR).[65] The CDR model has the same basic structure that has emerged in the previous cases. O'Rourke starts with the eminently reasonable assumption that command and control models of pollution control in which state agencies enforce legal regulations is unlikely to be sufficient to ensure citizens protection against exposure to toxic wastes, especially in a poor country where democratic rights are limited. Most ambitiously, he proposes that even in this inauspicious context, the interaction of a mobilized citizenry with state agencies can produce positive results, as least some of the time.

O'Rourke's analysis of one of the communities in which CDR worked in Vietnam will serve as a good concrete illustration. The village of Dona

---

[64] Baccaro and Papadakis (2005: 50–1).
[65] O'Rourke (2002; 2004).

Bochang was plagued by pollution from a nearby, Taiwanese-owned textile factory. Unlike some other communities O'Rourke studied, Dona Bochang enjoyed an extremely cohesive informal structure, built around the Catholic Church, and also maintained (somewhat paradoxically) good relations with the People's Committee of the local Communist Party. Nonetheless, all of the community's direct contacts with the factory, including village youth storming the factory gates, were ineffectual and the local environmental protection agency proved toothless. Only after mobilizing a combination of media exposure, informal pressure through the party, and continued pressure on the factory was the community able, with the help of the state agency, to get simple pollution emission improvements. At the same time, this process was important in strengthening the position of the environmental agency vis-à-vis other less sympathetic state agencies. In short, it took the interaction of variegated civil society mobilization and a variety of public institutions to produce positive change.

The commonalities and complementarities that range across this disparate set of cases are impressive. A priori, common threads running from nineteenth-century Irish famines through redistributive struggles on the Malabar coast of India to fighting against the ravages AIDS in Southern Africa and pollution in postsocialist Vietnam would seem unlikely. Yet, common analytical motifs have indeed emerged. Even more important, they are motifs with heuristically fruitful implications both for understanding the social roots of health-plus outcomes as well as for thinking about how to better integrate the institutional turn and the capability approach.

LESSONS FOR POPULATION HEALTH AND DEVELOPMENT THEORY

In the initial discussion of the societal support index, two sorts of interpretations were invoked as possibilities. In the first, societal support took the form of established social institutions providing support that expanded the capabilities of the citizenry. In the second, the ability of civil society to mobilize collectively propelled institutional and cultural changes that in turn fostered capability expansion. The case studies put the integration of these two processes at the center of the dynamics of societal success and failure.

Kerala, the TAC, and, in a more primitive way, famines, all make it clear that the role of civil society in transforming the behavior and even the structure of public institutions is as important in the long-run as the influences that flow in the opposite direction. Perhaps the single most important determinant of successful famine prevention is the ability of society, especially its less privileged members, to make the state respond. In Kerala, not just service delivery, but the character of the state itself is the product of the political mobilization of civil society, again particularly the less privileged. In South Africa, the TAC seems to have begun doing what the efficient state could not do in Botswana. Equally important, it has also begun to change the way in which the state relates to AIDS and AIDS victims. In short, the virtuous (or vicious) circles that connect public institutions and civil society appear particularly crucial to population health outcomes, and, by extension, perhaps to the process of development itself.

The cases also make the additional point that social relations and culture do not stop at the boundaries of the state. Both Kerala and Ceará suggest that the relevant transformation of social relations takes place within public institutions, changing the way that actors within those institutions see themselves and their relations to each other. Likewise, the character of the social ties and identifications that cross the boundaries between state and society play a key role in these cases. Swidler's analysis of Botswana makes these same points in a different way. When those within the state are seen, and see themselves, only as efficient regulators and service providers, they lack the ability to transform definitions of valued behavior.

If looking at the dynamics of health outcomes forces a less flatfooted way of thinking about policy makers, civic servants, and the organizations that they run, it also validates perspective on civil society that spotlights the role of culture. The rational transcendence of collective action problems may be part of what is going on in these cases, but the construction of affect-laden cultural ties built around social imaginaries and collective narratives is at least as central.

All of these dynamics are consistent with the basic assumptions of Sen's capability approach, but, except for the case of famines, they are left unexplored by the capability theorists themselves. Beyond stipulating the centrality of informed public deliberation, the capability approach leaves the role of collective action in generating capability expansion, especially collective action that requires oppositional mobilization, unexplored. Beyond acknowledging the necessity of public provision of infrastructure and collective goods, the task of figuring out what separates effective state apparatuses from ineffectual ones is also left for others to decipher.

The institutional and cultural analysis proposed here offers only a rudimentary beginning to building an understanding of the social roots of capability expansion, but something of this sort is absolutely necessary if the capability approach is to move from being a compelling statement of developmental aspirations to being a theory of the processes involved in achieving broad-based expansion of capabilities.

If a cultural/institutional approach to population health poses a challenge to proponents of the capability approach, its challenge to growth theorists who have taken the institutional turn is no less serious. One facet of the challenge is obvious. Currently, institutional analyses of growth have avoided engaging issues of social imaginaries, collective narratives, and most other cultural determinants of collective action.[66]

---

[66] There are exceptions, such as the use of ethnic fractionalization, but the theoretical frame in which these are introduced assumes that noneconomic identities are divisive and lead to irrational conflictive behavior. See Easterly and Levine (1997).

Proponents of the institutional turn may argue that as long as increased incomes are defined as the preeminent outcome in question, then firm protection of the fruits of individual effort combined with predictable public provision of rules and material infrastructure remain a parsimonious description of the institutional requirements of development. But the institutional turn has already outgrown this gambit. First, this minimalist version of the institutional turn leaves unexplained the origins of the institutions capable of predictably providing rules and infrastructure, a problem that has become central to the institutional turn. Beyond that, having accepted the idea that human development is cause as well as consequence of income growth,[67] growth theorists must face the necessity of providing institutional explanations for a range of outcomes that begins to rival the range considered by the capability approach.

There is, however, another, more specific, challenge posed to adherents to the institutional turn by the analyses offered here. It was pointed out earlier that a narrow institutional focus on property rights and other institutions closely tied to economic incentives is susceptible to slipping back into the simpler assumption that markets plus capital are sufficient for growth. Looking at the illustrative cases that have been considered here suggests that this devolution is not just a theoretical retreat, but unsustainable, even if development goals could be restricted to increased income.

Simple models of making markets work often involve trying to depoliticize allocational decisions. Yet, in the cases we have looked at here, depoliticizing may precisely undercut the very social mechanisms that are necessary, not only to achieve broader development goals and provide support in the event of unavoidable market failures but even to generate the kind of social change necessary to make markets work. Two examples should suffice to make the point.

O'Rourke's Dona Bochang case is one. A narrow version of the institutional turn approach to development in Vietnam would emphasize making the property rights of the Taiwanese textile owners more secure, especially vis-à-vis the Vietnamese state. In doing so it would, in all likelihood, inadvertently weaken the more diffuse property rights of the next door villagers, reduce the bargaining power of the environmental protection agency, and reduce the chances of controlling emissions. In a country where the World Bank predicted in 1997 that, barring better control of industrial pollution, toxic intensity would increase fourfold by 2010 leading to hundreds of millions of dollars of increased health care costs and correspondingly diminished human capabilities, this would be a serious weakness.[68]

Kerala illustrates the more complicated version of the argument. Prior to communist-led mobilization, the monopolization of property rights to land

---

[67] As in Boozer et al. (2003) or Helpman (2004).
[68] World Bank (1997); compare O'Rourke (2004: 42).

by a small group of unentrepreneurial Brahmin landlords prevented the operation of real markets for either land or labor. Agriculture in contemporary Kerala now comes closer to having the properties of a modern market system, despite continued aspirations for instituting a socialist model of development. Ironically, the political mechanisms necessary to transform the system into one in which property rights were more consistent with growth were generated by ideas, processes, and social imaginaries of a sort that would have been summarily excluded by a narrow policy focus on protecting property rights.

In short, the attainment of economic ends conventionally defined as apolitical may require the emergence of political institutions radically different from those customarily associated with the protection of property rights. Admitting such institutions into the potential mix of institutional theories of development, opens in turn the Pandora's box of social imaginaries, collective narratives, and other cultural forms inescapably implicated in collective action.

If the version of a cultural/institutional approach proposed here, which might be called successful societies institutionalism, throws up irritating challenges to both the capabilities approach and the institutional turn, it also offers an intriguing promise for heuristically productive synthesis. The preliminary forays offered here make clear the potential for building more satisfying cultural and institutional explanations of developmental outcomes that are central to capability expansion and also critical to economic growth. They support the idea that the full extension of the institutional turn in growth theory would also end up being an institutional-cultural theory of capability expansion. In an era when development theory is often condemned as being incapable of contributing to the well-being of ordinary citizens in the Global South, the possibility of such an integrated approach is an exciting prospect.

APPENDIX A. *Regressions on Life Expectancy at Birth – Poor Countries*

	(1) Income Only	(2) Education and Gini Indices Only	(3) Income, Education Index, and Gini Index	(4) Societal Support Index Only	(5) Income and Societal Support
Income[a]	10.13		7.10		5.89
	(9.29)**		(5.38)**		(4.95)**
Education index[b]		39.74	17.64		
		(8.59)**	(3.05)**		
Gini index[c]		−0.35	−0.39		
		(3.90)**	(4.89)**		

	(1) Income Only	(2) Education and Gini Indices Only	(3) Income, Education Index, and Gini Index	(4) Societal Support Index Only	(5) Income and Societal Support
Societal support index[d]				38.54 (10.02)**	25.36 (5.82)**
Constant	−19.88 (2.25)*	47.25 (8.60)**	7.88 (−0.90)	11.19 (2.18)*	−19.03 (−2.49)*
Observations	99	99	99	99	99
R-squared	0.47	0.51	0.62	0.51	0.61

Absolute value of t-statistics in parentheses.

* significant at 5 percent; ** significant at 1 percent

[a] Income is defined as the log of GDP per capita (PPP US$), 2002.

[b] The Education index (2002) is comprised of an adult literacy index (two-thirds weight) and a combined primary, secondary, and tertiary gross enrollment ratio (one-third weight). Its final value ranges from 0 to 1.

[c] The Gini index (2002) measures the extent to which the distribution of income (or consumption) among individuals or households within a country deviates from a perfectly equal distribution. A value of 0 represents perfect equality and 100 represents perfect inequality.

[d] The societal support index is the sum of a proxy for social provision of access to knowledge (the education index) and a proxy for reductions in social hierarchy (1 − Gini index/100). Its final value can range from 0 to 2.

Data Source: United Nations Development Program (2004) and author's calculations.

5

Responding to AIDS in Sub-Saharan Africa

Culture, Institutions, and Health

Ann Swidler

Peter Hall and Rosemary Taylor (Chapter 3, in this volume) suggest that we think of the health and happiness of individuals as depending on the resources they can mobilize to confront the challenges that face them. An analogous argument might apply to collectivities, from families and communities to national states. Examining the massive threats to human health created by the AIDS epidemic in sub-Saharan Africa, I ask what shapes the resources collectivities can bring to bear to meet the challenges of AIDS.

This chapter lays out broad questions about the role of institutions and culture in responding to AIDS. It draws on research during three visits to sub-Saharan Africa (Botswana in July 2003 and June 2006 and Malawi in June and July of 2004 and 2006), about seventy interviews with staff from nongovernmental organizations (NGOs) working on the ground on AIDS projects across sub-Saharan Africa, and an initial effort at mapping the universe of organizations responding to Africa's AIDS pandemic.

OUTLINING THE ISSUES

No one questions the enormity of the AIDS crisis on the African continent. The epidemiological models are inexact, but the best estimates are that of the approximately 33 million people currently infected with HIV, more than 22 million are in sub-Saharan Africa, with an estimated 1.7 million Africans newly infected in

This chapter draws on "The Politics of AIDS in Sub-Saharan Africa," presented at the Annual Meetings of the American Sociological Association, Atlanta, August 16–20, 2003. I am grateful for support from the Canadian Institute for Advanced Research (CIFAR) and from the Center for Health Policy, the Center for African Studies, and the Committee on Research of the University of California, Berkeley. Arlie Hochschild, Adam Hochschild, Ron Jepperson, Clark Leith, Ted Miguel, Kristin Mann, Susan Watkins, and the CIFAR Successful Societies Program members and Advisory Board offered valuable feedback on earlier drafts. Joanna Weinberg gave crucial advice on framing this chapter. Sarah Gilman, Kate Krontiris, Keyvan Kashkooli, Rachel Sullivan, and Perrin Elkind provided able research assistance.

2007.[1] Perhaps 17 million Africans have already died of AIDS, and in some places deaths among groups such as teachers, nurses, and soldiers threaten the collapse of entire institutional spheres.[2] Households and communities are exhausted by care for the dying, children are orphaned, and whole communities are devastated by the loss of those whose labor would have supported the old and the young.

The AIDS epidemic dramatizes the ways the vitality of social institutions can matter for health. AIDS is both similar to and very different from other health challenges nations face. On the one hand, capacities to confront the epidemic depend in part on the same resources – health infrastructure, national wealth, administrative competence, and political will – required to meet other public health challenges. On the other hand, in Africa HIV is transmitted primarily through sexual contact, so dealing with HIV/AIDS has not been purely, or even primarily a medical matter.[3] The well-worn techniques of international public health–vaccinations, clinics, visiting nurses, even sanitation and such amenities as wells, latrines, and nutrition – are largely irrelevant. Since AIDS prevention cannot be administered by a determined government or international public health authorities, limiting the spread of HIV has depended on deeper, more complex, and less well-understood social capacities than has the response to many other health crises.[4]

---

[1] The figures here come from UNAIDS (2007).

[2] UNAIDS estimated 13 million cumulative AIDS deaths in Africa as of the end of 2003 (UNAIDS 2005: 28), an additional 2.3 million in 2004 (p. 3), 2.4 million in 2005 (p. 17), 2.1 million in 2006 (UNAIDS 2006: 2), and 1.6 million in 2007 (UNAIDS 2007). UNAIDS (2007) now acknowledges, however, that earlier methods of serosurveillance based on data from antenatal clinics overestimated HIV prevalence, so the earlier numbers should be adjusted downward. See Barnett and Whiteside (2002); de Waal (2003); Lewis (2003); Poku, Whiteside, and Sandkjaer (2007) on the devastating consequences of the epidemic.

[3] An article in *The New York Times Magazine* (July 6, 2006) by Tina Rosenberg makes this point repeatedly. She quotes Peter Piot, director of UNAIDS, as saying, "The technology is doing O.K., it's moving. But we have grossly, grossly neglected the social, cultural and personal stuff that makes it work." Rosenberg concludes: "Without attention to the social, psychological and cultural factors surrounding the disease, we are throwing away money and lives. This is the new frontier. Twenty-five years into the epidemic, we now know how to keep people from dying of AIDS. The challenge for the future is to keep them from dying of stigma, denial and silence."

[4] The development of efficient disease-prevention technologies does not guarantee that political and cultural barriers to their use will be overcome: Cases of polio erupted following suspicions in Northern Nigeria's Islamic provinces that the vaccine could cause sterility; a modest whooping-cough epidemic has emerged in the U.S. because some parents remain unconvinced of the vaccine's safety; and governments from the U.S. to China have resisted giving addicts clean needles because they do not wish to acknowledge or legitimate illegal drug use. Like family planning but more-so (Cleland and Watkins 2006), AIDS prevention seems to require changes in some of the deepest, most intimate, and least understood aspects of human behavior. Individuals and communities in Africa and elsewhere have found it enormously difficult to change embedded social and sexual practices (see, for example, Caldwell, Caldwell, and Quiggin 1989; Caldwell 1999; Hunter 2002; Campbell 2003; Kaler 2003; Watkins 2004; Chimbiri 2007; Swidler and Watkins 2007; Tavory and Swidler 2009).

The challenge of AIDS in Africa also raises wider questions about the way states and cultural communities operate in a contemporary globalizing world. African states are notoriously permeable to outside influences.[5] Even though they differ greatly in their administrative capacities, political stability, and transparency, they are also almost universally poor, so that their health spending relies heavily on outside donors who provide not only funds but also administrative support, monitoring, and often the basic direction of policy. Thus the AIDS crisis in Africa is not just a local crisis, but a focus of intense transnational energy and effort.

Hall and Taylor suggest that health and well-being depend on the relationship between the nature of the challenges individuals face and two factors: the individual and collective resources they draw upon to meet those challenges and their inner resources or "psychic resilience." In a similar way, we may think of collectivities as varying in their resources – most obviously in the economic resources they can use to promote the health and welfare of their populations, but also, very importantly, the capabilities they can draw on to address problems.[6] Here the crucial skills might be those required for effective governance, from the technical skills required for administration (in the AIDS arena, collecting and analyzing basic data about the epidemic; developing and managing budgets, and the bureaucratic skills required to make administrative systems function) to the political skills required to focus attention on a problem or to coordinate action among competing agencies and multiple jurisdictions.[7]

AIDS is worthy of special attention in part because it appeared during an era in which an emergent "transnational citizenship" has made the welfare of all people everywhere seem to demand global care and concern. Although it lies outside the scope of this chapter, we should note that just as citizenship constituted individuals as entitled to benefits from the states of which they are members, the emerging rules of the global order – from international tribunals to transnational political campaigns – have increasingly created a global cultural understanding in which all individuals have human rights that transcend their nation-bound citizenship rights and every collectivity has claims on the world's conscience.[8]

---

[5] Chabal and Daloz (1999); Callaghy et al. (2001).

[6] Peter Baldwin (2005) has shown that the industrialized democracies have also differed sharply in the conceptual, legal, and institutional resources they have drawn upon in the AIDS fight.

[7] As Hurricane Katrina illustrated, complex bureaucratic and administrative skills can be in short supply in the wealthy, industrialized nations of the Global North, with potentially catastrophic results. Similar gaps in administrative competence, but also in public attention, planning, and political coordination have led to dramatic variations in deaths during heat waves, from many thousands of elderly French men and women who died in the summer of 2004 to the hundreds of deaths in Chicago in the summer of 1999, whose political and social causes are analyzed in Klinenberg (2002).

[8] Jane Jenson (this volume) describes the history of changing citizenship regimes as they affect health policy. Amartya Sen (1999) has been the most influential proponent of a new, transnational regime in which all people have fundamental claims to capacities that produce freedom,

Indeed, AIDS has in some ways been the poster child for a global commitment to health.[9]

Finally, more than many other health challenges, responses to AIDS have depended on the collective equivalent of individual psychological resilience. The ability of institutions to mobilize and motivate their populations has been vital in effective responses to the epidemic.[10] Much less is understood, however, about the capabilities of collectivities to mobilize their energies than about the psychological resilience of individuals. Focusing on responses to the AIDS epidemic, this chapter argues that collective capacities shape health at two levels: on the one hand, responses to the epidemic depend on such political goods as leadership, organizational capacity, and collective commitment. Without these, no solutions to health challenges can be defined or implemented. But AIDS also reveals a deeper connection between collective mobilization and individual health. The persistent failure of even the best-designed public health campaigns directed at individuals to change AIDS-relevant behaviors – and the striking success of the few programs that have mobilized political and moral energies to fight the epidemic – suggest that health depends on collectively-valued identities and moral meanings as much as on individual prudential calculations.

while John Meyer and his collaborators have noted that promoting individual well-being is increasingly assumed to be the purpose of global and national political institutions (see, for example, Frank and Meyer 2002). Michel Foucault (1988: 152) notes the same collective attention to individual health and well-being, but reverses the relationship, emphasizing that the well-being of individuals matters insofar as it affects the "strength of the state." Examples of the burgeoning literature on transnational political campaigns include Keck and Sikkink (1998); Khagram, Riker, and Sikkink (2002); Tarrow (2005). On emerging understandings of individual rights that transcend nations, see Soysal (1994); Meyer (1999); Hagan and Levi (2004).

[9] AIDS was already a high-profile disease with a voluble and politically effective constituency in the United States, Brazil, Australia, and elsewhere when, after the mid 1980s, the enormity of the global pandemic produced a torrent of organizational activity and an ever-widening flow of resources, much of it channeled through (or originating in) the NGO sector. On the history of responses to the AIDS epidemic, see Altman (1994); S. Epstein (1996) on the United States; Berkman et al. (2005) on Brazil; Dowsett (1999) on Australia; and H. Epstein (2007) on the global response as well as Lancaster (2008) on AIDS and U.S. foreign aid. There is a large literature on the ambiguity of the NGO concept and the conflicting evaluations of the role and effectiveness of NGOs. For examples, see Fisher (1997); Keck and Sikkink (1998); Callaghy, Kassimir and Latham (2001); Khagram, Riker, and Sikkink (2002); Ferguson and Gupta (2002); and Sharma (2006). See the work of John Meyer and his collaborators (Boli and Thomas 1997; Meyer et al. 1997; Boli and Thomas 1999) for the argument that NGOs have been primary creators and promoters of the emerging world culture. According to the Resource Flows Project (2004), which tracks funding for population activities, from 1995 to 2002 AIDS funding increased from 9 percent to 43 percent of population funding with more than 400 percent increases in resources for sub-Saharan Africa, and with an estimated 57 percent of population assistance flowing through NGOs. Thus, by analogy to individuals who vary in their access to networks of social support, nations differ in their capacity both to attract and to work effectively with the innumerable organizations, individuals, and agencies that might provide help in combating the AIDS epidemic.

[10] Altman (1994).

The argument of this chapter is multilayered, so it is best to outline it briefly here. I analyze the contrast between Botswana – wealthy and well governed – where AIDS-prevention efforts have largely failed and treatment with antiretroviral drugs was slow to get off the ground, and Uganda – much poorer and less well administered – yet one of the rare cases of success in both prevention and treatment. The argument begins with two ways in which Botswana and Uganda are similar: both have political leadership committed to fighting the epidemic, and both have governments that, in quite different respects, fit their local political cultures, creating what, following Steven Cornell and Joseph Kalt, I call "cultural match."[11] Nonetheless, Uganda's AIDS efforts differed in a critical respect from those of Botswana because Uganda proceeded by mobilizing its population at the grass roots, through local communities and organizations, while Botswana pursued AIDS prevention through a top-down program of information and education. The specific information and even the programs were similar, but the ways in which they activated (or failed to activate) local communities were very different.

The third step in the argument probes why such grass-roots mobilization has been so important for AIDS prevention, and how the lessons learned might apply to health more generally. Community mobilization may be necessary to create the "normative ferment" that can lead to change in socially significant behaviors. Communities also provide one source of solidarity that can reduce the shame and helplessness that often accompany illness, affecting people's motivation to protect their health. Finally, the AIDS struggle raises wider questions about human motives: while rational, prudential interests may motivate some health behaviors, a great deal of evidence suggests that the sense of moral identity, shared fate, and commitment to others may be more important.

VARIATIONS IN POLITICAL RESPONSE: PROBLEMS AND PARADOXES

When it comes to HIV and AIDS, epidemiological and political questions cannot be separated. From the role of sexual coercion and rape in the spread of HIV to U.S. support for an international property-rights regime that limits poor countries' access to inexpensive generic antiretroviral drugs, politics shapes the AIDS pandemic.[12] In theory, the response to AIDS should be greater where prevalence is higher; however, variations in political response often seem independent of epidemiological urgency. Thus Senegal, where infection rates are low (about 1 percent of adults) and where the dominant strain of HIV (HIV-2) is less infectious than HIV-1, has mobilized one of the most effective prevention programs in Africa.

---

[11] Cornell and Kalt (2000).
[12] On sexual violence see Epstein (2001); World Bank (2002). On AIDS and international intellectual property-rights regimes see Kapp (2002); Loff (2002); Love (2002; 2006); Klug (2005).

One of the many ironies of the African situation is that infection rates are highest in the continent's more developed southern region (South Africa, Namibia, Botswana, Swaziland, and Zimbabwe, along with the much poorer Lesotho, Mozambique, Zambia, and Malawi) and among the wealthier and better-educated.[13] Furthermore, while collapsed or failed states certainly create barriers to dealing with the epidemic, state competence is no guarantee of effective action, as the South African case suggests.[14] Thus searching for the sources of variation in effective response to the epidemic is both an intellectual puzzle and a gripping practical challenge.

A Political Paradox: Botswana versus Uganda

One of the most fascinating puzzles of African AIDS is the contrast between Botswana's response to the pandemic and that of Uganda and, more recently, Kenya. Ugandans mobilized early to counter HIV/AIDS, lowering HIV prevalence from 29.1 percent of ante-natal clinic attendees in 1992 to 11.2 percent in 2001, with an estimated 7.1 percent of the adult population infected in 2005.[15] The government instigated a broad social mobilization that linked the campaign against AIDS to a nation-building rhetoric and a sense of collective empowerment that galvanized political party officials, churches, international NGOs, and community-based organizations in what was seen as a struggle for collective survival.[16] Botswana meanwhile saw HIV prevalence rise from 18.1 percent of ante-natal clinic attendees in 1992 to 36.3 percent in 2001 and 37.4 percent in 2003. Newer methods of estimating HIV prevalence from population surveys give lower figures than ante-natal clinic data, but the latest UNAIDS estimates still find Botswana's HIV prevalence among adults 15 to 49 years of age unchanged at 24 percent in 2003 and 2004.[17]

---

[13] The income inequality associated with greater wealth might account for the dramatically higher HIV prevalence in Southern Africa, if men with money can afford multiple partners and poor women and girls seek additional income through transactional sex. Recent evidence of the strong positive relationship between wealth and HIV prevalence within countries suggests that greater wealth may increase rates of HIV infection by allowing both women and men to have multiple partners (see Shelton et al. 2006; Mishra et al. 2007).

[14] On variations in political response to the epidemic, see Boone and Batsell (2001), Buvé, Bishikwabo-Nsarhazab, and Mutangadurac (2002), and UNAIDS (2005). Lieberman (2007) argues persuasively that ethnic fragmentation reduces the intensity of nations' responses to the epidemic. Zartman (1995), Herbst (2000), and Bates (2008), among others, attempt to explain state weakness or failure in Africa, but state strength and competence do not appear to explain success in actually reducing HIV prevalence.

[15] UNAIDS/WHO (2002; 2005); UNAIDS (2007): 11.

[16] Synergy Project (2002a); Green (2003); H. Epstein (2007: 158–67).

[17] The "2006 Global AIDS Report" (UNAIDS 2006: Chapter 2, pp. 9–11) and UNAIDS (2007) explain that newer data from population surveys (Botswana's most recent survey was in 2004) give lower estimates of HIV prevalence than the earlier reliance on ante-natal clinic data from pregnant women: because women have higher infection rates than men, because ante-natal clinics typically over represent urban and peri-urban areas, and because pregnant women represent only those women having unprotected sex.

Botswana is in many other respects a public health success. The WHO estimates that skilled health personnel attend 98.5 percent of births in Botswana, while in Uganda the comparable figure is 38.3 percent.[18] The most successful democracy in Africa, Botswana was aware of the epidemic early on and mounted a substantial public health response. Yet throughout the 1990s and up to at least 2003, despite the intervention of a variety of international organizations and foundations (most notably the Merck and Gates Foundations, Bristol Meyers Squibb, and the Harvard School of Public Health), Botswana's HIV prevalence continued to climb, vying with Swaziland's for the highest in the world.

Botswana's success in combining political stability with economic discipline to raise its standard of living some tenfold in the last twenty years suggests that the problem is not lack of governance capacity.[19] And the serious public health campaigns Botswana has mounted suggest that the problem is not lack of public health effort – or even of information. As we shall see later, the difference rests ultimately on the success of Uganda in mobilizing collective solidarities in the cause of AIDS prevention, while Botswana's failure says a great deal about the limitations of a model of health behaviors as arising from individual concerns about personal well-being. The contrast between Botswana and Uganda thus provides an excellent focus for examining critically the standard explanations for more and less effective efforts to combat HIV/AIDS.

Leadership

The leadership of Yoweri Museveni, Uganda's President, is universally credited with initiating Uganda's all-out battle against AIDS. Despite Museveni's growing reputation for corruption and repression,[20] the first ten years of his

---

[18] UNAIDS/WHO (2002); UNAIDS (2002).

[19] On Botswana's economic and political success, see Acemoglu, Johnson, and Robinson (2003); Leith (2005). The discovery of diamonds shortly after Botswana's independence in 1966 provided the resources to finance public health, education, and infrastructure improvements. Elsewhere, however, natural resources such as oil or mineral wealth have been a "resource curse" (see, for example, Sachs and Warner 2001), triggering political instability and civil war. Botswana's political institutions are credited with making its resources contribute to development.

[20] Museveni's decision in late 2005 – against the advice of President Bush, among others – to run for another five-year term and, in early 2006, Uganda's first multiparty elections, held with the head of the major opposition party under indictment on what seem to be politically motivated charges, have badly tarnished Museveni's reputation. Here is one of the harsher indictments: "He has attacked and looted Congo; he has allowed fantastic corruption within his inner circle; he has harassed journalists and cracked down on political dissent; he has amended Uganda's constitution to allow himself to serve indefinitely. In November [2005], he jailed his strongest opponent in this month's presidential election, charging him with rape and treason. Once touted as one of the 'new leaders of Africa,' an American political analyst wrote recently in a damning confidential report to the World Bank, '[Museveni] over the last eight years, has increasingly resembled the old.'" (Rice 2006: 12).

leadership – from 1986 to the mid 1990s – saw dramatic reductions in HIV prevalence due to a massive social mobilization against AIDS. Museveni recognized early in his presidency that AIDS was a fundamental threat to his society. The (perhaps apocryphal) story is that when Museveni's guerrilla movement came to power in 1986, after the savage dictatorships of Idi Amin and Milton Obote, Museveni sent his top military men to Cuba for training. The Cubans, who have practiced draconian AIDS-control policies, immediately tested the Ugandans for HIV; Castro then drew Museveni aside to tell him that he was facing a looming disaster.[21] Museveni used his very effective political party, the National Resistance Movement (NRM) as a vehicle for spreading AIDS awareness. (Here we might note that political parties that emerge from peasant-based guerrilla campaigns develop special political capacities – witness the Vietnamese, the Cubans, and the Chinese communists). Museveni committed himself to address the issue of AIDS in every speech he gave, and he decreed that every party official, all the way down the five-level party hierarchy, should do the same.[22]

When it comes to leadership, however, Botswana is also far ahead of most other African countries in the openness and commitment of its leaders on the AIDS issue. Even though Ketumile Masire, Botswana's president until 1998, was reputed to be somewhat more conservative or traditional culturally and thus more reluctant to speak publicly about AIDS, he did so, and Botswana had a vigorous condom promotion program as well as an "ABC" (Abstain; Be Faithful; or use a Condom) campaign modeled on that in Uganda. Festus Mogae, president from 1998 to 2008, has been outspoken on the issue, commanding national and international attention for his commitment to the fight against AIDS. A 2002 study of the seven hardest-hit southern African countries notes that "Though Botswana's HIV/AIDS epidemic is relatively young, the government has been open about the epidemic and has in some sense 'claimed' it as an appropriate issue for government intervention."[23]

But even this critic credits Museveni's activist and inclusive politics in his early years: "In Uganda, Museveni presided over the enactment of a new constitution, intended to protect human rights. He reversed racist economic policies, welcoming back investors from India, who had been kicked out by Amin. He promoted an open political culture, grudgingly tolerated a raucous free press, and was one of the first African leaders to talk honestly about AIDS, a disease destined to kill more Ugandans than all the country's wars and dictators combined. He maintained a frugal lifestyle and encouraged his underlings to do the same. Only one political party was allowed, the ruling Movement Party, but Museveni reasonably argued that such strictures were temporarily necessary: Uganda's old parties had fractured along tribal and religious lines. 'There were numerous signs to indicate that a process was moving forward that was positive in terms of setting the stage for a genuine democracy,' says Johnnie Carson, the American ambassador to Uganda from 1991 to 1994, who has since become critical of the regime" (Rice 2006: 13).

[21] Garrett (2000).

[22] See the detailed political analysis in Putzel (2004).

[23] Whiteside et al. (2002).

Education and Information

Botswana has not ignored the epidemic. A synthesis of public opinion data from seven Southern African nations notes that in Botswana as elsewhere in the region knowledge of the epidemic is extensive. Many people (and in some countries a majority) report knowing someone who has died of AIDS in the last year. Wealthier than most countries in the region, Botswana stands out because its citizens give relatively high priority to government action against AIDS.[24] Widespread AIDS awareness and a sense of the importance of the threat have nonetheless failed to change behavior. Neither knowledge about how HIV is transmitted nor a general sense that the government cares about the epidemic has been sufficient to change health behaviors or to begin to turn the infection rate around. As one study of 1,372 students at the University of Botswana notes, "students have factual knowledge and information about HIV/AIDS, but their actual sexual practices and behavior do not reflect this high level of knowledge. Students engage in risky sexual behavior including sexual experience in early youth, unprotected sex, and casual sex with multiple partners."[25]

Money, Government Competence, Public Health Infrastructure

Botswana has an excellent system of public health. Not only is Botswana's government recognized as one of the least corrupt in Africa or elsewhere in the developing world, but it has also spent a good deal of its diamond wealth in socially egalitarian ways: providing universal, free primary education; moving rapidly toward universal secondary education; and providing an extensive set of local health clinics staffed by Family Welfare Educators, said to be respected senior women from their communities. The government of Botswana's AIDS/STD Unit has an exemplary system of Home Based Care that includes teams of nurses and counselors who provide support and assistance to caregivers, try to assure that people take their medications consistently, give nutrition counseling, and provide special food supplements where necessary.

Money has not been the problem in Botswana, at least not a shortage of money. Botswana is, as I have said, relatively wealthy by African standards with GDP/capita of about US$14,300 in 2007 and an estimated economic growth rate of 4.7 percent.[26] Because the country has honest, capable government and good infrastructure, it has also attracted sizable outside funding to combat AIDS, most notably $17 million plus free antiretroviral drugs from Bristol-Myers Squibb, and US$100 million (plus Merck's free antiretrovirals) that the Bill and Melinda Gates and Merck Foundations committed to the African Comprehensive HIV/AIDS Partnership (ACHAP) – this in a country with 1.7 million population of whom perhaps 330,000 are HIV positive.[27]

---

[24] Whiteside et al. (2002: 21).

[25] Seloilwe et al. (2001: 204). See the similarly disheartening evaluation in Chilisa (2001).

[26] This is Purchasing Power Parity (PPP) GDP/capita (Central Intelligence Agency 2008).

[27] Brubaker (2000); Grunwald (2002); Meldrum (2002); Motseta (2003); Ramiah and Reich (2005).

Public Health Campaigns of Various Stripes: Condoms versus Abstinence

The contrast between Botswana and Uganda does not rest on the kind of public health policy each pursued, at least at the level of explicit policy. Indeed Botswana had an ABC campaign modeled on that in Uganda.[28] Apparently public health messages were everywhere – on billboards, on buses, on the radio – a saturation effort so extensive that some observers believe it became counter-productive, so that no one listened anymore.[29]

There was, however, a difference in the public health approaches Botswana and Uganda actually implemented. Both Uganda and Botswana used the ABC approach; however, their efforts differed dramatically. Uganda mobilized its entire society, ultimately emphasizing locally rooted campaigns to reduce multiple partnerships: urging people to "Love Faithfully" and to practice "Zero Grazing." Following the advice of the international public health community, Botswana actively encouraged condom use. One informant reports having a videotape from 1987, taken in a village some distance from the capital, of a group of public health nurses singing "the condom song" and waving condoms above their heads as they danced.[30] Another educated, urban informant reported that concerts held to promote condoms to the young with music and dancing would end with people getting drunk and then going out and having unsafe sex.[31]

NGOs and Outside Funding

Uganda mounted one of the most effective anti-AIDS campaigns in the world.[32] One of the reasons for this success is certainly that Uganda encouraged a variety of NGOs, including faith-based and community organizations, as well as many international organizations to become involved in combating AIDS. Thus the first, organizational-level look at the contrast between Botswana and Uganda would focus on the NGO response.

One striking aspect of Botswana's situation has been the absence of an energized, vigorous, autonomous NGO sector. One of my informants noted that as of 2003 there were only twenty or so AIDS-related NGOs in the country, loosely coordinated under an NGO AIDS commission.[33] But when the modest outside funding that some of those organizations had received at their inception dried up, the organizations became largely inactive. In 2004 many

---

[28] A note on terminology: the dominant group in Botswana is the Tswana. An individual member of the group is a Motswana, plural Batswana; the language is Setswana.

[29] See Allen and Heald (2004: 1144).

[30] Interview # 18, April 3, 2003.

[31] Interview # 17, March 27, 2003.

[32] Synergy Project (2002b); Green (2003); Allen and Heald (2004); Low-Beer and Stoneburner (2004); Stoneburner and Low-Beer (2004); H. Epstein (2007).

[33] After ACHAP, the Merck/Gates-funded initiative, began offering small grants in 2004 many more organizations appeared, but there is no evidence that funding has in fact produced a more vocal civil society nor more openness about the epidemic.

community organizations emerged when ACHAP announced a program offering funding, but when that funding flagged, most of these organizations turned out not to have an autonomous base. Not only did ACHAP fail to stimulate a broad NGO response in Botswana, but in some ways it also further weakened local organizational capacities. Indeed, a Motswana informant noted that ACHAP had even begun competing directly with NGOs, offering the example of how, after a local group held a conference on how practitioners of traditional medicine might work with modern AIDS therapies, ACHAP hired someone to work with traditional medical practitioners (to add insult to injury, they hired an international, with no ties to the local practitioners – and worse, a woman trained as a "sangoma," a traditional sorcerer, looked down on by practitioners of traditional medicine).[34] A high-ranking member of one of the UN agencies in Botswana put the matter more bluntly, saying, "ACHAP has become a monster!" Thus despite its generous funding and ambitious goals, this major effort to transform AIDS in Botswana had remarkably little success in AIDS prevention and a very uncertain start in providing antiretroviral drugs.

Culture, Legitimacy, and the Problem of "Cultural Match"

The question of why vigorous NGOs did not emerge in response to the AIDS threat in Botswana is not just a question of the influence of outside funding behemoths. It goes deeper, to the link between culture, institutions, and health in Botswana. Another Motswana informant noted that "we Batswana are too modest, too humble, too polite."[35] What she meant is that there is little sense of outrage, or even of urgency about the AIDS issue in Botswana, despite incessant funerals, growing numbers of orphans, illness and deaths in every family. In a sense, Botswana's political culture is one of pride in and reliance upon an effective, capable government.[36] If one looks at Botswana's history – both its centuries-long success in avoiding the worst impacts of colonial rule, and its

---

[34] Interview # 36, July 15, 2003.
[35] Interview #27, July 4, 2003.
[36] Allen and Heald (2004: 1147) note both the top-down style of the government of Botswana, and its link to traditional sources of legitimation: "One of the new strategies to complement the ARV programme was called 'total community mobilisation'. This, as with so much else in Botswana, was designed as a top down intervention. An army of field-officers were to undertake door-to-door visits, and to talk at various community gatherings and hold workshops. During colonial times, local level government in Botswana had remained largely in the control of the *dikgotla* (sing. *kgotla*), the 'traditional' structure of chiefs and their associated councils. Since Independence, in 1966, as state control has become increasingly centralised, their power has been considerably eroded. Nevertheless, the basic structure of the *dikgotla* remains, with councils at all levels, from the sub-ward up to the ward, village, tribe and thence to the house of chiefs. It runs both in parallel with government bureaucracy and is incorporated into it, or rather side lined by it. *Dikgosi* (chiefs) still sit everyday in their courts and are paid a Government stipend but their powers of independent action are curtailed."

rulers' success in creating a stable, honest, administratively efficient modern state[37] – the tendency of contemporary Batswana to rely on government to take care of problems is understandable. And against the background of violent conflict, corrupt misrule, and economic chaos elsewhere on the African continent, Botswana indeed seems like a peaceful, well-governed paradise.

Botswana's success in building capable government nevertheless undermined the effectiveness of its AIDS programs. As two long-term observers of AIDS programs in both Botswana and Uganda note, "in Botswana, years of efficient, centralised government [have led] to a systematic disempowering of local councils"; however, in Uganda the local councils set up under Museveni's National Resistance Movement were elected and operated with considerable autonomy.[38]

In one respect, Botswana and Uganda are similar, I believe, scoring high on that elusive feature of compatibility between deep-rooted cultural patterns and contemporary institutions of governance that Steven Cornell and Joseph Kalt have called "cultural match."[39] Mikael Karlström has described the close cultural connections between Uganda's contemporary governing structure – a one-party democracy – and traditional Buganda political forms. The president of Uganda, Yoweri Museveni, has argued that Uganda is not yet ready for competitive democracy, but his National Resistance Movement has introduced a complex system of local elections on a nonparty basis.[40] Local politicians seek election, but as individuals rather than representatives of political parties. Karlström argues that – at least in the Buganda region – local people see this political system as democratic in the sense of embodying Ganda conceptions of civility and civic virtue:

the embodiment of these features [of Uganda's limited democracy] in the system of clans and king is viewed as the foundation of a "civil" and unified socio-political order. Such unity (*okwegatta*) is regularly advanced as a prime political value and as the underlying reason for clan activities and even the existence of clans. Less well educated Buganda were often surprised to discover that in my homeland there are no clans and would ask me, "How can you be united without them?"[41]

Unitary rule by Museveni's NRM allowed him to mobilize the Ugandan population in the AIDS fight, while local elections constrained officials to

---

[37] Both phases of Botswana's history are dramatic and reflect extraordinarily well on the royal family, the descendants of King Khama III, who went personally to ask Queen Victoria to make Bechuanaland a British Protectorate, to protect it from a threatened Boer invasion. Khama III's grandson, Sir Seretse Khama, became the first president of the newly independent nation, Botswana's George Washington, followed after his death by a democratic succession (Parsons 1998). See Acemoglu, Johnson, and Robinson (2003) and Leith (2005) on Botswana's economic success.

[38] Allen and Heald (2004: 1150).

[39] Cornell and Kalt (2000); see also Englebert (2000).

[40] Kassimir (1999).

[41] Karlström (1996: 492).

encourage, rather than exploit the collective goods created by NGO activity. As Karlström notes:

Since previous Ugandan governments ran local affairs through centrally appointed civil service chiefs, it is also the RC [Resistance Council] system which has provided Ugandans with their first significant experience of democratic governance at the local level. As I have tried to show, this pyramidal system of indirect representation is eminently assimilable to the Ganda Model of legitimate authority as constructed from the bottom up and founded on nested solidarities. It is also the first electoral system to resonate with the preference for regulated, as opposed to total, competition.[42]

Uganda's democracy not only empowered local communities. It created just the right environment for NGOs to flourish, constraining forces that elsewhere compromise NGO effectiveness. One of my interviewees, a Ugandan who founded a micro-lending NGO in Eastern Uganda, illustrates the "multi-layeredness" of an NGO's cultural and political embedding. He noted that local officials did not demand bribes because they all wanted to take credit for the NGO's successes to improve their chances in local elections.[43] Thus partial, rather than full electoral competition – and, not unimportantly, a political culture that resonates with traditional Ganda understandings of clan and kingship – seems, at least through the early 1990s, to have generated a political dynamic that encouraged, rather than discouraged public goods.[44]

Like Uganda, which reinstated the local powers of the Buganda kings, Botswana has preserved the *kgotla* system of local courts and customary law and has incorporated the eight Tswana chiefdoms into its constitution as a modern House of Chiefs, advisory to the national legislature. Members of the traditional royal line, as well as the local chiefs of each village, also continue to play a vital role in national life.[45] Perhaps most importantly, Botswana has assimilated the traditional *kgotla* style of consensus-based consultation under a *kgosi* or chief into the political culture of its contemporary democracy.[46]

In Botswana's case, however, its tradition of orderly, consensus-based democracy, even though it seems to have produced leadership with real vision and courage (both the first president, Seretse Khama, and the most recent president, Festus Mogae, come in for high praise, Mogae being regarded as far ahead of most others in his government on AIDS issues), has stood in the way of bold action on AIDS. Botswana's leaders have spoken out about AIDS and encouraged a wide variety of international collaborations, but the very traits that made Botswana's government such an African success story have stymied its AIDS efforts.

---

[42] Karlström (1996: 498–9).

[43] Interview # 7, August 2, 2002.

[44] Though see Mamdani (1996); Karlström (1999.

[45] Sir Seretse Khama, grandson of Botswana's great nineteenth-century ruler, King Khama III, was Botswana's first elected president. His son, Ian Khama, was the country's vice president and head of the Botswana Defense Force. In 2008, following elected presidents Ketumile Masire and Festus Mogae, he succeeded to the presidency.

[46] See the papers collected in Holm and Molutsi (1989).

One example is Botswana's vaunted freedom from corruption. I was told by frustrated internationals that any government purchasing requires an elaborate system of open bidding, slowing down attempts to streamline AIDS activities. Others from outside organizations trying to work with the government of Botswana reported that it was impossible to get standard procedures waived even in the AIDS emergency. Botswana's pride in its administrative competence proves a similar liability. Delivery of antiretroviral drugs was slowed by a shortage of doctors and nurses, yet both groups resisted having their tasks done by less qualified professionals. In an epidemic where drawing blood has been essential for monitoring the spread of the disease (sentinel surveillance), HIV testing, and managing antiretroviral therapy, Botswana has no phlebotomists – specialists in drawing blood but without the broad training of doctors or nurses – and the existing professionals resist having such unqualified people do their jobs.

In contrast, Uganda's limited no-party democracy provided a stimulating environment for the operation of a wide variety of NGOs and for an array of international collaborations. As Tim Allen, a social anthropologist with twenty-five years of experience in Uganda notes, "one of the most remarkable aspects of the HIV/AIDS campaigns in Uganda is the way they have involved everyone including international agencies, NGOs, government ministers and journalists, to pop stars, Catholic priests, local councils and soldiers. There has indeed been a considerable degree of mass mobilization."[47] In part, one might say, the state-building strategy of Museveni's National Resistance Movement, after a devastating civil war, was to mobilize around the AIDS epidemic in order to draw international assistance and to bring more of society under its purview. One Ugandan observer, Kintu Nyago, notes that Uganda's success against the epidemic depended on the "democratic reforms that characterised the post 1986 period. This new political climate unleashed people's creative energies to respond to this pestilence. This occurred through free debate in the media and the broader public realm, which helped demystify the disease, in addition to the formation of people-centered NGOs such as TASO [The AIDS Support Organisation] and the Aids Information Centre." He also credits the "decentralisation and the introduction of the Local Council system," noting the kind of collaboration that was encouraged between community groups and local-level party officials:

The women, youth and people with disabilities were particularly targeted for empowerment. This meant that scientifically proven information would smoothly flow from the top to the Local Council leadership, who would in turn disseminate it to a receptive population. It's this local coalition of the LCs, clan head, local imam and pastor, or bwana Mukulu [parish priest] together with Community Based Organisations that helped change the tide through community ownership of the anti-AIDS campaign.[48]

---

[47] Allen (2006: 20).
[48] Nyago (2003).

Tim Allen and Suzette Heald note the importance of Uganda's local councils in promoting behavior change:

Although members of these locally elected bodies were originally not paid salaries or stipends, they were able to make informal charges for their services. Most importantly, they derived their authority directly from the President, and were supported by the army. They were also given a great deal of latitude in deciding how to operate. They were supposed to act as advocates for their people at each level of the administration, collaborate with aid agencies and monitor security. In Moyo District, and in many other parts of Uganda they become active in promoting awareness of HIV/AIDS, often putting up their own health promotion posters. In some cases they also became active in not just promoting behavioural change, but in enforcing it.[49]

They note the sharp contrast with the way local authorities function in Botswana:

In addition to a hereditary chief or headman, each village [in Botswana] now has a range of elected village committees (including one for AIDS), who report to village chief and council but also, and more importantly, to the Village Development Committee and thence to government offices higher up the hierarchy. But the wheels of the bureaucracy grind exceedingly slowly. ... [C]hiefs can no longer act independently of this committee structure, nor committees independently of higher approval. In 2003, we heard of two cases where chiefs wanted to put up their own HIV/AIDS posters in their kgotla – but permission had to go up to NACA (the National AIDS Coordinating Agency) and then come down. In over two years in one case, and in over three in the other, no such authorization had come down. But these chiefs were exceptions. We did not see much sign of those few we visited in 2004 wanting to act.[50]

Uganda's democracy not only empowered local communities. It created the right environment for NGOs to flourish, constraining forces that elsewhere compromise NGO effectiveness. Botswana's political culture created effective government institutions but without the ability to mobilize local communities.

Solidarities and Silences

Bound up with issues of political culture and organizational style lies the problem of stigma. Over and over again, throughout Africa, the deep sense of shame about AIDS, the fear of isolation of people living with AIDS, and the reluctance of everyone from heads of state to local clergy to talk about the issue seems to stand in the way of effective prevention and treatment. Stephen Lewis, the UN special ambassador for AIDS, reported that when he urged Daniel arap Moi, Kenya's former president, to speak out about Kenya's AIDS crisis, Moi replied, "We don't talk about nasty things." In Uganda, Museveni's determination to speak openly about AIDS and about the changes in sexual practices necessary to prevent it is credited with breaking through the stigma

---

[49] Allen and Heald (2004: 1150).
[50] Ibid: 1147.

and silence surrounding the disease. And in Uganda as elsewhere in Africa, the few celebrities, such as musicians, who have been willing to come out as HIV positive are reported to have made an enormous difference.[51]

Stigma has indeed played a role in Africa's AIDS crisis, but the meaning of the term – both its nature and possible remedies – have been misunderstood in the West. In my view, this gets to the heart of the Botswana paradox, and the contrasting outcome of AIDS-prevention efforts in Uganda versus those in stable, peaceful Botswana. Stigma is a problem virtually everywhere.[52] My Ugandan informant reported that the taboo on discussing anything connected with sex among clan or family members creates special difficulties for the AIDS education his micro-lending NGO aspires to do. An informant who had done AIDS work in a South African mine reported that to be revealed as HIV positive would be "social death" within the macho community of miners, even though the mine authorities knew that 40 percent of the miners were infected.[53]

In Botswana, I heard again and again how stigma was slowing access to antiretroviral therapy, even though in theory the treatment was available free to anyone who needed it. Since people wouldn't acknowledge that they were HIV positive, they delayed therapy until they were desperately ill, thus overwhelming limited clinical facilities.[54] Nurses in the government's AIDS/STD Unit reported having to paint over the insignia on their vans in order to be able to enter the neighborhoods where they worked, having patients refuse home visits if the nursing staff wore uniforms, and having parents and other care givers refuse to acknowledge that their adult children were ill with AIDS even as those children died.[55] Funerals in Botswana routinely include a detailed recitation of the life and death of the deceased, including full detail about the final illness, but I was told over and over again that AIDS is never mentioned. Two of my interviewees, both nurses, reported having been assigned the funeral oration about the final illness of a family member because of their medical training, and then being told by the families that they could not mention AIDS.

Yet stigma, if it means discrimination or social rejection, is not quite the right concept to describe what is happening in Botswana. One informant, an influential director of AIDS services for a major mine, said that she became aware of the paradoxical nature of the situation when she realized that work units, which might be at full strength with ten workers, were requesting four additional workers. When she investigated, she found that the units actually

---

[51] See Eaton (2004).
[52] See Farmer (1992) on the association between AIDS witchcraft in Haiti; also Ashforth (2005). Campbell et al. (2005) like many others find that the association between AIDS and sexual immorality generates stigma.
[53] Interview 19, April 29, 2003.
[54] Interview #33, July 9, 2003. See also Grunwald (2002).
[55] Interview # 31, July 8, 2003.

had ten workers on the payroll, four of whom were too sick to work. So the mine foremen were carrying their sick workers, protecting them from losing their jobs, rather than firing them or discriminating against them in the usual sense.[56] In this sense the silence surrounding AIDS is partly denial, but it is partly a kind of protective refusal to push the infected person outside the relationships of solidarity upon which he or she depends. People recognize when they or their relatives are ill with the symptoms of AIDS, but they protect themselves and each other from the socially disruptive, public acknowledgment of the disease. There is thus a kind of protective tenderness behind the secrecy and suppression of AIDS stigma in Botswana.

If stigma does not result in discrimination or a loss of rights and benefits,[57] the meaning of variations in political and cultural response to the epidemic becomes clearer. What stigma and the resulting secrecy do is to prevent the direct mobilization of social solidarities to confront the realities of the epidemic, both for those who are infected and those who are at risk. Most analyses of the sources of effective response to health threats still assume, implicitly or explicitly, that information and education lead people (as autonomous, rational individuals) to make prudentially motivated health decisions. But as we have seen for Botswana, even universal or near-universal health information about HIV/AIDS risks does not lead, by itself, to behavior change. Botswana has done a good job of informing its people and alerting them to the danger they face. Their president has spoken out, according to a *Washington Post* report, "warning his people in fiery speeches that they are 'threatened with annihilation,' chairing his country's AIDS council, and badgering his health officials with questions about condom distribution in prisons and construction timetables for clinics."[58] Batswana are well informed; indeed they have been inundated with health messages about AIDS. They have had high-quality professional attention – respectful and caring – for people living with AIDS in the Home Based Care service of the AIDS/STD Unit of the ministry of Health. Then what is missing?

What is missing is precisely the activation of social solidarities, the sense of community and the mobilization of collective identities, that can create the elusive behavior changes (abstinence, partner reduction, and condom use) that can reduce the epidemic's devastation. As Tim Allen has noted, based on his twenty-five years of anthropological fieldwork in Uganda, "If declining HIV incidence is linked to behavioural changes in the most intimate aspects of social relations, then changes are required in understandings and expectations

---

[56] Interview # 26, July 4, 2003.

[57] Stigma as social isolation is also closer to Erving Goffman's (1963) original meaning. For him, a stigma was something that made a person a *defective interactor*, meaning that others could not smoothly enact the ritual proprieties of normal social interaction. It was this social defectiveness – and thus the isolation from the ritual encounters that affirm social solidarity – that made a particular trait a source of stigma.

[58] Grunwald (2002).

of accountability and duty – in other words, in what it means to act in a moral way."[59] Such mobilized solidarities may also be necessary to encourage people to seek out and persist with the antiretroviral therapies that can extend the lives of those living with HIV and AIDS.

The crucial difference is whether responses to AIDS activate the NGOs, community organizations, churches, and village authorities that have played such a crucial role in Uganda and in some of the other African societies that are starting to show declining rates of HIV infection. To give a sense of what this means, let me quote another informant, an AIDS activist from Zambia, describing how her organization, the Society for Women and AIDS in Zambia (SWAAZ) – an organization now numbering some ten thousand volunteers, organized into local chapters, with only a tiny paid staff – waged its campaigns:

When we go into an area to work on HIV/AIDS we sensitize the women about AIDS, we mobilize. But we go to the Health Ministry for the statistics and the data to know how many people are dying, how many are infected. When you go to a rural area you go first to the Ministry of Health. Then you go to the village head man. Then go to the village chief.

Last year [we] went to the Eastern region. First we had a workshop for all the chiefs. We had eighty-one chiefs there. And we told them that because they are guardians of traditions, they are influential. They were very excited, they all said, "Come to my village; come to my village."

Then we meet with the village headmen. A small village will have between one hundred and two hundred people. If they are close together we can put five villages together, and they can form subcommittees. And then, after a year, they have to hold elections. They are volunteers. They have to take the responsibility for mobilizing themselves. There has to be a contact person that SWAAZ communicates with. Then there should be a chairperson that is in communication with Lusaka, and he communicates to the other village leaders. You have to find someone who can write and read. And usually you use the address of the village headman, the church, the police if there is a police station nearby.[60]

Such bottom-up mobilization dispenses nothing more than information and exhortation – the same information and exhortation that has been offered in Botswana. But in Uganda, Zambia, and even to some degree in parts of Kenya and Tanzania, such collective mobilization is also producing that other elusive property – social solidarity – making new health behaviors, and the willingness to take life-saving drugs, part not only of protecting one's individual health but of participating in the collective process of saving one's community. The Botswana case demonstrates – as clearly as anything could – that individual prudential interests are not enough. Human beings seek participation in social community. And where to participate in that community as a full member is to maintain the smooth, polite, considerate, civil style that characterizes Tswana

---

[59] Allen (2006): 8.
[60] Interview 15, March 25, 2003.

social life, people will – and do – repeatedly choose death over the potential social isolation that would arise from openly acknowledging a dreaded
disease.[61] But civility and politeness are features of Ugandan political culture as
well. In the Ugandan case, however, the ferment of collective mobilization – by
churches, TASO, community organizations, government officials, and a multiplicity of NGOs – has at least in part broken through isolating stigma to produce profound changes in attitudes and behavior.

THE HEART OF THE MATTER

Uganda's success and Botswana's wrenching failure illustrate the intersection
of the political and the cultural, the institutional and the moral. Botswana's
success as a modern state has in part involved great receptivity to technocratic
advice. Botswana has imported legions of experts on matters from economic
policy, to investment strategy, to schooling and health care. Uganda has also
welcomed a variety of international actors as well as encouraging local nongovernmental and community organizations of all sorts. But in Uganda, the
president, Yoweri Museveni, made the fight against AIDS a national crusade.
He included the AIDS issue in every speech he gave; he insisted that all the
officials of the National Resistance Movement, down to the local level, discuss
AIDS in every speech and every public meeting. Uganda's National Resistance
Movement also authorized its Local Councils to enforce community moral
norms.[62] So the many public health messages were reinforced by a huge variety
of locally sponsored activities, like school groups putting on theater presenta-
tions about the danger of HIV and AIDS.[63]

The really crucial difference between Botswana and Uganda has not been
the vigor of their responses to the pandemic, or even their educational efforts.
Rather, Ugandans were led to see action against AIDS as part of a collective
narrative,[64] one that made them central players not only in protecting themselves as individuals, but in participating in a community that was endangered
and demanded heroic effort. Botswana may have done everything right, but
it did not create the sense of shared fate, of collective meaning, and of necessary sacrifice that could bridge the gap between the isolation of individual fear
and social stigma and the necessity for collectively shared action. This would
suggest that a broad social movement – the pattern of Brazil and Uganda,
but not of Botswana – makes the fight against AIDS not just a matter of individual prudence, but of a collective moral struggle, so that individual changes
in health behaviors are part of a broader sense of community morality, and

---

[61] On the link between Tswana conceptions of civility and the reluctance to acknowledge AIDS
as the cause of death at funerals, see Durham and Klaits (2002).

[62] Allen (2006): 23.

[63] See Obbo (1995); U.S. Agency for International Development (2002).

[64] I am indebted to Chaviva Hosek of the Canadian Institute for Advanced Research for this
phrase.

perhaps of a kind of nationalist mobilization on behalf of group well-being. The very competent, but more technocratic response in Botswana – however well-conceived and carefully carried out, however much information about the virus and warnings about its dangers were disseminated – simply couldn't match the political commitment and the moral enthusiasm, at all levels of the society, that galvanized Uganda.

CONCLUSION

The comparison between Botswana and Uganda raises a broader set of issues about responses to the AIDS epidemic, about culture and health, and finally about human behavior more generally. Several analysts have pointed out the failure of most – indeed nearly all – of the Western-inspired efforts at AIDS prevention in Africa.[65] One explanation is that public health experts exported strategies that had worked in Europe and North America, rather than grounding their strategies in local African conditions: condoms appeared to have led to dramatic reductions in HIV incidence in the Global North, so international public health authorities saw condoms as the best, and sometimes the only, effective AIDS prevention.[66] Another, somewhat broader view of the problem is that along with a reliance on condoms, Western experts advocated the whole set of policies and political commitments that had been important for prevention campaigns in the West, especially in the gay community.[67] Confidentiality, voluntary and anonymous testing, human rights, and freedom from stigma and discrimination were seen as the fundamental weapons for fighting AIDS.[68] Yet this standard recipe of human rights combined with HIV/

[65] See H. Epstein (2007); Potts et al. (2008). Catherine Campbell (2003), in a courageous book on an AIDS prevention project among prostitutes and miners in South Africa, explores failure in what was supposed to be a "best practice" project that lived up to all the ideals of "stakeholder buy in" and "participation."

[66] The most visible proponent of this view has been Edward C. Green (2003) who claims (p. 58), "Condom use was widely believed to be the best solution to sexually transmitted AIDS in the United States; it was even believed to have been responsible for reducing HIV infection rates among gay men in some key cities where infection levels among gay men reached extremely high levels." Green and others who agreed with him have been embraced by the proabstinence religious community (and of course by the Bush administration's PEPFAR program). This political embrace has cast the conflict as one between condoms and the ABC approach, while obscuring the really important factors at work.

[67] Writing in *The Lancet*, De Cock et al. (2002) note: "The approach to HIV/AIDS has its roots in the early history of the epidemic in the USA, when its pathogenesis and natural history were little understood, treatment options were few, and society was at best unresponsive and at worst discriminatory towards a focal epidemic spread by male-to-male sex and injecting drug use. During that time, when no treatment was available, an unusual coalition was formed between the gay community, medical and public health practitioners, and civil liberty proponents to avoid prevention measures that might 'drive the epidemic underground'" (p. 68).

[68] Allen (2004) notes that "the human rights of those who are HIV positive are privileged over those who are not. It is very understandable why this is the case, but in public health terms

AIDS information and exhortations failed to galvanize an effective response to the epidemic in Botswana.

The lessons of the American, Australian, and Brazilian gay communities' fight against AIDS – and the ways these lessons do apply directly to Africa's AIDS epidemic – have been widely misunderstood. Neither condoms nor protection of human rights were in themselves keys to reducing HIV transmission. These commitments were part of a much broader mobilization of gay communities in political, cultural, and moral response to the epidemic.[69] The social, political, and moral mobilization of gay men led to dramatic behavior change that turned back the tide of new infections. Using a condom signified not protecting oneself from other men who were dangerous; rather, practicing safe sex signaled gay men's pride in their identity, their love of other men, and their commitment to their community.[70] Gay men used condoms (public health officials in San Francisco estimate that at the peak of the safe sex campaigns, condoms were used in something like 95 percent of all gay male sexual encounters) because practicing safe sex enhanced their own identity as moral persons. That powerful identity rested in turn on deep identification with their community, and on the simultaneous pride (and fear) of a group that mobilized politically to demand respect and protection and to shape the medical and public-health response to the disease.[71]

The contrasting experiences of Uganda and Botswana also point to larger questions about the fundamental motivations for human behavior. Michèle Lamont has described "the world in moral order."[72] When asked about their sense of self and about what they value, French and American working-class men describe their desire to see the world as governed by a moral order and to see themselves as filling a valuable place in that order. So even the powerful

---

it is potentially counterproductive. Moreover, if the rates of infection occurring in southern Africa were occurring in a rich country, such as the UK or Canada, it would be surprising if extreme measures were not introduced. The extraordinary responses to the SARS virus in 2002–03 make that very clear" (p. 1127). See also De Cock et al. (2002).

[69] Dennis Altman (1994) analyzes the remarkable array of community organizations that mobilized in response to the AIDS epidemic and discusses the political opportunities and constraints that made such organizing more successful in some contexts than in others. He quotes from a French AIDS organization's pamphlet to suggest the general role played by such organizations: "One alone cannot change his or her behavior: a social movement and opinion leaders are needed" (p. 43).

[70] Writing of the Australian gay community in the 1980s, Dowsett (1999: 227) claims that "gay communities were working hard to create a 'safe sex culture' in their educational activities, using the idea of 'a community acting together to protect itself'. This notion of a safe sex culture is not merely a documentation of aggregated behaviour change; rather, it is a framework of ideas, practices, images, language, preoccupations and activities that insinuate safe sex directly into the centre of daily life for gay men. It means that any involvement in gay life is also an immersion in HIV/AIDS and in its key concern of developing, sustaining and living with safe sexual practice."

[71] See Altman (1994) and Epstein (1996).

[72] Lamont (2000).

engine of individual interests operates within a larger understanding of a moral order and the individual's place within it. Myra Bluebond-Langner, an anthropologist who studies decision making for dying children, has noted that when parents make decisions about how far to prolong treatment for their dying children, they act "not in terms of the weighing of risks and benefits, but in the construction of identities that can survive what the body may not."[73] That same commitment to the preservation of a moral identity, one affirmed by one's community, is also central to AIDS decision making. In the West, acting rationally in one's interest is considered part of an adequate identity, both for individuals and in many respects for organizations and nations as well.[74] Yet even in Europe and North America, with our long history of individualism, rational, individual self interest has played a surprisingly small role in reducing HIV transmission.

In Africa, despite the consistent presumption by international donors that rational self-interest is the fulcrum on which behavior can change (witness the commitment to Voluntary Counseling and Testing as the necessary prerequisite to behavior change and the persistence of the conviction that Information, Education, and Communication [IEC] will change behavior), the evidence is entirely in the other direction.[75] Uganda and other places that have mobilized moral solidarities on the ground have been able to dramatically reduce unsafe behaviors, but even the clearest knowledge of the most direct threats have been unable to overcome people's commitment to valued moral identities.[76]

As Hall and Taylor note, contemporary health researchers have gathered powerful evidence that, at the individual level, social support and social networks play crucial roles in health – strengthening the immune system,

---

[73] Bluebond-Langner (2003).

[74] See Dobbin (1994a; 1994b; 2004).

[75] In a February 10, 2004, Op-Ed essay in the *New York Times*, Richard Holbrooke and Richard Furman wrote: "Of all the mind-numbing statistics about H.I.V. and AIDS, the most staggering – and important – is this: 95 percent of those infected worldwide do not know they are harboring the most deadly virus in history, and are therefore spreading it, however unintentionally." Despite the U.S. commitment to the notion that individuals can't protect themselves and others without knowing their status, there is little evidence that knowing one's HIV status is linked to behavior change and no evidence that individuals' knowledge of their HIV status is necessary for effective prevention.

[76] Some of the most striking evidence comes from the debate over condoms. The effectiveness of consistent condom use in preventing HIV transmission is estimated at about 90 percent. In Africa, governments and NGOs have been quite successful in increasing the aggregate numbers of condoms distributed, with proportions as high as 85 percent of men in some places reporting condom use with high-risk partners. But this increase in condom use has had no measurable impact on HIV prevalence. Why? It appears that the very association of condoms with promiscuity, prostitution, and nonregular partners has made using condoms unacceptable with spouses or even steady boyfriends and girlfriends. Thus the semiotic coding of the condom makes it incompatible with intimacy and affection, even for those who know they risk infection (Agha et al. 2002; , S. Allen et al. 2003; Hearst and Chen 2004; Kaler 2004; Chimbiri 2007; Tavory and Swidler 2009).

speeding recovery from heart attacks, and promoting health behaviors.[77] This chapter, and this volume as a whole, address parallel phenomena at the collective – community or national – level and offer a possible reinterpretation of the efficacy of individual-level social support. The comparison of Botswana and Uganda suggests that individuals' ability to act rationally to protect their health – their ability to face frightening realities, to change socially significant behaviors, and even to value their own well-being – may depend both directly and indirectly on collectively-generated meanings. It is hard to identify the precise mechanisms at work here. But evidence from Uganda and Botswana, as well as the experiences of successful AIDS prevention in Brazil and in Australian, American, and European gay communities, suggests that people can make even difficult changes in behavior when they feel they are making a socially validated effort for a moral end. Furthermore, social solidarity may alter the shameful aspects of disease (and remember that illness in general is often experienced as a personal moral failing)[78] to allow people to take care of their own health and to ask or expect others to help them. We typically think of social support as aid and assistance – sometimes psychological – that others give us. But the major benefit of social support may be instead that it makes us feel valuable enough that we are worth taking care of.

The kinds of collective mobilization that happened in Uganda (and in some other AIDS-affected communities around the world) are in some ways specific to a particular national experience and the collective mobilization that a new regime and an assortment of local organizations and international NGOs were able to achieve. But at another level, the contrast between Botswana and Uganda reminds us that human flourishing is fundamentally tied to collective processes and more specifically to the ways collective meanings shape the significance of individual lives.

---

[77] See Keating and Hertzman (1999) and Berkman and Kawachi (2000) for major overviews of evidence and arguments.
[78] See Sontag (1978).

6

Responses to Racism, Health, and Social Inclusion as a Dimension of Successful Societies*

Michèle Lamont

OBJECTIVES AND CONTRIBUTIONS

This chapter informs one aspect of what makes societies successful: social inclusion. My focus is social recognition and cultural citizenship – who fits in, who belongs, who is "us" and who is "them." Societies that are inclusive are societies that make room for the social recognition of a variety of groups. They are societies that sustain competing definitions of a worthy life and a worthy person, which empower low-status groups to contest stereotypes and measure their worth independently of dominant social matrices. They are also societies where people do not have to pay a heavy toll (symbolic or material) for crossing group boundaries – for intermarriage, for instance.

I study one social process that leads to greater social inclusion: how ordinary members of stigmatized ethnic and racial groups respond to exclusion by challenging stereotypes that feed and justify discriminatory behavior and rebutting the notion of their inferiority.[1] This is what I call destigmatization

---

* I wish to thank CIFAR and the Racliffe Institute for Advanced Studies for supporting this research. My gratitude also goes to colleagues who have commented on this chapter or discussed it with me: Peter Hall, Lisa Berkman, Christopher Bail, Gerard Bouchard, Rich Carpiano, Wendy Espeland, Katherine Frohlich, Mary Jo Good, Christopher Jencks, Arthur Kleinman, Nancy Krieger, Mary Clare Lenon, Paul Lichterman, Bernice Pescosalido, Abigail Saguy, James Sidanius, Patrick Simon, Art Stinchcombe, David Williams, Andreas Wimmer, as well as the members of the Successful Societies Program for conversations around and/or feedback on this chapter. I also thank Joe Cook, Heather Latham, Sabrina Pendergrass, and Seth Hannah for their assistance.

[1] I build on Goffman (1963) who shows how individuals with discredited or spoiled identities take on the responsibility of managing interaction to prevent discomfort in others. Much of the literature on responses to stigma concerns the management of mental illness and HIV- and AIDS-based stigma, and the health impact of reactions to such stressors. See Link and Phelan (2001) for a review. More recently researchers have developed an interest in the broader moral context of stigma (Yang et al. 2007) and in stigma and social exclusion (Reidpath et al. 2005). This literature can inform our study of responses to ethnoracial stigma.

strategies.[2] This chapter explains and illustrates this notion and explores how such strategies may enhance social inclusion, and contribute to societal success.

This chapter also speaks to health inequality, another topic at the center of this collective volume. Considering destigmatization strategies can broaden our understanding of the effect of racism and discrimination on health. Research has clearly shown the impact of inequality and discrimination on physical and mental health.[3] However, social epidemiologists rarely consider how *responses* to inequality and discrimination can modulate this impact,[4] and those who consider them tend to have a thin understanding of the role of meaning and the cultural environment in shaping these responses.[5] My agenda is to illuminate the role of meaning and available cultural repertoires (or schemas) in the pathways leading to the production of the health gradient.[6]

It is reasonable to believe that how individuals interpret and deal with exclusion and stigmatization is a key intervening factor in how racism and discrimination affect their mental and physical health. Inequality and discrimination affect health behavior not only by influencing the frequency at which individuals experience negative life events and access to resources – to quality health care and decent housing – and not only by shaping lifestyles, but also by affecting feelings of worth and belonging, which in turn undermines physical and mental health through a variety of stress-related biological pathways, including psychoneuroendocrinological and psychoneuroimmunological mechanisms.[7] Perceived discrimination can bring about emotions such as shame, anger, distancing, privatizing, and stereotyping, as well as envy, resentment, compassion, contempt, pride, deference, and condescension.[8] These emotions are intimately tied to the experience of inequality and misrecognition and they contribute to the health gradient.[9]

---

[2] This notion is inspired by Essed's (1991) notion of "everyday racism." It also expands on Aptheker's (1992) definition of antiracism as rhetoric aimed at disproving racial inferiority.

[3] Williams (1997); Schnittker and McLeod (2005); Leigh and Jencks (2006). On income inequality, see Lynch et al. (2004). On discrimination, see Krieger (1999); Williams, Neighbors, and Jackson (2003).

[4] But Krieger et al. (1993) and Krieger (2001).

[5] For a critique of thin approaches to culture in the field of poverty, see Lamont and Small (2008).

[6] Following Sewell (2005: 131), I define cultural schemas as "society's fundamental tools of thought, but also the various recipes, scenarios, principles of action, and habits of speech and gesture built up with these fundamental tools."

[7] See Keating (Chapter 2, in this volume). The development of the hypothalamus-pituitary-adrenal (HPA) axis, the body's stress-response system, is affected by levels of control, status, dominance, hierarchies, and threats. The level of serotonin production, which helps maintain positive emotionality and reduce depression, is affected by feelings of belonging, participation, and social connection. For its part, the functioning of the frontal cortex, which controls decision making and the integration of emotion, cognition, and judgment, is tied to feelings of worth and affection and to identity formation. See also Keating and Hertzman (1999b); Suomi (1999), McEwen (2003); Boyce and Keating (2004).

[8] Skeggs (1997); Sayer (2005b): 950; Todd (2006).

[9] Archer (2000); Nussbaum (2001). See Wilkinson (1999) on emotions and the health gradient.

How members of subordinate groups respond to these emotions by internalizing their lower status and the stigma that comes with it or interpreting their situation so as to alter the status hierarchy or power dynamics must matter. Whether the social context broadly defined facilitates or hinders such a contestation (through its collective myths, cultural repertoires, institutions, and so forth) must matter as well, and can be regarded as an indicator of how successful a society is. In societies where no alternative valuation system is available, low-status groups are more likely to be resigned and passive, instead of resilient. The absence of readily available cultural options could affect their well-being, and a range of related health outcomes such as depression and suicide. The availability of empowering cultural repertoires sustains resilience.[10] It should be considered in explanations of cross-national differences in the health gradient to the same extent as welfare regime or political ideology.[11] Repertoires (collective myths, imaginaries, and so on) matter because they can energize, motivate, create excitement, and optimism.[12]

Considering responses to discrimination is crucial because individuals cannot be presumed to be passive recipients of discrimination. They have agency and their responses mediates the effect of discrimination on their well-being, as well as how exclusion occurs. The range of potential responses is circumscribed by the repertoires that are made available to them. Thus, it really matters what these repertoires are and whether they facilitate or constrain greater inclusion.

Psychologists have given consideration to the intrapsychological mechanisms with which members of stigmatized groups cope with stigmas that they believe are associated with them, such as privileging in-group comparisons.[13] They examine what leads people to improve their self-esteem and subjective well-being, focusing on elements such as goal attainment.[14] However, they do not consider how cultural contexts – such as widely shared views on the moral character of low-income or immigrant populations – influence coping. Conversely, even though some have studied the effect of subjective social status on various health outcomes,[15] psychologists have not considered the variegated frameworks through which people define status, including through

---

[10] For an approach to health that emphasizes resilience and assets, see Bartley et al. (forthcoming).

[11] Coburn (2004); Chung and Muntaner (2007); Navarro et al. (2006).

[12] Here I expand from Gérard Bouchard (Chapter 7, in this volume) on collective imaginaries and myths. Also see Bouchard (2003a).

[13] Steele and Crocker (1998). Psychologists Oyserman and Swim (2001) propose an agenda for studying how members of stigmatized groups react to stigma. See also Steele (1998); Clark et al. (1999); Crocker and Major (1989); Pinel (1999); Brickson (2000).

[14] For a review, see Twenge and Crocker (2002). Also Oyserman et al. (2002). On subjective well-being, see Diener and Lucas (2000). On new approaches to self-esteem that are organized around definitions of worth, see Crocker and Knight (2005).

[15] On subjective social status, see the work of Nancy E. Adler and her collaborators (for example, Goodman et al. 2001).

standards of evaluation that are autonomous from socioeconomic status. This chapter complements their work by tackling these questions.[16]

Social epidemiologists have spent considerable energy elaborating various frameworks to account for the production of the health gradient, and inequality in health more generally. These frameworks typically take into consideration psychosocial and material factors, networks, neighborhood effects, life course, access to health care, and policies.[17] Considering the effect of meaning and destigmatization strategies on health adds an important dimension to these explanatory frameworks. Indeed, I believe that meaning (manifested in cultural scripts, collective myths, taken-for-granted meanings, and folk classification systems) mediate some of the psychosocial mechanisms emphasized by influential social epidemiologists such as Marmot and Wilkinson, who attribute the health gradient to lack of control, autonomy, participation, and relative status.[18] Even though the community of health scholars is becoming aware of the importance of broadening research on the cultural factors and mechanisms affecting health, and some researchers are now introducing cultural elements into their analytical toolkits, their analyses often remain limited to cross-national or cross-cultural differences,[19] or to lifestyle and habitus.[20] This is not enough. We also need to explore how competing definitions of self-worth and status that prevail in different segments of the population and in different societies. These are likely to mediate the relationship between psychosocial mechanisms and health and how they interact with the environment – with immigration and redistributive policies for instance – as constraints and conditions mediating this relationship.

---

[16] It particularly complements that of British social psychologists have made headways on such questions. Henry Tajfel (1981) advocated a return to the content of stereotypes and "justificatory myths" of social inequalities. Condor (1996) applies qualitative methods to the examination of various aspects of racism and national identity in talk. See also Barrett (2005).

[17] Berkman and Syme (1979); Link and Phelan (1995); Kawachi (2000). For instance, for Krieger (2003), there are "5 key pathways through which racism can harm health, by shaping exposure and vulnerability to the following: 1) economic and social deprivation; 2) toxic substances and hazardous conditions; 3) socially inflicted trauma (mental, physical, sexual, directly experienced or witnessed, from verbal threats to violent acts); 4) targeted marketing of commodities that can harm health, such as junk food and psychoactive substances (alcohol, tobacco, and other licit and illicit drugs); and 5) inadequate or degrading medical care." Also Williams (1997); Adler and Ostrove (1999); Krieger (2001); Cockerham (2005); Link and Phelan (2005). Consensus has yet to emerge concerning the best model describing such mechanisms.

[18] Marmot (2004); Wilkinson (2005).

[19] For instance, Corin (1994); for a critique of these assumptions, see Gupta and Ferguson (1992) and Lamont and Thévenot (2000). Wilkinson (2005: 219) distinguishes between national "cultures of inequality" in terms of how "macho" they are. For his part, Marmot (2004) suggests that cultural changes affect societies as a whole, but internal differences within the population also matter.

[20] On lifestyle, see Dressler (1991); Trostle and Sommerfeld (1996); Frolich, Corin, and Potvin (2001); Nguyen and Peschard (2003); Cockerham (2005); Dressler, Ochs, and Gravlee (2005); Carpiano (2006). On lifestyle and habitus, see Veenstra (2005). Karlsen and Nazroo (2002) compare the impact of "ethnicity as identity" versus "ethnicity as structure" (defined in terms of racialization and class experience) on the health of ethnic minority people in Britain.

We need a framework for reaching a more comprehensive and detailed understanding of how meaning-making contributes to the process by which the environment "gets under the skin" to create disparities in mental and physical health.[21] This chapter does some of the analytical groundwork needed for such an explanation.

Meanings and cultural structures factor into our analysis at several levels. I consider: (1) personal and group identity and the transformation of the boundaries that define them; (2) frames and schemas concerning injustice and what is possible and how they shape strategies of collective action; (3) taken-for-granted views of the relationship between superordinate and subordinate groups; (4) available cultural models (scripts, repertoires) of how to lead one's life and of what defines a good life; (5) conceptions of status, recognition, moral order, and imaginaries that affect resilience and the capacity to respond to challenges; (6) broader cultural repertoires that define cultural citizenship, what makes one part of the collectivity, and how the characteristics of one's group measure up to such standards – particularly what is unquestioned and what is contentious about each of these cultural constructs.

Even though, in the absence of data, it is too early to reach conclusion about what responses to racism lead to the best health outcome, related literatures suggest a number of hypotheses. The first section describes theoretical tools and defines and illustrates destigmatization strategies by drawing on my earlier work on various groups of African Americans and on North-African immigrants living in France. The second section provides hypotheses on the relationship between destigmatization strategies and health. The third section discusses the broader agenda for the study of the health gradient and of successful societies.

DESTIGMATIZATION STRATEGIES

The empirical focus is the everyday narratives of ordinary people who are members of stigmatized groups – as opposed to intellectuals or social movement leaders or members – concerning how they understand similarities and differences between their group and dominant groups, and what they do in the course of daily life to transform the negative meanings associated with their collective identity, to challenge stereotypes about their group and to create, enact, or demand new forms of personal interaction.[22] Ordinary people face discrimination on a daily basis, and negotiate relationships, including the meaning of their ethnoracial identity, in the course of daily life.[23] In this

---

[21] Similarly, Johnson-Hanks (2002) integrates culture in demographic explanation of fertility and contraception.

[22] This chapter complements the large literature on resistance – for instance, Scott (1990); Mansbridge (1999); Silbey and Ewick (2003); Herzog (2004). I acknowledge that individuals may be victim of discrimination without being aware of it. These experiences may vary across social class, depending on the resources that individuals have at their disposal. This topic is beyond the scope of this chapter.

[23] Wimmer (2008).

context, they produce changes at the interactional level that are fed by the rhetoric and the efforts of broader social movements.[24] The sum of these microchanges can be considerable and contribute to greater social inclusion.

Borrowing from Jenkins, I use the term "social identity" to refer to a twin process of group identification and social categorization. Individuals differentiate themselves from others by drawing on criteria of commonality and a sense of shared belonging within their subgroup, as well as on a shared perception that members of other groups also have commonalities.[25] This is what Jenkins calls "group identification." This internal identification process must be recognized by outsiders for a collective identity to emerge. This is what he calls "social categorization" – the meaning given to a group by outsiders.

These two processes are at the center of my analysis. I study how individuals draw group boundaries – who is "in" and "out" – and define the meaning they give to their group – who is "us" and "them." This requires considering how they construct similarity and difference between themselves and others, as well as the types of evidence they give of equality or equivalence between groups ("we are the same or as good because ..."; "we are better because ...").[26] I also analyze the meaning of one's group to oneself – what it means for African Americans, for instance, to belong to their group (what defines their distinctiveness, their authenticity). Instead of focusing exclusively on direct responses to discrimination or racism, I study folk classification systems and everyday narratives about group boundaries and what makes people worthy.[27]

Responses to racism can range from efforts to assimilate to the dominant group and downplaying one's low-status identity, to affirming and celebrating differences. For their part, destigmatization strategies may include demonstrating that one does not present the negative characteristics associated with one's group, that negative views of this group are unfounded, and that the group has a great many strengths. Moreover, individuals may appeal to a wide range of evidence to demonstrate equality between groups, including shared morality or religion, similar earning or consumption capabilities, common physical characteristics ("we all have ten fingers"), citizenship ("we all have the same rights"), or the universality of human nature. Others also want to demonstrate the superiority of their group on spiritual, moral, or economic grounds. Although

---

[24] Mansbridge and Flaster (2007).

[25] Jenkins (1996). I thank Arthur Stinchcombe for pointing out to me the parallels between Jenkins's theory and Erik Erikson's classic essay, "The Problem of Ego Identity."

[26] My agenda is similar to that of Dressler, Oths, and Gravlee (2005) which draws on Bourdieu and focuses on "cognitive representations constructed out of an amalgam of socially shared understandings" (p. 214) – particularly racial folk self-categorization and self-identification – and their implications for health. These anthropologists are concerned with racial folk self-categorization and self-identification. My approach is inspired by developments in cultural sociology, cultural anthropology, and cultural psychology. See D'Andrade (1995); DiMaggio (1997); Schweder, Minow, and Markus (2002).

[27] See Boltanski and Thévenot (1991); Espeland and Stevens (1998); Lamont and Molnár (2002).

developing an encompassing inventory of destigmatization strategies is beyond the scope of this chapter, I identify several possible axes of comparison next.

1. We can differentiate strategies by their effect on the actors, that is, by the extent to which they produce self-empowerment, increased autonomy in self-definition, gains in recognition, maximization of self-actualization, and an increase in resilience or the capability to cope with change. Strategies can also result in improving the character of interactions with others, facilitating collective action, and enhancing security. Negative effects of destigmatization strategies can include low self-esteem, depression, passivity, and the absence of self-acceptance. I expect those to be present when individuals reject their group of origin and important aspects of their self-concept.

2. We can compare the extent to which strategies require strong group identification or maximizing the autonomy and distance of the individual from the group. Strategies that require strong and exclusive identification of the individual to the group may produce a rigidification of group boundaries, as opposed to greater social inclusion.

3. We can compare the degree to which strategies mobilize universalistic or particularistic rhetorics. Some strategies are based on universalistic criteria or supraindividual principles of similarity that are available to all, such as an affirmation of basic human rights. Others are particularistic and imply the inferiority of out-groups instead of appealing to shared supraindividual principles – it is the case for nationalist strategies. This axis speaks to the normative and political implications of strategies for communal life.

4. We can compare whether individuals privilege one type of strategy, or combine several types (for example, by simultaneously claiming common citizenship and common belonging to the human race as bases for equality). We can also compare whether they always favor more confrontational strategies, or switch between more confrontational and more conciliatory ones. Individuals may want to challenge stereotypes and affirm the value of their group under some circumstances, while conforming to dominant culture in others. They may want to "exit" when boundaries are strongly policed and "voice" when they are contestable (to borrow Albert Hirschman's categories).[28]

I provide a few examples of destigmatization strategies, including strategies for establishing equality and for contesting stereotypes, before proposing hypotheses concerning the impact of various types of destigmatization strategies on health. These examples are drawn from interview-based studies I have conducted. Destigmatization strategies often consist in redefining symbolic boundaries between groups – who is us and them. I use the interview setting

[28] Hirschman (1964).

as an experimental context in which I ask respondents to describe to me the taken-for-granted classification system in which they locate themselves. Although this approach does not capture boundary work in natural settings, it is an adequate approach for comparing the broad contours of boundary work of a number of individuals across a range of settings.[29]

Antiracism among Black Working-Class Men

In a previous study, I analyzed the destigmatization strategies of thirty randomly sampled African American blue-collar workers and low-status white-collar workers living in the New York area.[30] This study explored inductively how workers concretely define the boundaries between us and them and draw the lines between the worthy and the less worthy. It is in this context that African American workers were interviewed concerning what they believe made them equal to whites and what made them equal to "people above," that is, to middle- and upper-class people. The study revealed that workers emphasize various moral values as standards of worth (having a strong work ethic, having high moral standards, and being responsible and dependable as providers), and readily use religion as a proxy for moral character.[31] For instance, Abe Lind, a plumber on Long Island, chooses his friends on the basis of whether they "believe in God, to a large extent, [because] that's who they answer to, and they treat people fairly." John Lamb, a recycling technician from Georgia who recently moved to the North, describes his friends in the following terms: "We basically have the same background ... Baptists who have a lot of respect for people, believe in just doing the right thing." By privileging morality and religion as criteria for worth, these workers refuse to measure themselves solely by a socioeconomic yardstick that would put them at the bottom of the racial and class hierarchy. At the same time, they refute the view of their inferiority, at least in their own eyes. Their emotional and cognitive commitment to this alternative yardstick should have repercussions on their well-being, sustain their resilience, and lessen the subjective impact of their relatively low social status.

The African American workers were compared with forty-five white American workers. I contrasted the kinds of evidence both groups used to discuss equality between whites and blacks. I found that blacks used a much wider range of evidence of equality or similarity than whites, perhaps because racism and discrimination forces them to confront the question of their relative equality on a more regular basis than is the case for whites. White workers believed that blacks who make as much money as they do are equal ("if you can buy a house and I can buy I house, we are the same"). They also emphasized the universality of human nature as evidence of equality between racial groups,

---

[29] For more information on this approach, see Lamont (1992).

[30] Lamont (2000).

[31] Along these lines, recent surveys find that blacks embrace religious commitments more than whites (Smith and Seltzer 1992): 30.

and argued that there are good and bad people in all races. In the words of Billy Taylor, a white foreman employed in a cosmetic company, "I could have a problem with you as a black but I could have the same problem if you were white, or green, or yellow, or whatever. People are people. There's good cops, there's bad cops. There's good whites, there's bad whites."[32] Blacks also point to the universality of human nature and the market as an arbitrator of worth to ground racial equality. However, they also point to their status as American citizens, their ability to consume, and their competence at work to demonstrate their equality with whites. A black recycling plant worker for instance says:

Basically it comes down to, once you prove yourself that you're just as good as [your white coworkers] ... that you can do anything they do just as well as them, and you carry yourself with that weight, then people respect you, they kinda back away from you. I'm kind of quiet, I just go there, I don't miss a day on the job, I do what I gotta do, and I'm one of the best throughout the whole plant at what I do.

Black workers also rebut racism by referring to the fact that we are all children of God, have similar human needs (food, sleep), and a common physiology ("we all spend nine months in our mother's womb"). These are universalistic evidence of equality – available to all, independent of level of education, income, or civil status.

Workers' antiracist rhetoric draws on everyday experience – such as the common-sensical view that human nature is universal. It is in stark contrast with that produced in academia, popularized by school curriculum debates, and shared by a number of professionals, that multiculturalism or cultural diversity should be celebrated. This is an argument never used by the workers I interviewed. Perhaps the latter appeal less to workers than to professionals due to their desire to keep the world in moral order and to distinguish clearly the boundaries between what is permissible and normal and what is not.

The African American Elite

Another study concerned the destigmatization strategies of the African American elite.[33] It drew on interviews with ten individuals identified by other elite members as belonging to this highly select group in the mid 1980s.[34] These individuals included the poet Nikki Giovani, the Congresswoman Eleanor Holmes Norton, the civil rights lawyer Julius Chambers, the former U.S. Ambassador to South Africa James Joseph, and Thirman Milner from Hartford, Connecticut, who was the first black mayor of a New England town.[35]

---

[32] See also Lamont and Aksartova (2002).

[33] Lamont and Fleming (2005).

[34] For details, see Jackson, Thoits, and Taylor (1995).

[35] These individuals authorized us to reveal their identity. Interviews were coded thematically by the first author. She systematically looked for counterevidence and used matrix displays (see

Unlike their working-class counterparts, members of the African American elite do not draw on religion to cope with racism – as one of them puts it, he doesn't believe in "praying my way out of discrimination." Instead, elite African Americans emphasize using one's intelligence, competence, and education as the most effective destigmatization strategies. They frequently identify these qualities as their ticket out of social exclusion. This common theme animates the responses of both Congresswoman Norton, who coped with racism by showing that "you can out-do them, you can outlearn them, you can be smarter than them" and of James Joseph, an ambassador, who took to heart his mother's warning that "you have to be twice as smart to get half as good a job." Betty Lou Dodson suggests a similar strategy of competency, saying: "make sure that you know what you're doing ... Knowledge is power ... So you try to learn as much as you can about whatever it is you're doing." Thus, African American workers and elite members use different concepts of equality and have different views concerning how to achieve it.

Black Marketing Executives

A third case concerns African American marketing executives specializing in the African American market. Based on only eight interviews, this study shows that these individuals offer cues and cultural models to blacks about how to achieve full social membership. They believe blacks should use consumption to signal social membership (as citizens, middle-class people, and people of color): through consumption, African Americans transform the meanings attributed to the category "black," enact a positive vision of their distinct cultural identity (for example, as fashionable or proud black people), and affirm their distinctiveness. These marketing experts equate mainstream society with elite society, perhaps because acquiring expensive goods makes social membership undeniable. In their eyes, buying power is a true mark of personal worth and racial equality, as well as a powerful rebuttal to racism. Like elite African Americans who emphasize expertise and knowledge as key to social membership, these marketing specialists provide to most blacks an ambiguous message: that this membership is out of reach for most of them. Their narratives about what grounds equality across ethnoracial groups made no reference to other traits available to all, such as common humanity, shared physiology and needs, shared citizenship, or religion and our shared status as children of god. They do not challenge the class boundaries that define the American class structure. Instead, they reinforce the view that those who can consume are worthy, as they met the standards of cultural membership that prevail in American society. Thus they promote a particularist, instead of a universalist, definition of membership – one where membership is available to all.

Miles and Huberman 1994) to reveal patterns in the use of antiracist arguments. For details, see Lamont (2000: Appendix A).

North African Immigrants in France

A fourth case concerns North African immigrants living in Paris and shows that they mobilize cultural repertoires made available to them by the Muslim tradition in their responses to racism and discrimination. I conducted and analyzed interviews with thirty randomly sampled North African immigrants living in the Paris suburbs.[36] Lamont, Morning, and Mooney analyzed these interviews to understand more finely the destigmatization strategies used by North African immigrants.[37] We found that respondents rebut racism by drawing on their daily experience and on a *particular universalism*, a moral universalism informed by Islam. Even though French political ideology equates Republican universalism with antiracism, North African immigrants refute the notion of their inferiority by culling evidence of universal equality from their daily lives. Like African American workers, they point to traits shared by all human beings, such as common morality, human needs, biology, and destiny. Second, they refer to explicitly particularist and differentialist arguments and to conceptions of moral universalism informed by the Koran to disprove their inferiority in the eyes of the French: they stress that they adopt specific forms of moral conduct including tranquility, following a straight path, altruism toward the poor and the elderly, and rejecting an excess of freedom. They explicitly link these virtues to the five pillars of Islam and to the Koran more generally. This moral universalism is central to what defines a good Muslim and what makes some claim superiority over the French. Grounded in Islam, this moral universalism is in fact particularlist because it is not available to all.

Interviews do not refer to the principles of the Enlightenment and Republicanism, or to the right to difference. These themes are central in elite and popular antiracist rhetoric in France.[38] French civic culture does not appear to have penetrated the immigrant population significantly, as they seem not to have deeply internalized Republican and Enlightenment principles pertaining to the rule of law, human rights, and equality.[39] Undoubtedly, the high rate of illiteracy, the uneasy relationship that immigrants have with the educational system, and strong ethnic enclaves influence which cultural tools immigrants use to rebut racism. Considering which cultural toolkits are made most readily accessible to low-status population is an important complement to the work of psychologists who emphasize in-group comparison and neglect the broader cultural context in which concepts of self-worth are developed.

---

[36] Lamont (2000).

[37] Lamont, Morning, and Mooney (2001).

[38] Lamont (2000).

[39] Note that my respondents are first-generation immigrants and have not undergone socialization in the French educational system. A study of the destigmatization strategies of second-generation blacks living in France reveals a greater centrality of Republicanism and of their French identity and citizenship in this group. See Bickerstaff (2008).

THE IMPACT OF DESTIGMATIZATION STRATEGIES
ON MENTAL HEALTH

With these examples in mind, we can review the existing research on well-being, self-esteem, school success, personal efficacy, and health to generate hypotheses about the kinds of destigmatization strategies that are most likely to mitigate the effect of discrimination and racism on health. I am concerned with their impact on mental and physical health; nevertheless, most of the following examples concern primarily mental health and its correlates – self-esteem, resilience, and efficacy. I discuss the added value of considering meaning and cultural repertoires to the framing of the relevant questions.

But first, a note on measurement: The impact of different destigmatization strategies on mental health can be ascertained by comparing the health status (measured by a depression scale, the clinical global index, or others) of individuals who use various strategies. One could also use scales measuring mastery and self-efficacy – psychosocial coping/buffering factors that have been extensively linked to health and well-being (particularly depression). Or else, one could consider how the mental health status of one individual changes as she adopts different strategies or collect narrative accounts of how individuals perceive the relationship between their response to racism and their health. A more experimental approach could consist in monitoring cardiovascular and other reactions occurring while members of stigmatized groups are reading descriptions of various racist incidents and antiracist strategies.[40]

Negative health outcomes are correlated with numerous factors other than exposure to discrimination (for example, access to health care) and these factors work against establishing a clear causal relationship between destigmatization strategies and improved health. Moreover, the impact of daily hassles that are associated with discrimination may be profound, as these stressors tend to be persistent, chronic, and linked to life-long exposure. Their effect can be spread over the life course, which raises additional challenges.[41] The impact of destigmatization strategies may not be easily reflected in their short-term effect on mental health – especially given that health self-report is also affected by who the reference group is. These challenges should be kept in mind as we consider the relevant social psychological literature and future research agendas. Perhaps what we have learned concerning how to measure parsimoniously the impact of discrimination on health (in the work of Nancy Krieger for instance) can be of help in conceptualizing how to measure the effects of destigmatization strategies.[42] Analytical descriptions may also be particularly useful to capture the effects of cultural repertoires and meaning on resilience and capabilities, and related aspects of mental health.

---

[40] As illustrated by the study by Bennett et al. (2002) of the cardiovascular reactions of African American men to blatant and ambiguous racism.
[41] Hertzman and Power (2004).
[42] See also Yang and Collins (2004) on measuring mental illness stigma.

Social psychologists have produced a variety of findings about what types of racial identification sustain better correlates of mental health and well-being such as self-esteem, personal efficacy, and school success. Studies all suggest that how one relates to one's racial group influences various aspects of well-being. Strong racial identification predicts positive psychosocial and physical health. The more central race is to the self-concept of African Americans, the more positive is their mental health.[43] Thinking positively about one's group also has desirable outcomes: adolescents who are culturally connected to their racial group and think highly of it report the highest level of adjustment.[44] Similarly, Canadian First Nation tribes with the lowest suicide rate are those that keep alive and celebrate their traditional culture; Gérard Bouchard (Chapter 7, in this volume) also suggests this association.[45] Such findings lead us to predict that greater awareness and pride in collective identity and traditions is correlated with better mental health outcomes for a variety of racial and ethnic groups. This pride would act as a buffer when experiencing racism and discrimination and would foster resilience and strengthen capacities to meet life's challenges. To illustrate with the case of North African immigrants living in France: individuals having access to positive collective myths and cultural repertoires celebrating the moral virtues of the group (perhaps through their commitment to Islam) would show greater resilience when experiencing discrimination. Although neglected by social psychologists, there is an added value to considering the cultural toolkits on which destigmatization strategies hinge and that are mobilized by individuals to make sense of the exclusion they face and to respond to it.

Social psychologists also show that higher academic self-concept and achievement among African American adolescents is found among those who have a racial-ethnic self-schema that emphasizes that one is a member of both an in-group and the larger society, or a member of an in-group that must fight to overcome obstacles to attain larger societal resources.[46] Students who

---

[43] Sellers et al. (2003) measure racial identity using a centrality scale and a public regard scale: "The revised centrality scale consists of three items assessing the extent to which race was an important part of how respondents defined themselves. Sample items include, 'Being black is a major part of my identity,' and 'I feel close to other black people.' The revised public regard scale consists of two items assessing the individual's perceptions of how positively or negatively other groups view blacks. The items were, 'In general, other groups view blacks in a positive manner,' and 'Blacks are considered to be good by society.'" (pp. 306 and 311). Caldwell et al. (2002: 1325). On collective self-esteem scale, see Luhtanen and Crocker (1992) and Crocker et al. (1994). For their part, Williams and Harris-Reid (1999) find only relatively weak effects of ingroup identification with mental health.

[44] Chatman et al. (2001). Also, Sellers et al. (2003) show the impact of (positive) "private regard" for one's racial group on health outcomes. Feliciano (2005) also finds that children of immigrants who have not abandoned their immigrant ethnic culture have the greatest educational success, which is correlated with well-being.

[45] Chandler et al. (2003).

[46] Wong, Eccles, and Sameroff (2003); Shelton et al. 2005. See Noh et al. (1999) for contradictory results.

succeed the least do not have racial-ethnic self-schemas. Alternatively, they only have in-group self-schemas and the latter do not connect to the larger society.[47] Comparable conclusions can be drawn from Prudence Carter's research that compares low-income African American and Latino students in a multiracial high school. She finds that those who succeed best are cultural "straddlers" who master the cultural capital most valued by teachers, as well as the forms of nondominant cultural capital valued by the students.[48] Their biculturalism allows them to do well in two competing status hierarchies. Applied to the case of African American workers, these results suggest that individuals who have a strong sense of group identity *and* are well-integrated in American mainstream culture are most resilient and most empowered to claim social membership. Individuals who are less aware of and proud of their collective identity may be less in touch with common cultural reper-toires of resistance on which they could draw to make claims. And indeed, Mario Small's study of community participation across various generations of residents of public housing project serving a Latino population in Boston supports these conclusions.[49] This study shows the importance of intergener-ational exposure to collective frames for explaining differences in degrees of collective involvement – the very type of collective meanings that are beyond the disciplinary toolkit mobilized by social psychologists.

Complementary results concern more exclusively the impact of awareness of racism and discrimination on mental health. Both denial of racism and acceptance of the notion of white superiority are inversely related to health.[50] Students who are aware of the existence of racial discrimination are better protected against its effects.[51] Children who are made aware of racial barriers and socialized to be proactive toward blocked opportunities have a greater sense of personal efficacy than those who are not – and we know that self-mastery has been extensively linked to well-being (particularly depression).[52] If being aware of racism and of discrimination has a positive impact on health outcome, it is likely that being familiar with the historical struggle of one's group against exclusion also contributes to resilience. Exposure to such narra-tives may have an effect that goes beyond the simple awareness of discrimina-tion that is of concern to social psychologists.[53]

---

[47] Oysterman et al. (2003).
[48] Carter (2005).
[49] Small (2004).
[50] Jackson et al. (1996).
[51] Sellers et al. (2003).
[52] Bowman and Howard (1985): 139.
[53] Neighbors and Jackson (1996: Chapter 8). Neighbors et al. (1996). According to Schnittker and McLeod (2005), "Discrimination has stronger effects on physical health among persons with self-blaming rather than system-blaming attributional styles, and among those who accept dis-crimination rather than challenge it." Based on data from African American college-age men of high socioeconomic status, the literature on "John Henryism" also suggests that "a strong behavioral predisposition to directly confront barriers to upward mobility" is associated with positive health outcomes (see Bonham, Sellers, and Neighbors 2004).

In another direction, the work of Jennifer Crocker and colleagues shows that people whose self-worth is contingent on God's love have better well-being outcomes than those whose self-worth is contingent on other criteria such as appearance and academic achievement.[54] This research suggests the importance of looking closely at the effect of various destigmatization strategies on mental health, and at whether these strategies are universally available.

Another example of the role of cultural repertoires in sustaining group identification and destigmatization strategies comes from my previous work, which showed that compared with middle class people, working-class people mobilized criteria based on moral character and solidarity rather than money and education in their evaluation of what defines a worthy person, so as to value more highly their own positions.[55] This is more the case among French workers than among American workers, in part because Catholicism, Republicanism, and socialism make repertoires of social solidarity more readily available to workers in France than in the Untied States.[56] Such cultural repertoires facilitate, or are conditions for, lower-status groups to develop feelings of self-worth despite being lower in a status hierarchy. I hypothesize that this ability to develop a sense of self-worth somewhat autonomously from the dominant matrixes plays an important role in sustaining resilience, individual self-efficacy, and the ability to react collectively to challenges, which in turn would affect mental health.

All societies do not make the cultural tools necessary to sustain alternative matrixes equally available. The nationalist movements in Québec, Brittany, and Scotland provided well-defined repertoires for collective affirmations. In contrast, the ubiquitous celebration of economic success in American society may facilitate individualistic destigmatization strategies for better endowed individuals but may lead to passivity and withdrawal for those who are less well-endowed. The former may respond to the stigmatization of their identity not by attempting to change the meaning associated with their group, but by trying to improve their own position within a given hierarchy, perhaps while drawing on narratives of upward mobility, passing, forgiveness, and reconciliation. It is notable that American workers have a greater sense of personal distress than their counterparts in countries such as Japan and Poland; however, professionals have higher self-esteem in the United States.[57] Considering the relative availability of different cultural schemas concerning empowerment could help us make sense of the health gradient, but also of the fact that among the advanced industrial societies, the association between GNP, well-being, and health is nonlinear. Societies that allow for the coexistence of various matrices for defining worthy or meaningful lives could very well be the most successful if success is defined in terms of health outcomes.

[54] Sargent, Crocker, and Luhtanen (2006).
[55] Lamont (2000).
[56] Lamont and Thévenot (2000).
[57] Kohn (1987); Kohn et al (1990).

THE FUTURE AGENDA

Social epidemiologists have been studying the effect of various ecological elements on the health/inequality nexus. They have given particular attention to range of mechanisms and factors such as social cohesion and integration, networks, residential segregation, and income inequality. They have also spent considerable energy exploring how relative status, as opposed to absolute status, affects psychosocial orientations and their impact on health.[58] But contexts have material, social structural, and sociopsychological components, as well as cultural components.[59]

The task at hand has been to add specificity and parsimoniousness to our understanding of how cultural templates influence the health gradient, and to explore how various cultural and noncultural (for example, psychosocial) factors interact with one another. Earlier treatment of cultural explanations of health outcomes concentrated on cross-cultural or cross-national differences, rather than analyzing the supply side of ideas and how they vary across national contexts.[60] This literature presumes that to each nation correspond cultural differences that can explain cross-national differences. This essentialist approach, akin to the old national character argument, has been widely criticized and rejected in favor of an approach that considers the relationship between space and cultural similarities an empirical issue, as opposed to simply describing certain countries as more materialistic or solidaristic.[61]

More recently, epidemiologists have also drawn on broader sociological theory and on the work of Pierre Bourdieu in particular, to consider the effect of lifestyle and habitus on health. These approaches are more attuned to recent developments in cultural sociology, but they generally also ignore the role of

---

[58] House (2001); Marmot (2004).

[59] Epidemiologists often operationalize context as including the following: psychosocial factors (social capital), behavioral factors (for example, tobacco use, physical activity), public health (assessment, policy development, and funding of programs), access to health care services, housing, environmental factors (for example, hazardous waste), political factors (for example, community political participation), education (related to socioeconomic status), and employment (including employment opportunities); see for instance Hillemeier et al. (2003). For Ashmore, Deaux, and McLaughlin-Volpe, contexts are "the general and continuing multi-layered and interwoven set of material realities, social structures, patterns of social relations, and shared belief systems that surround any given situation" (2004: 103).

[60] See footnote 19 in this chapter. That the epidemiological literature so readily draws parallels between the behavior of rhesus monkey and that of humans raises issues concerning the rather minimalist causal role it gives to culture as an intervening dimension. The position of George Davey Smith (2003) is illustrative of broader trends in the field. He suggests that the impact of psychosocial factors is mediated by long-term exposure to domination over the life course, which leads to the embodiment of discrimination. A comprehensive view of the literature on inequality strongly suggests that structural/material domination goes hand in hand with cultural/semiotic subordination (in Bourdieu 1984, for instance). For a review, see Lamont and Small (2008).

[61] For instance, Corin (1994); for a critique of these assumptions, see Gupta and Ferguson (1992) and Lamont and Thévenot (2000).

cultural repertoires in empowering and constraining various types of responses to discrimination and racism. By using the analytical tools developed by recent scholarship – concepts such as cultural structures, schemas, and repertoires, symbolic boundaries, and scripts of personhood – it is possible to analyze the relative availability of cultural schemas across environments.[62] Although much work remains to be done to fully develop the theoretical implications of this line of thinking, this chapter has outlined some of the analytical groundwork needed to elaborate an explanation that would include cultural repertoires, and consider their interactions with structural, psychosocial, institutional, and biological explanations of health outcomes.

Cultural structures – whether scripts, narratives, frames, repertoires, or identities – are intermediary between the social psychological processes and the health outcomes that have attracted the attention of social epidemiologists. Broader cultural templates having to do with injustice, definitions of a good life, and how status correlates with worth, are likely to influence the effect of discrimination on health. Whether stigmatized groups react to racism by fighting or exiting, and whether and how they identify with their group, is influenced by the cultural repertoires they have access to. And various strategies will have different effects on actors – empowering them, buffering them from the wear and tear of everyday life, or else, weakening their resolve, their self-efficacy, and sense of entitlement. These are precisely the questions that are not considered by psychologists concerned with well-being.

This chapter has framed questions and provided analytical tools and means for answering them. The next stage will be to develop a more systematic empirical program to tackle these questions, building on some of the hypotheses developed here. We need to be more empirically specific concerning what kind of social context facilitates or hinders the contestation of dominant frameworks – through its imaginaries, boundaries, institutions, and so forth. Societies that allow for the coexistence of various matrices for measuring meaningful lives are those that are most inclusive, and in part, most successful.

More generally, it will be important to carry out a systematic comparison of the destigmatization strategies of groups located in various national contexts

---

[62] For a review of conceptual tools for cultural analysis, see Lamont and Small (2008). Different national settings can present group boundary patterns that are organized around various dimensions, with religious, linguistic, or ethnoracial components being more or less salient in structuring conflict and political mobilization. The salience of these dimensions is sustained by structural factors as well as by the social representation of groups and by identificatory dynamics. Thus, in the United States, strong class boundaries separating the poor from others overlap with strong racial boundaries separating blacks from nonblacks (Gans 1999), which also translate into clear patterns of residential segregation across racial groups and into low rates of intermarriage (Kalmijn 1991; Lamont 2000; Pattillo 2005). At the symbolic level, whites and blacks experience strong group identification and group categorization (McDermott and Samson 2005) and have different patterns of religious affiliation (Emerson and Smith 2000). They also display differentiated patterns of cultural practices and tastes. See Lamont and Bail (2005).

and to compare how strategies vary with the porosity of the boundaries that separate superordinate and subordinate groups across societies. In particular, one should consider how variations in the *range* and *salience* of evidence (or criteria such as race, class, status, or moral character) are used by stigmatized groups in different contexts to establish their value in relation to that of dominant majority groups. By "range," I mean the number and diversity of such criteria. By "salience," I mean the extent to which individuals are using given criteria when comparing groups (whether they are present at all, and how much they are present compared to other criteria). Based on the comparisons of white and African American, and white and North African workers (described above), it appears that range and salience vary according to the strength of ethnoracial boundaries low-status groups face: the more group members perceive discrimination, the more they are likely to draw on a wider range of evidence to demonstrate their equality and to combat the daily indignity of misrecognition.

It should be noted that not all destigmatization strategies lead to greater inclusion. Indeed, effective strategies may include affirming the cultural distinctiveness of a group, limiting intergroup interactions (for example, intermarriage), and defending the institutions that are essential for its survival – hospitals and schools that serve populations in their native language for instance, as in the case of Canadian francophones living outside Quebec. In such a case, the strengthening of group boundaries may lead to empowerment, but perhaps also to isolation and ghettoization if the group is not sufficiently engaged with mainstream culture – if it lacks in cosmopolitanism. Reaching a balance between self-affirmation and engagement with the out-group may be crucial to attenuating the impact of discrimination on health outcomes.

7

Collective Imaginaries and Population Health

How Health Data Can Highlight Cultural History

Gérard Bouchard

This chapter on health, society, and culture in Québec has its own story, which is worth telling as a way of a summary. At the outset, my goal was to elicit how culture (particularly collective imaginary broadly construed as a package of values, beliefs, and ideals wrapped up in myths – see discussion later) can at least indirectly impact population health. Accordingly, I engaged in an attempt to recreate the cultural trend of Québec society between 1850 and 1960 with a view to comparing it with the health pattern (as mirrored in mortality rates). Soon, this endeavour came across two major obstacles. First, historians strongly disagree on the interpretation of Québec's cultural past. I had to choose between two diametrically opposed theses or paradigms (I will call them "Survival" and "Modernist"), a choice I was unwilling to make on the basis of the available evidence. Second, as we shall see, both theses fail to fully account for the shape of the health trend during the period.

In the face of the first puzzle, I finally decided to reverse my approach and to use the sociocultural/health framework backward: rather than traveling the interaction chain from culture to health, as was initially intended, I simply used the health record as a landmark from which I could make inferences about the sociocultural trend. This decision was based on the assumption that the sociocultural/health framework is robust enough so that the health data during the period should provide useful hints about the sociocultural dynamics at work. This about-face led me to go well beyond the two conflicting paradigms and to develop a third historiographical pathway promoting what I call an "integrative" or "synthesis" paradigm. As for the second hurdle, it led me to rethink the complex relationship between culture and the social dynamics

I express my thanks to Peter Hall, Michèle Lamont, and the other members of the CIFAR Successful Societies Group for their valuable comments on earlier versions of this chapter. I am also grateful to Paul-André Linteau who has helped to improve this chapter in various ways. Finally, I acknowledge the kind support of Robert Bourbeau and his team at the department of demography of the Université de Montréal.

broadly construed. Finally, on both counts, the understanding of the health/ culture relationship somehow benefits from the analysis.

As it is now, this chapter can be seen as a journey into the web of interactions between sociocultural factors and health, against a controversial historical backdrop. Three points emerge from this investigation: (1) the study of the collective imaginary, as advocated here, provides valuable although incomplete insight into the deep cultural dynamics of a society; (2) even though the collective imaginary undoubtedly affects the well-being (including health) of a population, the extent of its impact and the way it is played out remain somewhat unpredictable and difficult to pinpoint; and (3) health data can substantially contribute to better understand sociocultural dynamics and to advance the historiographical reflection.

A number of recent studies have compellingly established a causal relationship between social variables and population health.[1] In this regard, scholars agree to single out factors and processes like social participation or any form of inclusion ("bowling together"), a sense of security, autonomy, and control (which involves a capacity for action and interaction), a strong identity. Yet, from there, one immediately suspects the underlying role of culture. Self-esteem, self-reliance, and recognition feed into autonomy. Deep-rooted motivation based on values and ideals is conducive to strength, undertaking, and achievement. A sense of belonging and shared perceptions is a prerequisite for social trust, solidarity, and connectedness, whereas a coherent worldview and vibrant traditions are associated with all these factors. Likewise, ethnicity, race, language, and religion are known to be related to risks of disease and premature death.[2] At the individual level, intensity of purpose, meaning, and hope has been associated with healthy psychological and biological development.[3] Conversely, being denigrated and stereotyped, feeling a sense of worthlessness and despondency, or lacking a direction in one's life can alter mental and physical health. Therefore, insofar as any social fabric needs symbolic foundations, it follows that a concern for population health might also involve some consideration for collective imaginaries. Quite significantly, in their study on social conditions of health, Berkman et al. have included values and norms among the major determinants.[4]

In Russia, the dramatic rise of the mortality rate and ill-health after the 1960s has been linked to the waning of old national myths (celebrating acceptance and suffering) that eroded the authority of the State and of other institutions and created a context of uncertainty, depression, and anomie.[5] In the

---

[1] For appropriate references, see the introduction, and chapters by Hertzman (Chapter 1), Keating (Chapter 2), and Lamont (Chapter 6).

[2] In their analysis of infant mortality in the city of Ottawa for the year 1901, Mercier and Boone (2002: 98) conclude that these cultural factors were the stronger predictors of infant deaths.

[3] As shown in Chapter 2 in this volume by Daniel P. Keating.

[4] Berkman et al. (2000).

[5] Eberstadt (1981).

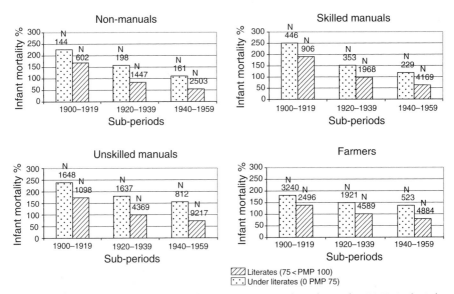

FIGURE 7.1. Infant mortality and literacy (measure based on the PMP index) by occupational groupings – Saguenay, 1900–59. N = number of individuals involved.
Source: The calculations are based on 381,915 birth, marriage, and death records from the BALSAC Population Register.

opposite direction, our colleague Peter Evans, in Chapter 4, underlines the role of the collective imaginary as an important dimension to the remarkable performance of the Kerala State in India as well as the Ceara State in Northeast Brazil with regard to health-plus. Finally, numerous studies have shown a close relationship between level of literacy and mortality rates, namely infant mortality (see Figure 7.1 for an example related to a region of northeastern Québec). In short, one could say that in many ways culture impacts the individual and collective capacity to cope with and adapt to a hostile environment conducive to morbidity (through deprivation, dependency, stress, and other factors).[6]

In the light of this assumption that somehow culture is linked and potentially instrumental (or detrimental) to health, this chapter will cautiously venture in a mostly uncharted territory by examining the case of Québec society and culture during the period 1850–1960. And, from now on, in order to stress the specific role of culture within or beyond the social (depending on whether the latter is defined in a broad or in a restricted way), I will use the expression "sociocultural/health framework."[7]

[6] For other relevant references and comments, see the introduction of this book by Peter Hall and Michèle Lamont.
[7] In this regard, sociology as well as social history conveys an old ambivalence. In some cases, the notion of social is broadly construed and refers to all aspects of collective life, all kinds of

COLLECTIVE IMAGINARY AS ARTICULATION OF REASON
AND MYTH

Insofar as values, ideals, and beliefs (or myths) matter for a society to function, it makes sense to look into the prevailing symbolic framework produced and reproduced by the prominent intellectuals (novelists, poets, playwrights, social scientists, historians, philosophers, theologians, priests, filmmakers, and other artists) to highlight part of the social praxis and its various correlates (among them: the health trend). After all, collective imaginaries can be seen as being located near the beginning of the cultural chain that leads to individuals' perceptions, motivations, and identity. Since I intend to capture the cultural dynamics through the study of collective imaginary, it is in order to describe first the approach that I have developed in my research.

By this concept of collective imaginary, I refer to the representations through which a society provides its members with a definition of selfhood and otherness, a vision of their past and their future, as well as a territorial appropriation. The prime function of intellectuals is to elaborate these symbolic configurations. Altogether, they set forth ideas that are parts of systems of thought. By and large, these systems can be understood as heterogeneous and sometimes unlikely combinations or alliances of reason and myth. At the outset, I posit that all attempts to frame a political thought or simply to account for collective reality – past and present – are faced with dichotomies leading to contradictions between competing principles or conflicting requirements such as freedom/equality, localism/universalism, historical determinism/ voluntary human action, individual/community, idealism/pragmatism, and elites/popular classes. The function of myth is precisely to act as a mediating mechanism and to allow reason to, one way or another, overcome these contradictions. Myth does that by inserting a third component that makes the original dichotomy look like and function not as an inescapable opposition but as a functional leverage, which also becomes a source of dynamism or energy. Therefore, myth appears to be a central feature of any structure of thought, whatever its origin or form (folk tale, philosophical system, scientific theory, literature, political discourse, or day-to-day identification strategies).

The kind of configurations reason works out and the extent to which they prove to be successful make room for a first typology:

1. Reason[8] can achieve cohesion by just suppressing one term of the contradiction (Soviet dictatorship officially sacrificed freedom for equality; in the Jacobin France, equality took precedence over diversity and

---

relationships in which individuals are involved, all instances – material or symbolic – which seem to operate beyond them. According to a more restricted meaning, the social mostly relates to status and stratification, the uneven distribution of wealth, prestige, and power, or the relationships which link individuals to each other.

8 The concept simply refers to the basic operations of the intellect in its most formal endeavour meant to both bring out and establish cohesion in the universe.

citizenship abolished ethnicity; all fascisms gave preference to the nation over the individual for the sake of moral purity). This is the *radical* thought.[9]

2. Reason can tolerate and try to accommodate contradiction by creating a positive tension as well as a source of dynamism and achievement. For instance, the powerful myth of the American dream, combined with a deep sense of individual responsibility, tends to conceal or to make acceptable the acute social inequalities that violate a foundational idea of the United States. This is the *organic* thought – organic in that it is flexible, constantly moving, renegotiating the relationships between its conflicting components. Its major propriety is to increase the global collective efficacy, namely by dampening the divisive forces and channelling potential collective discontent into accomplishment attitudes.

3. Finally, it may happen that reason fails to articulate contradictions when, for whatever reason, the myths that are activated prove to be ineffective. Then, the resulting system of thought, rather than enabling or empowering individuals and groups, instills uncertainty, self-doubt, stagnation, even inhibition. Good examples of the latter can be found in the history of Ireland, Peru, and Québec prior to the middle of the twentieth century, as well as, predictably, in any society which has experienced a long period of lethargy or unsuccessful endeavours. This is the *equivocal* or *fragmentary* thought, plagued by open, unarticulated contradictions, incompatible propositions, and inefficient myths.

Along with this first typology, another emerges based on the kind of myths called on to overcome contradictions. Myths can be projecting, predisposing to action, invention, change, or risk-taking. They can also be depressing, inclining to just the contrary. From this, one understands that myth is not addressed here from the standpoint of veracity (true/false) but as a symbolic device, which proves more or less effective in securing adhesion and mobilizing people toward a common goal beyond contradictions.

Against this backdrop, myth should not be primarily understood as a gross, pernicious, deliberately falsified rendition of reality, although it sometimes – if not often – happens to be just so. According to my approach, the universal essence of myth is a representation or a set of representations that carry and promote in a durable way meanings, values, beliefs, and ideals, which are embodied in historical events, individuals, places, or objects. It is in the nature of myth to always combine, in various degrees, an empirical and a fictional component. Yet, again, its efficiency is mostly contingent upon the appeal that, as a symbolic device, it exerts on both imagination and reason. At its apex, a myth may owe more to fiction than to empirical reality. It then enjoys a wide consensus and acquires a taboo-like status. As a result, any

---

[9] One can see that the radical thought may feed into authentic democratic regimes as well as into the opposites.

criticism leveled against it is likely to be rejected as iconoclastic, unethical, even preposterous.[10]

Therefore, it is fairly safe to say that myth acts as an indispensable and universal device of any social life – there is no such thing as a myth-free or a myth-less society (to pretend to the contrary would be another myth). As a collective mechanism, myth matters because, in ordinary circumstances, it fulfills vital societal functions. It creates bonds between groups, communities, cultures, genders, and races. It alleviates lines of conflict. It moves a society forward by reducing the anguish that individuals may experience when looking toward their past or their future. And it holds a nation together in times of crisis. Myth is everywhere, and not only in the so-called primitive tribes (as the Levi-Strauss[11] approach would wrongly suggest). Yet, societies vary greatly with respect to the nature, structure, and efficiency of their myths, and to their capacity to overhaul them when they become obsolete or detrimental.

Such a definition of myth also carries a strong concern for its social correlates in at least two directions. Upstream: the context, the social relationships and the power struggle, which condition its emergence and promotion. Downstream: the extent to which it succeeds in penetrating institutions, shaping individuals' and groups' perceptions, identity, and behaviors, and pushing collective action in one particular direction. The assumed linkage with the determinants of population health[12] rests on this downstream side.

In order to qualify these comprehensive symbolic configurations that I call collective imaginary, various scholars have used the word "narrative." I prefer to restrict this concept to its literal meaning: the narration of an event or any feature that belongs to the past. Only in a metaphorical and quite arbitrary way, it has come to designate a fictional account, a collective representation, an identity, a discourse, an ideology, a belief, a myth. Because of these extensions, the concept has become overloaded. So, collective imaginaries include narratives, but they are much more than that. Conversely, I reject the concept of *social* imaginary because it is too limited – as well as potentially confusing. Quite often, it relates to the representation of social facts, processes, or mechanisms, excluding other major components of collective imaginary such as memory, utopias, territorial perceptions, archetypes, discursive strategies, and so forth.[13] Besides, as I just said, the analysis of imaginaries requires us to

---

[10] Admittedly, this is a broad definition of myth and I think it has to be so. The concept is intended to capture a quite polymorphic reality. It must also testify to the wide range of a type of thought generally – and wrongly – restricted to the so-called primitive or archaic societies. Reason has been over-celebrated by the Enlightenment and some deconstruction is in order. Besides, I can't think of any other concept in social sciences which fits the definition provided above.

[11] Levi-Strauss (1958).

[12] A more detailed discussion of what precedes can be found in Bouchard (2003b).

[13] Castoriadis (1987) uses the concept of social imaginary, but in a quite different way, to underline the agency of human beings whose autonomy is demonstrated by their capacity to define their destiny and to act accordingly. In this perspective, the social imaginary becomes a

investigate their social grounding (both upstream and downstream), hence the necessity to preserve the distinction between the symbolic and the social.

For some scholars, social imaginary does not extend to the whole of a society or a culture, which makes the concept even more problematic. This is the case, for instance, with the philosopher C. Taylor for whom social imaginary excludes the ideas, doctrines, worldviews, and theories produced by the learned culture, unless they become widespread among the whole population and infiltrate its culture.[14] Whereas intellectuals' minds are said to be fed with formalized, articulate ideas, "ordinary people" deal with legends, stories, myths, and the like. Obviously, this conception creates a hierarchy between collective representations on the basis of their social background, in such a way that some are assumed to be "imagined" while others are not. From both a methodological and a theoretical standpoint, this kind of normative pronouncement, which grants a strange privilege to the learned culture is difficult to justify. Sophisticated products of intellectuals are certainly different from contents of popular culture; however, the former are no less discursive strategies ultimately based on beliefs, values, and myths; they are simply wrapped up in a different, more elaborate discursive apparatus.

Finally, collective imaginaries should not be confused with identity, although they provide the symbolic contents from which the latter is built. Collective imaginaries belong to the sphere of discourse made available by intellectuals, whereas identity refers to representations once internalized and re-processed by individuals or social groups.

My approach to collective imaginary partly proceeds from a criticism of a well-known Western dogma establishing reason (*logos*) as a self-sufficient mechanism, as the only legitimate way to build rigorous and dependable bodies of knowledge and thought, at the expense of myth. Since the nineteenth century, however, major thinkers have begun to seriously question this a priori.[15] I want to join this growing tradition of thought that somewhat paradoxically asserts that rationality can be viewed as one of the most powerful myths of the Western civilization: the (never demonstrated) general belief that, through reason, every question can be answered, every problem can be solved. Actually, behind the operations of reason, myth is always active – including in science where it provides the very foundations of paradigms. In other words, the *muthos*, which had been generally condemned and chastised in the Greek philosophical tradition, is making a comeback. This invites us to take a fresh look at its relationship with the *logos* (I will shortly report on the research I have conducted on the Québec cultural past, following these guidelines).

---

blueprint for social change through reform or revolution. As one can see, there is a programmatic, almost normative dimension to this definition.

[14] Taylor (2002: 91–2; 105–7).

[15] Among the most prominent, one thinks of Hegel, Schopenhauer, Nietzsche, Freud, Jung, Berlin, Adorno, and all the Frankfurt School.

THE SOCIOCULTURAL/HEALTH FRAMEWORK ENCAPSULATED:
IDENTITY DEPRIVATION AND PHYSICAL DISORDERS AMONG
QUÉBEC INDIANS

For the sake of the overall argument, I shall begin with a story I collected in the course of my research on Indian (Innus) communities living in northeastern Québec. It seems appropriate to report this story at length because it so perfectly exemplifies at a small scale the whole approach that I am trying to implement at the larger scale of Québec society. It is the personal account of a leader of an Indian reservation in Québec, as he told it to me a few years ago. I find his story all the more meaningful because, since then, I have been able to collect a number of similar stories:[16]

My grandfather and my father were hunters. I was born during the winter in the territories, like most of my brothers and sisters. Every year, in the first part of my life, I used to accompany my family to the woods. When I grew older though, I had to stay in the Reservation to attend school. I was strongly motivated, I wanted to be the first Indian here to get a university degree: it was my dream. And, finally, after years of hard work and painful experiences, that's exactly what I did. I graduated in management with quite good marks. My family was very proud of me and I was quite proud as well of my accomplishment. Eager to make a career, I applied for a number of jobs in my field but, to my great surprise and despair, I was unable to get any. I found nobody willing to give me a chance. This was my first real encounter with racism, and a very brutal one. I felt that a very basic human rule had been violated, and my life itself was shattered. At that time, I had gotten married and had children. I felt a lot of shame when I had to come back to my community, unemployed and unable to support my wife and kids. How was I going to explain my failure to my family, relatives, and friends? My own wife was in shock. All of them, they were so disappointed. Sure, they were kind enough to try very hard to conceal their feelings; but I knew too well.

The next part of my story is really sad. I started drinking, went from unskilled, low-paid jobs to unemployment to low-paid jobs again. I did not recover from my disappointment, my sense of failure, and the guilt that came with it. I got depressed, turned to drugs, was sent to detoxication a few times, to no avail. I had lost my appetite, I was suffering from insomnia, I developed strange ailments and did not even bother to get treated. Along the way, I separated from my wife and my children, and kept going from bad to worse. I was riding straight and fast down the road to suicide.

That's when my grandfather came in. It was at the end of the summer, twenty years ago. I remember this day as though it was yesterday. September used to be the beginning of the hunting season, when all my family and relatives gathered and went back to the ancestral territory to live the only life they knew and liked, as did their forebears for centuries, if not thousands of years. I had long been cut from all that. At that time, my grandfather had himself relinquished hunting because he was too old, but on that day of September, he said to me: "That's enough, I am taking you with me to the woods." I was surprised; he really seemed to care for me, so I went along. Besides, what did I have to lose? [I should mention that at this point of his narration, the man was crying like a child and he did so until he was finished with his story.]

---

[16] I could not record the interview. What follows is a reconstitution from my very detailed notes taken during and immediately after the fact.

In retrospect, it is easy now to understand what he has done for me. Just the simplest things. What is amazing is that he did it, all those right things, instinctively. First, we drove and walked for a few days (it was really tough for me, I was out of shape, out of breath) and we reached the old family hunting place. Then, he just showed me where we used to camp, where I was born, where he taught me as a kid how to capture squirrels and how to fish, where I used to play with my brothers and sisters. He showed me the place where other families would join us at Christmas to pray and to celebrate and to exchange gifts. He took me to a brook where he said I sure would have drowned had my mother not saved me. All those things that I had forgotten.

He was giving me back a sense of place, of a territory, I was re-discovering my roots, my identity, my past. He reinserted me into a history through my family tree, into a community of belonging, and the strongest one: blood-based. And then, the miracle occurred. Suddenly, I was no longer from nowhere, I was no longer a nobody drifting through empty time and place. I was someone, I was me again.

After a few weeks, we came back from the woods and, from then on, I never drank and never took drugs again. And all my ailments progressively disappeared. Later on, I went back to school, took another craft, and pledged to devote all my life to helping people from my community who where living through the same nightmare as I had. And I went back to my wife and my children. Now, my life has a purpose and I feel very lucky. Because, what I have experienced, sir, is worse than being whipped.

From the point of view of this chapter, the relevance of this informant's experience is obvious. Through part of his life, this remarkable man had traveled both ways on the sociocultural/health pathway: first, losing his symbolic landmarks, and then, almost miraculously recovering them. His story highlights, concisely and at the individual level, every aspect of the complex dynamics involving the socio-cultural determinants of disease. However, since his testimony is extracted from an incomplete research, I cannot extend this analysis here. I only thought this extract would fit in because, somehow, it epitomizes the issue that I intend to tackle at a much broader scale and over a longer time period. I will only add that this case, along with many others, have led to the implementation, in native communities, of formalized therapy programs reproducing the pattern that the old hunter had devised for his despondent grandson: return to the woods, rediscovery of roots, reinsertion into a territory and a community (real and symbolic), recreation of a belonging, reacculturation to old traditions, rituals, and ways of life, and finally, experience of pride and self-esteem.

Turning now to the Québec society between 1850 and 1960, I am obviously engaging in a much more difficult endeavor since, to my knowledge, nobody has ever attempted to establish a macro scale linkage between (1) cultural or symbolic mechanisms and processes and (2) population health. This involves testing the sociocultural/health framework by relying on older, longer term historical data. These data may be incomplete and include distorted information, with some blanks, and a set of suspected associated factors (values, myths, symbols, beliefs), which hardly lend themselves to quantification. My analysis may include a good deal of estimation and – presumably – more distortions. However, as I have discovered very early, the major difficulty in confronting cultural and health trends lies in the fact that, even though it is possible to build virtually undisputable evidence for the latter, the case is much more complex for the former. Indeed, it happens that the interpretation of Québec cultural past for the period 1850–1960 is highly controversial, most historians being divided, as I said, between two conflicting schemes. Which one is to be retained?

Another obstacle comes from the fact that it is very difficult (1) to determine how a given symbolic content (a value, an ideal, or a myth) set forth by a group of intellectuals works its way through the sociocultural web to finally reach the individuals in their daily life and (2) to estimate the extent of its impact on the day-to-day behaviors. In other words, through what pathways does collective imaginary relate to well-being and ultimately affect health? Finally, needless to say, I must also renounce causality analysis and settle for plausibility based on logical inference and coincidental evidence. Notwithstanding these major snags and limitations, I thought that the challenge was worth an attempt.

QUÉBEC: ONE PAST, TWO NARRATIVES (IN SEARCH OF A CULTURAL TREND)

I have alluded to conflicting interpretations of Québec's cultural past among historians and other social scientists. This is the first hurdle with regard to analyzing Québec's sociocultural history between 1850 and 1960. In keeping with an old and robust intellectual tradition, this period has been widely characterized as the time of "survival." From the 1960s onward, however, another interpretive framework has emerged that I will call here Modernist. These two encompassing narratives radically differ in their account of cultural and social change in Québec, which raises the question: which one must be taken as the right or the best framework of reference for the sociocultural/health analysis? I offer a very brief presentation of these two narratives, thus sacrificing many nuances and variants.

The Survival Thesis

The Survival thesis (or paradigm) has for a long time enjoyed a wide consensus and it is still very much alive in Québec (in the public in general, as well as in the media and in major parts of the social sciences, but less and less among the professional historians) and outside Québec. According to this view, the change of colonial regime (from France to Great Britain) that took place in 1760 after the British military victory on the Plaines d'Abraham in Québec City was a catastrophe and, one could say, the founding event of contemporary Québec. The "Conquest," as it was going to be and is still known, is blamed for having broken a dynamic, healthy (some say normal) historical course. Besides, the British rule immediately appeared to threaten the existing culture and institutions (language, religion, schools, judiciary system) of New France. From then on, Canadian Francophones entered an era characterized by a fear of disappearing, a great uncertainty about their present and future, not to mention a second-class status in the new Canadian society.

This deep feeling sparked a social and political movement – the *Patriotes* – which, from the beginning of the nineteenth century and for three decades, advocated decolonization, political sovereignty, and republican democracy mostly inspired by the American model. The movement, however, was crushed in 1837–8 by the Imperial army when it culminated in an insurrection. To many, this major setback marks the second watershed in Québec history, in that the military defeat, coming after the Conquest of 1760, persuaded the larger part of the Francophone elites that they must come to terms with the British rule and give up their political dream of a decolonized, sovereign State.

Soon, following through, a new generation took over and promoted a vision of Québec's future in terms of conservatism, past-oriented attitudes, and nostalgia of the Golden Age of New France.[17] Somehow, the new motto was: brace for the past and forget the future. It also meant that French Canadians[18] would relinquish their hope for a political emancipation and settle for a cultural survival through traditions, language, religion, memory, literature, and the arts, under the spiritual leadership of the Catholic Church. As the thesis goes, they were forging the dream of a great collective destiny as a free, modern nation-State. They also made it a duty to replicate, even in a slavish way, the culture of France along with its norms, models, and so forth. They were a very fragile people with an uncertain future, and, in every matter, they took a self-protective attitude. The fight for the nationality – that is to say, ethnicity – became an everyday battle that took precedence over almost everything else on the collective agenda.[19]

A defensive, subdued mood settled in the conquered society. A widespread discourse promoted by the Church and its allies among the petite-bourgeoisie taught that French Canadians should obey the designs of Providence. They had to accept the British domination, to come to terms with the fact that their minds (*mentalité*) were more suited for spiritual rather than material matters, and to behave accordingly – which meant: to leave the leadership of industry and finance to the Anglophones, to concentrate on farming and craftsmanship, to avoid wasting energy in trying to climb up the social ladder, to be a socially inferior but spiritually and morally superior people, to distrust and turn their back to the dangerous, ill-inspired European ideas like progress, modernity, secularism, and the like.

Such was the blueprint after which, according to the Survival thesis, French Canadian elites successfully modeled the present and the future of their society for more than one century. As a consequence, to the French Canadian intellectuals of the 1940s and 1950s who had opened their mind to modernity, the

---

[17] Which covers the period from the outset of the French settlement at the beginning of the seventeenth century through 1760.

[18] The name French Canadians appeared around 1840–50 (perhaps a little earlier) to designate the Francophones of Québec and Canada. Prior to that time, they used to call themselves "Français" or "Canadiens."

[19] More on this in Bouchard (2000: 99–110).

Survival period appeared very backward, gloomy, depressive (and depressing), even shameful, and they resolved to get rid of it and carry out major changes in their society. From this new mood came two labels: first, the *Grande Noirceur* (literally, the Great Darkness), which from then on, has designated the period of French Canadian history between 1850 and 1960;[20] second, the *Révolution tranquille* (Quiet Revolution), which refers to the deep, spectacular social, cultural, economic, and political overhaul that took place during the decades 1960 and 1970. In the minds of the majority of Québécois,[21] these two terms have come to shape a twofold vision of the past: a humiliating period followed by glorious decades of "normalization."[22]

Significant statistical evidence seems to provide a rough empirical valida-tion of the Survival narrative. Indeed, major indices based on comparative data attest to the underdevelopment of this society and dovetail with the con-cept of Grande Noirceur.[23] For instance, at the Canadian level, various literacy measures (based on the ability to sign, to read, or to write) place the Québec Francophones well behind the Canadian Anglophones (taken at large or by provinces). According to the 1891 Canadian census, Québec had the highest proportion of illiterates among the age group 20+; in 1921, the overall pro-portion of illiterates was twice that of Ontario. French Canadians also read less and were the most poorly equipped in public libraries. Statistics of school enrollment yield a similar picture. Among adults born between 1916 and 1936, the proportion of those who did not reach the ninth grade at school was 41.5 percent in Montréal, 30.7 in Toronto, and 22.9 in Vancouver. These discrep-ancies widen when the comparison is extended to large American cities.

Likewise, in the 1950s, access to university among the age group 20 to 24 was restricted to 3 percent among Francophones as opposed to 11 percent in the Québec Anglophone community. During the same period, among the major ethnic groups in Canada, only Italians were less educated than French Canadians. Many intellectuals living in those years, along with a number of present-day analysts, join in lamenting the sheer mediocrity of the literary and artistic production prior to the 1940s, with a few exceptions.

A few economic insights are available. According to Canadian censuses for the period 1931–61, French Canadians of Québec were heavily under-represented in the nonmanual categories of the occupational structure and overrepresented in the manual unskilled. They also occupied the lowest rungs with respect to earnings and income, ownership of financial institutions and big companies, and overall management and control of economy, particularly natural resources.

---

[20] Often, the expression also takes a more restricted meaning: 1900–60, or even 1930–60.
[21] From 1960 onward, French Canadians of Québec began to call themselves Québécois (see later).
[22] Most of the time, this word is avoided in the common discourse, but the idea is almost always lurking.
[23] Most of what follows comes from Bouchard (2004: 252–5).

The Modernist Thesis

The Modernist narrative took shape in the early 1960s and the new framework made headway during the following decades, achieving a dominant status nowadays among professional historians. Again, I will stick to the key tenets at the expense of refinement. Basically, the Modernist approach rejected the backward, depressing, and defensive vision of the Survival paradigm. In doing so, it has used the powerful analytical tools made available by the emerging new social and cultural history in Québec to dispel a number of gross and groundless historical accounts. Indeed, there is no doubt that, most often, the Modernists historians have hit the right buttons, as evidenced by a number of well-documented insights that take on a new meaning under the lens of the present questioning.

For instance, they have rightly insisted on highlighting major, heretofore disregarded or simply unknown facts, such as the onset of fertility decline as early as the 1860s (well in advance of the majority of European populations), the rapid pace of industrialization and urbanization (with the urban outnumbering the rural population from the 1910s),[24] the participation of French Canadians in economic growth (though most of the time as second-rank actors), a rapid expansion of secularized labor unions, the early rise of a consumer culture, the ethnic diversification of Québec population (particularly in Montréal), the persistence of liberal and modern thought throughout the period, and, thanks to the importation of European and American books, the circulation of secular, progressive ideas. The Modernists also opposed the widespread views that Francophone Québec had been a priest-ridden society, reluctant to modernize; that most peasants refused to integrate agriculture into the national or international markets; that they turned their back to the capitalist ethics; and so forth.[25]

Other less known or less visited facts crop up, like the spectacular, steady increase in the circulation of daily newspapers from 1901 onward (it more than doubled only in the subsequent twenty years), or the precipitous decline of clergy recruitment (from as early as 1930s in the Saguenay region where a wealth of historical data has allowed a very accurate measurement).[26] Between 1901 and 1961, the Québec active population in the primary sector went from 34.6 percent to 11.4 percent, while the GDP experienced a sevenfold increase. During the period 1926–1961, the mean personal income jumped from C$360 to C$1489. A strong take-off also occurred in the farming sector after the Great Depression, followed by a sustained growth. In addition, a waning of

---

[24] This proportion went from 39 to 75 percent between 1901 and 1961, thanks to a growth rate that surpassed the Canadian average for some decades. During the same years, the population of the Montréal Island shows a nearly fivefold increase (from 360,838 to 1,747,696).

[25] For a good example of this scientific trend, see the balanced and richly documented view offered by Linteau et al. (1979; 1986).

[26] See Bouchard et al. (1988); Bouchard and Thibault (1995).

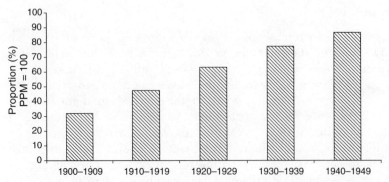

FIGURE 7.2. Evolution of literacy in Québec (proportion of PPM = 100). Only individual records containing three mentions or more have been used. Number of marriage records considered: 278,950. Number of individuals involved: 89,341. Number of individual mentions: 367,271.
Source: BALSAC Population Register (reconstituted family records).

core religious beliefs (at least from the 1940s) and a sustained increase in the overall literacy level (from 32 to 87 percent between 1900–9 and 1940–9) have also been documented (Figure 7.2).[27] Even the change in the occupational structure began well prior to 1960 – for instance, the overrepresentation of French Canadians in the manual unskilled group declined from 3.3 in 1931 to 2.8 in 1961.[28]

In short, the Modernist narrative tended to show that, in its own way, the French Canadian society had evolved culturally, economically, and socially at the same pace and along similar pathways as any other parts of the Atlantic world, particularly North America. Not surprisingly, this kind of fresh historical account by a new class of very competent young historians drawing on hard facts and figures was greeted with great enthusiasm by the emerging, well-educated baby boomers who reached adulthood in the 1960s, at the time of the Montréal World's Fair. All in all, the Modernist paradigm can be considered as a much needed corrective to the reductionist Survival account.

The Missing Narrative

Both the Modernist and the Survival narratives have been the target of harsh criticisms. For instance, it is obvious that the Survival paradigm fails to take

---

[27] According to a new index based on all the signatures in the family reconstitution records (unpublished data extracted from the BALSAC population register). The new index, rather than being binary (able/unable to sign), is a percentage expressing the degree of one's mastery of literacy. For a detailed presentation, see Bouchard and Larouche (1989).

[28] Porter (1965: Table 1, p. 87).

into account important, undisputable facts. Apart from those aforementioned pertaining to urbanization, industrialization, or fertility trend, it is not true that the French Canadian elites gave up attempts to advance the national agenda (or whatever cause) through political action, nor that they renounced great American (meaning: Continental) dreams, nor that they gave up fighting against economic and social domination. Important fragments of this society demonstrated resilience and dynamism – which does not mean that their actions were successful. As a corollary, if the Grande Noirceur was not that dark, then the change carried out by the Quiet Revolution could not have been that dramatic; so, the great myth of the 1960s could use some deconstructive work as well.

One must also keep in mind the strategic dimension of the Survival thesis. It is obvious that this gloomy narrative, which has emerged mostly in the 1950s, has served the sociopolitical agenda of a new elite engaged in a power struggle against the very conservative Duplessis regime and its clerical allies.[29] *Cité libre*, a very influential periodical established in 1950, became the launching pad of the new ideas that constituted the blueprint of the Quiet Revolution. Its contributors included well-known figures such as P. E. Trudeau (future prime minister of Canada), René Lévesque (future premier of Québec), along with a group of young social scientists trained in the United States and Europe. All of them shared the same objective of modernizing Québec. Needless to say, projecting a depressing picture of the past and the present of their society was very instrumental to their cause – and neglecting the brighter sides was part of the game. The set of reforms they advocated (and were about to inform the Quiet Revolution) were then presented as the logical response.

On the other hand, over the years, the Modernist approach has developed a tendency to downplay or even to disregard the negative traits and to promote a rosy version of the French Canadian past. In its most radical embodiment (to be found usually in nonprominent scholarship), it came to depict the so-called Survival (pre-1960) society in a very idealized way, as modern, open-minded, liberal, censorship-free, individualistic, secularized, not-so-religious, democratic, rational, well in tune with the progressive Western worldview, not backward in any way – actually, one could hardly find so perfect an equivalent society elsewhere. This kind of exaggeration has hurt the immense progress brought about by the Modernist history and it has sparked some antipathy in the field.

More precisely, it came under attack on the ground that it downplays the overall conservatism of the elites, the still important power of the Catholic Church, the evidence of xenophobia, the living legacy of colonialism, and

---

[29] Maurice Duplessis was the premier of the province of Québec between 1936 and 1939; he was reelected in 1944 and remained in office up to his death in 1959. His name is nowadays widely associated with one of the most conservative and less democratic periods of Québec history.

major features of collective underdevelopment. One critic has gone so far as to denounce the sheer opportunism of this revisionist historiography.[30] Some Modernists have also set forth an interpretation of the Quiet Revolution that has been challenged. The counterargument is that, if the French Canadian society had developed as any other Western society prior to 1960, where is the need for a revolution in the 1960s? From this perspective, the Quiet Revolution appears to be no more than a politically motivated mythical construction. Here, a lot of scholars (including myself) disagree. It is hardly questionable that, partly as a result of a new collective imaginary, the 1960s witnessed a number of fundamental changes. Higher education became widely open to the middle and working classes. The provincial State apparatus underwent major reforms. Secularization made important headway (in schools, politics, medias, and elsewhere) and newly created government agencies along with the civil society itself took over the Church everywhere. Following a new collective agenda, Québec Francophones asserted themselves in just about every domain of activity: economy, education, science, literature, and the arts. Indicators of underdevelopment disappeared or abated, remarkable performances were recorded in major areas (development of an entrepreneurship soon operating at the world scale, control of big corporations, average wage increase, dramatic shifts in the occupational structure), a new identity as well as a new vision of the past took shape, and at last, most Québécois, for two or three decades, felt good. To sum up, the post-1960 Québec society exhibited a remarkable capacity to adapt, to change, and to overhaul its collective imaginary to make it attuned with the challenges of the times.

One must particularly emphasize the new identity that emerged as part of the so-called neonationalism, that is, a complete rejection of the submissive and inward-looking mood of the old French Canadians. Pride, self-confidence, and achievement-impulse replaced what were perceived as the trademarks of the preceding period: fatalism, resignation, apathy. The decades 1950–70 witnessed a surge of radical thought advocating clear choices: urban life over rural, change over status quo, State over Church, Québec over Canada, Québec as a nation of the New World rather than a simple extension (or replica) of France, large-scale capitalism over family business. Intellectuals also succeeded in mobilizing the population around very effective myths that closely resonated with economic, social, and cultural urgencies of that time – social equality, modernity, secularism, "américanité," "québécitude," political sovereignty, economic emancipation, scientific development, opening to the world.[31] Along the way, and quite significantly, in order to mark this important transition, Québec Francophones jettisoned their former name and decided to call themselves Québécois. From then on, an original trajectory began, which led to a quite unprecedented achievement: a very strong nationalist movement that

---

[30] Rudin (1997).
[31] More on this topic in Bouchard (2003c).

took itself the initiative to enlarge its boundaries with a view to include all people living in Québec regardless of their ethnicity. At the same time, the former French Canadian minority in Canada gave way to a Québec nation wherein Francophones posited themselves as a majority.[32]

Yet, all these criticisms of the Modernist history must be received with caution since this scientific strand, beyond some basic premises, is far from homogeneous and its agenda has evolved over the years. Besides, one has to consider here the heart of the matter. Many historians and social scientists in Québec and elsewhere used to think and to teach that the underdevelopment of the French Canadian society prior to the Quiet Revolution originated primarily in a *mentalité* unfit for capitalism and modernization. Thanks to the Modernist history, this simplistic, never-demonstrated thesis has largely been sidelined in exchange for much more scientific accounts. Finally, the Survival thesis has wrongly aggravated the pessimistic and depressive view that Québec Francophones had already developed about themselves after 1840. Again, altogether, the Modernists contributed to promote a more balanced image supported by solid empirical data.

These remarks are meant to illustrate the difficulty I am facing here. In order to link the cultural trend of Québec with its health record, as already pointed out, one and only one consistent historical account is required. It should not come as a surprise that this condition cannot be met: many nations are plagued with conflicting narratives, just as social sciences everywhere experience permanent analytical and theoretical divides. To resolve this conflict, I introduce two sets of additional data. First, I will bring in new cultural evidence coming from the research that I have conducted on the collective imaginary of the French Canadian society between 1850 and 1960. As I have noted, this is an original foray into the cultural framework of Québec past, and it will hopefully shed a new light upon a much disputed terrain.

Second, I will resort to the sociocultural/health framework but in a reverse way. Rather than confronting the cultural and the health variables to bring out the impact of the former on the latter, I will use the health data to highlight the cultural trend. In so doing, I have to assume that, based on the wealth of scholarship produced so far, the sociocultural/health framework is robust enough that I can use the health record to somehow alleviate the ambiguity surrounding the cultural trend. At the same time, I am fully aware that there is no determinism at work here; I only expect health data to provide some hints as to fruitful directions to go and relevant inferences to make. This way, the analysis is expected to yield useful information about the sociocultural evolution of the French Canadian society and to bring some clarification to the controversy between the Survival and the Modernist paradigms.

---

[32] Needless to say, the interpretation of the Quiet Revolution by Québec historians will remain for a long time a very tricky business. For the time being, I think that one of the best available accounts have been provided by Linteau (2000).

Thereafter, I will explore whether and how these two inputs – collective imaginary analysis and health data – correlate together, how both of them articulate with the two conflicting paradigms, and to what extent they help break our deadlock.

THE 1850–1960 FRENCH CANADIAN IMAGINARY: INEFFECTIVE MYTHS, FRAGMENTARY THOUGHT

The study of collective imaginary, as outlined in the first part of this chapter, provides a powerful tool to capture the mood of a society while avoiding the subjective and impressionistic judgments that often plague that kind of research. That is what I have done in two recent books, wherein I have analyzed the prevailing system of thought and national myths in the French Canadian society between 1850 and 1960.[33] The basis of my investigation was a sample of the most prominent intellectuals who were active during this period and whose works are considered today as classics.[34] I sum up the main findings.

To begin with, all of these writings (essays, historical works, novels, and so on) reveal the same axes of tension and contradiction around a common set of conflicting ideals and orientations that were never reconciled nor efficiently articulated. These are:

1. Rural versus urban setting (or agriculture versus industry), as the authentic, natural mission of French Canadians;
2. Status quo versus change (or conservatism versus liberalism, or tradition versus modernity), as the most appropriate orientation for a small nation and a minority culture;
3. State versus Church, as the predominant authority in the secular as well as in the spiritual sphere;
4. Elites versus popular classes, as the legitimate detainees of collective authority;
5. Large-scale capitalism versus small family business, as the ideal moral pathway to social and economic development;
6. Québec versus Canada, as the prime center of political life and collective belonging;
7. Individuals versus nation (or community), as the primary reference of society and politics;
8. Materialism versus spiritualism (or intellectualism), as the norm, the right driving force of private and public life;

---

[33] Bouchard (2003a; 2004).

[34] First, I studied the discourse of settlement ideologies and utopias through well-known representatives of frontier (colonization) literature during the period. Then I conducted an in-depth analysis of five leading figures who have imagined and promoted an identity as well as a destiny for the French Canadian nation (Arthur Buies, Edmond de Nevers, Édouard Montpetit, Jean-Charles-Harvey, and Lionel Groulx).

9. Québec as an extension (a clone?) of France and Europe in America versus a settler society part of the New World with an original, distinctive past and future.

Along each of these dichotomies, the sampled intellectuals never really made up their minds – or more exactly, and strangely enough, they took every stance *simultaneously*, which is typical of what I call the fragmentary thought. For instance, reduced to its skeleton, the typical reasoning would go like this:

- The future of Québec, as with any other Western society, unquestionably belongs to industry and capitalism, but we should also secure the predominance of agriculture and avoid the hardship of urbanization by establishing the manufactures in the countryside;
- The French Canadians are predestined to excel internationally not in the economic careers but in the intellectual life (arts, literature, science); however, compulsory public education (up to 14 years old) must be rejected in the name of individual and family rights;
- French Canadians should free themselves from the detrimental cultural dependence upon France as the source of norms and models in arts, science, and thought; nevertheless, they should also keep imitating French cultural life because of its tremendous wealth and obvious superiority;
- Québec must enjoy a complete political autonomy, but within a united Canada;
- French Canadian businessmen, just like their Anglophone counterparts, should assert themselves in the wide economic world and aim at no less than the summit; in doing so, however, they must comply with the precedence that must be given to Catholic morality and, preferably, confine themselves in the handicraft sector and small family enterprises.

The ambivalence of this equivocal/fragmentary thought went even further. As I have explained, when faced with contradiction, reason may call to myth as a mediating device. One finds numerous examples of this mechanism in French Canadian intellectuals' writings. Yet, a number of the myths put forward were really far-fetched, very unlikely to capture ordinary people's minds. Witness this view, expressed a few times by a very influential figure, canon Lionel Groulx. Modernity and capitalism, he wrote, have destroyed the old Christian body of sacred traditions and replaced it with materialism, egotism, rivalry, and so forth. As a result, decadence is everywhere and a major catastrophe that will return the entire world to chaos is impending. Fortunately, Francophone Québec will be miraculously preserved since its Providential mission is to rekindle the civilization and rediffuse the old values in their original purity. By the same token, Groulx was revealing why Québec had been created as a cultural minority in North America and why it had been kept from engaging into modernity: in its wisdom, the Mighty God had chosen to spare it for the Great Day.

One also thinks of Edmond de Nevers's lofty vision of French Canada becoming an Athenian republic of the arts and science, shining all over the world; but he also held that access to college education was much too easy in Québec and that this aberration should be remedied. Besides, at the same time, he was working very hard to set up a huge project aiming to direct French Canadians to the wild North where they would colonize the virgin part of the province of Québec and become happy farmers – which was their authentic mission on earth. Finally, he also promoted the vision of a modern, dynamic, fearless industrialized and urbanized Québec becoming a leading part of an enlarged North American Republic.

Yet, beyond this amazing inconsistency, what is really striking in these writings is the amount of contradictions that crop up even among the myths set forth to overcome the conflicting ideas. Again, a few examples:

- To advocate a vigorous recovery (a social and economic "decolonization") of the Francophone nation while condemning the State, the democratic institutions, and the political action as dangerous, corrupted, frivolous. In other words: to engage in a very difficult, enormous collective task while rejecting the most powerful available tools.
- To invite French Canadians to demonstrate boldness, self-reliance, risk-taking, but at the same time to remind them how fragile, powerless, and incompetent they are as individuals and as a nation, and why they should avoid uncertain endeavors, leaving to others the responsibility of innovation and change.
- On the one hand, to celebrate the exceptional virtues of the French Canadians, proud heirs of the heroic founders of the glorious New France, and on the other hand, to repeatedly remind them of their lack of courage, intelligence, capability, and dignity, as members of a lousy and corrupt nation that fully deserves its downtrodden condition and gloomy destiny.
- To urge French Canadians to take their fate into their own hands and to put an end to their socioeconomic predicament through a vibrant collective effort, but also to persuade them that they must accept their social and economic woes since Providence governs the course of history and not the individuals themselves through their action.
- The French Canadian nation has a great future (1) as a faithful, modest, and grateful replication in the New World of the immortal French civilization, (2) as an original nation in America, breaking new ground, inventing itself, enjoying freedom to forge its own great destiny, away from the declining, atrophied Old World (France included).

Still about contradictory ideas and myths, two more notes deserve mention. First, according to a typical pattern, in the course of their writings, these intellectuals went back and forth between one assertion and its antithesis (sometimes even within the same article or book chapter) as though they were unaware of their contradictions. Very rarely would they pause and try to come to terms with their inconsistent propositions. And when they did, they often worsened their case rather than get things straight. Second, what finally emerges from this huge body of inconsistent writings is a gloomy discourse, a sense of despondency, of collective incapacity, reflected in what I have called depressing myths that (particularly in Groulx's writings) typically depict the French Canadians as victims, sacrificed people, even martyrs – and happy to be so.

On a brighter side though, I should also recall that all of these thinkers set out to devise a great vision of the French Canadian future – one could say: to carve out a "manifest destiny." Indeed, all of them ambitioned to construe a collective agenda designed to free and to develop their nation. In this respect, it is interesting to note that the major items of the Quiet Revolution's program were put forward well before 1960 (more precisely from the end of the nineteenth century onward), including the reform of education, the control of economic resources, and the call for collective self-esteem – actually, a redefinition of national identity. Even the powerful 1960s slogan "Maîtres chez nous" was forged in the 1920s. In each case, however, entangled as they were in counterpropositions and conflicting ideals, these schemes did not yield the much desired results. Not surprisingly, the alternate dreams, rather eccentric, did not materialize either. Therefore, failure imposed itself both as a major fact and as a central discursive theme. Canon Groulx, again, is a fascinating case in point. Just prior to his death, he reflected on his long itinerary (born in 1878, he died in 1967) and he summed it up by referring to "the complete failure of my life" (my translation).

What precedes must be viewed in a wider perspective. A pervasive threefold symbolic configuration informs these writings. First, the great (one is tempted to say: foundational) trauma of 1760; second, the successive, fruitless attempts to restore the broken equilibrium, to heal the injured nation, leading to an overwhelming sense of failure; and third, the longing for a reconquest. Hence, this three-step timeline: (1) golden age, (2) downfall and disenchantment, (3) dreams of and failed attempts to reconquest. Interestingly, this triad echoes one of the greatest archemyths[35] present in the cultural history of many nations of the New World. One thinks, among others, of the dream of the Great Columbia in Latin America, the quest to recover the stolen sea in Bolivia, the mourning of the lost northern land in Mexico, the shame of the destroyed ecological garden in New Zealand, the happy years of the first republic in Haiti, the memory of the Deportation ("le Grand Dérangement") among the Acadians in eastern Canada. In every case, the narrative assumes a past golden age and then a trauma followed by a period of an unsuccessful struggle fueled by a spirit of reconquest (a magic, widespread and powerful myth in the writings of French Canadian as well as Québécois intellectuals even nowadays).[36]

Other factors intervened at the identity level. For a long time, English Canadian politicians and intellectuals have diffused disparaging stereotypes

---

[35] I call archemyth a comprehensive symbolic construction acting as a matrix which integrates and commands a whole set of complementary myths.

[36] It is also worth noting that this archemyth, by and large, reproduces the structure of the millenarist thought, so widely spread in the cultural past of the Western Christian world.

about French Canadians. Over the years, the latter somehow have internalized this discourse buttressed by the prestige of the economically and politically dominant ethnic group.[37] As a result, collective recognition was extremely low and, to some extent, self-despise replaced self-esteem.

To sum up these findings, for all the resilience that fostered the dream and successive programs of reconquest, what pervades the sample of writings is a depressed mood, a deep sense of powerlessness, a negative, inhibiting self-image, a widespread conviction that the French Canadians have failed to make their own destiny and have been left on the margins of history. This conclusion is entirely consistent with a large body of literature on colonialism, particularly the sociocultural effects of a prolonged political and economic dependency.[38] It is also consistent with what happened after 1960: the emergence of a new, much more assertive ("radicalized") collective imaginary.[39] In other words, my analysis seems, in its own way, to validate major tenets of the Survival thesis over the Modernist interpretation, which means that the aforementioned analytical deadlock persists. Of course, this statement is based on the assumption that the collective imaginary defined by the pre-1960 French Canadian intellectuals has deeply impregnated the mindset of groups, classes, and institutions during the whole period – I will come back to this later.

THE HEALTH RECORD

Against this backdrop, what picture emerges from the health data? Using mortality (infant mortality and life expectancy) as a proxy, I have reconstituted the health trend and confronted it with the cultural background. Due to a scarcity of data, there is not much to say about the years 1850–90. From then on, available evidence shows that infant mortality was exceptionally high.[40] Up to the 1940s, Québec had by far the worst record among the Canadian provinces. Between the end of the nineteenth century and 1930, the rates in Montréal and Québec city were as high as they were in seventeenth-century

---

[37] This so-called "Québec bashing" discourse has been analyzed namely by Vallières (1969) and Bouthillette (1972) as well as in many articles published in the 1960s by the Québec leftist periodical *Parti pris*. A more recent insight can be found, among others, in Potvin (1999). Historically, a major milestone of this discursive thread is the Durham Report of 1839 (Report on the Affairs of British North America) in which the British governor of Canada wrote that the French Canadian people had no history and no literature. He also estimated that the only way to remedy their inferiority was through assimilating to the English race.

[38] Among others: Fanon (1961); Memmi (1963); Berque (1964). I mention these authors since they were quite influential among the 1960's Québec leftist intellectuals.

[39] Basically, the old dichotomies were all broken while a whole new set of myths was promoted (see "The Missing Narrative").

[40] The following figures are based on Gauvreau (1914); Groulx (1943); Henripin (1961); Copp (1978: Chapter 6); Authier (1992); Turmel and Hamelin (1995); Gaumer and Authier (1996); Guérard (2001); Bourbeau and Smuga (2003); Baillargeon (2004). For some data, I have also used the BALSAC population register. Other data comes from the Canadian Human Mortality Database (CHMD).

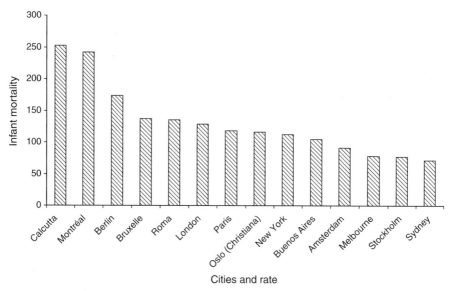

FIGURE 7.3. Infant mortality in 1911 (o/oo).

New France. According to Copp, infant mortality in Montréal averaged around 333 percent between 1897 and 1911.[41] A comparative British investigation by the Registrar General for the year 1911 (source, methods unknown) puts Montréal just behind Calcutta among a sample of major Western cities (Figure 7.3).[42] In the early 1920s, its rate of infant mortality doubled the level of Toronto.[43]

A few regional insights suggest that the years 1895–1912 were particularly bad everywhere in Québec. The Saguenay region (northern Québec) provides a good example, just as the Mauricie (central Québec) does. In the city of Trois-Rivières, the rate during the period 1890–1930 reached peaks of 300 percent (1899–1901, 1935, 1938). These figures compare to the worst scores observed in rural France in the seventeenth and eighteenth centuries. In the city of Ottawa, at the border of Québec and Ontario, an infant mortality rate of close to 400 percent was observed between 1890 and 1900.[44] From the data provided by the authors, one can estimate a rate of 480 percent among the French Canadian segment of this city.[45]

[41] Copp (1978: 93).
[42] For a similar comparison (and identical conclusions), see Mercier and Boone (2002: 490).
[43] Gaumer and Authier (1996: 276).
[44] Mercier and Boone (2002).
[45] There is an ongoing discussion about possible differential registration practices among the Catholics and the Protestants. For various reasons, the former are suspected of overdeclaration of infant deaths. While the suspicion appears grounded, it is very unlikely that this factor weighs heavily on the comparison.

As to life expectancy at birth, for the year 1921 (no available data prior to that year), an interprovincial comparison shows that Québec again ranks last with a score of 52.4 (Canadian average: 57.1). Besides, in all these measurements, the rates within Québec were significantly worse for French Canadians than for other ethnic groups. For instance, in Montréal, between 1895 and 1930, French Canadian infant mortality surpassed Anglophones' rates by a coefficient varying between 1.4 and 1.7.[46] Still in 1950, infant mortality rates were respectively 22.7 percent among French Canadians and 15.8 percent among all other Québecers.[47] A number of other studies concur on the sharp, long-lasting discrepancy between French Canadians and other ethnic groups within Québec.[48] Finally, a significant gender gap shows up during the twentieth century in favor of females who scored better with regard to both infant mortality and life expectancy, a largely unexplained fact (data not reproduced). Similarly, more expected cleavages appear between occupational groups and social classes.[49]

As a provisory conclusion about the decades 1880–1920, one could say that these facts and figures concur with a collective imaginary that generates apathy, stagnation, powerlessness, and hinders autonomy, self-esteem, and sense of control, thus at least indirectly contributing to ill-health (through the channels described here in Chapter 2 by Daniel Keating and in Chapter 1 by Clyde Hertzman and Arjumand Siddiqi). With respect to the historiographical controversies mentioned previously, they also add significant evidence to the Survival thesis and, presumably, to the image of the Quiet Revolution as a dramatic watershed of Québec history. Somehow, they suggest an analogy between the Québec case and what happened in Russia's post-Soviet transition where the lack of a strong collective imaginary (or narrative) based on mobilizing myths, undoubtedly contributed to accelerate the economic and institutional breakdown and, as well, prevented or delayed a smooth and energetic reshaping and recovery process. From the same perspective, an opposite scenario can be found in the recent history of some Eastern European countries where robust identity and traditions took hold during the decades of active resistance against totalitarianism (one thinks of the Czech Republic or Hungary). Each case, in its own way, exemplifies the impact of a vibrant

[46] Gaumer and Authier (1996: 274, 282). For a similar comparative view with the United States, see Rochester (1923).

[47] Henripin (1961: 14). Most data on infant mortality for the end of the nineteenth century and the early 1900s come from contemporary compilations that are considered dependable despite several flaws (see, for instance, the evaluation offered by Tétreault 1991: 46–54). Besides, they are consistent with well-criticized data of later years and they fit the overall mortality pattern.

[48] Among others: Thornton and Olson (1991; 2001); Olson and Thornton (2001); Baillargeon (2004: 40). Also, the annual reports of the Bureau d'Hygiène et de Statistiques of the city of Montréal.

[49] See, for example, Figure 7.4; also, Henripin (1961).

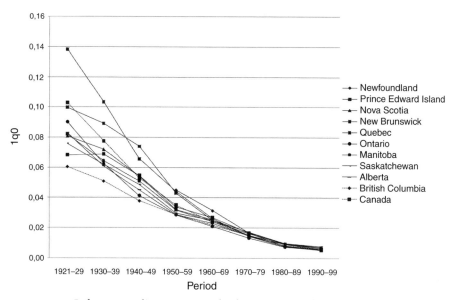

FIGURE 7.4. Infant mortality rate ($1q_0$), both sexes, Canada and provinces, 1921–9 to 1990–9.

collective imaginary – or the lack of it – on the functioning of institutions and the course of a society.

However, the Québec health data tell a very different story for the period 1920–60. Not many historians seem to have paid close attention to the curves of infant mortality and life expectancy during this period and its significance in terms of societal dynamics. I would dare to say that a lot of scholars just assume that, as almost everything else, the catching up with other Canadian provinces for this major social indicator took place from the 1960s onward, thanks to the Quiet Revolution. Yet, the reality is quite different. For both indices, the interprovincial gap had almost disappeared in the 1960s (Figures 7.4 and 7.5). A sharp decline of infant mortality started early in the twentieth century and continued steadily over the period.[50] Even the remote Saguenay region, sometimes said to be rather backward, experienced a sharp recovery from the 1910s onward (Figure 7.6).

What is directly targeted in this chapter, however, is the impact of culture per se (and indirectly the social). Consequently, it could be advisable to remove from the calculations the mortality at low ages (1–15) on the ground that, in this case, the causal diseases might be mostly the effect of material or technical factors like feeding practices, hygiene, infrastructure (sewer, pasteurization), or availability of medical services (like vaccination), as opposed

[50] Gaumer and Authier (1996: 274–5).

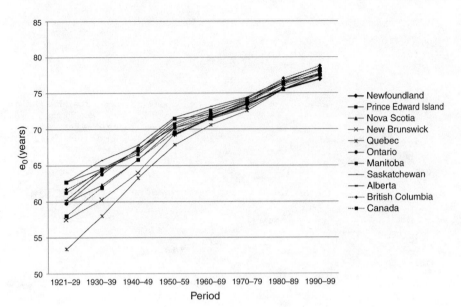

FIGURE 7.5. Life expectancy at birth (e_o), both sexes, Canada and provinces, 1921–9 to 1990–9.
Source: Canadian Human Mortality Database (CHMD), 2004.

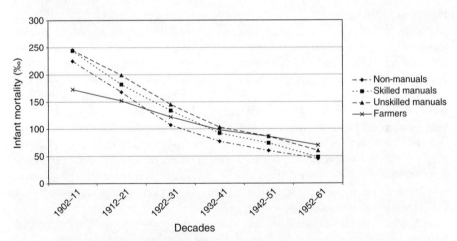

FIGURE 7.6. Infant mortality by occupational group (Saguenay region).
Source: BALSAC Population Register, 2005 (BALSAC Project).

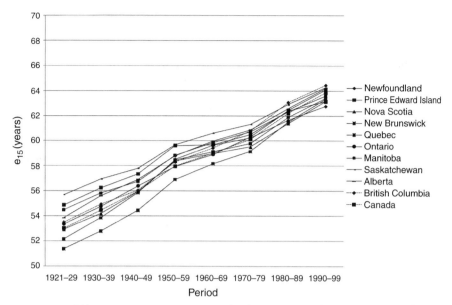

FIGURE 7.7. Life expectancy at age 15 (e_{15}), both sexes, Canada and provinces, 1921–9 to 1990–9.

to the strictly sociocultural processes and mechanisms listed earlier.[51] Yet, the new curves (Figure 7.7) assume quite the same shape (with a faster recovery for women after 1939 – graph not included). This suggests that even mortality at very low ages might be relevant to the same explanatory mechanisms, whatever they are.

As a result, the analysis is still faced with a very puzzling paradox: a depressive collective imaginary all along the period, coupled with a sharp improvement in health indices from the 1910–20s onward, implying a dynamic sociocultural pattern. The more one stresses the depressive cultural picture in order to account for the gloomy health record prior to the 1910–20s, the more difficult it becomes to account for the spectacular takeoff that took place in the following decades – since no well-known equivalent breakthrough occurred in the meantime in the collective imaginary. Two ways are offered to get out of this conundrum: (1) to reject (or substantially modify) the sociocultural/health framework, (2) to revise the interpretation of Québec sociocultural trend in

---

[51] There seems to be no clear agreement among researchers as to whether infant mortality should be removed or not from the social/health framework analysis. One interesting note about this: it could be expected that the rapid decline of infant mortality in Québec would have been slowed down by the Great Depression, which is not the case (see Copp 1982: 130–1; also, Figure 7.5).

such a way as to reach a better fit with the health data. As already indicated, I have decided to take the latter option and, in so doing, to reverse the global sociocultural/health framework approach in order to test its analytical potential in the area of historical and social sciences. This choice, quite consistently, leads us to question the Survival paradigm (as well as the collective imaginary analysis) for the period between 1910 and 1960 and to look for additional data supporting an alternative scheme.

We already know about features of modernization, which have undoubtedly contributed to health-plus: urbanization, industrialization, and economic growth have increased literacy and improved standards of living,[52] fertility decline alleviated the pressure on overcrowded households, secularization fostered more mundane concerns and changed the attitude toward infant deaths,[53] and so on. Besides, various studies have shown that, as has been observed in many other cases, the community networks survived urbanization, providing families with a valuable safety net.[54] Other favorable factors must be mentioned: nationalism per se created a strong solidarity, being a cultural minority fed into a vibrant collective identity, local democracies and powerful religious institutions offered stable and living environments, and there is indication that the relatively low level of economic inequality in the countryside fostered social trust.[55]

However, one has to be careful not to overstretch this line of reasoning since, even though all those factors were undoubtedly conducive to health-plus, they were present well before 1910–20 – how then to explain that they were kept inactive for so long? And what could have suddenly switched them on? Likewise, the evidence of underdevelopment provided earlier remains true for decades after the 1920s. Finally, there still is this dumbfounding phenomenon

---

[52] There are several clear signs of economic improvement among the Montréal working class, such as the increased utilization of public transportation facilities, the growing access to electric power supply, the wide diffusion of radio and movies, the betterment of housing, the emergence of mass consumption.

[53] For instance, it is well known that, traditionally, the Catholic Church praised the acceptation of children deaths and family sufferings as a way to secure a better place in Paradise.

[54] See, for instance, Lamontagne and Falardeau (1947); Tremblay and Fortin (1964); Garigue (1971); Fournier (1983); Ferretti (1992). A similar phenomenon has been observed in many other industrial cities outside Québec during the same period (Bouchard (1986); Fournier (1989): 182–5).

[55] I have conducted a comparative research on the Saguenay region (based on the distribution of the real estate ownership value) which yielded relatively low Gini scores, varying between 0.43 and 0.48 during the period 1879–1949; actually, they were the lowest in a sample of towns and villages of English Canada and the United States, where all the Gini scores fall between 0.63 and 0.91 (Bouchard 1998: 680). Unfortunately, there is no Gini data available for other regions of Québec. Apart from that, there are a number of studies providing valuable insights and documenting quite sharp inequalities (for instance, Hanna and Olson 1990), on the social landscape of Montréal in 1901, but in the absence of a comparative apparatus, there is not much that can be inferred here.

of a sharp inflexion in the mortality curves whereas the structure and content of collective imaginary (at least as reflected in the intellectuals' writings) show no sign of a concomitant shift. Since the new prevailing Québec imaginary began to emerge only after World War II as a first step toward the Quiet Revolution, one obviously needs to rethink not only the relationship between collective imaginary and health but also the whole issue of the social articulation of symbolic frameworks.

A fair appraisal of the whole picture at this stage would probably give something like this: the road opened by the Modernist approach, as bolstered and widened by the health data, helps alleviate the aforementioned paradox of which major parts nevertheless remain. In other words, we still have a long way to go in terms of empirical research and analysis.

CONCLUSION

From this rather bumpy itinerary through the interplay of culture, society, and health, two lessons finally come to light.

A Complex, Unpredictable Journey: From Collective Imaginaries to Behaviors – and Backward

The first lesson pertains to the impact of collective imaginaries upon the social life (one is tempted to say: the "praxis") and, more generally, to the interactions between the cultural and the social. The contents of a collective imaginary, defined as a mixture of myths and rational constructions, may show a poor fit with the dynamics of the day-to-day life and the representations that ultimately drive individual identities and behaviors. This leads to reject a view of imaginaries as monolithic and making a direct, predictable impact on the social life in general and on health in particular – we have seen that a depressing imaginary does not necessarily inhibit social dynamism, as witnessed by the sharp and sustained decline of mortality after 1910–20 and other elements of modernization prior to 1960. Again, this raises the question: how do cultural repertoires or meta-narratives impregnate identities and condition individual and group behaviors?[56] One suspects the intervention of various kinds of agencies or mediating devices (such as family and kinship, peer groups, social classes, school, media, unions, Church, State, and other institutions) that can deflect, mitigate, or even overturn a collective imaginary by redefining, filtering, and selecting among its contents. In other words, there is no straightforward trickle down process from above – that is, from those broad symbolic configurations created by national intellectual elites. Rather, one pictures a complex, unpredictable dynamics of diffusion and constant

---

[56] Swidler (1986).

reprocessing between various networks and environments related to different social layers.[57]

In this respect, collective imaginaries still matter a lot since, ultimately, all individuals somehow tap into them to foster their identity. However, they are one cultural factor among others insofar as their contents are submitted to at least two mechanisms of appropriation and translation: one by social groups and institutions that act as brokers (this is the locus of power struggles), the other by the individuals themselves through negotiating and identifying (or reidentifying) strategies operating at the micro level, the kind which is analyzed by Michèle Lamont, namely under the label of destigmatization strategies.[58] Besides, one must also allow for a reverse impact from below[59] since the intellectuals themselves are socially situated and act under influence, feeding their discourse with impulses, experiences, emotions, and intuitions originating in their collective environment. Those comments draw attention to the role of intellectuals and their location in the discourse production and diffusion process. It might be useful to retrieve here Gramsci's distinction[60] between the *classic* or *traditional* intellectual rooted in and operating within the learned culture (while wittingly or unwittingly catering to the hegemonic class) and the *organic* intellectual working much closer to the popular classes and heralding a new, emerging societal order – or, more simply, promoting a different repertoire.

As a result of all these buffering, reprocessing, and countering effects, it makes sense to picture, for instance, a society where the elites' culture could be characterized by a depressed mood, while the popular or the mass culture would manifest dynamism and resilience – or just the other way around. Along this path, many other scenarios, just as plausible, come to mind. And, of course, one can imagine a situation where two or more collective imaginaries are conflicting at the macro level within a society, a phenomenon that, again, drives the analysis toward the field of power struggle.

In this chapter, collective imaginaries are looked at from a macro perspective as formal discourses constructed by intellectuals. At this level, one primarily deals not with the constant individual strategy-making and negotiating processes taking place on the "reception" side but with the contents, the myths

---

[57] This strongly resonates with the analytical framework advocated by Steensland (2006) in his study of the cultural categories which condition the public discourse and the fate of projected policies.

[58] Lamont (2000). See also Lamont et al. (2001); Lamont and Aksartova (2002); Lamont (Chapter 6, in this volume). Individuals, at any time, are assumed to choose what fits their needs and expectations among symbolic material (toolkits) made available to them by the culture of their society (models, symbols, values, ideals, norms, and the like). The outcome determines their capacity to adequately respond to any challenging situation.

[59] As the reader can see, I am not comfortable with this "above and below" terminology. A much better way would be to envision a sphere wherein a number of actors interact in an unpredictable way through different media and channels, at various scales, and with uneven leverage.

[60] From his *Quaderni del carcere* (1930–5).

that fuel them. Yet, it is important to realize that the micro level, day-to-day discourse can be very effective and successfully compete with the more formal construction of the learned culture, thus significantly impacting the social life (and well-being) in their own way.[61]

These remarks may help defuse at least part of the paradox that I came across during my research. They also point to a new research agenda on Québec cultural past. Obviously, the study of collective imaginary must go well beyond the production of the intellectuals' discourse to embrace the aforementioned complex, multilayer interactive processes of negotiation, definition, and redefinition that unfold at and between the macro and the micro levels. In the case of Québec, more refined accounts are needed of the way major inputs such as improved living standards, fertility decline, and literacy growth have affected the day-to-day life of ordinary people.

The Case for a New Paradigm

The second lesson relates precisely to the state and the future of Québec historical research. Contrary to what has become a quite standard approach, this chapter intended to use the sociocultural/health framework not to account for health as impinged upon or driven by collective mechanisms but to better understand the cultural historical course of a society. This reversal, combined with an investigation of collective imaginary, has proved fruitful insofar as it has contributed to foreground some major disregarded facts (notably the spectacular break in the mortality curves during the decade 1910–20) and to ignite a search for new ones. In so doing, it has brought about a useful insight into the lasting interpretative controversy about Québec's past, thus opening the road toward a more complex and balanced scheme apt to better integrate the conflicting evidence. By the same token, it invites researchers to distance themselves from the simplistic versions of both the Survival and the Modernist views.

As already mentioned, the Survival thesis fails to account for the early twentieth century health reversal and for other important changes that occurred prior to 1900. The Modernist thesis has its own predicaments. It downplays evidence of underdevelopment and backwardness prior to and after 1910–20, and it disregards the strength of the depressed, equivocal collective imaginary prior to 1960. Finally, more troubles might loom for both theses if, some day, more and better sociocultural, economic, and health time series data become available for the period 1850–80.

Those two paradigms, born decades ago, may have exhausted most of their scientific potential; insofar as they have antagonized the historical field, they

---

[61] A spectacular example of such a competing process between "above" and "below" narratives (or macro versus micro levels) can be found in the religious life of contemporary Poland to the point where popular beliefs come to contradict and oppose the official Catholic creed. See Zubrzycki (2006).

have become somewhat counterproductive. They may also have outlived their premises; other, more pressing issues and concerns now occupy the Québec agenda, and they speak less to modernity than to postmodernity: values, citizenship, pluralism, symbolic foundations of the social link, and the like – to which I would add inequalities, power struggles, and institutional change. For these reasons, one feels a need for a new analytical framework. Indeed, there is now room for an overarching view, an integrative or synthesis paradigm promoting a *new social history* writ large. This paradigm should be integrative in at least two ways: (1) by articulating both conflicting and new evidence about Québec past into a broader picture that would resonate with the challenges of our times, (2) by combining the cultural strands of the last decades (including the so-called linguistic turn) with the traditional social history that has suffered a dramatic setback since the 1980s – along the lines suggested, for instance, by Sewell.[62]

[62] Sewell (2005).

8

Making Sense of Contagion

Citizenship Regimes and Public Health in Victorian England

Jane Jenson

Successful societies protect and foster the health of their populations. This volume is premised, moreover, on the knowledge that health status depends on much more than the availability of health care for the treatment of individuals. Instead, much of health depends upon avoiding the dangers of social interaction, whether these take the form of contagion, environmental pollution, or unequal social status. International panics in recent years about that the next flu pandemic is only the latest in a long line of efforts to anticipate and prevent the spread of infection. The "epidemic of obesity" among children as well as adults is only one example of attention to social as well as physical conditions that lower the chances of individual good health and therefore societal success. The Public Health Agency of Canada, created in response to the 2003 scare about Severe Acute Respiratory Syndrome (SARS), is only one example of an institutional and structural reform based on the recognition that personal strategies for health cannot address threats affecting entire groups and populations.

Such long-standing concerns about intersections between individual and societal well-being is the domain of public health. International organizations seek to promote it, national governments institutionalize it, medical science debates it, and social science as well as epidemiology tracks its variable patterns over time and space.[1] Studies of public health practices reveal them to be widely diverse. There have consistently been major variations among societies in the diagnosis experts draw from aetiological knowledge as well as the prophylactic strategies they adopt.

How might we understand such variation in interpretations and practice? One account might be framed in terms of knowledge, and what is available

[1] In Chapter 1 in this volume, Hertzman and Siddiqi provide several examples of the epidemiological variations in patterns of public health across countries and across socioeconomic status (SES) groups as well as their correlation with politically generated efforts to alter the distributional gradient of well-being.

in medical science for fostering health and well-being. The availability of vaccines against a wide variety of childhood and other diseases has clearly had effects on not only child mortality but also life expectancy rates. Another might focus on individual-level social relations and their cultural content, via which greater value is ascribed to some persons and ways of being than to others, thereby generating the wear and tear of everyday life for those ranked as less worthy. Useful as both these accounts are, it is necessary to supplement them. The claim of this chapter is that politics matters for explaining cross-time and cross-space variation in public health practice. In particular, the chapter argues that shared political narratives about collective solidarity, belonging and merit – expressed among other places in ideas about citizenship – have consequences for governments' actions and policies, including for the ways that they understand threats to public health, sources of disease and protective mechanisms deployed to limit ill-health.

The goal of this chapter is to contribute to understanding why "we don't act on what we know." In other words, the question is: why is social knowledge, about which there is little scientific debate, not quickly translated into effective public policy? The chapter argues that specific public health choices follow from the particular narratives and practices of citizenship deployed in modern states. For one historical case, that of nineteenth-century England, it tracks the partial implementation of public health measures despite near consensus about what interventions were needed and demonstrates that such processes are profoundly shaped by broader societal debates about the role of the state and its responsibilities vis à vis citizens. The options considered to be available and the choices made are constrained by the political discourse as well as institutions and interests of the time.[2]

ANALYTIC TOOLS FOR THINKING ABOUT POLICY VARIATION

Better medical science has generated greater capacity to explain disease and propose helpful strategies for improving public health. Vaccinations against most common diseases were invented by the early decades of the twentieth century, and public health efforts have been organized around mass campaigns at both the national and international level since then. Nonetheless, references to the science alone cannot provide full accounts of public health initiatives. For example, in the early nineteenth century epidemiologists such as Louis René Villermé had statistically documented the relationship between income inequality and health outcomes, but these studies did not much influence policy in nineteenth-century France or Britain, where environmental causes (such as miasma) were preferred over explanations derived from the social determinants of disease and in particular poverty.[3]

---

[2] Jenson (1986; 1989); Hall (1989: 383–6).
[3] Villermé's analyses provided classic epidemiological findings about health gradients: "In 1826, he demonstrated across Parisian districts a gradient in mortality in close accord with the

Nor do all examples of stubborn inattention to scientific findings come from the days when modern medical science was in its infancy. Contemporary epidemiologists and the population health perspective have documented the stubborn persistence of income and class gradients in health outcomes, which they term "modernity's paradox."[4] Such findings provide "strong arguments for a focus on social and economic determinants and for investments in the sectors that 'produce health' such as education, income, and housing."[5] In other words, this science leads to proposals to intervene to change the unequal *distribution* of access to a range of goods and services. Much public health policy remains focused, however, on what produces ill-health.

This chapter examines a historical moment when social knowledge exhibited a relative consensus about actions needed to promote health, but that knowledge was not translated into effective public policy for many years. Examination of this example, now well behind us in time, reveals the extent to which seemingly simple interventions to promote health by ensuring access to clean water and sanitation can be chronically limited by ideas about the responsibility of states and markets, about rights, about governance and about solidarity across social classes. It teaches a lesson for understanding societal success. Just as health care is inadequate to produce health, knowledge about health is insufficient to prompt appropriate action by political authorities. In the intellectual battles over the meanings of epidemiological results and about the long-term consequences of social marginality, in which we are now engaged, it is helpful to remember this example. It is one, and hardly an exceptional one, in which the norms of citizenship carried as much if not more weight in the structuring of public policy than did either medical or social scientific knowledge.

IN PUBLIC HEALTH, "POLITICS MATTERS"

Historians of science and of society have pointed out that politics matter in the history of public health.[6] As Peter Baldwin recounts in detail, at least since the 1940s and the work of historians following Erwin Ackernecht, a popular contention has been that authoritarian and liberal states favored different aetiology and prophylaxis for the spread of disease and its prevention.[7] Because

---

percentage of rents too low to tax; in 1840, in a six-year study of the textile town of Mulhouse, he found striking gradients by occupation" (Susser 2000: 882). As the chapters by Keating (Chapter 2) as well as Hertzman and Siddiqi (Chapter 1) in this volume indicate, the interpretation of gradients still provokes scientific controversy.

4 Keating and Hertzman (1999).

5 Kickbusch (2003: 385). See also Evans (Chapter 4, this volume) who argues too that much more than health policy has long-term effects on population health.

6 Dorothy Porter (1999: 1–2) describes the classic public health literature as one that deploys a narrative of linear progress. Her book disputes this position by adopting a more sociological account, anchored in historical thinking about state formation. See also Peter Baldwin's (1999) massive history of varying strategies to fight epidemics.

7 Baldwin (1999: 12ff. and passim).

public health interventions involve a tension between individual liberty and the collective good, nineteenth-century liberals supposedly tended toward sanitarian interventions that interfered least with individual behavior (such as building sewers and providing clean water) and, therefore, also tended to explain that disease resulted from lack of public hygiene. In authoritarian states, there was less concern for interference in the lives of individuals. Therefore quarantines were supposedly more acceptable and theories of interpersonal contagion most popular. Summarizing the Ackernechtian explanation, Baldwin writes: "it was not the nature of the disease which specified how it would be prevented and limited, but the kind of political regime under epidemic attack."[8]

In his cross-national comparison of public health policies in France, Britain, Germany, and Sweden from 1830 to 1930, Baldwin rejects the Ackernechtian stance as too simplistic. His account of the three major public health threats in nineteenth-century Western Europe – cholera, smallpox, and syphilis – led him to propose a set of three general factors that combined in variable ways in each society to generate public health strategies:

Though politics was certainly part of the story, a simple Ackernechtian reading of prophylactic strategies cannot explain the polymorphous divergence of the precautions imposed across nations. As supplement and replacement, other factors have been adduced here: geoepidemiological location, both in terms of positioning vis-à-vis the epidemic currents of contagious disease and in those of the topography required to make certain preventive strategies work; and commercial interest and administrative capacity, both of which had implications for various tactics.... Such factors were the general conditions within whose ambit prophylactic decisions were taken, but only a historical accounting of the precise steps behind every such choice can explain any specific outcome.[9]

In other words, after identifying a number of large structural and institutional conditions, Baldwin sends us back to a classic method of detailed historical recounting.

While not disputing the validity of his method or his detailed analysis, and indeed engaging with his challenge to "amend or supplement a political interpretation of ... public health and statutory intervention,"[10] I argue here that attention to the regime level of analysis – rather than the distinction between authoritarian and liberal political systems that preoccupied the Ackernechtians – helps to put some general order into the variable and even contradictory practices Baldwin found. In particular, by focusing on the "citizenship regime" it provides an account of the difficulties English sanitarians faced in advancing toward full implementation of their position through the mid-Victorian years as well as some of the opposition it provoked. Norms

---

[8] Baldwin (1999): 13).
[9] Baldwin (1999: 550).
[10] Baldwin (1999: 35).

about citizenship rather than topography, state capacity or commercial interests are proposed as explanatory factors for both the process of implementation of the sanitary idea and the mobilization in opposition to some forms of compulsory behavior imposed by sanitarians on noncitizens.

POLITICS AND CITIZENSHIP REGIMES

Public health interventions involve fundamental matters touching on individual rights, the role of the state, and its respect for the liberty of individuals while ensuring the foundations of social solidarity – what the French revolutionaries termed *fraternité*. Public health policy is, in other words, a matter of citizenship.

This chapter uses an historical-institutionalist approach to substantiate its claim that the particular content of the citizenship regime at any point in time operates as a set of institutionalised ideas working "to constrain the normative range of legitimate solutions available to policy makers."[11] This claim follows from a standard premise of that approach: in order for policies to be adopted, "they must fit with the underlying norms and values of the society."[12] More specifically, the chapter describes the ways in which ideas and practices of the citizenship regime constrained the translation of medical knowledge into policy action, despite the existence of a broad-based consensus on what should be done.

The discourse of citizenship provides a narrative about inclusion and exclusion and the practices that stem from it.[13] These have varied widely over both the long term – when, for example, only men who could take up arms for the nation could be citizens and women were thereby excluded – and the short term, in which, for example, ideas about the rights and duties of citizenship altered significantly with the widespread ideological shift toward neoliberalism in the 1980s and 1990s.[14] The notion of citizenship regime is helpful for tracking

---

[11] Campbell (1998): 385); Hall (1993); Thelen and Steimo (1992).

[12] Campbell (1998: 380), describing Peter A. Hall's position.

[13] This analysis can be seen as a specific case in which practice is shaped by collective imaginaries and vice versa. An historical-institutionalist approach requires linking discourse to institutions as well as to interests. But even more philosophical approaches argue that ideas – or imaginaries – are anchored in practice. As Charles Taylor (2002: 107) says of social imaginaries, "the relation between practices and the background understanding behind them is therefore not one-sided. If the understanding makes the practice possible, it is also true that the practice largely carries the understanding. At any given time, we can speak of the 'repertory' of collective actions at the disposal of a given sector of society." Bouchard (Chapter 7, in this volume) also raises questions about the effects of institutions on collective imaginaries and cultural repertoires.

[14] Sewell (Chapter 10, in this volume) provides a consideration of neoliberalism. On the consequences of neoliberalism for citizenship regimes, see for example, Jenson and Saint-Martin (2006).

changes in understandings of citizenship across time.[15] It focuses attention on the institutional arrangements, rules and understandings that guide and shape concurrent policy decisions and expenditures of states, problem definitions by states and citizens, and claims making by citizens.[16]

To map both the institutional arrangements and ideas it is helpful to see a citizenship regime as composed of four elements:

- *A responsibility mix:* Citizenship involves the expression of basic values about the responsibility mix, defining the boundaries of state responsibilities and differentiating them from those of markets, of families and of communities. The result is definition of "how we wish to produce well-being," whether via purchased welfare, the reciprocity of kin, collective support in communities (both virtual and spatial), or collective and public solidarity, that is state provision. The state's portion is the citizenship portion, and its size can vary significantly across time and in different places.
- *A definition of rights and duties:* Through formal recognition by the state of particular rights and duties (civic, political, social, and cultural; individual and collective), a citizenship regime establishes the borders and boundaries of inclusion and exclusion of a polity. When certain needs are met via an extension of rights, the role of the market as well as family and community sectors have less responsibility for them. If, however, the state refuses any responsibility, then the other sectors will be pressed to fill the gap and take up their duties.
- *A prescription of governance practices:* Among these are democratic rules, including the institutional mechanisms giving access to the state, the modes of participation in civic life and public debates and the legitimacy of specific types of claims making. It sketches routes to representation, the ways in which legitimate voices are recognized and actors provided entry into the policy process.
- *A definition of who belongs:* This involves identity and membership, in both the narrow passport-holding sense of nationality and the more complicated notions of multiple feelings of belonging to several public communities. These feelings of belonging will set the boundaries of inclusion and exclusion into full citizenship.

The specific content of each dimension of any citizenship regime is established through political action, which arises from competing ideas as well as the interests of actors and institutions within which they act.[17] Therefore, even

---

[15] For the concept of citizenship regime and its application see, inter alia, Jenson and Phillips (1996; 2002); Yashar (1999); Papillon and Turgeon (2003).

[16] While this definition is directly adapted from Esping-Andersen's (1990) depiction of a welfare regime, it is hardly different from some definitions of culture deployed in organizational institutionalism. For example, "by 'culture' [Frank] Dobbin meant the shared conceptions of reality, institutionalized meaning systems, and collective understandings that guide policy" (Campbell 1998: 381).

[17] The notion of ideas and norms about citizenship used here is different from, although by no means contrary to, what Bouchard (Chapter 7, in this volume) calls the collective imaginary

though a regime is a temporarily stabilized set of discourses and practices that represent the contemporary play of power relations, there is almost always competition from other actors seeking inclusion, recognition, and opportunities to realise their own aspirations. Dissonance is to be expected. Ideas about science as well as social justice will clash as scientists and other experts and as social movements and political formations press the state to adopt one kind of social knowledge rather than another. State institutions themselves are likely to be traversed by conflict even as they move to recognize and act on some ideas and actors, consigning others to the margins of influence.

This chapter demonstrates that public health interventions were constrained by ideas about citizenship (who is responsible for what, what rights, who has access, who belongs), such that the consensus around the "sanitary idea" was not fully implemented for more than four decades. This is, then, an analysis that agrees that politics matter in order to understand public health practices. It illustrates these patterns of constraints by tracking the history of public health with respect to contagion in England in the nineteenth century.[18] It will document that a sanitarian approach to public health had garnered wide support in England by the third decade of the nineteenth century, and that it certainly fit the *reformed* citizenship regime better than the alternative, which was based on limiting contagion by quarantine. Nonetheless, it was only partially, and according to its promoters, inadequately implemented in the various pieces of legislation dealing with public health of the mid-Victorian period. Full implementation of the sanitary idea only could occur when the predominantly liberal citizenship regime, and particularly the institutions of governance and ideas about the responsibility mix, had undergone significant adjustment. This did not happen until after 1870. In that same decade as well, social mobilization arose against the most illiberal elements of the sanitary idea. As citizenship became more inclusive in the last three decades of the century, it became more difficult to treat noncitizens, particularly women and the working class, in the draconian ways that sanitarians had themselves promoted when citizenship was a status reserved for middle-class property owners by the Great Reform of the first decades of the nineteenth century.

MID-NINETEENTH-CENTURY ENGLAND: ONLY PARTIAL IMPLEMENTATION OF THE SANITARY IDEA

In Britain, life expectancy had increased significantly in the eighteenth century, but in the second and third decades of the nineteenth-century urban life brought ill health and early death. Longevity continued to increase in the

---

("representations through which a society provides its members with a definition of selfhood and otherness, a vision of their past and their futures, as well as territorial appropriation"). Indeed, the dimension of "belonging" in the citizenship regime covers similar ground.

[18] Scotland and Ireland followed different public health policies at this time (Hamlin and Sheard 1998).

countryside, while life expectancy "in such cities as Manchester, Glasgow, and Liverpool [was] falling to levels not seen since the mediaeval Black Death."[19] Moreover, the rates stuck at those low levels until the 1870s. In 1871 average life expectancy was still hovering at 41 years, the level it had achieved in 1821. In the largest cities (over 100,000), the rate had not recovered from its plummet between 1821 and 1851, and had stabilized at a rate lower than where it was in 1821. It was only after 1870 that substantial new gains were made.

Smallpox was still a scourge, despite Edward Jenner's discovery of how to vaccinate against it in the previous century. Venereal diseases threatened reproductive health as well as longevity in general. But cholera was "the classic epidemic disease of the nineteenth century." Four pandemics swept out from Asia to Europe during the nineteenth century.[20] The disease was carried from British India to Britain itself on water and rail. Landing in the "mushrooming towns and cities of a society in the throes of rapid urbanization, it took advantage of overcrowded housing conditions, poor hygiene and insanitary water supplies."[21] In the first pandemic of the early 1830s, most European governments acted in the same way, using traditional policing methods to enforce *cordons sanitaires* that had served to combat earlier plagues.[22] Ships were quarantined, ports shut down, and travel restricted. In the next pandemics, however, English practices would diverge from those of the rest of Europe.

SANITARIANS AND PUBLIC HEALTH

At the time experts in the international public health networks did not have a shared diagnosis of the mechanisms spreading cholera and other epidemics such as yellow fever.[23] There were three main aetiological positions. One described contagion by contact between infected individuals, and therefore the prophylactic strategies were quarantine or vaccination.[24] Another argued that bad air – in the form of miasma – arising from filth and rot was the mechanism of infection and prescribed vastly improved public sanitation infrastructure to eliminate the sources of disease. A third position with respect to cholera was that transmission occurred by contaminated water, and therefore providing

---

[19] Szreter (1999: 147).
[20] Evans (1988: 124–5).
[21] Evans (1988: 124).
[22] Ibid.: 139.
[23] Porter (1999: 81–2); Eyler (2001). The cholera bacillus was identified only in the 1880s by Robert Koch (Baldwin 1999: 139). The bacillus thrives in warm water and is passed on the excreta of the sick and other carriers, entering the body through the mouth (Evans 1988: 127). Until the 1880s (and even after) the precise role of water in transmitting the disease was hotly debated (Eyler 2001).
[24] Edward Jenner's vaccine against smallpox had been available since 1798. Quarantine had been standard practice for centuries.

sanitary water supplies and waste disposal was the way to limit the spread.[25] Even though the second and third aetiology of contagion were quite different, one pointing to air and the other to water as the carrier of infection, they both agreed on what to do. This convergence meant that by the middle of the nineteenth century English policy makers had moved clearly away from any general reliance on quarantine and were firmly on the side of the sanitarian paradigm.[26] Many historians term this position the "sanitary idea."

The 1848 Public Health Act was a landmark piece of legislation. It followed more than a decade of public inquiry, expert reports, and public discussion about what to do about public health. It was promoted by Edwin Chadwick, at the time a high-level civil servant and who continued to be a well-known public intellectual through the whole of the middle of the century. But what Chadwick promoted was no more than the consensual position.[27] There was little dispute that cleanliness of water, streets, housing, and persons was important. Indeed, "it was a commonplace of educated opinion by the beginning of the 19th century."[28] The various inquiries, royal commissions, statistical reports, and scientific research piled up evidence confirming the strong correlation between lack of sanitation and disease. There was consensus about the need to build sewers and provide clean water; "public health was not a party matter, nor was the need for comprehensive sanitary legislation controversial."[29]

But there was no consensus about how to do it. Ideas about the proper arrangements of government and governance to ensure clean water and functioning sewers were controversial and partisan. At issue were fundamental questions about the citizenship regime's responsibility mix and governance: the role of public versus private provision and central versus local control. When the pioneering legislation actually passed in 1848, it was an adulterated version of the full sanitary idea.

The act constituted an effort to implement the sanitary idea in a citizenship regime dominated by liberal notions of the responsibility of states

[25] In 1854 Dr. John Snow famously removed the handle of the Broad Street pump, and infection rates declined (McLeod 2000).

[26] Scotland focused instead on the improvement of poor relief, and Ireland sought to coordinate and expand provision of infirmaries (Hamlin and Sheard 1998: 591).

[27] The 1848 Act was inspired by the miasmic approach of its main author, Edwin Chadwick, who had the support of recognized experts of the time. For example, William Farr, statistical superintendent of the General Registrar Office, in the 1840s and 1850s carefully mapped patterns of cholera and found that they varied by height of land. This finding allowed him to postulate that a specific, nonliving zymotic material caused each of the class of diseases that included cholera (he labeled the zymotic material cholerine). These epidemic, endemic, and contagious diseases were most prevalent in urban slums, prisons, and port towns because "in such places the air was ladened [sic] with organic matter from respiration, perspiration, decomposition and putrification." The concentration of miasmata – the airborne particles – would decrease as one climbed out of the river basin (quoted in Eyler 2001: 228).

[28] Szreter (1997: 705).

[29] Hamlin and Sheard (1998: 589).

and markets and the role of the central state. The 1848 Public Health Act contained numerous sanitary clauses about the cleansing of sewers, sanitation of houses, supervision of lodging houses and slaughterhouses, and maintenance of pavements. It created a new central department, the General Board of Health under a nominated president, and permitted the establishment of local boards of health. Each board of health was empowered to appoint a surveyor, an inspector of nuisances, a treasurer, a clerk and an "officer of health" who had to be a legally qualified medical practitioner. The General Board had no powers to enforce local action where the clauses of the act were not first adopted locally, however.[30]

Indeed, as enacted, the 1848 act provided mechanisms for governance that virtually ensured it would not achieve its intended effects. "Smoke prevention and insanitary burial grounds, both seen as important health problems, were jettisoned. Metropolitan London was left out ... Scotland and Ireland were left out ... To retain some independence from parliamentary interference, Morpeth[31] bargained away most of the provisions to guarantee health."[32] Such compromises were necessary because of party differences about good governance. "[T]he Tories saw the Home Office or some other cabinet office as planning the needed works and enforcing standards. Influenced by Chadwick, Morpeth and the Whigs were wary of too much parliamentary accountability in technical matters. As models they looked to the Privy Council ... or the Poor Law Commissions – administrations independent of parliamentary interference," and under local control.[33] The act therefore left to local rate payers the decision whether to establish a health board as well as the power to elect its members.[34] It also maintained the existing relationship between the public and private sectors. Responsibility for carrying out the improvements in the water supply – the key to success – remained in the hands of the private companies that already owned the rights to water distribution and sewage collection. As historian Dorothy Porter put it: "the creation of a public health system in Britain was founded upon a political economic philosophy which intended to use statutory regulation to enhance the free operation of market relations."[35] There were, unfortunately, few market incentives to provide clean water or sewers to the poor who did not have the wherewithal to pay for them.[36]

---

[30] Baldwin (1999: 138–9).
[31] Lord Morpeth who carried out the political negotiations around the act, was in charge of the Office of Woods and Forests, where much urban refuse was dumped.
[32] Hamlin and Sheard (1998: 589–90).
[33] Hamlin and Sheard (1998: 589).
[34] The act did include an option for the central government to impose a board of health on a municipality where mortality exceeded 23/1,000 (Hamlin and Sheard 1998: 590). London was excluded from this law, in part because any objective reducing the rate to 23/1,000 seemed vastly too ambitious (Tanner 1999: 37–8).
[35] Porter (1999: 121). As a liberal influenced by the utilitarians, Chadwick supported leaving sanitation in private hands (Hamlin and Sheard 1998: 589).
[36] Szreter (1997: 707).

The result of such compromises was a very partial implementation of the sanitary idea with respect to access to clean water and sewers:

Chadwick had envisaged every urban house connected to a clean water supply and to a water-borne mains sewerage system. ... Plenty of new mains water supply pipes were laid under dug-up streets from the 1840s onward, but the Royal Sanitary Commission found as late as 1871 that most provincial cities were only just then beginning to build the integrated sewerage system necessary to avoid contamination from wastes.... Furthermore, except where the wealthier residents paid for it in their suburban villas, little effort before the last quarter of the nineteenth century was devoted to connecting-up, en masse, individual homes to the enhanced water supplies.[37]

Public health interventions to prevent ill-health and the spread of disease involved more than these public health acts, of course. Two other areas of action are illustrative of the mid-nineteenth-century view of citizens, their rights and responsibilities, and of the ways in which the citizenship regime structured public health interventions in their lives. These are the treatment of international travellers, the vast majority of whom were of middle-class or even aristocratic background. The other was the treatment of noncitizens. The sanitary idea applied quite differently to the two groups.

International travel was booming in the nineteenth century, with movement back and forth between the colonies and around the world as international trade ballooned. An unintended but important consequence of heightened rates of population mobility was the geographic spread of disease. Cholera, for example, spread from Asia to Europe as waves of pandemics, approximately every five years from the 1820s until 1890s. Faced with this and other contagious diseases, governments had to decide how to respond, and particularly whether to impose quarantines on travelers from ports known to have cases of these deadly contagious diseases. If the British government concurred with the choice of most of the other European countries in the cholera pandemic of 1826–37, in later ones it diverged sharply.

Throughout the rest of the nineteenth century, the British steadfastly refused to align with strict quarantine practices favored by Continental governments, making instead the same commitment to liberal sanitarian practices that had underpinned the Public Health Act. "Throughout the 1880s and nineties, during the interminable disputes that pitted the British against most other nations over precautions to be imposed in the Middle East, the contrast was between the fundamentally sanitationist approach taken by the British and their Indian allies and the quarantinism of the major continental powers."[38]

They invented what Peter Baldwin terms the English system of neoquarantinism, passengers arriving at a port of entry who exhibited signs of disease could be detained (quarantined), but passengers appearing healthy were free to continue their travel, as long as they provided details of their destination

---

[37] Szreter (1997: 708–9).
[38] Baldwin (1999: 194).

and notified authorities of any subsequent illness.[39] This preference for medical surveillance and notification contrasted with the observation quarantines advocated by many other European governments. These latter involved detaining for a fixed period of time all passengers arriving from infected ports, whether they exhibited signs of illness or not.[40] Travelers to England, many of whom would be British citizens, were assumed to be sufficiently responsible that they could be relied upon to notify authorities. The same practices applied within the country; the English system in general relied on citizens reporting illness to authorities, disinfecting their homes and linens, refraining from taking public transportation, and so on. Public authorities intervened only when they judged individuals did not, or would not, fulfill their duty to avoid affecting others. In many cases, the poor and working class were judged to lack this sense of duty.

The second example provides a sharp contrast, therefore. In these same years, individuals lacking full citizenship were treated as legitimate targets for state interference, and compulsion was the norm. Even in liberal Britain, non-citizens could be subject to the type of surveillance and compulsion as were subjects in authoritarian systems. One example that contradicts the expression an "Englishman's home is his castle," comes from the program of a pioneer public health professional. London's activist medical officer of health in the 1850s, John Simon, displayed no compunction about overseeing the lives of the poor: he had "inspectors examining hundreds of houses at regular intervals, thus transforming what had been envisaged as temporary visitations during epidemics into a system of permanent and periodic sanitary superintendence of the dwellings of the poor."[41]

Children, and particularly children of the poor, were also targets of state intervention. The 1853 Vaccination Act closely followed on the pioneering Public Health Act of 1848. The law required parents to have their children vaccinated against smallpox, and the children of the poor were particularly sorely treated.[42] That they were the main targets of enforced mass public vaccinations is evidenced by the fact that responsibility for overseeing the program was assigned to the local Poor Law guardians, tasked with ensuring

---

[39] Baldwin (1999: 152–3).
[40] Baldwin (1999: 196).
[41] Baldwin (1999: 240).
[42] "Vaccination was hardly a matter of 'clean needles': at that time it did not involve needles at all. Instead, the infant's skin was scored with a lancet in several places and viral material rubbed into the wound. Eight days later, the parent was required to bring the child back: those who had developed vesicles [blisters] had the lymph harvested for direct application to another child. This 'arm to arm' method was cheaper than vaccination with calf lymph but was, unsurprisingly, much resented by the poor, who could neither prevent their children from being used as a sort of petri dish for the cultivation of vaccine material nor choose the source of the material smeared into their own child's wounds. (The better-off had their children vaccinated privately, with calf lymph or lymph taken from a child whose pedigree they knew.)" (Pedersen, 2005: no page).

that all infants born within their district were vaccinated against smallpox. Vaccination provoked mobilization by working-class (and likely disenfranchised) parents as well as by middle-class liberals. They generated an antivaccination movement that railed against an authoritarian state:

For compulsory vaccination hit the poor in particular: it was the poor who had to be vaccinated at the despised Poor Law hospitals, the poor whose children were smeared seriatim with lymph of unknown provenance, the poor who would find it hard to pay the fines levied on resisters, and the poor who went to prison if unable to find the cash. Small wonder, then, that working-class opponents saw the Acts as 'class legislation' – a form of tyranny suffered by respectable and vigilant parents for no better reason than that they were poor.[43]

Although raising standard Victorian tropes about bodily purity, this mobilization also opposed vaccination in the name of citizenship: "the rhetoric of political rights were [sic] employed by the anti-vaccinators, who raised questions about the rights of parents and of citizens and called attention to the 1853 Act's differential application to middle- and working-class children."[44]

FITTING THE "SANITARY IDEA" INTO THE AGE OF REFORM'S CITIZENSHIP REGIME

At each point of policy choice from the 1830s through the 1870s, public health policy makers selected the action that (1) involved the least challenge to a responsibility mix in which the private predominated over the public sector and the local over the center, (2) assigned responsibility to individuals as well as the state for maintaining public health, (3) focused draconian intervention and compulsion on those excluded from full citizenship. These choices meant that private interests installed water and sewers for those able to pay the price, that local ratepayers were able to choose low taxes over healthy environments, that individuals became monitors of their own health, unless they were not citizens, in which case their houses and their bodies were subject to the kind to intrusion commonplace in the authoritarian systems of Continental Europe.

These patterns were not chance events. They followed from the new narrative of citizenship, profoundly different from the eighteenth-century version, that was institutionalized in the 1830s and 1840s in a wave of legislation and other public actions covering much more than public health. The policy instruments for public health described in the previous section made good sense within the narrative of citizenship deployed in Britain after the 1830s, years sometimes termed the Age of Reform. Examining these norms of citizenship helps explain why the 1848 Act was only a pale imitation of the sanitary idea, why an English system of neoquarantinism was developed and why house inspections and compulsory vaccination overseen by the Poor Law

---

[43] Pedersen (2005).
[44] Robinson (2006: 471).

guardians were considered a modern and scientific public policy for dealing with the health of the poor.

By the end of the eighteenth century a collective narrative describing a nation of merchants and manufacturers developed in opposition to the "Old Corruption." This idiom was understood at the time both in its narrow sense of the widespread use of pensions, sinecures, and gratuitous emoluments deployed by the government for purposes of bribery and reward and in a wider sense by radicals to designate systematic reliance on sinecures, nepotism, and closed corporations, such as the East India Company and those handling municipal affairs. The old and reviled system depended on ties to the Crown, the aristocracy, and the Tory Party, encapsulating a profoundly premodern and non-Weberian view of the state.[45] Radicals opposed to the Old Corruption constructed

different sets of values and frames of references. In this regard the radical, revolutionary nature of Victorian liberalism and reform becomes more apparent, as do the real bases of 'Victorianism': not sexual prudery or an apology for capitalist exploitation but the imposition of rationality and "modernity" upon the irrational and pre-modern – a gain for the ordinary man, not a loss – as well as individuality, the coincidence of merit and reward, and the extension of responsibility and privacy.[46]

The Age of Reform consecrated a new position for the middle class and its rights to representation.[47] Reform rested on recognition of the modern social structure of Britain, with its reliance on agricultural improvements, international trade, and industrial production, much of which occurred in rapidly expanding cities. The middle classes of small property owners, shopkeepers, and professionals gained political power.

Citizens' political rights changed profoundly. The design of the Reform of Act of 1832 reshaped the governance dimensions of the citizenship regime. The parliamentary franchise was enlarged by lowering property restrictions, thereby enfranchising the middle classes, and providing representation to large industrial cities, such as Birmingham and Manchester.[48] The parallel Municipal Corporations Act of 1835 laid the foundations for municipal government, inventing democratically based corporate bodies (rather than ad hoc private corporations) that could undertake local public projects financed by rate payers. A key idea of reform was to allow the middle-class English to escape from the burdens of the Old Corruption's expenditures and to keep taxes at a reasonable level. This was the patriotic position. A quantitative analysis of two centuries of the iconography of John Bull, the symbol of patriotic

---

[45] See Rubenstein (1983: 55; 57–8; 86). S. H. Beer classifies the defence of the Crown as an "Old Tory" position and of the unreformed House of Commons as "Old Whig." Both contrast with Liberal and Radical positions (1957: 614ff.).

[46] Rubenstein (1983: 86).

[47] Beer (1957: 630).

[48] Lizzeri and Persico (2004: 737).

Britishness, maps the changing representations in the popular press of the claims of ordinary citizens. From 1784 until 1832 by far the most important issues raised by John Bull were the tax burden and the civil list. The latter disappeared after 1832, but the tax burden remained the priority.[49]

Social rights were also fundamentally redesigned, via the debate about and then passage of the New Poor Law in 1834. Still excluded from political citizenship by reason of their lack of property, the poor who were not able to provide for themselves lost their previous rights to some measure of relief and were consigned to the "modern" workhouses, populated almost exclusively by the old, lone parents and their children, and the most feckless of men. The governance structure of the citizenship regime ensured that workhouse conditions would remain harsh; administration at the local level provided every inducement for the Boards of Guardians to act as guardians of the rates rather than the poor.[50] The new law, including the institutionalization of local management, "dramatically cut the nation's expenditure on welfare payments to the sick, old and poor from 2% of the national product … to only 1%."[51]

Sanitarians saw their policy proposals as directly linked to social welfare and the citizenship rights of the "deserving poor." Indeed, "the maximum sanitationist program implied change on a revolutionary scale, granting to the poor living conditions largely achieved by the well-off."[52] Others reasoned in terms of the responsibility mix of citizenship. For example, Edwin Chadwick advocated his policies for improving health and preventing disease as the best way to halt the major cause of poverty, which he saw as being acute infectious diseases fatal to male breadwinners. Loss of a breadwinner could result in an increase in the population of the workhouses. The sanitarian position was one, then, that could offer to keep families intact and capable of maintaining themselves. Dorothy Porter summarizes the relationship between the citizenship regime's vision of family, market and public responsibilities this way:

Reducing the cost of destitution and poverty by preventing the premature mortality of breadwinners was one feature of a new theory of government which asserted that efficiency and justice could only be obtained through the scientific and rational organization of the affairs of state. Policy-making should become a managerial practice. Edwin Chadwick was the central figure in bringing this approach to the management of public health with his "sanitary idea."[53]

---

[49] Taylor (1992: 96–9).

[50] The structure of interests was built into the franchise for welfare spending which was reformed in 1818–19 as well as 1834. Only property owners (including absentee ones) could vote on tax levels, whereas previously entire vestries (including, therefore, the potential receipts of poor relief) had sometimes voted on relief levels. As Lizzeri and Persico (2004: 739) put it: "by 1834 property owners had taken a dominant role in voting on issues related to poor-law spending."

[51] Szreter (1999: 147).

[52] See Baldwin (1999: 142). See also the quotes from parliamentary debates in Hamlin and Sheard (1998).

[53] Porter (1999: 121).

Such changes in citizenship norms and public actions that put an end to the Old Corruption were followed by significant changes in policy that reflected the interests of the newly enfranchised urban middle classes and the ideas upon which they relied. Total government spending as a percentage of GDP (after accounting for spending on war) remained stable from 1790 to 1890, while total taxation as a portion of GDP decreased after 1800 and did not rise again until after 1870. There was, however, a major shift in the composition of spending. Although poor relief fell, local spending as a proportion of government spending began to climb, albeit slowly.[54]

Such patterns track the shift in political power from the Crown and aristocracy to the urban middle classes. The latter had a clear interest in some public goods being provided. If the poorest of the poor (those excluded from citizenship rights) were sequestered in workhouses, vast numbers of the working poor shared urban space, water and air with the enfranchised middle classes.[55] In this situation, then, theories of miasmatic transfer of disease made sense of a situation in which property owners in industrial cities might succumb to contagious disease alongside the poor. As the 1844 report of the Parliamentary Committee of Inquiry into the State of Large Towns and Populous Districts put it, miasma did not stay put: "The presence of such emanations, whether they be derived from stagnant ditches, open cesspools, or from accumulation of decaying refuse, is a great cause of disease and death, not confined to the immediate district in which they occur, but extending their influence to neighbourhoods, and even to distant places."[56]

Nonetheless, as we have pointed out, the sanitary idea was not fully implemented. Nor were policy communities unaware that their hopes had been derailed. Indeed the 1857 foundation of the Social Science Association, in which Chadwick and many other liberal reformers were active, was explicitly framed as a response to the perception that the "stream of reform" had been "chilled if not frozen."[57] Rather than forward movement and progress in sanitation and public health, there was a "prolonged period of municipal inactivism from the 1830s until the 1870s."[58]

The limits on the sanitary idea's prescriptions for water, sewers, and urban cleanliness in general followed from two dimensions of the citizenship regime itself – those of governance and the role of the state. Building the full infrastructure would have required going against the mid-Victorian citizenship regime's norms for the responsibility mix, with its commitment to private

---

[54] Lizzeri and Persico (2004: 710–12).

[55] William Farr wrote in 1838, "the epidemics which arise in the east end of the town [London] do not stay there; they travel to the west and prove fatal" (quoted in Lizzeri and Persico 2004: 714). Moreover, while the wealthy could move to suburban villas, the newly enfranchised middle-income rate payers often still lived within the central city (Szreter 1997: 705).

[56] Quoted in Lizzeri and Persico (2004): 742.

[57] Goldman (1986: 116 and passim).

[58] Millward and Sheard (1995); Szreter (1997: 706).

over public action, and preference for local choice rather than central institutions of governance. "In the name of local self-government, a virtual rebellion among this class [the 'shopocracy'] of ratepayers took place against those clauses of the 1848 Public Health Act that threatened to force towns to spend on improving their water supply."[59] The result was that the clauses were rarely used and indeed were rescinded in 1858. This occurred despite the availability via the popular local press of statistical and other evidence of contagion patterns documented and reported in the General Registrar Office reports prepared under the supervision of William Farr.[60]

Despite having plentiful social knowledge, in the form of increasingly popular statistical analyses, resistance to full implementation of the sanitarian program for water and sewers predominated. It came from municipal voters who were caught between two sets of interests: for a healthy environment and for low taxes. The latter interest generally won out; opposition to implementing the sanitary idea came from market-favoring citizens and political forces and they managed to hold back the achievement of its goals for decades. The Municipal Reform Act of 1835 had given political power to a "diverse and growing amalgam of petty capitalist rate-payers, with their numerous doctrinal and congregational differences [who] could all agree on only one thing: not to spend each other's money if at all possible."[61] It was local elites and rate payers eligible to vote in local elections who revolted against the dictates of the "clean party."[62]

Moreover, improvements that were made often privileged commercial and industrial expansion over general public health. Water mains were installed, and the volume of constant-pressure water supply (necessary as an industrial raw material) vastly improved. But the sanitarians' key idea of connecting every dwelling to a supply of clean water and a sanitary sewer was not realized, and therefore the 1872 Public Health Act had still to promise to guarantee "the right of each Briton to pure air, water and soil."[63]

THE RECONFIGURED CITIZENSHIP REGIME AFTER 1870: PROGRESS FOR THE SANITARY IDEA; OPPOSITION TO SANITARIANS

By the time the 1875 Public Health Act was passed, the citizenship regime was already substantially changed. Although not as all-encompassing as the move from the Old Corruption to the Age of Reform, there were a number of significant internal adjustments to its liberalism that made it more inclusive and legitimated a more active state, albeit still a local one.

---

[59] Szreter (1997: 708).
[60] Szreter (1997: 705); Eyler (2001: 229–30).
[61] Szreter (1999: 148).
[62] Porter (1999: 120).
[63] Baldwin (1999: 149).

The Politics of Water and Sewers in the 1870s

When the consolidating Public Health Act was passed in 1875, "much that had been permissive became imperative."[64] Municipal governments, for example, were obliged to create a local health board and hire a local health officer as well as provide adequate local water and related health services. Rate payers could no longer use cost control as an excuse to avoid setting up a board. The Vaccination Act of 1871 also required action, mandating the employment of vaccination officers by the local authorities.[65] In the last three decades of the nineteenth century there was a significantly reduced reliance on the private sector to provide access to clean water, sewers, and other improvements, at the same time that the momentum of public spending on water, public health, gas and electricity, roads and trams, and education increased, both as capital expenditures and current costs.[66]

This new politics of public health cannot be explained by any new scientific consensus; the principles of the sanitary idea remained the same and still rested on an agreement about prophylactic strategies masking differences about aetiology. Parts of the public health movement still relied on the miasmatic version of sanitarianism, as they had in the 1840s. Some sanitarians resisted germ theory formulations and as late as "the early nineties, reputable British public health experts were still rejecting Koch's bacillus as the cause of cholera, appealing instead to atmospheric conditions or simple filth."[67] On the other hand, as early as the 1860s William Farr, who had started by being convinced by theories of miasma, had been converted to transmission by water (John Snow's argument) and even gave his zymads "additional properties of life, until they became nearly indistinguishable from living organisms," such as Koch's bacillus.[68]

Fuller implementation came not from new scientific knowledge but rather with major changes on several dimensions of the citizenship regime. Most obviously, political rights were expanded. Formal political rights were extended to whole new population groups in the parliamentary franchise reforms of 1867 (an 88 percent increase in the size of the electorate) and 1884 (bringing household suffrage). Parallel municipal franchise reforms in 1869 and 1888 reduced residency and rate-paying requirements, in effect giving the vote to laborers who rented housing.[69] But beyond that, as the next paragraphs describe, governance practices were redesigned, both by the inclusion of many more voters from the ranks of the working poor and by restrictions placed on local authorities' capacity to resist. Second, the norms about the responsibility mix were altered, and they brought much greater legitimacy for the state to assume

---

[64] Hamlin and Sheard (1998: 590).
[65] Durbach (2005: 8).
[66] Millward and Sheard (1995: 503ff.).
[67] Baldwin (1999: 184).
[68] Eyler (2001: 230).
[69] Lizzeri and Persico (2004: 737–9).

responsibility for delivering a healthy environment to citizens. The changes involved were, in other words, institutional and normative; they shifted patterns of interests as well as ideas.

Still reluctant to take greater responsibilities for governance on itself, the central government in the 1870s was nonetheless newly willing to *oblige* municipal authorities to ensure services were available as well as find the revenue sources to pay for them, something it had refused to do in the compromise legislation of 1848 and 1858.[70] Parliament was actively legislating in a wide range of areas that changed governance patterns in the citizenship regime by assigning new responsibilities to local authorities. These included the 1870 education act establishing school boards, an 1875 housing act (Artisan Dwelling Act), and an 1856 police act.

New local governance practices took shape and the new activism had several origins. One was the obligations imposed on local authorities, just described. Another source was the redistribution of rights that widened access to political participation. Newly enfranchised tenants had a real interest in their rented housing being linked to the sewer and water mains and to the cleanliness of that water and functioning of the sewers. This institutional reform shifted the balance of local political power in a major way, breaking "the hold of rate-payer 'economy' over municipal politics" that had shaped local politics in most cities for more than three decades.[71] Elected municipal politicians could see a clear political interest in responding to these constituents, and they did not tarry in adjusting their program.

Yet the addition of new voters alone can not account for the enthusiasm with which municipal leaders threw themselves into building infrastructure. These decades in British politics are sometimes labeled those of "municipal socialism" and "gas and water socialism." Terms chosen to represent the wide scope and large ambition of municipal action, the local authorities' policies and programs owed more to liberal principles of human improvement and classical visions of successful societies than they did to left-wing thought.[72] What happened in these decades was that the investment in the infrastructure that the sanitarians had long been advocating could finally be married to a normative position on citizenship that not only permitted but also virtually required increased spending. John Bull significantly reduced his focus on and opposition to the tax burden in the years 1876–85.[73]

---

[70] See Millward and Sheard (1995).

[71] Szreter (1999: 149).

[72] The great liberal politician and mayor of Birmingham from 1873 to 1876, Joseph Chamberlain, became a leader in this movement, innovating not only in his political programme appealing to the newly enfranchised but also in the forms of local governance. He pioneered in the use of large, long-term, low-interest loans to finance improvements as well as in setting up municipal monopolies for services, whose profits would finance infrastructural costs (Szreter 1998: 709ff.).

[73] Taylor (1992: 99).

Ideas of the "civic gospel" providing new norms of behaviour and citizen engagement for prosperous citizens provided goals and standards other than those of saving taxes. "The 'civic gospel' spread with something of a rivalry now developing between the town halls of many of Britain's great 'city states' during the last quarter of the century, as they competed with each other for salubrity, sanitary provision, healthy amenities and the lowest death rates." Good citizenship no longer enjoined a common effort to save money. "[E]xplicit parallels began to be drawn by the confident city fathers with the cultural achievements of the city-states of classical Greece and Renaissance Italy, as models for the corporate conversion of mere industrial prosperity into positive human progress, civilisation, art and learning."[74]

Social gospelers were not the only ones to turn back to Greece for ideas. British social thinking became centred on a form of Platonic idealism, that flowered into an "emphasis on corporate identity, individual altruism, ethical imperatives, and active citizen-participation."[75] The result was a consensus reaching from the social collectivism advocated by Helen Bosanquet and leading members of the Charity Organization Society (who invoked "the companionship and assistance" of friendly societies, cooperatives, and trade unions) to the Fabianism promoted by Beatrice and Sidney Webb.[76]

These normative positions could easily sustain claims for spending to realize the sanitary idea and policy action was immediate: local authorities received subsidized loans for sanitary activities from the central exchequer at a rate that increased eightfold, from eleven million for the years 1848–70 to eighty-four million for the period 1871–97. "Whereas Britain may ... have underinvested in its cities in the classic industrial revolution period, such could not be said of the late nineteenth century. The public sector played a central role in its expansion; its share was half in the early 1870s but it was accounting for nearly three-quarters by the early years of this [twentieth] century.... investment in roads, public health, and water supply all showed a rise."[77]

Citizenship and Bodily Integrity – Opposition to Sanitarians

If the sanitary idea finally made good headway in municipal politics with respect to sewers and water after 1870, the same cannot be said for its scientific knowledge imposed on noncitizens in the mid-Victorian years. Middle-class, mostly male reformers had proudly developed their institutions for social knowledge

---

[74] Szreter (1999: 149).

[75] Harris (1992: 118) obviously takes issue with A. V. Dicey's characterization of the years after 1870 as a transition from individualism to collectivism. See also Harris (1992: 137; 123ff.).

[76] "The Webbs, for example, wholly shared the Bosanquets' belief that private and public virtue were not independent, that 'state-conscious idealism' was the goal of citizenship, and that social-welfare policies should be ethically as well as materially constructive.... But they claimed that the deviant or needy individual could far more easily be provoked into self-improvement from within the context of state social services than if left to his own unaided efforts" (Harris, 1992: 133; also 131–3).

[77] Millward and Sheard (1995: 504–5).

where medical experts, statisticians, and other social observers met to discuss and promote reform. By the late 1860s, their actions and even their bastions were under assault from social movements acting in the name of the excluded and those seeking full citizenship. Two movements for more inclusive citizenship, in the form of both political rights and the basic civil right of bodily integrity for those excluded from citizenship, challenged some sanitarian practices. They explicitly rejected a number of fundamentally ill liberal norms of the citizenship regime with regard to noncitizens, developed at a time when the status was conferred almost exclusively on middle-class male property owners. In other words, as the citizenship regime was altered, providing new rights and reshaping governance, some of the practices of sanitarians were contested by appealing to the norms of the new regime.

Two examples illustrate this process. The Compulsory Vaccination Act of 1853, covering all infants born in England and Wales, had resulted from the research work and lobbying by some of the most prominent sanitarians of the time, organized in the London Epidemiological Society.[78] The 1853 legislation was reformed in 1867 and then in 1871. The third reform's policy design demonstrated the same governance practices that had finally prompted massive infrastructural investments: central authorities placed obligations on local authorities by mandating them to hire and pay for vaccination officers.[79] All three laws, but especially the third, provoked civil disobedience on the part of working-class parents as well as much public outcry in the streets and the press. The vaccination officers were feared and reviled as representatives of authoritarianism and the poor law.

Opposition did not focus, therefore, on its costs to taxpayers, as it might have in earlier decades. Rather, "resistance to compulsory vaccination was mobilized not only by Liberal reformers, but by members of a large and politically active working class who lobbied for their rights as English citizens."[80] Resisters made explicit links to the broadest issues of citizenship, that is the representation of the very nation, when they asked rhetorically as one pamphleteer did, whether "'Englishmen, Scotchmen and Irishmen' were 'fit to enjoy Home Rule over their own bodies, and over the bodies of their offspring.'"[81] Antivaccinationists explicitly targeted the sanitary idea and the citizenship regime of the mid-Victorian years. They accused legislators, for example, of treating working-class babies as a "nuisance" and the working class in general as "conduits of disease."[82] But they reserved perhaps their greatest opprobrium

---

[78] Among other members were the by now familiar William Farr and John Snow (Evans 2001: 226).

[79] Local authorities resisted the 1853 law, and such nonenforcement caused the central government to impose higher fines and other mechanisms of coercion in the second and third pieces of legislation (Durbach 2005: 2–10).

[80] Durbach (2000): 46.

[81] Ibid. In this sense they were contesting in the name of what Bouchard (Chapter 7, in this volume) calls the collective imaginary.

[82] Durbach (2000: 50, 49).

for the way the law was enforced. Relying on the Poor Law guardians put vaccination, in the eyes of its working-class opponents, in the same basket as the menace of the workhouse and the cutbacks in poor relief that were, as we have seen, a major element of the citizenship regime from the 1830s on.

One part of their repertoire confronted the sanitarians directly, by disputing the very statistics used to justify small pox vaccination and arguing it harmed more than it helped.[83] But perhaps the argument that carried the most weight was the one calling for sanitarians to live up to their aetiological position, and this in an ironic twist. The emergence of germ theory in the 1870s and 1880s provided anti-vaccinators with "a new, authoritative medical language to articulate what they continued to identify as smallpox's material and social cause: dirty environments and compromised constitutions."[84] Thus they could make claims to the very sanitary idea that had promoted the hated system in the first place, doing so by distinguishing themselves from the "undeserving" poor.[85] They could argue that as citizens who were responsible – and there-fore almost by definition "clean" – working-class parents ought to be able to make their own decisions about their children's bodies. They could make claims in the name of the more inclusive citizenship regime for the respect of their bodily integrity and against the surveillance and intervention of well-meaning but ultimately interfering middle-class sanitarians. Faced with unre-lenting dissent and noncompliance, the law was changed following the report of the royal commission appointed in 1889. Beginning in "1898 any parent who could satisfy two justices or a police magistrate that he or she 'conscien-tiously believed' that vaccination would be harmful to their child was granted exemption from the Act."[86]

The second example of opposition to sanitarians' limited view of citizenship rights comes from the opposition to the draconian forms of surveillance and attacks on bodily integrity in the Contagious Diseases Acts. These were fre-quently seen as similar to the Vaccination Acts in respect to their interference with the bodily integrity of those whose rights were unrecognized.[87] The mobi-lization for repeal pitted the proponents of the sanitarian paradigm, whose liberal principles of minimal interference to ensure the removal of sources of infection and nuisances had been set aside in this case, against a mobilization for recognition of the women's right to bodily integrity and autonomy.

Britain's three Contagious Diseases Acts passed in the 1860s targeted pros-titutes in garrison towns who supposedly spread disease to the army, thereby

---

[83] Durbach (2005: 2; 47).
[84] Durbach (2005: 150).
[85] Durbach (2000) develops in detail the ways in which the antivaccination campaigns embedded this distinction between the "respectable" and "undeserving" within the working class itself.
[86] Pedersen (2005).
[87] Durbach (2000: 45, 49) documents the quite explicit connection that antivaccinationists made to the Contagious Diseases Act, as well as the similar sense of horror at the treatment of women as not respectable (for example, p. 59).

weakening it at the very time that Britain's identity as a nation required a large imperial presence. The acts resulted from an alliance between military leaders whose interest was in a healthy fighting force and medical men who propounded regular examination as the key to controlling venereal diseases. After trying first to institute compulsory examinations of soldiers, and failing when opponents argued it "contravened men's self-respect" – understood as a citizenship right – attention turned to prostitutes. Targeting prostitutes serving enlisted men, the 1864 Contagious Diseases Act required any allegedly diseased prostitute to undergo an inspection. If infected, she could be held in a lock hospital for up to three months. The 1866 Contagious Diseases Act empowered a special police force to order bimonthly inspections for up to a year. Changes in 1869 required registration of prostitutes, increased inspection locales and the number of towns targeted, and upped incarceration in a lock hospital from three to nine months. The methods deployed were much closer to Continental Europe's quarantinism than to England's emphasis on noninterference.[88]

This state strategy of policing and quarantine was vehemently opposed by civil society groups.[89] Josephine Butler, one of the leading activists for repeal, exposed the link between women's lack of the basic civil right of bodily integrity and the sanitarian position on filth and nuisance:

This legalisation of vice, which is the endorsement of the "necessity" of impurity for men, and the institution of the slavery of women, is the most open denial which modern times have seen of the principle of the sacredness of the individual human being. ... An English high-class journal confessed this, when it dared to demand that women who are unchaste shall henceforth be dealt with "not as human beings, but as foul sewers" or some such "material nuisance," without souls, without rights, and without responsibility.[90]

The campaign to repeal the Contagious Diseases Acts erupted in the bastion of positivism and liberalism frequented by sanitarians, the meeting of the Social Science Association in Bristol. This conflict that began in 1869 was "to the evident amazement of the doctors and civil servants of its Public Health Department – the very men whose scientific rationalism had led to the

[88] For detailed analyses see Walkowitz (1980) and Baldwin (1999: 372–4), in which Britain's position on venereal disease is described as being closer to the Continental model than it was, for example, with respect to cholera.

[89] In 1869 repealers founded the National Association for the Repeal of the Contagious Diseases Act, followed immediately by the creation of the Ladies' National Association for the Repeal of the Contagious Diseases Act. This second association was a linchpin in the long campaign for repeal and its initiatives were supported at various points by all leading activists for women's rights, including Josephine Butler, Harriet Martineau and Florence Nightingale. The repealers argued points of principle rather than simply focusing on medical effectiveness, as the public health experts had. As Josephine Butler put it, the issue was "the autonomy of the individual" (quoted in Jeffreys 1987: 185).

[90] Quoted in Jeffreys (1987: 185).

introduction of the Acts in the first place."[91] The Social Science Association represented a middle class whose popular sentiments and social knowledge were composed of a "widely flourishing culture of popular 'social science', operating through the medium of national and local sociological and statistical associations."[92] It provided "a social vision ... dominated by the belief that middle-class progress could be universalized."[93]

This positivist world view shaped the collective narrative and practices of citizenship. It was, therefore, a logical institution in which to debate the issues raised by the Contagious Diseases Acts; compulsory medical examinations and incarceration for resistance to them infringed a basic civil right of citizenship. For several years, disputes over citizenship, and particularly women's civil right to bodily integrity, was intense. Eventually, the powerful movement for repeal transmogrified into the movement for women's political rights of citizenship, representing the liberal and moral feminism that opposed flagrant manifestations of a double standard and claimed for all women, no matter their class or calling, the right to be treated as fully human.

The long campaign and eventual repeal of the legislation in 1886 signaled, in other words, one of the ways in which the citizenship regime was becoming more inclusive and the practice of differential treatment of citizen and noncitizen favored by sanitarians could not be sustained.

SUMMARY AND CONCLUSIONS

In the cross-time comparison presented here, it has been possible to observe several patterns that help make sense of some of the different prophylaxis choices that were made during the mid and late Victorian period, the reasons for their partial and then full application, and the mobilisations against sanitarians' preferences for heavy-handed restrictions on noncitizens.

First, England's commitment to the sanitarian paradigm from the 1830s through the 1870s was stronger than that found among its Continental neighbors. This commitment matched well to British norms of citizenship, which in the Age of Reform had become not only more liberal but was also more inclusive of urban middle-class ideas and interests and involved a commitment to a modern, technocratic and evidence-based policy process. Other norms of this same citizenship regime, however, worked to limit the full translation of the sanitarian medical paradigm into policy. Norms for the responsibility mix and governance stressed private provision, deemphasized Parliamentary imposition and sustained beliefs in local authority. They allowed middle-class rate payers to trade off their interest in low taxes against spending on public goods such as clean water and sewers, in which they also had an interest both for themselves and for their environments more generally. This trade-off became less

[91] Goldman (1986: 129–30).
[92] Goldman (1986); Harris (1992: 120).
[93] Harris (1992: 120).

sustainable in the 1870s, as decision makers developed new ideas about "great cities" and responsible citizenship. Politicians and municipal institutions had every interest to respond to the demands of the newly enfranchised voters, whose economic circumstances never allowed them to entertain the hope of a personal escape from the overcrowded and filthy cities. But in addition the blockages to the sanitary idea coming from the dimensions of governance and responsibility mix were lifted and the paradigm could be more fully implemented.

Second, some of the mixed patterns in prophylaxis – the "polymorphous divergence of precautions" – that Peter Baldwin[94] emphasises take on a clearer meaning when the citizenship status of the targets of intervention is factored into the analysis. In Britain through the mid-Victorian years even sanitarians were quite willing to act as the Continent's authoritarian quarantinists did when the target was a poor person without political rights or a woman lacking recognized civil and political rights. Draconian measures such as confinement in a lock hospital and compulsory unsanitary vaccination were overturned via mobilization in around claims for citizenship and eventually gave greater responsibility over their own bodies and those of their children to those who had been subject to the sanitarians' ministrations.

Third, this example demonstrates that no medical paradigm is fully hegemonic. Even as the sanitarians were promoting public health interventions to fight miasma, alternative scientific theories were competing for recognition. Eventually, "the good" science drove out "the bad" and the bacteriological basis for cholera and other contagious diseases was accepted. The result was not consensus, but rather a set of new disputes about the role of dirt and the importance of cleanliness, several of which maintained the familiar distinction between prophylactic strategies for citizens and for noncitizens. In other words, over the nineteenth century there was little reduction in the widespread middle-class fear that the lives of the popular classes were defined by dissolution and dirt. Male workers were now citizens, but working-class wives and poor women were still fair game for inspection and regulation of their daily life, particularly with respect to that key female activity of childbirth and child rearing.[95] Both the germ theory paradigm and lingering miasmatic thinking provided a "scientific" basis for middle-class social workers and doctors working for the state or private philanthropic agencies to regulate working-class and poor women's housekeeping, child rearing, and hygiene. But that is another story.[96]

---

[94] Baldwin (1999: 550).

[95] As Dr Harold Kerr, assistant medical officer, Newcastle upon Tyne, said in 1910 (quoted in McIntyre, 1997: 724): "The terribly heavy death rate among young children in our town is of course due to a certain extent to the relative unhealthiness of our surroundings, but that is by no means the chief cause. The factor that is of primary importance is maternal mismanagement ..., every visitor in the homes of the working class knows only too well the hopeless ignorance of the majority of the mothers in regard to everything connected with the rearing of healthy offspring."

[96] For some of that story see Jenson (1986).

9

The Multicultural Welfare State?

Will Kymlicka

INTRODUCTION

One of the most important challenges facing contemporary Western societies concerns increasing ethnocultural diversity. Three interrelated, big, slow-moving trends are dramatically transforming Western societies: (1) the increasing ethnic and racial heterogeneity of the population; (2) the increasing politicization of ethnocultural identities, and the rise of "identity politics" or "recognition politics"; and (3) partly in response to the first two trends, the increasing adoption of "multiculturalism" policies to accommodate politicized ethnocultural groups. In short, there are diversity-related changes in demographic composition, in political mobilization, and in public policies.

The implications of these trends for population health are potentially enormous. Studies often reveal significant inequalities in health outcomes across ethnic and racial groups, and even though the precise causal explanations remain debated, there is growing evidence for the importance of social factors, alongside more traditional genetic or economic explanations. Only a small fraction of these variations are explained by differences in gene frequency across groups, such as the greater genetic disposition of Ashkenazi Jews toward Tay-Sachs disease or of Caucasian people with light skin pigmentation toward melanoma. These disease-specific genetic idiosyncrasies – which are as likely to affect dominant groups as subordinate ones – do not explain the tendency of ethnic and racial minorities to have worse health across a broad range of illnesses.

A more significant factor is undoubtedly the fact that racial and ethnic minorities often have below-average per capita incomes, or unequal access to health care, both of which strongly affect health outcomes. But even when

This chapter grows out of an ongoing project with Keith Banting (Queen's University), and draws on our coauthored work and on research conducted in collaboration with Richard Johnston (Pennsylvania) and Stuart Soroka (McGill).

controlling for socioeconomic status and access to health care, the evidence suggests ethnic and racial minorities often suffer from worse health outcomes,[1] and this suggests that a significant causal role is played by what Hall and Taylor call "the structure of social relations."[2]

According to Hall and Taylor, the structure of social relations can be understood along two key dimensions: vertically, there are forms of "social hierarchy" that differentially accord social status to individuals; and horizontally, there are forms of "social connectedness" that link individuals to broader networks of friends, neighbors, colleagues, and various civic, economic, and political associations. These two dimensions play an important role in determining both the challenges of daily life that people confront and the social resources they can access in dealing with those challenges. Ethnic and racial diversity are important to both, and are likely to become more so in the future.

The significance of race for social hierarchy is obvious. Ideologies of racism and ethnocentrism have profoundly shaped status hierarchies in the Western world for centuries, and many studies have shown that ethnic and racial minorities continue to experience stigmatization. This experience is a stressful one, which over time contributes to the "wear and tear of daily life," with demonstrable adverse health outcomes.[3]

The impact of ethnic and racial diversity on social connectedness is perhaps less obvious but is increasingly a matter of intense scholarly debate. Robert Putnam has recently argued that as societies become more ethnically and racially diverse, individuals become socially *dis*connected, less likely to join formal or informal networks and associations. As diversity increases, people become less trusting of others. Moreover, this distrust is not just of people from other racial and ethnic groups, but also of members of one's own group, such that one neither "bridges" to members of other groups nor "bonds" with members of one's own group. Rather, one simply retreats from social connection altogether. As Putnam puts it, "Diversity seems to trigger *not* in-group/out-group division, but anomie or social isolation ... people living in ethnically diverse settings appear to 'hunker down.'"[4] The resulting diminution of people's social networks and social capital further contributes to the wear and tear of daily life, with demonstrable adverse health consequences, and not just for those at the bottom of a status hierarchy.[5]

---

[1] For overviews, see Williams (1999); Karlsen and Nazroo (2002); Krieger (2003).

[2] See Chapter 3 in this volume by Peter Hall and Rosemary Taylor for the ideas in this and the following paragraph.

[3] Williams (1999); Karlsen and Nazroo (2002). These adverse effects of status hierarchies are found not only in relation to health but also in relation to a broad range of developmental goals such as education (for example, Steele 1999).

[4] Putnam (2007: 149).

[5] For studies linking social capital to health outcomes, see Kawachi and Kennedy (1999); Kawachi et al (1998).

As Western societies become more diverse, we urgently need to gain a better understanding of these dynamics of social hierarchy and social connectedness, and how they shape people's vulnerabilities and capacities. For example, what sorts of "everyday destigmatization strategies" help protect the members of racial minorities from the injuries of racism?[6] What sorts of bridging and bonding strategies are available for citizens in diverse neighborhoods to preserve the vitality of their social networks and associational life?

These questions represent a compelling research agenda for the future. But they are complicated, and perhaps even overshadowed, by another concern. For many commentators, the greatest challenge of ethnic and racial diversity is not its impact on the social resources available to individuals and neighborhoods, but its impact on the collective capacity of society generally to produce public goods, including education, health care, and the welfare state. The concern here is not with the resiliency of individuals or groups, but with the very capacity of society to adopt health-promoting public institutions and public policies.

In the modern Western world, the core of these health-promoting public institutions and policies has been the national welfare state. It has had the task of promoting health both directly, through the provision of accessible health care and public health campaigns, and indirectly, by reducing the socioeconomic inequalities that are known to adversely affect overall health outcomes. Western welfare states differ significantly in the extent and effectiveness of their efforts to promote health and human development; nevertheless, in a broad historical and comparative perspective they have been responsible for an increase in longevity and well-being that is unparalleled in human history, and studies consistently show that population health is better in countries with more generous welfare states.[7]

A crucial question, therefore, is whether current diversity-related trends are eroding the viability and functioning of the national welfare state. As we will see, many commentators fear that diversity is having this effect. If so, the long-term effect of increasing diversity on population health may be not only to erode the social resources that individuals and communities draw upon, but also to erode the public services and income supports provided by the welfare state.

In this chapter, I will explore this emerging debate on the impact of ethnocultural diversity on the welfare state. Even though I believe that this debate is largely misconceived, it contains some important lessons for how we theorize the role of social relations, cultural scripts, and public institutions in promoting health and human development.

---

[6] See Lamont's chapter on destigmatization strategies (Chapter 6).

[7] For the variable effectiveness of Western welfare states in promoting health outcomes, including the impact of both direct health care spending and of policies aimed at reducing socioeconomic gradients, see Chapter 1 in this volume by Hertzman and Siddiqi. For the general correlations between the size of the welfare state and population health, see Zambon et al. (2006); Chung and Muntaner (2007).

DIVERSITY AND THE WELFARE STATE

Why do commentators fear that the increasing salience of ethnocultural diversity will erode the welfare state? Part of the answer lies in the link between the welfare state and ideologies of nationhood. The national welfare state is precisely a *national* institution, and its historic evolution is tied up with ideas of nationhood and national identity. In fact, the link between the welfare state and national identity runs in both directions. On the one hand, governments and other political actors appealed to ideas of common nationhood and national solidarity to justify and legitimize the welfare state. Citizens were told that they should be willing to support the welfare state because its beneficiaries are conationals to whom we have special obligations: they are "one of us." On the other hand, the welfare state also served to reproduce and diffuse ideas of nationhood. Access to common national educational and health care systems, and to other social rights (pensions, unemployment), gave concrete substance to ideas of common nationhood. Participating in the institutions of a national welfare state provided an important source of common experiences and loyalties that helped to bind together the otherwise disparate populations of Western countries.[8]

In short, the welfare state both presupposed and perpetuated an ideology of nationhood. In that sense, the welfare state must be understood in relation to what Gérard Bouchard calls a "collective imaginary," with its accompanying cultural scripts that inform people about the nature of their collective moral order, with its sense of mutual rights and responsibilities.[9] Indeed, the mutually supportive relationship between the welfare state and ideas of nationhood can arguably be seen as one of the most successful examples of the construction of a well-functioning collective imaginary that has enabled modern societies to deal effectively with a range of challenges to health and well-being.

However, many commentators today worry that the trends toward increasing ethnic diversity, identity politics, and multiculturalism policies are eroding this collective imaginary, undermining the national identities and solidarities that have historically sustained the welfare state. There are actually two concerns here:

1. Ethnic/racial diversity as such makes it more difficult to sustain redistributive policies, since it is difficult to generate a common sense of national identity and feelings of national solidarity and trust across ethnic/racial lines. We can formulate this as the hypothesis that the larger the size of ethnic/racial minorities as a percentage of the population, the harder

---

[8] Conversely, a group's exclusion from equal access to the welfare state provides a clear symbol that its members weren't "one of us," and weren't full members of the national community. An example concerns the way African Americans were effectively excluded from New Deal-era welfare state programs (Katznelson 2005).

[9] See Chapter 7 in this volume by Bouchard for a discussion of this idea.

it is to sustain a robust welfare state. I will call this the heterogeneity/
redistribution trade-off;

2. The multiculturalism policies adopted to recognize or accommodate
   ethnic groups tend to further undermine national solidarity and trust,
   since they emphasize ethnic differences rather than national commonalities. We can formulate this as the hypothesis that the more a country
   embraces the multicultural politics of ethnic recognition, the harder it
   is to sustain the politics of economic redistribution. I will call this the
   "recognition/redistribution" trade-off.

The first hypothesis argues that the very presence of sizable ethnic/racial
diversity erodes the welfare state, regardless of what sorts of policies governments adopt to manage that diversity. The second hypothesis argues that the
typical way in which Western governments today manage diversity – namely,
by attempting to accommodate it through multiculturalism policies, rather
than ignoring or suppressing it – worsens the problem.

If these hypotheses are true, the historically mutually reinforcing relationship between the welfare state and nationhood is challenged in both directions. Not only will the welfare state become less able to draw upon feelings
of national solidarity to legitimize its demands on citizens, but it will also
become less able to perpetuate and diffuse national identities. As the practices
and ideologies of multiculturalism penetrate the institutions of the welfare
state such as schools and social services, they will become instruments for dif-
fusing ethnic particularism rather than shared nationhood, further reducing
the national solidarity upon which the welfare state depends.

If either of these hypotheses is true, we face a serious and growing problem
because there is no reason to expect either that ethnic/racial minorities will
diminish as a percentage of the overall population in most Western countries, or that these groups will abandon their claims for multicultural accommodations. On the contrary, there is every reason to expect that minorities
will continue to grow as a percentage of the overall population. For example,
indigenous peoples are the fastest growing segment of the population in countries like Canada, the United States, or Australia, with a higher birth rate than
the nonindigenous population. Also, immigration into the Western democracies will continue to grow, partly to offset the declining birth rate and aging
population, and partly because there are limits on the state's ability to stop
would-be migrants from entering the country. Similarly, there is every reason to expect that minorities, whether they are historically rooted or newer
migrants, will continue to press demands for recognition, which grow out of
deep forces of contemporary societies.[10]

So if there is a tendency for either heterogeneity and/or multiculturalism
to erode the welfare state, the problem is likely to get worse. If either of these

---

[10] For a discussion of these forces, including the postwar human rights revolution, the desecuri-
tization of state-minority relations, and democratization, see Kymlicka (2007).

hypotheses were true, the very idea of a multicultural welfare state – a welfare state that respects and accommodates diversity – would be almost a contradiction in terms.

This worry has been labeled as the "progressive's dilemma."[11] Social democrats, it is said, are faced with a tragic trade-off between sustaining their traditional agenda of economic redistribution and embracing ethnocultural diversity and multiculturalism. The belief in such a trade-off is creating a major political re-alignment on these issues. In the past, most resistance to immigration and multiculturalism came from the right, who viewed them as a threat to cherished national traditions or values. Today, however, opposition to immigration and multiculturalism is emerging within the left, as a perceived threat to the welfare state.[12]

THE CASE FOR A TRADE-OFF

But are the hypotheses true? Why have so many people come to believe that ethnic/racial heterogeneity threatens the welfare state, and that multiculturalism policies exacerbate the problem? I will start with the heterogeneity debate, and then look at multiculturalism.

The Case for a Heterogeneity/Redistribution Trade-Off

In one sense, the idea that ethnic/racial heterogeneity can weaken the pursuit of a robust welfare state is an old one. Karl Marx argued that racial divisions within the working class in the United States would undermine its capacity to demand progressive reforms, and this has been a recurring theme in American politics.[13] Yet, until very recently, no one has attempted to systematically test the impact of heterogeneity on welfare state levels.

Attention to ethnic/racial heterogeneity as an explanatory variable initially emerged in two discrete geographical contexts. First, development economists pointed to ethnic and tribal diversity in attempting to explain the poor economic and social performance of countries in sub-Saharan Africa, including the poor provision of public goods, such as public education.[14]

The second context concerns the United States, where ethnic and racial heterogeneity has been invoked to explain differences in social expenditures across cities and states within the country.[15] These studies consistently show, for example, that the higher the proportion of African Americans within a

---

[11] Goodhart (2004); Pearce (2004).
[12] For an overview of the debates within European social democratic parties on these issues, see Cuperus, Duffek, and Kandel (2003).
[13] For a discussion of the history of this argument, see Lipset and Marks (2000).
[14] For a sampling of these studies, see Easterly and Levine (1997); Nettle (2000); Easterly (2001); Miguel (2004); Miguel and Gugerty (2005).
[15] Plotnick and Winters (1985); Alesina, Baqir, and Easterly (2001); Hero (1998); Johnson (2001); Soss et al. (2001; 2003); Hero and Preuhs (2006).

state, the more restrictive state-level welfare programs such as Medicaid are. More recently, Alesina and Glaeser have extended this analysis to the cross-national level, arguing that differences in racial diversity are a significant part of the explanation why the United States did not develop a European-style welfare state.[16]

Based on these two experiences, several scholars have concluded that there is a universal tendency for people to resist interethnic redistribution.[17] Explanations differ as to why this tendency exists. Some simply view it as a brute preference or taste.[18] Others argue that ethnocentrism is a genetically determined disposition, since evolution would select for ethnic nepotism. From an evolutionary perspective, it is rational to make sacrifices for those who are more likely to share one's genes, but irrational to help those who do not, and ethnicity is in effect an extended kin-group. If the increasing level of ethnic and racial heterogeneity means that citizens can no longer see the national community being served by the welfare state as essentially coextensive with their own ethnic group, support for national-level redistribution will diminish.[19]

Others offer a more nuanced account for this tendency. Even if people are willing in principle to make sacrifices for cocitizens who are not coethnics – perhaps motivated by some sense of common citizenship or shared patriotism – they are only likely to do so if they trust the would-be recipient to reciprocate. However, this sort of trust is difficult to generate across ethnic lines. For one thing, it is easier to sanction "defectors" within one's own ethnic group than to sanction members of other ethnic groups.[20] Also, trust can be seen as a component of social capital that develops in associational life, and as we've seen Putnam argues that the sort of associational life that generates social capital is lower in ethnically heterogeneous neighborhoods.[21] Yet other analysts emphasize electoral dynamics, such as the challenges ethnic cleavages can play for the formation of a united and powerful labor movement and associated labor-based political parties.[22]

Whatever the explanation – whether seen as an inherent genetic disposition or as a predictable byproduct of social capital deficits or electoral dynamics – there is an increasing tendency to assume that ethnic/racial heterogeneity erodes redistribution. The sort of collective imaginary of common national identity and solidarity that can underpin a strong welfare state is seen as unsustainable under conditions of growing ethnic and racial heterogeneity. Although the main evidence for this assumption comes from two specific contexts – namely,

[16] Alesina and Glaeser (2004).
[17] It is important to distinguish episodic humanitarian charity in response to disasters from ongoing institutionally compelled redistribution. The debate concerns resistance to the latter.
[18] Luttmer (2001).
[19] Salter (2004).
[20] Miguel and Gugarty (2005).
[21] Putnam (2007); also Goodhart (2004).
[22] Stephens (1979); Alesina and Glaeser (2004).

sub-Saharan Africa and the United States – it is increasingly treated as a universal tendency. The strongly racialized dimension of U.S. welfare politics is no longer seen as an anomaly – a pernicious legacy of the peculiar American history of slavery and segregation – but rather as a normal, even inevitable, reaction to the simple fact of ethnic/racial heterogeneity.

Based on this assumption, scholars have drawn rather dire predictions about the future of the welfare state across the Western democracies. If it is the mere presence of ethnic and racial minorities that has weakened the welfare state in the United States, then increasing immigration threatens to do the same in Europe. As early as 1986, Gary Freeman predicted that immigration would lead to "the Americanization of European welfare politics,"[23] and more recent studies have reiterated his doubts about "whether the generous welfare state [in Europe] can really survive in a heterogenous society."[24]

This is the basic case for a heterogeneity/redistribution trade-off. It begins with strong empirical evidence from two specific contexts – Africa and America – where negative correlations between ethnic/racial heterogeneity and public spending have been found in several studies. This evidence is then combined with some speculations about the underlying evolutionary or sociological mechanisms at work, and the conclusion is drawn that there is a general tendency for heterogeneity to erode redistribution.

This basic case has some initial plausibility, but it is not water-tight. The empirical evidence is drawn from two contexts that are arguably atypical. In the sub-Saharan context, the artificiality of state boundaries, combined with the weakness of state institutions at the time of independence, meant that states had no usable traditions or institutional capacity for dealing with diversity. In the American context, racial animosity had been sedimented by centuries of slavery and segregation, whose maintenance depended on state-sponsored ideologies and practices that dehumanized blacks. One could argue that neither of these contexts provides a reliable basis for predicting the impact of, say, increasing Turkish immigration on the German welfare state, or increasing Philippine immigration on the Canadian welfare state. Where minorities are newcomers rather than historically enslaved groups, and where state institutions are strong rather than weak, the impact of increasing heterogeneity may be quite different.

The Case for a Recognition/Redistribution Trade-Off

Much of the literature to date has focused on the link between levels of ethnic/racial heterogeneity and the welfare state. But for public policy purposes, this is a rather academic debate. A country simply finds itself with certain ethnic/racial minorities, and unless it is willing to contemplate genocide or ethnic cleansing, this must be taken as a given. For most policy makers, therefore, the crucial

[23] Freeman (1986: 62).
[24] Alesina and Glaeser (2004: 180–1). See also Faist (1995); Goodhart (2004).

issue is not what level of ethnic heterogeneity is desirable, but rather how we should respond to the ethnic heterogeneity that already exists in our society.

In the past, ethnocultural diversity was often seen as a threat to political stability, and hence as something to be discouraged by public policies. Ethnic minorities were subject to a range of policies intended to either assimilate or marginalize them. Today, however, many Western democracies have abandoned these earlier policies and shifted toward a more accommodating approach to diversity. This is reflected in the widespread adoption of multiculturalism policies for immigrant groups, the acceptance of territorial autonomy and language rights for national minorities, and the recognition of land claims and self-government rights for indigenous peoples. I will refer to all such policies as multiculturalism policies or MCPs.

This trend has generated the second main worry that I wish to discuss – namely, the fear that there is a trade-off between multiculturalism policies and the welfare state. MCPs publicly recognize and institutionalize heterogeneity, and if we assume that heterogeneity weakens the welfare state, this negative impact may be compounded by policies that heighten its public visibility and political salience (and by the ethnic political mobilization needed to get these policies adopted). Critics worry, therefore, that there is conflict between the "politics of recognition" and the "politics of redistribution."

These critics generally acknowledge that defenders of MCPs do not *intend* to weaken the welfare state.[25] On the contrary, most defenders of MCPs are also strong defenders of the welfare state, and view both as flowing from the same underlying principle of justice. The conflict between MCPs and the welfare state is not so much a matter of competing ideals or principles, but of unintended sociological dynamics. MCPs, critics worry, erode the interpersonal trust, social solidarity, and political coalitions that sustain the welfare state.

Why have so many critics assumed that there is a recognition/redistribution trade-off? In the case of the heterogeneity/redistribution trade-off, the argument rests on empirical studies from Africa and America, which are interpreted as reflections of a universal trend. In the case of the recognition/redistribution trade-off, by contrast, there are no empirical studies that have revealed a negative correlation between the adoption of MCPs and the welfare state. No one has attempted to empirically test the recognition/redistribution hypothesis. Instead, the argument for a recognition/redistribution trade-off is conjectural. Critics have speculated about a range of mechanisms by which MCPs could inadvertently erode the welfare state. We could summarize these mechanisms under three headings:

The corroding effect: One line of argument suggests that MCPs weaken redistribution because they erode the underlying collective imaginary of

---

[25] In discussing the recognition/redistribution hypothesis, I have drawn in particular on the writings of a set of critics whose works have become widely cited in the literature: Todd Gitlin (1995); Wolfe and Klausen (1997; 2000); Richard Rorty (2000); Brian Barry (2001). When referring to "the critics," I have these authors in mind, as well as the many commentators who have endorsed their arguments.

nationhood that sustains trust and solidarity amongst citizens. MCPs emphasize differences between citizens, whereas the ideology of nationhood requires emphasizing our commonalities. Citizens have historically supported the welfare state and been willing to make sacrifices to support their disadvantaged cocitizens, because they viewed these cocitizens as "one of us," bound together by a common national identity and common sense of belonging. However, MCPs are said to corrode this overarching common identity. MCPs tell citizens that what divides them into separate ethnocultural groups is more important than what they have in common, and that cocitizens from other groups are therefore not really "one of us."

According to Wolfe and Klausen, in the early days of the British welfare state in the 1940s and 1950s, "people believed they were paying the social welfare part of their taxes to people who were like themselves." But with the adoption of MCPs, and the resulting abandonment of the "long process of national homogenization," the outcome has been growing "tax resistance," for "if the ties that bind you to increasingly diverse fellow citizens are loosened, you are likely to be less inclined to share your resources with them."[26]

The crowding out effect: According to a second argument, MCPs weaken proredistribution coalitions by diverting time, energy, and money from redistribution to recognition.[27] People who would otherwise be fighting to enhance economic redistribution, or at least to protect the welfare state from right-wing retrenchment, are instead spending their time on issues of multiculturalism.

Todd Gitlin gives an example of this. He discusses how left-wing students at UCLA fought for what they deemed a more inclusive educational environment, through greater representation of minorities in the faculty and curricula. At the same time, however, they largely ignored huge budget cuts to the state educational system that were making it more difficult for minority students to even get to UCLA. As he puts it, "much of the popular energy and commitment it would have taken to fight for the preservation – let alone the improvement – of public education was channeled into acrimony amongst potential allies."[28] This "channelling of energy" is captured nicely in one of his chapter titles: "Marching on the English Department while the Right Took the White House."[29]

The misdiagnosis effect: A third line of argument suggests that MCPs lead people to misdiagnose the problems that minorities face. It encourages people to think that the problems facing minority groups are rooted primarily in cultural "misrecognition," and hence to think that the solution lies in greater state recognition of ethnic identities and cultural practices. In reality, however, these "culturalist" solutions will be of little or no benefit, since the real problems lie elsewhere.

---

[26] Wolfe and Klausen (2000: 28).
[27] Barry (2001: 325).
[28] Gitlin (1995: 31).
[29] Gitlin (1995: 126).

This argument comes in two different forms. One version claims that the focus on cultural difference has displaced attention to race, and thereby ignored the distinctive problems facing groups like African Americans. Barry, for example, argues that "one of the most serious mistakes by multicultural-ists is to misunderstand the plight of American blacks." He goes on to quote Kwame Anthony Appiah's observation that

it is not black culture that the racist disdains, but blacks. There is no conflict of visions between black and white cultures that is the source of racial discord. No amount of knowledge of the architectural achievements of Nubia or Kush guarantees respect for African Americans.... Culture is not the problem, and it is not the solution.[30]

The rhetoric of MCPs lumps all ethnic groups together, as equal victims of cultural misrecognition, while obscuring the distinctive problems faced by those racial groups that suffer the consequences of segregation, slavery, rac-ism, and discrimination.

A second version of the misdiagnosis argument claims that the focus on ethnic or racial difference has displaced attention to class, and thereby made pan-ethnic alliances on class issues less likely. On this view, the real problem is economic marginalization, not cultural misrecognition, and the solution is not to adopt MCPs but rather to improve people's standing in the labor market, through better access to jobs, education and training, and so on. The multicul-turalist approach encourages people to think that what low-income Pakistani immigrants in Britain need most is to have their distinctive history, religion, or dress given greater public status or accommodation, when in fact their real need is for improved access to decent housing, education and training, and gainful employment – a need they share with the disadvantaged members of the larger society or other ethnic groups, and that can only be met through a pan-ethnic class alliance.

Both versions of the misdiagnosis argument claim that MCPs do not simply divert energy from more pressing issues of race and class (that is the crowding out effect), but that they distort people's understanding of the causes of disad-vantage, by failing to acknowledge the reality of racism and class inequality. (A Machiavellian version of this argument suggests that right-wing political and economic elites have in fact promoted MCPs precisely in order to obscure the reality of racism and economic marginalization.)

This then is the basic case for the existence of a recognition/redistribution trade-off.[31] At first glance, all three of these suggested mechanisms have some

---

[30] Appiah quoted on Barry (2001: 306).

[31] There are other accounts in the literature. Nancy Fraser, for example, who coined the "Recognition versus redistribution" terminology, suggests that recognition and redistribution conflict because the latter is de-differentiating (that is, aims at reducing differences between groups, by creating greater similarity in life conditions), whereas the former is differentiating (that is, affirms group boundaries) (1998; 2000). But it's not clear why reducing differences in economic circumstances should conflict with recognition of differences in cultural identities

plausibility. Yet here again, the case for a trade-off is not water-tight. For one thing, as I mentioned earlier, there is as yet no empirical evidence for the existence of such a trade-off.

Some critics would respond that the evidence is plain to see. After all, the thirty-year period that has witnessed the rise of MCPs has largely coincided with the period of retrenchment in many social programs across the Western democracies, and this hardly seems like a coincidence. On the other hand, the restructuring of the welfare state occurred throughout the Western democracies, affecting countries that strongly resist MCPs, like Germany and France, as well as pro-MCP countries, like Canada and Australia. It is not at all clear that the presence or absence of MCPs had any bearing on whether or how the welfare state was restructured. Indeed, as I will discuss later, some pro-MCP countries resisted the retrenchment of the welfare state better than some anti-MCP countries. So the existence of a general link between MCPs and the welfare state is not self-evident.

And once we think about it, the three more specific critiques of MCP listed previously are not self-evident either. One can imagine plausible arguments in the other direction. The corroding argument, for example, assumes that there were high levels of interethnic trust and solidarity that are now being slowly (or quickly) eroded by MCPs. In reality, many Western societies had low levels of interethnic trust, manifested in a long history of exclusionary and discriminatory policies toward minorities, and MCPs are intended precisely to combat this preexisting problem. On this view, recognizing and accommodating minorities can help overcome a legacy of division and distrust, and thereby build the basis for a new and more inclusive national imaginary.

Similarly, in response to the crowding out argument, defenders of MCPs have argued that the struggle for MCPs may actually have helped to reinvigorate the left, which had been progressively losing ground to the right well before the rise of multicultural politics.[32] And finally, in response to the misdiagnosis argument, defenders of MCPs argue that any adequate diagnosis of the disadvantages facing minorities requires attending to a range of different dimensions – including race, class, and culture – and that it is a mistake to ignore any of them. The theory and practice of multiculturalism is intended precisely to supplement and enrich our conceptual tools and political spaces for arriving at a more adequate diagnosis of the full range of injustices faced by different groups in our society.[33]

---

and practices. If we ask why the former conflicts with the latter, Fraser's answer would, I think, end up invoking one or more of the three mechanisms I have listed here.

[32] Van Cott argues that this is true of the left in Latin America, which has been revitalized by the struggles for multiculturalism, and which has capitalized on promulticultural coalitions to build more effective opposition to neoliberalism (2006).

[33] For versions of these responses, see Tully (2000); Parekh (2004); Zurn (2004). As with the critiques of MCPs, these responses are entirely speculative.

In short, none of the arguments for the alleged harmful impact of MCPs on the welfare state are self-evident. Here again, more research is required before we make any definitive judgments about the recognition/redistribution trade-off.

TESTING THE TRADE-OFFS

Any attempt to systematically confirm or refute the two hypotheses would require a long-term undertaking, in part because the existing data are insufficient to test the claims. We do not have reliable cross-national data over time on many of the crucial variables, such as levels of (different types of) ethnic heterogeneity, or levels of (different types of) MCPs. Even the data on welfare spending are not as consistent as one would like.

Nonetheless, there are some more preliminary tests that can be conducted regarding the two hypotheses. The following section describes some recent findings from studies that were conducted by, or in collaboration with, several colleagues.

Testing the Heterogeneity/Redistribution Trade-Off

As I noted earlier, those who believe that there is a heterogeneity/redistribution trade-off invoke it both to explain the historical weakness of the American welfare state and to predict the likely future of European welfare states as immigration increases. Skeptics respond that the racialization of American welfare politics is an idiosyncratic product of the history of American race relations and need not be a harbinger of the impact of immigration on European welfare politics.

Is there a way to test this dispute? In a recent study, three of my colleagues have analyzed the relationship between immigration and change in the level of social spending across OECD countries from 1970 to 1998.[34] In this study, immigration is measured using United Nations' data on "migrant stock," the proportion of the population born outside the country. To analyze the role of migrant stock in the evolution of the welfare state, the study begins by adopting the most sophisticated existing models of the factors associated with variation in social spending (in particular, the models developed by Swank and Huber and Stephens).[35] These models incorporate a range of factors that have been shown to be important determinants of social spending, such as the proportion of the population older than 64, the percentage of women in the labor force, and strength of the political left in government. However, as I noted earlier, these models have not typically included ethnoracial heterogeneity as a variable. So this study adds migrant stock to the model, to see what effect, if any, it has on social spending.

---

[34] Soroka, Banting, and Johnston (2006).
[35] Huber and Stephens (2001); Swank (2002).

If a heterogeneity/redistribution trade-off existed, we would expect that those countries with higher levels of migrant stock would exhibit either a decrease in social spending, or at least slower rates of growth compared to countries with lower levels of immigration. However, the study revealed that there is no relationship between the proportion of the population born outside the country and growth in social spending over the last three decades of the twentieth century, controlling for other factors associated with social spending. There was simply no evidence that countries with large foreign-born populations had more trouble sustaining and developing their social programs over these three decades than countries with small immigrant communities.

This finding has been confirmed in a more recent study we conducted,[36] and in a separate analysis conducted by Peter Taylor-Gooby. He too finds that once the other factors that affect social spending are controlled for, the size of immigrant groups has no statistically significant effect on social spending in Western Europe. He concludes that there is, as yet, no evidence that immigration will have the same effect on European welfare states that race has historically had on the American welfare state.[37]

Our recent study also examined the impact of two other (nonimmigrant) forms of ethnoracial diversity: namely, indigenous peoples (for example, American Indians, Maori, Sami) and national minorities (for example, Scots, Catalans, Flemish, Quebecois). Here again, in both cases, there is no correlation between the size of the minority and change in welfare spending over the past thirty years. Countries with larger indigenous populations or national minorities had no more difficulty sustaining their welfare spending than countries with smaller such groups.[38]

In short, attempts to test the heterogeneity/redistribution trade-off beyond the United States and Africa have found little support for this hypothesis.[39] One might argue that this simply reflects a time lag: perhaps the corroding effects of heterogeneity have not yet had time to show up. Welfare states are large, slow-moving entities that do not change overnight. For this reason, it is

---

[36] Banting et al. (2006).

[37] Taylor-Gooby (2005).

[38] Banting et al. (2006).

[39] Alesina and Glaeser (2004) claim to find a strong cross-national correlation between heterogeneity and welfare spending, but their findings are distorted by serious inconsistencies in the way heterogeneity is measured. The classification of ethnic groups in their Index of Ethnolinguistic Fractionalization varies significantly across countries. For example, the U.K. data ignores national minorities in Scotland and Wales, as well as white immigrants such as the Irish. As a result, the index is only measuring "racial" differences: white 93.7 percent; Indian 1.8 percent; Other U.K. 1.6 percent; Pakistani 1.4 percent; Black 1.4 percent. In Canada, however, the index subdivides the white majority into a range of different ethnic and linguistic subgroups, including French 22.8 percent; British 20.8 percent; German 3.4 percent; Italian 2.8 percent; Dutch 1.3 percent; and so on. As a result, the index is not a consistent measure of either the diversity of the ethnic origins of a population or its politically salient ethnic identities.

useful to look, not only at welfare spending levels, but also at public support for the welfare state. As Markus Crepaz notes, we can view public attitudes as the "canary in the mine." If heterogeneity is going to have an eroding impact on the politics of redistribution, this will likely show up first in a drop in public support for the welfare state, before it shows up in actual changes in spending levels. Crepaz's research shows, however, that there is no clear tendency for increasing immigration to erode support for welfare spending in the Western democracies. After a comprehensive analysis of cross-national data on public attitudes, Crepaz warns against extrapolating from the American experience. The challenge posed by immigration to European welfare states is unfolding when they have reached maturity and are embedded deeply in public expectations, unlike the American experience in which racial heterogeneity hampered movement toward a more comprehensive welfare state from the outset. As a result, he concludes, "there is little evidence that immigration-induced diversity will lead to an 'Americanization' of the European welfare state."[40]

So we have found little support for the idea that ethnoracial heterogeneity exercises a systematic downward pressure on the welfare state. The correlations regarding African Americans in the United States, or "tribal" groups in sub-Saharan Africa, cannot be taken as universal tendencies that apply to other types of groups in other countries.

However, these studies do reveal one note of caution, relating to the case of immigrants: the *pace of change* does seem to matter. When the analysis examines the relationship between *growth* in the foreign-born population and *change* in social spending as a proportion of GDP between 1970 and 1998, an interesting result emerged: countries with large increases in the proportion of their population born outside the country tended to have smaller increases in social spending. Social spending as a proportion of GDP rose in every country in the sample during this period, including in countries with substantial growth in migrant stock. But the growth was smaller in countries that saw a significant increase in the portion of the population born outside the country, other things held constant.

Although there is still much work to be done in this field, these preliminary findings are suggestive. There is no evidence here that countries with large minority populations have greater difficulty in sustaining and enhancing their historic welfare commitments. But large changes do seem to matter. As in other areas of social life, it is the pace of social change rather than the fact of difference that stands out here as politically unsettling.

Testing the Recognition/Redistribution Trade-Off

To test the heterogeneity/redistribution trade-off, the studies I've just described have used several existing databases that give the size of various ethnic/racial

---

[40] Crepaz (2007).

minorities in different countries around the world. These databases all have their limitations, to which I will return, but they enable us to plug variables such as the size of immigrant population or the size of indigenous population into models of welfare state spending.

To test the recognition/redistribution trade-off, we would need to find comparable databases that measure the level or depth of multiculturalism policies in different countries around the world. We could then plug the extent of MCPs into these models, to see whether in fact ethnocultural recognition erodes economic redistribution.

Unfortunately, there are no such databases. To my knowledge, no one has attempted to systematically measure the extent to which different countries have adopted different types or levels of multiculturalism policies. To test the hypothesis, therefore, Keith Banting and I have constructed such an index. This involved several steps. We first developed a representative list of multiculturalism policies; we then checked to see which countries had adopted which policies and on that basis categorized countries as stronger or weaker in their level of MCPs. Finally, we then asked whether countries that have adopted strong multicultural policies over the last two decades have, in fact, experienced a weakening or even just slower growth in their welfare states compared to countries that have resisted such policies.

This is a complicated process, and the details are described elsewhere.[41] However, as an illustration, let me focus on the case of immigrants. We began by selecting the following eight policies as the most common or emblematic of a multicultural approach to immigrant integration:

1. Constitutional, legislative, or parliamentary affirmation of multiculturalism;
2. The explanation/celebration of multiculturalism in school curriculum;
3. The inclusion of ethnic representation/sensitivity in the mandate of public media or media licensing;
4. Exemptions from dress codes, Sunday-closing legislation, and the like;
5. Acceptance of dual citizenship;
6. The funding of ethnic group organizations or activities;
7. The funding of bilingual education or mother-tongue instruction;
8. Affirmative action for disadvantaged immigrant groups.

The first three policies celebrate and publicize the ethnocultural diversity brought to a country by its immigrant groups, the middle two reduce legal constraints on immigrant groups maintaining their identity and culture while participating in their new country, and the final three represent forms of active support for immigrant communities and individuals. The list is inevitably partial; one could think of other possible policies to include if one wanted to expand the list. Others might want to adopt a more restrictive list, applying

---

[41] Banting et al. (2006).

the term MCPs only to policies that recognize minorities in a very specific way (for example, through legal exemptions to common laws).[42] However, we believe that this list is a fair representation of the sorts of policies that have been adopted or debated by various countries, defended by advocates of multiculturalism and attacked by their critics.

We then examined twenty-one established democracies, to see which of these eight policies had been adopted. A country that had adopted six or more of these policies was classified as "strong" in its commitment to MCPs; a country that had adopted two or fewer of these policies was classified as "weak"; countries falling in-between were categorized as "modest." The resulting groupings of countries are reported in Table 9.1.

The second step was to examine how the three groups of countries fared in terms of change in the strength of their welfare state between 1980 and the end of the 1990s. Is it true that countries that adopted strong multiculturalism policies for immigrants had more difficulty than countries that resisted such approaches in maintaining and enhancing their welfare states over the last two decades of the twentieth century? Table 9.2 provides a first cut at the issues. There is no evidence here of a systematic tendency for immigrant multiculturalism policies to weaken the welfare state. Countries that adopted such programs did not experience erosion of their welfare states or even slower growth in social spending than countries that resisted such programs. Indeed, on the two measures that capture social policy most directly – the level of social spending and the redistributive impact of taxes and transfers – the countries with the strongest immigrant multiculturalism policies did better than the other groups, providing a hint that perhaps multiculturalism policies may actually ease possible tensions between heterogeneity and redistribution. This conclusion has been tested in multivariate analysis with the same result.

As part of this study, we conducted a similar process for indigenous peoples and national minorities. In each case, we identified a list of representative MCPs applicable to such groups, categorized countries as strong, modest, or weak in their level of MCPs, and tested whether strong-MCP countries experienced more difficulty sustaining their welfare state compared to other countries. Here again, as with immigrants, there was no evidence that engaging in a strong politics of recognition entailed a trade-off with a politics of redistribution.[43]

---

[42] For alternative ways of defining MCPs see Appendix 1 in Banting et al. (2006).

[43] In the case of substate national groups, for example, we chose the following six policies as emblematic of a multicultural approach: (1) federal or quasi-federal territorial autonomy; (2) official language status, either in the region or nationally; (3) guarantees of representation in the central government or on constitutional courts; (4) public funding of minority language universities/schools/media; (5) constitutional or parliamentary affirmation of multinationalism; (6) international personality (for example, allowing the substate region to sit on international bodies, sign treaties, or have their own Olympic team). If a country has adopted most or all of these, we categorized it as strong; if only one or two, as weak; and if in-between, as modest. Here again, strong-MCP countries fared as well as the other countries on welfare

TABLE 9.1. *The Strength of Multiculturalism Policies in Democratic Countries*

Strong	Australia, Canada
Modest	Belgium, Netherlands, New Zealand, Sweden, United Kingdom, United States
Weak	Austria, Denmark, Finland, France, Germany, Greece, Ireland, Italy, Japan, Norway, Portugal, Spain, Switzerland

TABLE 9.2. *Multiculturalism Policies and Change in Social Redistribution*

Multiculturalism Policies	Social Spending Average Percentage Change	Redistribution Average Percentage Change
Strong	42.8	11.8
Medium	3.8	−9.2
Weak	18.3	10.6

Notes: Change in social spending represents change in public social expenditure between 1980 and 2000. Based on data in OECD SocX. Change in redistribution represents change in redistributive impact of taxes and transfers between the early 1980s and 2000 or near years. Based on data provided by the Luxembourg Income Study.
Source: For details of the calculations, see Banting et al. (2006: Appendix 2.2).

As with the heterogeneity hypothesis, critics might argue that the hypothesized negative effects of MCPs have simply not had time to show up in spending levels.[44] To address this worry, we need to see whether there has been a drop in public support for the welfare state, even if it has not yet affected actual changes in spending levels. This question has been examined in a recent study by Markus Crepaz. Drawing on public opinion data from a variety of surveys across the Western democracies, Crepaz asks whether states with higher levels of MCPs have seen an erosion in public support for redistribution, in comparison with countries with lower levels of MCPs. Here again, the results are encouraging: he finds no evidence that adopting MCPs erodes trust, solidarity, or support for redistribution.[45]

In short, we have found no support for the claim that there is an inherent trade-off between policies of ethnocultural recognition and economic redistribution. It is possible that there are localized circumstances where particular forms of recognition erode particular forms of redistribution. But given the overall results, it is equally likely that there are other circumstances where the

state measures. For the relevant evidence, as well as the policies/categories for indigenous peoples, see Banting et al. (2006).
[44] Van Parijs (2004).
[45] Crepaz (2006).

politics of recognition enhances redistribution. It would be of great interest to identify these localized cases of either mutual interference or mutual support between recognition and redistribution. But the evidence to date provides no support for the bald claim that "a politics of multiculturalism undermines a politics of redistribution."[46]

RETHINKING THE UNDERLYING MECHANISMS

These results are preliminary and require further testing, but assuming that the basic findings hold up, they raise important questions about the underlying processes that structure relations of belonging and solidarity. As I noted earlier, predictions that ethnic heterogeneity and MCPs erode redistribution are often explained by reference to various underlying mechanisms, some of which have intuitive plausibility. If the predicted trade-offs have not materialized, does this mean that these mechanisms do not exist, at least not in any strong form? Or is it the case that these mechanisms do exist, and generate the predicted effects, but that there are other equally powerful mechanisms operating in the opposite direction, offsetting these effects?

Answering this question would require a much broader research project. However, let me make some tentative speculations.

In the case of the *heterogeneity/redistribution trade-off*, two of the main mechanisms cited were (1) evolutionary explanations that invoke a disposition to help those who share our genes, and (2) sociological explanations that invoke the difficulties of generating trust and social capital in ethnically mixed populations.

The first explanation is, I think, easier to dismiss. There may indeed be a biological disposition to make sacrifices for those who are one's genetic kin (for example, for one's children, brothers and sisters, even cousins and uncles), but there is no plausible way to understand coethnics as one's kin in the literal sense. It is true that ethnic groups are often described metaphorically as an "extended family," but this is just a metaphor, not a description of actual genetic ties. I don't know what it would mean to say that a typical Frenchman living in Marseilles "shares genes" with a typical Frenchwoman living in Paris, but insofar as we can make sense of this, he is just as likely to share genes with Italians in Piedmont or Spaniards in Catalonia, given the actual historical patterns of settlement and mobility in that region of the world.

Moreover, it is important to note that the most commonly cited cases of the negative effect of heterogeneity on welfare do not in fact track ethnicity. In the United States, for example, the evidence shows that Greek Americans are willing to make sacrifices for other whites, such as Swedish Americans, but not for African Americans. Yet this intrawhite redistribution is clearly interethnic. If there is an inherent disposition to resist redistribution to those who

---

[46] Barry (2001: 8).

are not one's coethnics, it should apply equally to other white ethnic groups as to nonwhite ethnic groups.

The fact that feelings of solidarity in the United States and other Western democracies often track racial categories rather than ethnicity is sometimes obscured by the inconsistent way that studies measure ethnic diversity. For example, the data used by Alesina and his colleagues often treat all whites as forming a single ethnic group, even when they manifestly have multiple ethnic origins.[47] This tendency to treat whites as an ethnic category accurately reflects the popular discourse and folk classifications used in many countries, where it is true that white immigrants are automatically presumed to be "one of us," no matter how recently they arrived and no matter what their ethnic origins, whereas nonwhite immigrants have difficulty being accepted even when they have culturally assimilated. Indeed, in some European countries the term "immigrant" is reserved for people from non-European countries, as if whites from another European country could not possibly be considered an alien or foreigner.

The strength and pervasiveness of this tendency to draw racial boundaries around our circle of solidarity is often taken as evidence of a "natural" genetic tendency to favor one's coethnics. In fact, however, it shows the opposite – namely, that socially constructed ideologies of racial categorization have much more power than facts about genetic ties and consanguinity. The fact that white Americans today downplay ethnic differences amongst themselves, while marking racial differences with blacks, is testament to the power of a particular historical narrative – a particular collective imaginary – about "who we are." It would have been possible for English settlers in America to treat the Irish or the Slavs as "alien others" with whom they shared no common blood or genes. And indeed for a period of time this was the case. But these ethnic differences over time have been transcended in the name of constructing a sense of shared American national identity, albeit one that continues to exclude Blacks.[48]

There was nothing inevitable about this construction of a shared identity that includes whites while excluding blacks. Indeed, as Michèle Lamont shows, a different pattern emerged in France, where it is Muslim Arabs rather than black Africans who have been defined as the main "other" who fall outside the collective imaginary.[49]

The point here is not simply that a socially constructed narrative can change how people treat those who are ethnically distinct, but rather that the very question of who is perceived as ethnically distinct is itself determined by a cultural script, not by some biological fact about blood and genes. By ignoring differences in national origin amongst whites, the index used by Alesina et al. is measuring a cultural script about who counts as ethnically distinct in a

---

[47] See note 39 in this chapter.
[48] See Ignatiev's study of "How the Irish Became White" (1995).
[49] Lamont (2000).

particular country, not some actual fact of diverse origins consanguinity. The evolutionary explanation of the heterogeneity/redistribution trade-off misses this dimension entirely.

The second explanation of the heterogeneity/redistribution trade-offs – namely, deficits in social capital – is more interesting. According to this explanation, (1) ethnic diversity erodes feelings of trust, and (2) this weakens support for social redistribution. My colleagues have attempted to test this hypothesis in a study of public attitudes in Canada.[50] Data for the analysis come from a special national survey, combined with census data about the local communities in which Canadians live, including the ethnic composition of their neighborhoods.

To test the first proposition – that ethnic diversity erodes trust – the survey adopted a measure of interpersonal trust known as the "wallet question." Respondents were asked: "Say you lost a wallet or purse with $100 in it. How likely is it that the wallet or purse will be returned with the money in it if it was found by a [neighbour/police officer/clerk at the local grocery store/stranger]?" This measure does reveal a tension between the ethnic diversity of the neighborhoods in which Canadians live and the level of trust they have in their neighbors. As Figure 9.1 shows, the larger the presence of visible minorities in the neighborhood, the less trusting is the majority even when one controls for other factors that influence trust levels, such as economic well-being, education, gender, and age. Members of racial minorities, in contrast, are much less trusting where the majority is very dominant, but are less affected by changes in the ethnic composition of the neighborhood. The two lines cross when the racial minority percentage is just a little more than half. Beyond that point, the average racial minority respondent is more interpersonally trusting than his or her "majority counterpart." So, sustaining trust across racial differences is a challenge in Canada, a pattern that parallels Putnam's results in the United States,[51] and MORI results in Britain.[52]

Many analysts stop at this point, assuming that diminished trust necessarily weakens support for redistribution. This turns out not to be true, at least in Canada. In addition to measuring trust levels, the survey explored respondents' support for the welfare state through a battery of questions about specific social programs. Analysis of the data revealed virtually no relationship between ethnicity and the ethnic complexion of neighborhoods on the one hand and support for social programs on the other. Compared to factors such as income, gender, and age, all of which do influence support for social spending, ethnicity and the ethnic composition of respondents' neighborhood virtually disappear.[53] Moreover, to the extent that there are even hints of a

---

[50] Soroka, Johnston, and Banting (2004).

[51] Putnam (2007).

[52] Goodhart (2004).

[53] The impact of ethnicity and ethnic context is decisively small. In effect, moving from a community populated completely by the majority to a community split evenly between the

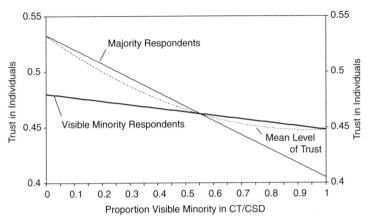

Trust = 0.533 -0.053 *REth* -0.128*CEth* + 0.096*REth*CEth*

FIGURE 9.1. Ethnicity and interpersonal trust in Canada.

relationship, it is the minorities, not the majorities, that are less supportive of redistribution. There is no evidence of majorities turning away from redistribution because some of the beneficiaries are ethnic "others." This suggests that the sort of trust that emerges from local associational life (and that might be reduced in mixed neighborhoods) is not the most relevant for sustaining support in national-level welfare programs. [54]

In short, the social capital story identifies a real mechanism at work – interpersonal trust may be harder to sustain in ethnically mixed populations – but the putative link between trust and the welfare state is not supported, at least in this study. Any attempt to link reductions in street-level social capital to the weakening of national political institutions like the welfare state will obviously require filling in a number of intermediary steps, and we don't yet know what those steps are, or how ethnic heterogeneity affects them. The evidence from this study suggests that, in Canada at least, there are other factors at work that buffer the welfare state from heterogeneity-induced variations in trust at the micro level.[55]

So there are unanswered questions regarding the heterogeneity/redistribution trade-off. It is not clear how widespread the phenomenon is or what mechanisms underlie it. Although a growing literature suggests that such an effect exists in particular times and places – and we can see evidence of that

majority and minorities leads to a decrease in aggregate support for unemployment benefits and health of about .0025 percent.

[54] Rothstein and Stolle (2005); Crepaz (2007); Hooghe (2007).

[55] The recent cross-national study by Kesler and Bloemraad (2008) suggests that multiculturalism policies may themselves be one of these intermediary factors that mitigate, or even entirely offset, the potentially negative effects of immigrant diversity on trust, membership, and participation.

every day in countries suffering from ethnic conflict and racist violence – we cannot assume that it is a universal tendency. More research is required before any definitive judgement can be made.

This applies even more forcefully to the case of the recognition/redistribution trade-off. As we have seen, critics of multiculturalism policies have identified three possible mechanisms: the corroding, crowding out, and misdiagnosis effects. The latter two can easily be dismissed. The idea that multiculturalism claims crowd out redistribution claims depends on the assumption that the pursuit of justice is a zero-sum game. This is a common assumption, but surely false as a generalization. For example, it is sometimes assumed that countries that work hard to assist the elderly must therefore be shortchanging the young, or that countries that devote more resources to foreign aid must therefore be shortchanging the poor at home – resources devoted to the former must come at the expense of the latter. In reality, countries with generous policies toward the elderly also tend to have generous policies regarding the young, and countries with generous foreign aid programs also tend to have generous domestic welfare programs. The same dynamic applies to most welfare state issues: the pursuit of justice in one dimension helps build a broader political culture that supports struggles for justice in other dimensions.

A similar objection can be raised to the alleged misdiagnosis effect, which depends on the related assumption that sensitivity to justice is zero-sum: people who develop a finely tuned sensitivity to cultural injustices must therefore be tone-deaf to claims of economic injustice. I suspect, however, that sensitivity to the different dimensions of injustice is as likely to be mutually reinforcing as competing.

So the crucial issue concerns the first proposed mechanism (that is, the corroding effect). In its usual form, the argument goes like this:

- -Multiculturalism policies emphasize diversity;
- Emphasizing diversity undermines the sense of common national identity;
- The welfare state depends on feelings of national solidarity.

Defenders of multiculturalism policies have a number of possible responses here. One response, advocated by some postnational or cosmopolitan theorists, is to accept that MCPs erode national identity, and hence jeopardize the national welfare-state as currently understood but to argue that we need to separate out redistribution from ideas of nationhood. Redistribution, on this postnational model, should be seen as an obligation owed to human beings as such, based on their universal personhood and human rights, rather than their status as "conationals," or their shared membership in some "national" collectivity.[56] On this view, we cannot truly accommodate heterogeneity and multiculturalism if we continue to pursue the nation-building goal of turning immigrants into "national citizens."

---

[56] See, for example, Soysal (1994).

One difficulty with this suggestion – apart from the fact that it has no hope of being adopted in the foreseeable future – is that connecting redistribution to personhood rather than nationhood is more likely to lead to a leveling down than a leveling up. Contemporary welfare states typically operate on a model of "egalitarianism amongst ourselves, humanitarianism for others." All human beings should have their basic human needs met, for example through foreign aid for the poor abroad, or through emergency medical care for visitors and tourists in our country. But amongst conationals, we aim for more than this, including equality of economic opportunity, equal capacity to participate in political life, and some minimal sense of a common standard of living. If we disconnect redistribution from nationhood, and assume that visitors and conationals should be treated the same way, the result may not be to extend egalitarianism to nonnationals, but rather to reduce intranational redistribution to mere humanitarianism.

Most defenders of multiculturalism policies, therefore, wish to argue that MCPs are consistent with maintaining national welfare states, and hence that MCPs need not erode feelings of national solidarity. But we can distinguish two different versions of this argument. One version, advanced by David Miller, accepts that MCPs on their own erode feelings of national identity, but insists that MCPs can be supplemented with nation-building policies that offset these corroding effects. Such nation-building policies include, for example, language-training programs, citizenship education in the schools, the shared celebration of national heroes and holidays, and citizenship ceremonies for immigrants. According to Miller, "radical" defenders of multiculturalism promote MCPs without simultaneously promoting nation building, and the inevitable result is to erode national solidarity and national redistribution. But a more "moderate" multiculturalism combines MCPs with nation-building policies, so that the corroding effects of the former are offset by the bonding effects of the latter.[57] So Miller's argument accepts that the existence of a corroding effect, but seeks offsetting mechanisms.

A second version, however, offers a more robust defense of MCPs. Both the postnational view and the Miller view accept that MCPs on their own erode national solidarity, although they differ in how to transcend/offset that effect. But one could argue that multiculturalism can itself be a tool for building national solidarity, in two ways.

First, MCPs can help to combat the stereotypes and stigmatizations that currently erode feelings of solidarity across ethnic and racial lines. Critics of MCPs assume that by heightening the public salience of ethnicity, they necessarily reinforce perceptions of difference and otherness, creating and reinforcing boundaries between citizens. But the reality is that such boundaries are already intensely marked in contemporary societies and are often accompanied by deeply rooted feelings of prejudice, fear, indifference, and contempt

---

[57] Miller (1995; 2000).

deriving from a long history of racism and colonialism in the West. The power of such boundaries, and their corrosive effects on solidarity, are no less powerful for being "private" and informal.

Under these conditions, the adoption of MCPs can be seen as a destigmatization strategy. They may heighten the public salience of ethnicity, but they do so precisely in order to contest the inherited stigmas that create feelings of distrust and antipathy between citizens. MCPs, on this view, focus on our differences, but they do so in a way that allows us to see each other as equally worthy of national membership and of the rights and responsibilities of citizenship. They direct attention to our differences in order to reconstruct our understanding of them, to see the stigmatized others as a legitimate part of the larger "we." Put another way, the crucial question is not whether MCPs draw boundaries between citizens, but rather what is the nature of these boundaries, and whether they are the sort of boundaries that undermine feelings of solidarity and perceptions of common national membership.

I would argue that MCPs almost always have this reconstructive and destigmatizing goal in contemporary Western democracies. The emergence of MCPs in the West in the last forty years is directly linked to the human rights revolution, and to the postwar commitment to the equality of races and peoples.[58] MCPs have been demanded by historically marginalized groups as a way of challenging inherited racial and ethnic hierarchies, and the sort of public recognition they provide is often designed in light of the sort of informal stigmatizations that persist. That is to say, MCPs do not necessarily protect those aspects of a group's culture that are seen by group members as most essential or valuable – rather, they often recognize those aspects of a group's culture and history that have been most dishonoured by the larger society. (This explains the tendency for "recognition politics" to merge into "redress politics" and demands for the acknowledgment of historic injustice.)

Viewed this way, the adoption of MCPs can be seen as an indirect tool of nation building, intended to enhance solidarity by reducing the inherited antipathies that currently prevent people from feeling solidarity across ethnic and racial lines. Of course, whether MCPs actually achieve this intended goal is another question. We can easily imagine scenarios in which the adoption of MCPs would backfire and reinforce the perception of minority groups as needy, undeserving, ungrateful, and dependent. Some critics seem to assume that such unintended restigmatizing effects are inevitable.[59] But the evidence mentioned earlier suggests that MCPs have not systematically had this effect, and that MCPs can enhance, rather than erode, national solidarity.

MCPs may be able to build national solidarity in a second, more direct, way – not simply as a by-product of reduced prejudice, but also as a focal point for national pride. The decision to adopt MCPs can be seen precisely as a collective

---

[58] I explore this link between MCPs and the human rights revolution in Kymlicka (2007).
[59] Fraser (1998); de Zwart (2005).

national project – it is something that we as a nation chose to do, a national project that we can take pride in. Indeed, it can be seen as one of the nation's defining characteristics – it is one of the things that makes us a distinct nation.

I would argue that multiculturalism plays precisely this role in Canada. Affirming multiculturalism has become part of what it means to be Canadian (as distinct from being American), and, more specifically, part of what it means to be a "good Canadian." It is un-Canadian to oppose multiculturalism, a betrayal of the national code. Opposing multiculturalism in Canada is not only or even primarily an attack on particular minorities, it is an attack on the symbol and substance of Canadian nationhood.

It is sometimes said that Canada has adopted a distinctly multicultural form of nationalism, one in which the national identity has been modified (and thinned) to be more inclusive of ethnic heterogeneity. I would put it the other way around: Canada has adopted a very nation-centered form of multiculturalism. Minorities can legitimately seek to benefit from Canada's multiculturalism policies, but they are expected to do so *qua Canadian* – it is *as a Canadian* that they can claim multicultural rights and privileges, as part of the exercise of Canadian citizenship, and as part of the playing out of a national narrative. In those (few) cases where minorities don't follow the script, and instead assert multiculturalism as an inherent right divorced from being Canadian, there is often a backlash from the larger society.[60] Perhaps for that reason, most immigrant groups play along with the script, and insist that they have no greater desire than to be good Canadians, and that the enacting of their ethnic identities in public space is their way of proudly and loyally "being Canadian." Under these conditions, multiculturalism is indeed a tool of nation building,[61] and not simply something

---

[60] For example, a backlash erupted when an Aboriginal leader (Matthew Coon-Come) asserted defiantly that he "wasn't a Canadian," yet nonetheless expected recognition of various rights from the Canadian state. The same sort of resentment arises when Anglophone Canadians are asked to make accommodations by Quebecois nationalists who, it is widely believed, don't really want to be part of the country.

[61] This capacity for multiculturalism to be deployed as a tool of nation building has been bemoaned by some postmodernist critics. On their view, the emancipatory potential of multiculturalism depended precisely on the possibility that it would not be contained with nationalist ideologies, and that it would push us toward a new postnational order that abandoned oppressive fantasies of national cohesion. Instead, multiculturalism has been used to buttress and relegitimize the nation-state, and invoked as a tool for normalizing, civilizing and disciplining minorities as national citizens (for example, Day 2000; Kernerman 2005). Whereas the social-democratic left (like Barry and Miller) criticizes MCPs for eroding national solidarity, the postmodernist left criticizes MCPs for relegitimating nationhood. From my perspective, postmodernists are right that multiculturalism has often become a tool of normalizing minorities as national citizens. However, I would argue that this is legitimate so long as (1) the conception of national citizenship respects the legitimate minority and cultural rights of all groups; (2) the means used to promote this national identity are morally permissible; and (3) the resulting sense of national solidarity is used to advance legitimate public goals, including redistribution. I try to defend such a "left-liberal" account of multicultural nationalism in Kymlicka (2001).

that must be offset by other nation-building policies.[62] As a result, any putative corroding effect is likely to be small.

CONCLUSION

If the arguments in this chapter are sound, it suggests a number of lessons for how we think about successful societies in an era of diversity – some specifically about the issue of multiculturalism policies and others with more general implications.

In terms of the policy debate around multiculturalism, the clearest lesson is simply that we need to avoid premature judgments about the inevitability of trade-offs between recognizing diversity and sustaining the welfare state. The evidence summarized here suggests that a variety of relationships between ethnic heterogeneity, multiculturalism, and the welfare state are possible, and that under some circumstances robust forms of minority rights can be combined with robust redistributive commitments. More generally, the evidence suggests that there is no inevitability at work, the future is open, and policy choices count.

None of this as yet provides a positive argument in favor of MCPs. The evidence here simply disputes one familiar objection to those policies – namely, that they unintentionally set in motion sociological dynamics that erode the welfare state. If we set aside that concern, we are still left with questions about the intrinsic merits of these policies. In previous work, I have argued that many (but not all) of the sorts of multiculturalism policies adopted recently by Western democracies respond to legitimate moral claims by ethnic minorities, providing appropriate acknowledgment and remedy for historic wrongs, reducing unjustified barriers and stigmatizations, and helping to ensure greater fairness in the ways societies recognize and accommodate the diverse languages, identities, and practices that exist within their borders.[63] There is also some encouraging evidence that these policies are (in at least some cases) working to enhance the capabilities of members of minority groups, with beneficial effects on health and human development – for example, in reducing Aboriginal suicide rates or in improving the educational performance of immigrant children.[64]

---

[62] This one of the crucial differences between multiculturalism in Canada and in most Continental European countries. In the latter, multiculturalism was initially seen as an obligation of hospitality to guests, rather than an attribute of shared national citizenship. One reason for this difference is that most European countries, until recently, hoped or expected that migrants would go home, and multiculturalism was seen as preparing them (and their children) for such a return. Also, viewing multiculturalism as a duty of hospitality to guests absolves the majority from having to rethink their national identity in a more inclusive way.

[63] Kymlicka (2001; 2007).

[64] See, for example, Chandler and Lalonde (1998) and Berry et al. (2006). But see Marc (2005), who notes that the evidence to date is insufficient to draw general conclusions about the effectiveness of MCPs.

These are complex questions, and there are certainly grounds for debate about how well MCPs are working to enhance the legitimate claims and interests of minorities. But this indeed is where the debate should be – MCPs should be evaluated primarily on their own terms, as attempting to fairly accommodate ethnocultural diversity – rather than rejected on the basis of unsupported speculation about their unintended side-effects.

The analysis in this chapter may also have a more general lesson about the nature and role of collective imaginaries and cultural scripts in sustaining successful societies. If ethnic heterogeneity and MCPs have not had the corrosive effect that many commentators feared, it is partly because one of the key elements of the modern social imaginary – namely, the ideology of nationhood – has turned out to be more adaptable than many people supposed, capable of incorporating ideas of diversity and recognition. The evidence in this chapter suggests that there is greater scope for reconciling ideas of nationhood and recognition of diversity than is often realized. Scripts of nationhood may not be as inherently homogenizing as many commentators suppose, and claims to recognition are often tied to, and nested in, larger national narratives.

This tells us something important about the nature of modern collective imaginaries. It used to be assumed that the idea of nationhood could only serve as an effective focal point for people's identities if it was a "thick" conception of nationhood, based on a dense constellation of shared values, beliefs, historical myths, and other ethnic, religious, and cultural similarities. In the past forty years, we have seen a dramatic "thinning" of national identities, as they have been stretched to accommodate demands for inclusion by a range of historically disadvantaged groups, including religious, racial, indigenous, linguistic, ethnic, and regional minorities. At each step along this process, commentators have feared that the thinning of national identity to make it more inclusive would undermine its power to create meaningful loyalties and solidarities. And yet, at the start of the twenty-first century, it seems clear that thin national identities are still capable of generating the sort of solidarity that enables societies to adopt institutions that effectively promote health and well-being. Even when national identities have been redefined as multicultural, disavowing any pretense to ethnic purity and cultural homogeneity, they can still serve as key elements in broader social imaginaries. Just as social scientists have long noted the power of weak social ties, so we can talk about the power of thin collective identities. Yet precisely how thin collective identities serve this function is less clear. An important topic for future research, therefore, is to examine in a more fine-grained way the relationship between nationhood, ethnic diversity, and multiculturalism, across a wide range of contexts, to see how they interact and mutually influence each other. This can help identify the potential room for creating new scripts that both generate solidarity while accommodating diversity.

10

From State-Centrism to Neoliberalism

Macro-Historical Contexts of Population Health since World War II

William H. Sewell, Jr.

The previous chapters of this book have shown that a society's institutional frameworks and cultural repertoires have a major impact on population health. But, as Hertzman and Saddiqi remarked in Chapter 1, such institutions and cultural repertoires also have a past and a future. The trajectory of a society's population health over time depends on the history of its institutions and cultural structures. It is, for example, well established that socioeconomic inequalities matter enormously to health outcomes – Link and Phelan call such inequalities a "fundamental cause" of disease.[1] But even if we agree that inequality is a permanent feature of human societies, it is also true that class structures and social institutions change significantly over time. Historical changes can restructure the very parameters within which the determinants of population health have their effects. Jane Jenson's study of citizenship regimes in this volume illustrates this point starkly: sanitary policies known to be capable of greatly improving the health of British urban populations could not be applied systematically as long as that country's liberal citizenship regime remained in place. It was only when the citizenship regime was transformed by historical changes in the British political system in the years after 1870 that major improvements in urban population health were attainable.

The aim of this chapter is to trace out a set of changes in institutional and cultural frameworks that have conditioned health outcomes on a global scale since the end of World War II. It argues that during these years there has been a major transformation in the architecture of world capitalism – a shift from what I call a state-centric to a neoliberal paradigm of capitalist political economy – and that this shift has had important implications for population health. By

---

[1] Link and Phelan (1995).

I would like the thank Alice Kessler-Harris, Moishe Postone, George Steinmetz, and my colleagues in the Successful Societies Program for their comments on earlier drafts of this manuscript. Peter Hall's comments have been especially helpful.

capitalist political economy, I mean to designate not just an "economy" made up of production, consumption, and markets but also an evolving historical configuration of political structures, economic regulations, technologies, market forms, class relations, and social imaginaries that together provide a framework for economic activity. There are, to be sure, important variations at any given time in the political economic patterns of different countries. But it is striking how much these patterns have, historically, shifted in tandem on a worldwide basis. Capitalism is an inherently world-spanning structure that, in spite of differences from place to place, evolves as an interdependent whole. This chapter attempts to account for the most recent of the epochal shifts that have periodically restructured the capitalist political economy.

There are good a priori reasons to believe that an account of capitalism's shift from a state-centric to a neoliberal political economic paradigm should have an important bearing on population health. The political economy of capitalism should be linked to population health through four distinct pathways that have been discussed repeatedly in this book. First, it is obvious that capitalism's dynamics largely determine levels of economic prosperity and rates of economic growth in the contemporary world – and we know that, other things equal, economic affluence has a strong positive effect on health. Second, it seems generally to be true that public provision of goods relevant to health – for example, water supply, sanitation, medical care, housing, education, alleviation of poverty, or control of environmental pollution – has a significantly positive effect on health. But one of the major trends in the transition from a state-centric to a neoliberal form of capitalism has been a shift in the balance away from public and toward private provision of economic goods in general, including those strongly relevant to health. Third, the nature and extent of material inequalities – loosely speaking the inequalities of class – are a fundamental cause of variation in population health. Although advocates of neoliberalism claim that unfettered capitalism produces high levels of economic growth, which tends to improve population health, its critics claim that unfettering capitalism also tends to increase class inequality, a factor that is unfavorable to population health. In the recent history of capitalism, how to strike a proper balance between growth and material equity has been a central issue and a major form of variation among countries. Fourth, it is arguable that recent changes in capitalism, by generally freeing resources and enterprise from state regulation, have increased the insecurity and consequently the general stress levels of the population. If this is true, it should have a negative effect on population health by increasing the "wear and tear" experienced by individuals in dealing with the challenges of daily life. In short, although it may be argued that neoliberalism has had a health-enhancing effect on the world's population by improving efficiency, increasing the gains of trade, and fostering enterprise, such enhancements may be limited or even nullified by other effects of neoliberalism – the shriveling of public provision, a rise in socioeconomic inequality, and an increase in general insecurity. For all these reasons, an account of transformations in the political economy of global capitalism since World War II seems eminently relevant to an inquiry into the effects of institutions and cultural frameworks on population health.

Although this chapter attempts to grasp changes in the political economy of the world as a whole, the world of capitalism is hardly flat. Within world capitalism, the economic developments, regulatory policies, and economic ideologies of the wealthiest nation states are vastly more influential than those of the poor and "underdeveloped" countries. Consequently, the story I tell may seem American or Euro-American centered. But this is because the story is capital-centered, and American and European capital has (with an important assist from Japan since the 1970s and China in the past decade) dominated the history of the world economy as a whole during the period since World War II. Even though I attempt in this chapter to relate American or European developments to the quite different histories of Asia, Africa, Latin America, the Middle East, and the former Soviet bloc, the controlling structures of world capitalist development in the years since World War II have disproportionately embodied the interests and the sociopolitical outlooks of the wealthiest states and of their political and economic elites.

THE RISE OF THE STATE-CENTRIC PARADIGM

The shift from a state-centric to a neoliberal political economic paradigm is a product of the past three decades or so, but this transformation must be seen in the perspective of the long-term history of capitalism. As numerous scholars have argued, the history of capitalist economic growth is characterized not by a straightforward incremental expansion of capital accumulation, technological development, and per-capita income, but by a more cyclical rhythm.[2] The history of capitalism since the sixteenth century has been marked by long-term shifts – for example, in leading sectors (from maritime commerce, to textiles and steam power, to chemicals and electricity, to consumer durables, to informatics) and in economically dominant or hegemonic states (from the Netherlands, to England, to the United States). My periodization in this chapter emphasizes changing paradigms of institutional governance of the capitalist economy. Schematically, the first phase of capitalist history was characterized by a mercantilist paradigm, associated with maritime and colonial rivalries between Spain, the Netherlands, England, and France in the seventeenth and eighteenth centuries. This gave way to a nineteenth-century liberal paradigm emphasizing internal laissez-faire and external free trade, enforced by British industrial and maritime dominance. This was followed by a state-centric paradigm that flourished most fully in the decades immediately after World War II, and finally by a neoliberal paradigm whose contours are still being formed in the present.

---

[2] Kondratieff (1935); Mandell (1980); Wallerstein (1974; 1980; 1989); Arrighi (1994).

Toward the end of the nineteenth century, British dominance and the liberal paradigm with which it was associated were challenged by the rise of the economic wealth and power of the United States and Germany; by the erection of high tariff barriers that reversed the drift toward free trade; by the growing scale of industrial production that led to the formation of trusts and cartels, thereby undermining the economic assumptions on which a laissez-faire economic regime was based; and by intensified colonial and military rivalries that threatened the long nineteenth-century peace. The inferno of World War I incinerated the intellectual prestige of nineteenth-century liberalism and made the United States, not Britain, the leading economic power and the world's major creditor. The years following World War I produced no single dominant economic paradigm, but state regimentation of production and exchange during the war emergency itself set precedents that were taken up in various later experiments, of which the most startling was the establishment of a socialist economy in the Soviet Union. Once the Great Depression of the 1930s struck, numerous state-imposed experiments, both ad hoc and systematic, were attempted. These included the American New Deal, Swedish social democracy, and the various fascisms – Italian, German, Japanese, Spanish, and Portuguese.

After World War II, a more or less coherent state-centric paradigm of economic governance was elaborated under American leadership. This state-centric paradigm presided over a period of unprecedented economic boom that lasted from the late 1940s to the early 1970s.[3] Having been spared the enormous wartime destruction visited upon Europe and Japan, the United States emerged from the war as the dominant power militarily, politically, and economically. Indeed, the surge of wartime production in the United States had not only jolted its economy out of the Great Depression but also enabled it to grow by two-thirds between 1940 and 1945. By the end of the war, the United States by itself had a sizable majority of the world's industrial capacity and most of the world's gold reserves – the War had made the United States the world's universal creditor.[4] The United States also assumed the dominant leadership role in managing the world economy. It provided generous aid to the defeated powers and – via the Marshall Plan – to the rest of Europe. It granted aid to countries in the underdeveloped world and guaranteed the Breton Woods postwar monetary agreements, which maintained fixed exchange rates between the world's major currencies. This generosity was in part inspired by political self-interest. In the context of the Cold War rivalry with the Soviet Union, assuring generalized prosperity acted as insurance against the potential popularity of communist parties both in Europe and in the developing world.

---

[3] As Hobsbawm (1994) points out, its only plausible rival in the history of capitalism was the great liberal boom a century earlier, in the 1850s and 1860s.

[4] Hobsbawm (1994: 285); Brenner (2006).

During this period of American hegemony, the core countries of the world capitalist economy all elaborated some sort of Keynsian welfare state. Although American spokesmen insisted rhetorically on the importance of free enterprise, the forms of capitalist political economy that emerged in the postwar all over the world were distinctly state-centric – a far cry from the liberal structures that had predominated in the nineteenth century. Governments in the wealthy countries took on a central role in guiding and regulating the economy – using fiscal policies to ensure full employment, limiting income inequality by means of highly progressive taxation, reducing social risks by introducing state-supported old age and disability insurance, unemployment insurance, housing, and medical care, and various forms of income supplements. Sometimes, as in France, governments nationalized key industries and elaborated comprehensive national economic plans. Everywhere they established labor relations regimes that recognized unions but steered them toward pragmatic bread-and-butter issues and cooperation with management. The precise form of government guidance of the economy varied a great deal, but the principle that the maintenance of economic prosperity and full employment was a prime state responsibility was universally accepted. Welfare states tended to expand in this period whether a conservative, centrist, or leftist party was in office. The welfare states established in different countries varied considerably in their features. Peter Hall and David Soskice, for example, distinguish the "coordinated market economies" of contemporary Continental Europe and Japan from the "liberal market economies" of the Anglophone world.[5] Many of the policies adopted in the postwar period had been experimented with between the two world wars, but it was only after the defeat of fascism and the onset of the Cold War "containment" of communism that a stable, state-centric political economic paradigm was put into place in all the economically advanced countries of the "free world."

This new state-centric paradigm – which has been dubbed "Fordism" by scholars – delivered solid economic security and rapid economic growth in the 1950s and 1960s.[6] The generalized prosperity, combined with the establishment of comprehensive welfare systems, made possible rapid advances in population health. Economic growth during this "Golden Age," as Eric Hobsbawm calls it, was powered by the spread of mass production techniques and corporate economic organization – which had initially been perfected in the United States – to the economies of Western Europe and Japan.[7] The advanced economies grew above all by mass-producing and mass-marketing automobiles, refrigerators, washing machines, radios, televisions, and other consumer durables. In Europe and Japan, where relatively few consumer durables had been produced before the war, the market demand for such commodities was limited

[5] Hall and Soskice (2001). See Esping-Andersen (1990; 1999) for a somewhat different classification.
[6] Aglietta (1979); Boyer (1986); Lipietz (1987).
[7] Hobsbawm (1994).

only by the purchasing power of the working population. Purchasing power was assured by a self-sustaining economic virtuous circle. Buoyant demand led to full employment and the expansion and modernization of plant, which drove up productivity, which enabled wages to rise, which insured continually rising demand. The U.S. economy was powered by the same virtuous circle, but because it started from a much higher base, rates of growth in the United States in the 1950s and 1960s were lower than those of Western Europe or Japan.

Yet by the end of the 1960s, signs of strain were beginning to show in the world economy. Inflation rates, which previously had been kept under control, were increasing ominously and labor unrest – most spectacularly in the French "events" of 1968 and the Italian "hot autumn" of 1969 – challenged the implicit labor compromise upon which the boom had rested. Meanwhile, the monetary agreements established at Breton Woods came apart between 1971 and 1973, when the U.S. Treasury's gold reserves, whose abundance had guaranteed the system's functioning, began to run low. In the spring of 1973, the entire system of fixed exchange rates was abandoned, and currencies henceforth floated on the international market. In the fall of 1973, the Arab-Israeli Yom Kippur War led to an Arab oil embargo. Dramatic rises in the price of oil caused an acceleration in what was an already troublesome bout of inflation. Over the course of the 1970s, Western economies were beset with a hitherto unobserved combination of inflation with economic stagnation (dubbed "stagflation") that proved impossible to resolve with existing Keynsian techniques of economic management. All this turbulence at the level of institutions of global economic management was matched by a marked slow-down in rates of economic growth, profits, productivity, and real wages. Robert Brenner argues that profit rates in the European and American economies, which of course dominated the world in the 1950s and 1960s, had already begun to sag by the late 1960s under the weight of excess capacity, and that it was this problem that made the economic crisis so difficult to resolve – indeed, he argues that excess capacity continues to plague the world economy to the present.[8] Excess capacity was represented most strikingly by the rise of Japanese producers, who by the 1970s were competing very effectively with European and American corporations in such high-end goods as automobiles and electronics. In the course of the 1970s, the entire Golden Age political economic-paradigm appears to have reached its limits and entered into a sustained crisis. Neither bureaucratized mass-production industry, nor the Keynsian welfare states that ensured more-or-less full-employment and mass consumption, nor the labor accords on which they rested, withstood the crisis of the 1970s.

The response to this crisis of the state-centric mass-production economy in the leading capitalist countries was at first confused and piece-meal, but it was

[8] Brenner (2002; 2004; 2006).

eventually far-reaching and creative. Capitalists in the wealthy European and North American countries abandoned the industries in which they were no longer competitive; adopted new, more decentralized, organizational forms, featuring part-time work, consulting, and outsourcing; applied new computerized technologies in both manufacturing and management; developed multinational corporations, many of which moved substantial portions of their manufacturing to low-wage countries; integrated design, advertising, and production ever more tightly, for example by increasingly producing for niche rather than mass markets; and specialized increasingly in service industries, especially financial services.[9] Wages, which had been rising steadily from the late 1940s to the mid 1970s, have essentially stagnated from the late 1970s to present, even after profits began to climb again in the 1980s. In part because of the potential and actual competition of low-cost labor outside the capitalist core states, the power of trade unions receded everywhere.

This profoundly restructured economy became increasingly globalized, in several senses. International trade rose as a percentage of total world GDP. This trade became ever more global in the sense that Asian economies joined North America and Western Europe as major producers for the world market – and not just Japan, but also South Korea, Taiwan, Singapore, Hong Kong, Malaysia, Thailand, Indonesia, and eventually China and India. There was also a rise in international migration. Multinational corporations, making use of the possibility for instantaneous computerized communications, developed globally integrated production systems, in which tasks were assigned to employees working in different countries – with, for example, routine parts production assigned to Mexico and Malaysia, design to Sweden, engineering specifications to Germany, final assembly to Canada, financing and marketing to the United States and Great Britain. And finally, a globalized market, also taking advantage of computerized communications, emerged in financial services. An important stimulus to the growth of financial markets was the possibility of large-scale speculation on currencies once the Bretton Woods accords broke down. This global financial market, increasingly based upon mathematically abstruse devices such as derivatives, boomed in spite of the generally lackluster overall performance of the world economy.[10] Global finance increasingly escaped control of even the most powerful countries and, especially by means of speculation in currency futures, effectively challenged the economic sovereignty of nation states.

It is a fascinating but somewhat mysterious fact that the communist countries of Eastern Europe, which had experienced about the same rate of economic growth as Western European countries from the late 1940s to the mid 1960s, experienced a slowing of growth at about the same time as the non-communist countries. (This is also when, as Hertzman and Siddiqi point out in

[9] On these changes, see, for example, Harvey (1990); Reich (1992).
[10] LiPuma and Lee (2004).

Chapter 1, health outcomes in Eastern and Western Europe began to diverge.) One might well explain the slowing of growth in the Global South after 1973 as a consequence of those countries' economic dependence on the stagnating wealthy capitalist countries. But since trade between Eastern European communist countries and the rest of the world was quite restricted, and since the communist economies were governed according to very different principles than economies in the "free world," it is hard to argue that the Soviet and East-European slowdown could have been a result of the slowdown in the West – especially since their slowdown, which dates from the mid 1960s, preceded that in the West by about a half-decade. One hypothesis is that both Soviet bloc and Western capitalist economic growth in the postwar period were, in spite of the immense differences between the two economic systems, characterized by analogous state-centric models of mass industrial production, managed in a top-down hierarchical fashion, and that the rigidities of this model began to outweigh its advantages in both the East and the West at about the same time. In any case, the previously parallel developments in the East and West diverged increasingly from the 1970s on. In the East, the command economy system proved immune to fundamental reform. Although the story is obviously complicated, the increasing sclerosis of the Soviet-style economies was a crucial factor in the eventual collapse of the communist political regimes.

Most states in the Global South had their own versions of state-centric economic models in the 1950s through the 1970s – what has been called the developmentalist state. Sometimes borrowing ideas from both capitalist and communist models, most states in the Global South imposed some form of state planning and developed programs of import-substitution in an attempt to foster industrialization. Although the record of the developmentalist states was uneven, they generally were able to participate in the overall economic expansion of the Golden Age. In Africa, for example, the annual GDP growth rate was a substantial 5.4 percent from 1965 to 1973.[11] In the 1970s, however, growth rates began to falter in the Global South as well. In this decade, many of the developmentalist states took on heavy loads of debt to keep the efforts at industrialization and import substitution going. By the 1980s, especially in Africa and Latin America, these debts became too big for many of the states to handle (in part because the expected productivity gains had not transpired, in part because the interest rates on their loans increased sharply). Countries unable to service their debts were subjected to IMF and World Bank structural adjustment programs that, among other things, required them to dismantle their developmentalist states (about which more later). By the 1990s, the Third World developmentalist state was as much a thing of the past as the communist state.

In short, the world economic crisis that became irreversible in 1973 marks a transition between distinct periods of world economic history. In

---

[11] Hoogvelt (2001: 174).

the course of the 1970s, the various state-centric economic architectures that had provided impressive levels of economic growth in most areas of the world – the Keynesian welfare state, the communist command economy, and the Third World developmentalist state – entered into a profound crisis. After a period of institutional turbulence and uncertainty during the 1970s, a new neoliberal global order began to take shape in the 1980s and eventually became hegemonic in the 1990s. This global shift reshaped the economic, political, institutional, and cultural forms of world society. In doing so, it also reshaped the cultural and institutional contexts of efforts to improve population health.

CULTURAL TRANSFORMATIONS

I have mentioned that political economic paradigms are cultural as well as institutional. But shifts in cultural repertoires, although intimately related to institutional shifts, were never simple reflections of the latter. Cultural repertoires or social imaginaries enjoy a certain autonomy from their institutional and material environments. Explaining the shift from a state-centric to a neoliberal political economic paradigm therefore requires an examination not only of the institutions that condition production and exchange but of the course and rhythms of cultural change as well.

   The economic transformations of the Golden Age profoundly affected the structures of people's lived experience, most obviously in the economically advanced core of Europe, North America, and Japan.[12] The mass economic insecurity of the interwar period faded away in the context of sustained economic growth and ever-expanding state welfare protections. Political passions that had embroiled Europe, North America, and East Asia in the interwar period by no means disappeared, but they were far less heated in the postwar era. The redistributive spending of governments, together with steadily rising wages and an outpouring of mass-produced goods, meant that the entire populations of the wealthier countries were lifted into what, by prewar standards, would have been inconceivable affluence. One of the consequences of this new affluence, combined with the reduced social inequalities ushered in by Keynsian welfare states, was an impressive improvement in population health. It was in the 1950s that the leading causes of death shifted from infectious diseases to the diseases of old age – because of improvements in sanitation, diet, housing, and medicine, people were now living long enough to die of strokes, heart disease, and cancer. During the Golden Age, populations of the wealthy countries shifted massively from rural to urban areas and rural areas became far less isolated with the generalization of the automobile and the spread of mass media. Advertising – already important between the wars – emerged as

---

[12] Hobsbawm (1994) gives a brilliant account of what he calls the "social revolution" of the postwar decades.

an increasingly dominant general cultural force. The combination of general affluence and sharply rising proportions of the population in school led to the development of distinct youth cultures with ever-greater economic and cultural salience. Although the world lived in the shadow of possible nuclear holocaust, the powerful upward thrust of economic growth and the profound social changes it brought about clearly injected a general optimism into the cultures of the countries of Western Europe, North America, and Japan.

The communist countries of Eastern Europe and the Soviet Union also experienced a period of sustained economic growth in the first postwar decades. Especially after the death of Stalin in 1953, political oppression was relaxed appreciably. The communist states assured full employment, economic security, and equitable provision of health-related goods. The Berlin rising of 1953, the Hungarian Revolution of 1956, the "Prague Spring" of 1968, and a succession of Polish popular mobilizations make it clear that communist rule in Eastern Europe was sustained by the threat of Soviet armed force. But at least until the later 1960s, these regimes assured social stability and steady economic progress, including major improvements in population health. Communism in China was, of course, a much more volatile affair. Periods of relative calm alternated with periods of catastrophic hyperactivity – the "Great Leap Forward" of 1958–60, which ended in famines that killed some thirty million,[13] and the "Great Proletarian Cultural Revolution" of 1966–76, which was by no means as deadly but effectively traumatized virtually the entire Chinese population.

The fundamental historical experience of the former colonial countries – which in this era began to be called the Third World – was decolonization. This was a long process, beginning in Indonesia and India in the immediate postwar years and not completed until the withdrawal of U.S. forces from Vietnam in 1975 and the collapse of the Portuguese empire in Africa at about the same time. But the arrow of history seemed to be pointing in a single direction in these years. The newly independent states of Asia and Africa gained formal sovereignty, exchanged ambassadors with other states, and claimed their seats in the United Nations. The leaders of a number of the most important new states attempted to forge a middle way between the liberal capitalism of the United States and the communism of the Soviet Union. Their program was characterized by strong developmentalist states with economies that combined socialist and market capitalist features. In the decolonizing Third World, the postwar years were – at least for the educated elites – a period of surging optimism.

If the economic watershed of the postwar world was the early 1970s, the cultural watershed came earlier, at least in the West. Over the course of the 1960s, there was an inchoate but powerful challenge to existing cultural and political norms, one powered above all by youth, and particularly by

[13] Yang (1996).

university students.[14] The youth revolt was made possible by the fundamental economic transformations of this era. The rapidly growing economies of the West and Japan were, as Daniel Bell pointed out in *The Coming of Post-Industrial Society,* increasingly based on knowledge – science and technology, obviously, but also marketing, advertising, forecasting, management, and the like – rather than on direct productive labor.[15] Sustaining this pattern of economic growth required the production of university graduates. Especially in the 1960s, university student populations burgeoned in all the economically advanced countries. Given the seemingly unshakable economic prosperity of this period, students generally were confident about gaining suitable employment upon graduation; they felt free to explore the full range of available opportunities of university life – intellectual, political, and cultural – in a way that later generations of students, facing a far more competitive and uncertain job markets, did not. Students in the United States were stimulated by the great political causes of the Civil Rights movement and opposition to the Vietnam War. Indeed, the Vietnam War became a major political issue in student movements all around the world. Both in the United States and elsewhere, student political activism was combined with experimental lifestyles, characterized by rock music, psychedelic drugs, and, crucially, the sexual revolution. The student population increasingly included nearly as many women as men and the extended period of adult autonomy without adult responsibility, combined with the increased availability of contraception – most emblematically "the pill" – resulted in fundamental and permanent changes in the sexual behavior of young adults. From the 1960s forward, the age of marriage rose, as did rates of premarital cohabitation, divorce, and single parenthood. By the end of the 1960s, the entire question of relations between the sexes was put into question by the modern feminist movement – and by the newly assertive gay liberation movement as well.

The predominant theme of the 1960s movements is probably best captured by the term "liberation," initially used by Third World struggles for "national liberation" but applied widely to struggles of all sorts. The students involved in the movements of the 1960s may have been enabled by the expansive Fordist capitalism of the 1950s and 1960s, but having no memories of the prewar or wartime eras, they felt little gratitude for the high prosperity and generalized economic security of the time, which they tended to take for granted as givens of the modern world. Instead, they were highly critical both of the stultifying conformity of contemporary corporate culture and of lingering racism, capitalist exploitation, and colonialism. Liberation was an elastic notion that encompassed both psychic liberation from the conformist norms of contemporary capitalist societies and political liberation from racial,

---

[14] For a general account of the revolts of the 1960s, see Horn (2007). On the role of youth, see also Hobsbawm (1994); Eley (2002).
[15] Bell (1999 [1973]).

colonial, and class oppression. In fashioning their discourse of liberation, the student radicals drew on extremely diverse sources: Marxism, the American Civil Rights movement, anticolonial struggles, the theater of the absurd, hedonistic rock music, the beatnicks, and the theories of such high intellectual figures as Guy Debord and Herbert Marcuse.[16] American and European universities became the chief nexus of a conjuries of novel movements by the late 1960s, both politically charged (like the antiwar movement, the environmental movements, ethnic and racial movements, the women's movement) and relatively apolitical (like the hippies, Eastern religions, communes, and assorted human potential movements).

If student radicalism had its strongest initial upsurge in the United States, its most spectacular single moment was the "events" of May and June 1968 in France. Beginning as a dispute within the universities, this struggle burgeoned into a general strike that paralyzed the entire country and seemed to threaten the continuity of the Gaullist Fifth Republic. This uprising, like its American counterparts, had an important component of lifestyle experimentation and a strongly liberationist bent.[17] The style of May 1968 was captured in a famous poster, which declared: "It is forbidden to forbid." There were also massive youth and student movements in Britain, Germany, and Italy in 1968. In Italy, as in France, the movement also spread into the factories; the Italian movement was particularly long-lived, and like the French "events" it also seemed at times to threaten the existing regime.[18] Yet, by the early 1970s, the students' and workers' rebellions were in retreat everywhere in the West. Societies had been shaken and an entire generation of students had participated in radical political and lifestyle experiments that would, in one way or another, mark them for life. But the student movements, unlike the labor movements of earlier decades, had few concrete reforms to show for their efforts. Their most significant effects were on the cultural assumptions and social norms of their societies – on relations between the sexes, on styles of emotional expression, on opinions about environmental pollution or militarism, on personal goals and imaginations. They were an important source of the "postindustrial values" that researchers like Ronald Inglehart began to study in the 1970s.[19]

One of the most important cultural and political changes of the 1960s was an expansion in the number and character of the groups – especially as defined by race, ethnicity, gender, or sexuality – that felt entitled to declare their existence and solidarity and to make claims against states. The student movement in the United States arose in symbiosis with the movement for Civil Rights for blacks. The lunch counter sit-ins of 1960 were launched by students and it was students, both black and white, who were the crucial militants in the Student

---

[16] Marcuse (1991 [1964]); Debord (1994 [1967]).
[17] Le Goff (1998); Ross (2002).
[18] Tarrow (1989).
[19] Inglehart (1977).

Nonviolent Coordinating Committee (SNCC) and the Freedom Summer voting rights project.[20] Moreover, the first of the American campus revolts, the Berkeley Free Speech Movement of 1964, arose out of a dispute about on-campus solicitation of funds by Civil Rights organizations.[21] In its initial integrationist form, the Civil Rights movement based its claims on the formal citizenship rights of African Americans, attempting to make them equal participants in the post–New Deal democratic order. But in the mid 1960s, the Civil Rights movement was transformed by a rhetoric of Black Power or Black Nationalism, inspired in part by the anticolonial liberation struggles under way at that time in Africa. This represented a fundamental shift in the movement's style and claims – toward militancy and separatism and toward an emphasis on victimization and, through the invocation of "Black Pride," what might be called the repair of spoiled identity.[22] The model pioneered by Black Nationalism had a surprising resonance among other groups – various ethnic groups, women, gays, Native Americans, and so on. An interesting case in point is the Jews. It was only in the wake of the Six-Day War of 1967 that Holocaust discourse suddenly took off, making the suffering of the Jews at the hands of the Nazis the crucial node of Jewish identity for the first time. This was true in the United States, as Peter Novick has noted in *The Holocaust in American Life,* but elsewhere as well – for example, in France.[23]

Both the Civil Rights frame and the quasi-nationalist frame were widely adopted outside the United States over the course of the ensuing decades. Whether aborigines in Australia, First Nations in Canada, Maoris in New Zealand, West-Indian or Pakistani immigrants in Britain, Breton or Occitan nationalists in France, women or gays or the disabled or the deaf in various countries, all kinds of groups in the 1970s and 1980s claimed the status of oppressed minorities,[24] attempted to instill pride in their ranks, worked for recognition by states and in the public sphere, and claimed various forms of legislative recompense. This was clearly an extension of democracy in that it allowed all kinds of groups to name their oppressions and to organize themselves both to restore their injured pride and to gain access to political or economic resources they had previously been denied. As Will Kymlicka points out in Chapter 9 in this volume, this political program, which has come to be known as multiculturalism, found considerable resonance among the growing minority populations across the whole range of advanced democratic countries. A few countries, with Canada in the lead, have adopted multiculturalism as an official state policy. If carried out effectively, multicultural democracy could lead not only to more equitable economic and political outcomes, but to

---

[20] McAdam (1982; 1988).
[21] Heirich (1971); Freeman (2004).
[22] Goffman (1963).
[23] Novick (1999); Wolf (2004).
[24] Of course, one of these "minorities" – women – actually constitutes a majority in most of the world's countries.

an enhanced sense of dignity, participation, and well-being among the various minorities that have been slighted in the past.

But another side to the upsurge of multiple cultural identities must also be acknowledged. Under the dispensation of postwar Fordist democracy, the nation was understood as an essentially homogeneous body of active citizens with equal rights, who worked, expressed their opinions (above all at the polls), paid their taxes, raised their families, and counted on the economic security guaranteed by the state and the big business corporations. The citizen-worker was implicitly gendered male in this Fordist social imaginary and differences of ethnicity and race were also submerged under the egalitarian ideal. "John Q. Public," the incarnation of the average citizen in American political cartoons of the era, was conventionally portrayed as a bespectacled, balding, white, middle-aged, middle-class, white-collared taxpayer dressed in a hat, a necktie, and a somewhat rumpled suit. The alternative figure was the blue-collar citizen, with overalls, work shirt, and muscular body – but also invariably white and male. It was by means of such figures that the formal equality of all citizens was envisioned in the public mind. Such a social imaginary was, clearly, exclusionary. But it also underwrote a Fordist political order that assumed a certain solidarity among citizens, including universal provision of social security, unemployment insurance, other New Deal government benefits, and the right to collective bargaining. These universal entitlements were assumed in the form of equal citizenship symbolized by John Q. Public.

John Q. Public, with his suit, white shirt, tie, hat, and respectability could hardly have been expected to survive the 1960s. Indeed, he in some ways perfectly symbolized the bureaucratic conformity that was the obsession of the student radicals. The new claimants spawned by the 1960s based their claims not on their presumed likeness to other citizens but on their difference. Their moral standing was based essentially on a claim to victimhood – to having been denied rights and respect that should be owed to a citizen. In this emerging political imaginary, the internal solidarity of the oppressed group and its moral claim to political recognition and resources was far more intense than the claims that could be made on behalf of the society as a whole – especially since the supposed "society as a whole" had been revealed as actually benefiting a specific category. This tendency to seek the status of victim was enhanced in the 1970s, when the hopes for a Marxist-style workers' revolt faded. The complaints against the state and corporate capitalism that had been general on the left in the 1960s now tended to gravitate toward the claims of identity groups of some sort, resulting in a fracturing of the social imaginary.

In the 1970s, the far-reaching changes in culture and political discourse that had developed in the previous decade interacted with the post-1973 economic transformations. The new economic circumstances surely helped fuel the fracturing of the social imaginary that initially began in the 1960s as part of a polymorphous search for liberation. The grim realities of the new economic regime began to manifest themselves in the latter half of the decade. Both North American and Western European countries experienced extensive deindustrialization and widespread unemployment. This structural unemployment tended to be particularly severe among disadvantaged minorities – for example, African Americans in the United States, North Africans in France, Turks and Yugoslavs in Germany, and West Indians and South Asians in Britain – all of whom had been strongly concentrated in urban industrial employment during the Golden Age. This simultaneously increased both the grievance level of minority groups and the resentments of native white male workers, who, even if they were lucky enough to be employed, found themselves criticized by minorities at the same time that their own employment became increasingly insecure and their wages were stagnating, at best. At the same time, the women's movement was challenging men's traditional authority both in the family and in the workplace and the unions that had been the mainstay of workers' power both in the state and in the enterprise declined in membership and self-confidence. From having been recognized in the social imaginary as representing the epitome of the modern democratic citizen and the progressive foundation of the nation itself, white working-class men increasingly became a disgruntled minority that regarded itself as victimized by feminism and by racial and ethnic minorities. This resentment has had important political consequences: for example, in the United States by the 1980s a majority of white working-class men voted for Ronald Reagan and in France sizable but varying proportions have voted for the far right National Front.

In America, the fizzling out of liberationist hopes in the 1970s gave rise to an upsurge in religious experimentation among certain participants in the youth revolts. A fascination with "Eastern" religious practices had been an aspect of the 1960s movements all along. But as the 1970s wore on, religious experimentation was increasingly divorced from political goals and became an end in itself. There was a flowering of alternatives, from transcendental meditation, to Hindu Ashrams, to various syncretic "New Age" spiritualisms, to more conventional forms of evangelical or fundamentalist Christianity or orthodox Judaism. This turn to religion was alarming or simply befuddling to the secularist majority of leftists. But the turn to religion, no less than the simultaneous turn to identity politics, was a sign that the modernist state-centric imaginary that the left shared willy-nilly with its "corporate liberal" nemesis was losing its grip. Revolutionary and radical reformist politics had always regarded state action – legislation or administrative enactment – as the prime means of improving the world. The turn to religion marked a search for more spiritual, personal, and communal forms of betterment, to which state action was largely irrelevant.

This turn to religion was a prominent feature of American culture in the 1970s and 1980s, but it was by no means characteristic of all countries in this period. There was no significant religious upsurge in Europe, where church attendance continued a long and steady decline. But the 1970s did see a rise of religious fundamentalism in many portions of the world. Jewish fundamentalism became an increasingly important political force in Israel. In India the Hindu fundamentalist Bharatiya Janata Party, which governed the country from 1998 to 2004, also dates its rise to the 1970s – the period of Indira Ghandi's Emergency Decrees, which greatly tarnished the reputation of the secularist Congress Party. Sikh fundamentalism also thrived in the late 1970s in the Punjab; it was Sikh fundamentalists who assassinated Indira Gandhi. Pentecostalism made major breakthroughs in traditionally Catholic Latin America in the same years. It was also in the 1970s that Islamic fundamentalism became a mass movement all across the Middle East. Although groups like the Egyptian Islamic Brotherhood had been in existence for decades, political developments of the 1970s greatly swelled the numbers of Islamists. The defeat of Arab forces in both the Six Day War of 1967 and the Yom Kippur War of 1973 were experienced as a profound humiliation. The decline of once promising secularist Middle Eastern regimes into cynical and corrupt dictatorships – for example in Egypt, Syria, Iran, and Iraq – and the abysmal economic performance of non-oil-producing Middle Eastern states made the Islamist call for religiously based moral and political reform plausible and widely popular. The overthrow of the Shah of Iran in 1979 by a popular Islamist uprising made the longing for a powerful Islamic state seem increasingly realistic. The history of the rise of religious fundamentalism is, of course, different for each of these cases. But I think it is at least arguable that Indian Hindus and Sikhs, South American Pentecostals, Middle-Eastern Muslims, Israeli Jewish fundamentalists, and American religious seekers and Evangelicals were all, in one way or another, experiencing and reacting to the decline of a basically secular progressive state-centric social imaginary that had seemed to secure political order, both in the world at large and within the various nation states in the 1950s and 1960s.

Doubts or misgivings about the state-centric Golden Age social imaginary can also be seen in a very different realm: in the rise of new vocabularies of social analysis that emerged in the 1970s. These trends in the social sciences have a double interest. On the one hand, they are yet another indication of how pervasive the cultural changes of this period were. But they also matter because they tended to limit social scientists' ability to grasp the sort of macro socioeconomic changes that were transforming their own world in these years – and hence to leave social analysis relatively defenseless against the neoliberal offensive when it came. In the 1950s and 1960s, the social sciences were underwritten above all by modernization theory, in one or another of its guises. For modernization theorists, the widely varied societies that made up the world were destined to converge on a common pattern dominated by modern science and technology, industrialization, and rational bureaucratic administration – that is, on the state-centric world envisaged in the dominant social imaginary of the Golden Age. The task of the social sciences was to understand the complex structures and processes of modern societies and to chart out the course by which traditional societies could be brought to the goal of modernity. The favored means of the social sciences in carrying out these tasks was a basically positivist scientific methodology that itself performed the modernity toward which society was inevitably evolving.[25]

The upheavals of the late 1960s and the 1970s, however, subjected all of the presuppositions of modernization theory to systematic doubt. The inevitability of social progress toward an ideal of modern rationality seemed a mockery when advanced American technology was being used to rain napalm on Vietnamese peasants. The supposed superiority of technological reason seemed refuted by the diminishment of human possibilities that putatively characterized life in industrial society and by the ravages caused to the natural environment by technological "progress." The lifestyle experiments of the 1960s suggested that the study of non-Western or past societies was important less as a means of charting out pathways to the modern world than as a way of exploring the still potent multiplicity of human potential. The scientific method that was supposed to lead social scientists to truth was itself denounced as an exercise in bureaucratic administration, a means of replicating rather than criticizing the status quo. History, rather than following a single charmed path, now seemed both open and perilous. As the 1970s wore on, the predictability that was supposed to characterize rational modern society seemed to be giving way to flux on nearly every front.

Over the course of the 1970s and into the 1980s, critical social scientists unraveled the reified categories and the structural determinism at the core of the modernization paradigm. Antideterminist thinking took a number of different forms. The linguistic or cultural turn, which eventually swept through many disciplines in the human sciences, stressed the constitutive power of language and other symbolic forms and therefore stood as an alternative to the old paradigm's fundamental economic determinism.[26] Poststructuralism put in question the very possibility of coherent and purposeful human action – asserting that knowledge claims were "undecidable" or that knowledge was determined by the play of power.[27] In the 1980s and 1990s, adepts of postmodernism or poststructuralism tended to celebrate the fragmentary character of life as itself liberating.[28] There was a definite elective affinity between the fracturing of the leftist social imaginary into various identity groups and the epistemological fracturing carried out by postmodernism and poststructuralism. Meanwhile, the cultural turn was accompanied by a general upsurge of interest in the place of human action or agency in the social world, an attempt to see how social structures and social forces were not givens but were actively produced by the human individuals who were the constituents of the social world.[29]

All of these forms of social analysis had a strong affinity with the post-1960s left; they could be interpreted as an extension into the epistemology

---

[25] Steinmetz (2005).
[26] A phenomenally influential text was Geertz (1973).
[27] Derrida (1974); Foucault (1979).
[28] For an extreme case, see Deleuze and Guattari (1983).
[29] See, for example, Giddens (1976); Bourdieu (1977).

of the human sciences of the 1960s movements' opposition to bureaucratic rationality and the rigid conformity of corporate capitalism. But as critique, these theoretical movements were interestingly out of phase. The new social thought of the 1970s and 1980s was implicitly criticizing state-centric capitalism at the very time that the state-centric paradigm was being displaced by a more decentered, flexible, and globalized form of capitalism and by a fracturing of social identities. It can be argued that these forms of analysis, which tended to celebrate the impermanence and malleability of existing social forms as epistemologically and politically liberating, may have been complicit, albeit unwittingly, in the construction of the contemporary consumerist and neoliberal capitalist social imaginary.[30]

But the reaction against reified structures in social analysis was not confined to the cultural turn or to the political left. Politically neutral intellectual movements included social network analysis, which developed an important presence in sociology, and the rational choice movement, which gained adherents in political science, economics, sociology, and philosophy. Both of these currents embraced quantitative and mathematical techniques but sought, in quite different ways, to build up larger structures from microfoundations.[31] Finally, the most politically successful of all the post-1970 attempts to return to the microfoundations of social behavior was a resurgent microeconomics, which took the individual facing choices in the market as its microfoundational bedrock. Microeconomics, like rational choice and network analysis, had practitioners of all political persuasions, but one of its important variants, which was distinctly probusiness and anticollectivist, developed a close working relationship with the right wings of the U.S. Republican and the British Conservative parties in the 1970s (about which more later).

The fact that apolitical and conservative social scientists were as involved as leftists in attempting to rethink the social order from a micrological standpoint implies that this effort cannot have been simply a product of 1960s-generated leftist illusions. It was, rather, spurred by developments in the world, where a state-centric political economic paradigm – with its bureaucratized firms, confident social and economic forecasting, expanding welfare states, full employment, cooperative labor relations, and generalized sense of stability – was coming apart. The collapse of the old structures and the gradual and incomplete emergence of more flexible and less bureaucratic social relations seemed – to social analysts of all political leanings – to require a reformulation of theoretical categories from the bottom up. I would argue that these conceptually and politically various new modes of social thought were all responses to what Raymond Williams would call a shared "structure of feeling" – a distinctly experienced but difficult-to-articulate sense that important social changes were afoot in the 1970s, that the old reified and static

---

[30] I have argued this point at greater length in Sewell (2005: 53–62).

[31] Olson (1965); Granovetter (1973); Schelling (1978); Padgett (1993).

categories of modernist social science could no longer grasp the more volatile realities that were emerging in the social world.[32]

THE NEOLIBERAL OFFENSIVE

For most people who lived through the 1970s, whether intellectuals or common citizens, the socioeconomic changes of these years were confusing and disorienting. They certainly disoriented the left. University students, the major constituency for social and political experimentation in the 1960s, became notably more cautious as the job market shrank. This caution was accentuated in the 1980s and 1990s as the economic divide between jobs requiring higher education and those that did not became ever more stark. Deindustrialization – the decline of heavy industries in the most economically advanced countries – undermined the power of labor unions, which had been most deeply entrenched in precisely these sectors. By the 1980s, many unions seemed more intent on maintaining some semblance of the status quo for their own members than on championing a wider progressive agenda. Left-of-center political parties and intellectuals were also disoriented by the socioeconomic changes of the 1970s. The possibility of socialism was tarnished by the failure of the Cultural Revolution in China, the stagnation of the Soviet Union, and the evident cynicism of the apparatchiks who dominated Soviet bloc countries. In the West, Keynesian economic policy, which had served admirably during the long postwar boom, seemed to have no effective answer to the economic crisis. Social democratic programs, premised on the increasingly disarticulated synthesis of big government, big business, and big labor, lost momentum in the face of fiscal difficulties and public skepticism. Parties of the right generally were no less confused. They, too, had accepted the logic of state-centric economic management and expanding welfare entitlements. For most of the 1970s, neither the right nor the left could offer compelling alternatives – both were essentially engaged in attempts to muddle through.

Political initiative was regained, eventually, by a radically reconstituted right, which came to power above all through the elections of Margaret Thatcher as prime minister in Britain in 1979 and Ronald Reagan as president in the United States in 1980. Both Thatcher and Reagan arrived in office with programs very different from those of their parties' previous leaders. They ran against big government and the welfare state. They slashed taxes for the wealthy, which they claimed stifled private initiative. They vigorously attacked labor unions and whittled back their legal rights. They privatized many state services and, in Britain, sold off publicly owned enterprises and housing to private parties. They deregulated various industries, crucially including banking and finance. They attempted to roll back the welfare state, with mixed results – it turned out that citizens were quite attached to their benefits.[33]

[32] Williams (1977).
[33] Pierson (1994).

They also pursued aggressive and jingoistic foreign policies – which had no intrinsic connection with free-market economics. Finally, they denounced policies that "coddled" the poor, and they promised to crack down on crime and disorder. In a period during which most politicians had attempted to muddle through without any clear ideological compass, Reagan and Thatcher were self-confident, indeed zealous, advocates not only of a new set of economic and social policies, but a new social imaginary as well.

Both the new policy orientation and the new social imaginary were something of a throwback to nineteenth-century liberalism – hence the common label "neoliberalism." In addition to laissez-faire economic doctrines, derived essentially from nineteenth-century neoclassical economic theory, neoliberals espoused a set of social policies meant to restore the conditions for laissez-faire. This meant rolling back welfare provisions, undermining the power of labor unions, decreasing the level and the progressiveness of taxation, privatizing publicly owned enterprises, and deregulating private businesses. This economic and social policy was also wedded to a specific social imaginary. Neoliberals insisted on the importance of economic liberty, on the power of the market to distribute resources optimally without intervention or regulation by the state, on the leading role of the entrepreneur in economic progress, and on the moral and practical superiority of individualism and sturdy self-reliance over social provision. It exalted the enterprise of creative individuals and denigrated the social – indeed, Thatcher famously declared that "society" does not exist. It attacked head-on the notion that government should protect citizens against the hazards and risks inherent in capitalist society. It engaged in what Jacob Hacker has called a "personal responsibility crusade" that attempted to shift the risks of modern capitalist life from governments and corporations to individuals.[34]

These neoliberal policy doctrines and the accompanying social imaginary had been nurtured during the period of Keynesian ascendancy by a dedicated band of conservative thinkers of whom Friedrich Hayek and Milton Friedman were probably the best known.[35] This contrarian tendency found refuge during the Keynesian era in such well-funded think tanks as the Institute for Economic Affairs and the Center for Policy Studies in Britain and in the prestigious but maverick economics department at the University of Chicago in the United States.[36] When Keynesian ideas were discredited by their apparent inefficacy in combating stagflation in the 1970s, free-market economics presented an alternative to the unsatisfactory status quo. The entering wedge of neoliberal economics was monetarism, which insisted that control of inflation by means of restricting the monetary supply should be the prime concern of economic policy. This, of course, meant a willingness to accept high levels of unemployment in order to contain inflation. Monetarism was increasingly

[34] Hacker (2006).
[35] Hayek (1976 [1944]); Friedman (1962).
[36] Cockett (1994); Fourcade-Gourchinas and Babb (2002).

supported not only by professional economists, but by powerful Wall Street and City of London financial interests and by the financial press in both Britain and the United States. It is arguable that neoliberalism in general and monetarism in particular were especially taken up in the 1970s by representatives of upper-class interests as part of a self-conscious campaign for restoration of class power, privilege, and profits and was encouraged by the disarray of leftist political forces.[37]

It is an indication of the rising general plausibility of neoliberal ideas that it was Paul Volcker, an appointee of Democratic President Jimmy Carter, who initiated monetarist policies at the Federal Reserve in 1979, about a year before the election of Reagan. But it was the nearly simultaneous victories of Thatcher and Reagan that enabled neoliberalism to become the new common sense. This double political victory was, in my opinion, profoundly consequential for the subsequent course of world history. Thatcher's and Reagan's systematic and radical application of neoliberal policies and their unflagging preaching of the neoliberal social imaginary created a momentum that the rest of the world could not resist. The United States was, of course, the world's greatest economic and military power; it had long been the unchallenged leader of the "free world" in the Cold War; and it had the decisive voice in the Bretton Woods institutions that remained after the collapse of the system of fixed monetary exchange – the World Bank and the International Monetary Fund – and therefore had great leverage over economic policies in the world at large. Even had the United States been the only advanced capitalist country to adopt a neoliberal agenda, the world-historical effects would surely have been significant. But the fact that another leading country had taken a sharp neoliberal turn even before Reagan's election made the shift seem more than simply an American peculiarity – especially since Thatcher's neoliberalism was more zealous, articulate, and ideologically consistent than Reagan's. Indeed, Britain's close alliance with the United States in these years in both economic and military affairs closed off the one possibility that could conceivably have repulsed an American neoliberal offensive – a European Community united in defense of more solidaristic social and economic policies. Moreover, the fact that the two biggest and most powerful financial marketplaces in the world – Wall Street and London's "City" – were both under the control of neoliberal governments, encouraged a hypertrophic development of the financial industry, which came to dominate the capitalist economy as a whole in the early 1980s. Financial markets increasingly gained power over the economic policy of officially sovereign governments by means of speculative currency trading and subjected industry ever more closely to the free-wheeling stock and bond markets. Since 1980, states have been increasingly outflanked by international finance; labor movements have declined and workers' incomes have followed suit; manufacturing has become

---

[37] This claim is argued quite effectively by Duménil and Lévy (2004a) and by Harvey (2005).

increasingly internationalized; and the status and wealth of top corporate officers has risen exponentially.[38]

Looking back, we tend to think of these changes as inevitable – as being driven by unstoppable forces of economic and technological change that we usually label economic "globalization." But it is at least arguable that our contemporary social and economic landscape might have looked very different had it not been for the simultaneous victories and the long tenures in office of Reaganite Republicans and Thatcherite Conservatives. Moreover, these political successes were highly contingent, hardly the products of any iron law of history. For example, had it not been for the Iranian hostage crisis, Reagan might well have lost the 1980 election to Carter. And the alliance between Christian fundamentalists and libertarian capitalists that has been crucial to the rise of the Republican Party in the United States is, to put it mildly, strange. Nor was there anything in the logic of the ongoing transformations of capital that somehow dictated the emergence of a neoliberal hegemony.

It is certainly true that no capitalist country could have avoided serious economic reconstruction: the deep and systemic economic crisis of the 1970s made major changes inevitable. The sharp declines in transportation costs and the development of a world-spanning computerized network of communications would certainly have led to an intensified internationalization of trade and production. Significant deindustrialization in the core also was surely an inevitable consequence of advancing automation and the new possibilities for relocating production to countries with lower labor costs. And the fact that the United States could no longer afford to underwrite a system of fixed currency exchange rates was bound to lead to a rapid growth of international currency and capital markets, which were burgeoning well before 1980. But the reconstructed model of capitalism that emerged in the 1980s need not have taken a specifically neoliberal form.

Indeed, as the typologies of Hall and Soskice make clear, orthodox neoliberalism has not made a clean sweep of the field in the present.[39] Continental European countries have generally retained their extensive welfare states and some of them have also retained large and powerful labor movements. Sweden, for example, has very profitably followed socioeconomic policies that diverge in significant respects from the dominant neoliberal model. Like all advanced capitalist countries, it has been buffeted by intensified foreign competition and has responded by incorporating globalized enterprise, high technology, and flexible production systems. It has internationalized its capital markets. It has also experienced significant deindustrialization and an upsurge of immigration from the Global South. Sweden's response to these changes was not

---

[38] In 1970, the average remuneration of the one hundred best-paid U.S. CEOs was about forty times as much as the remuneration of the average American wage earner. By 1990 they were making almost four hundred times the average wage and by 2000 over one thousand times (Duménil and Lévy 2004b: 117).

[39] Hall and Soskice (2001).

to cut back its welfare state but to expand it. It has achieved steady growth in GDP and relatively high employment levels – the latter thanks largely to its "active labor market policy," which features extensive state-supported retraining of redundant workers. Its trade union membership has actually risen rather than fallen since the 1970s.[40] Its welfare state has expanded to include state-supported child care and generous maternity leaves that make it easier for women to remain in the labor force. This latter policy has also resulted in fertility rates much higher than the currently very low European norm.[41] And, of particular importance from the point of view of this volume, it has attained enviable levels of population health. There is no reason to think that an economic model analogous to Sweden's could not, in principle, have become hegemonic within the world economy in the years after the great economic crisis of the 1970s – had political forces been arrayed differently. But overwhelming U.S. military hegemony, the sheer weight of the U.S. economy, and the British and U.S. domination of world finance, have resulted in the ascendance, on a world level, of a neoliberal economic and political imaginary rather than what might have been an equally viable globalized social democratic economic imaginary.

So thoroughly had the Anglo-American and world economies been transformed by the 1990s that even the fall from power of the British Conservatives and the American Republicans failed to reverse the momentum of neoliberalism. Bill Clinton and Tony Blair both promised what Blair called a "Third Way," that would combine the best of both neoliberalism and social democracy.[42] A political economic paradigm combining free trade and liberalized labor markets on the one hand with increased investment in labor-force education, an enhanced but fully portable safety net, and extensive aftermarket income redistribution on the other might have been able to square the circle of free markets and social democracy – indeed, some of this has actually been accomplished in Canada. But with the dramatic failure of Clinton's universal health insurance proposal and the loss of control of the House of Representatives to the Republicans in 1994, the social democratic initiatives came to an end. From 1994 to the end of his presidency in 2000, it was neoliberal initiatives, such as balancing the budget, encouraging global free trade, and ending "welfare as we know it" that dominated Clinton's agenda. Thus, by the time Blair was elected as British prime minister in 1997, the social democratic side of Clinton's original agenda was already in eclipse; any possibility of a concerted Third Way effort by the two countries that launched the neoliberal turn was nullified by the realities of American domestic politics, whatever Clinton's real preferences may have been. Robert Rubin, a Wall Street

---

[40] Eley (2002: 391).
[41] Esping-Andersen (1999).
[42] The most systematic advocate of the "Third Way" has been Anthony Giddens (1998). See also Tony Blair's own Fabian pamphlet (1998). The promise of Clinton's early years may be seen in a book written by his first secretary of labor, Reich (1992).

insider who became secretary of the Treasury in 1995, was the most powerful figure in the cabinet in Clinton's later years and became the chief architect of the so-called "Washington Consensus" that essentially codified neoliberalism in matters of international financial policy and imposed it on the world as a whole. The prestige of U.S. policies in these years clearly benefited from the prolonged American economic boom that lasted for the entire term of Clinton's presidency – before turning into the "dot com" bubble that began to deflate in the fall of 2000. Clinton's and Blair's policies reversed in various ways some of the harshness and the overtly probusiness bias of their predecessors.[43] But they certainly failed to develop a coherent alternative to the regnant neoliberal imaginary either domestically or internationally. And the redistribution of income and political power from the working and middle classes toward the super-rich went on uninterrupted in both countries right through the 1990s.

The growing international hegemony of neoliberal economic policies and their associated social imaginary has put the welfare states of Continental Europe under considerable pressure to reduce or at least curb the rise of social spending and to open up their labor and capital markets. Much of the neoliberal initiative in Europe has come from the European Union, which has from the beginning been more favorably inclined to neoliberal measures than have most of the member states.[44] The pressure to neoliberalize has led to important disputes within these countries between those favoring more rapid and thorough market reforms and those defending the status quo. It has made Europeans feel constantly on edge about the threatened "Americanization" of their societies. But given the noisiness of the debates, it is surprising how little the Continental welfare states have actually changed in the three decades since the accession of Thatcher and Reagan. Nor has this aversion to adopting the full neoliberal program resulted in economic decline. Rates of growth of GDP per capita were a little lower in the 1990s in the Euro zone than in Britain and the United States, and unemployment remains higher in Europe. But it is not clear that ordinary Europeans were worse off than ordinary Americans, even after a decade of slower economic growth. In 1999–2001, the Euro zone GDP was 69 percent of the American. Half of the gap in GDP can be accounted for by the difference in hours worked: Euro-zone Europeans work fewer hours per week and take many more days of vacation (guaranteed, of course, by their welfare states) than do Americans.[45] It is far from clear that Americans, if they had the option, would not prefer the extra leisure, which would alleviate the wear and tear of daily life, to the extra work and income. Likewise, much of the United States' advantage in per capita growth since 1980 is a consequence of a rise in the number of hours worked by Americans,

---

[43] A clear example would be Clinton's environmental policies, which consistently valued environmental responsibility over narrow business interests.

[44] Offe (2006).

[45] Boltho (2003: 8–9).

not of greater productivity per hour worked.[46] Finally, because a dispropor-
tionate share of the increased income in the United States has gone to the very
wealthy, it is not clear that families at the median in the United States have any
income advantage over Germans, or French, or Dutch families at the median
in those countries. In short, even though the ideological initiative has passed
to Anglo-American neoliberalism, the advanced countries of the European
continent have both preserved their welfare states and held their own economically by comparison with the United States. Their citizens also have longer
life expectancies than Americans.[47]

Of course, the countries of Western Europe are all relatively wealthy and
have robust legal and economic institutions and dense, efficacious states. This
has enabled them to adapt to neoliberalism on something like their own terms.
It has been in areas of the world with weak, dependent, or collapsing states –
most of them located in the Global South or, after 1989, in the former Soviet
sphere – that neoliberalism has had the biggest impact. The most important
instruments for imposing a neoliberal economic architecture on such states have
been the International Monetary Fund (IMF) and the World Bank. Created at
the Bretton Woods conference at the end of World War II, the IMF is the
international lender of last resort for states experiencing fiscal difficulties and
the World Bank finances development projects in the Global South. Both are
located in Washington, and in the early 1980s both became what Joseph Stiglitz
calls "missionary institutions" for "market fundamentalism."[48] In the early
1980s, when neoliberals took over these institutions, numerous states in the
Global South were experiencing difficulty repaying the sizable debts they had
contracted in the 1970s. These debts arose when the big Wall Street investment
banks were awash in recycled oil money from the Middle East and, unable to
place it profitably in the stagnant U.S. economy, lent enormous sums to Third
World governments.[49] When interest rates rose dramatically with the imposition of monetarism in the late 1970s and early 1980s, many of the debtor countries teetered on the edge of default, which, in turn, threatened the solvency
of the great Wall Street banks and hence the entire world capitalist financial
system. At this juncture, the IMF brokered a refinancing of the loans, but on
terms that required a thorough neoliberalization of the debtor countries' states
and economies. From this point forward, in order to get needed loans, debtor
states were required to lower inflation, cut government expenditures, open
their capital markets, trim back expenditures on welfare and education, institute more flexible labor laws, and privatize industries and services.

---

[46] Schor (1991).

[47] In 2007, the U.S. life expectancy for males and females combined was appreciably below
that of the European Union as a whole, which includes poorer Eastern European as well as
Western European countries. There are ten Western European countries whose life expectancies exceed that of the United States by more than one year.

[48] Stiglitz (2002).

[49] Harvey (2005: 27–8).

The chief economist at the IMF in the early 1980s was Ann Kruger, best known for her recasting of a wide range of government programs as harmful "rent seeking." This notion underwrote the IMF's systematic attack on "big government" in its client states.[50] This IMF initiative, which was known euphemistically as "structural adjustment," spelled the effective end of what remained of the developmentalist states in the Global South. Some of the larger and more prosperous countries, like Mexico and Brazil, had sufficient hardiness and bargaining power to weather the storm and retain effective state apparatuses. But elsewhere, most particularly in sub-Saharan Africa, the already fragile states were essentially dismantled, with generally catastrophic results. The highly authoritarian "strong states" of East and Southeast Asia, which had generally avoided taking on debt in the 1970s, escaped almost entirely from the process of structural adjustment in the 1980s, although some of them were forced to submit to such reforms after the East Asian currency crisis of 1997. The irony that these countries, with their robust authoritarian states, generally had admirable growth rates in the 1980s, whereas the states that most abjectly accepted structural adjustment generally stagnated at best, seems not to have penetrated the consciousness of IMF officials.[51]

When the Berlin Wall fell in 1989 and the Soviet Union disintegrated in 1991, the IMF applied essentially the same formula to the former communist states, under the popular slogan "shock therapy." These were, of course, societies that lacked markets, contracts, private property, stock markets, and a system of business law. The idea of shock therapy was that a quick but painful transformation to free enterprise would set off rapid economic growth and result in solid, prosperous democratic societies. The results were far different from the expectations. Even in Hungary, Poland, and the Czech Republic, relatively prosperous countries with a strong memory of market economies and the rule of law, shock therapy resulted in some years of serious economic regression before growth finally set in. In Russia, where the IMF was deeply involved, the experience was downright catastrophic.[52] Between 1990 and 1999, the GDP of Russia actually fell by a shocking 54 percent.[53] Immediate freeing of state-administered prices resulted in a quick bout of inflation that obliterated people's savings. Premature privatization – that is, privatization undertaken before an adequate legal or regulatory regime had been installed – usually resulted in rigged sales that transferred former state property into the hands of those who had directed the enterprises under communism; these new owners often stripped the enterprises of whatever assets might be sold and deposited their gains in foreign accounts. The middle class and the working class were both despoiled. What had once been an industrial power became, in

[50] Kruger (1974); Stiglitz (2002: 13); see also Evans (1997a).
[51] This paragraph is based primarily on Stiglitz (2002).
[52] The account that follows is taken mainly from Stiglitz (2002). But see also Klein and Pomer (2001); Silverman and Yanowitch (2000).
[53] Stiglitz (2002: 143).

the course of a single decade, an impoverished, deindustrialized, oil-exporting state dominated by a handful of Mafia capitalists. And, as Hertzman and Siddiqi have already pointed out in Chapter 1 in this volume, Russian population health was absolutely devastated in these years.

THE GLOBAL CONTOURS OF A NEOLIBERAL PRESENT

The previous section has sketched out the emergence and the rise to global hegemony of a neoliberal political economic paradigm with a distinctive social imaginary and a specific array of social and economic policy prescriptions. The triumph of this paradigm has had powerful effects, but one must be careful not to attribute all of the leading features or trends in the contemporary capitalist economy to its neoliberal ideological and institutional framework. Although political economic paradigms impose a certain coherence on economic life, they never entirely master capitalism's inherently dynamic and restless tendencies. New and unforeseeable innovations repeatedly transform relations of production and exchange and pose ever-new problems of economic regulation and social reproduction. Paradigms must adapt themselves to such recurrent surprises and must also deal with long-term underlying trends of the capitalist economy. Neoliberalism, for example, has had to cope with the effects of a relentless advance of automation, a process that goes well back into the state-centric era. The shape of capitalism at any given time is always a joint product of capitalism's inherent rhythms and the organizing logics of the prevailing political economic paradigm.[54]

The distinctive characteristics of the neoliberal paradigm include a greatly enhanced role for markets in the allocation of resources, both within and between nation states; increased international mobility of capital; the emergence of a more flexible, less hierarchical, and more globally distended forms of business enterprise; a clear shift in leverage, on a global basis, away from labor and toward capital; a spectacular increase in the size and power of global financial markets; a concomitant reduction of the ability of states to determine effectively their domestic economic fates; and a pervasive disinclination to spend public money on programs designed to enhance the population's economic security. This neoliberal paradigm, which is still a work in progress, has not attained anything approaching the degree of solidity and predictability that characterized the state-centric paradigm in the 1950s and 1960s: for example, the years since 1980 have witnessed a major recrudescence of bubbles and financial crises. But the greater volatility of the neoliberal political economic paradigm should not be surprising: neoliberalism is not *aiming* at solidity and predictability, but at flexibility and agility. Occasional crises are, from the point of view of neoliberalism, a reasonable price to pay for the increased efficiency thought to be entailed by a shift from bureaucracies to markets.

---

[54] On capitalism's inherent rhythms, see Sewell (2008).

This new political economic paradigm has interacted with the underlying trends and rhythms of capitalism to create a global neoliberal reality, one that the world's population experiences in the everyday. This neoliberal world is, in a number of respects, more thoroughly capitalist than the one it has replaced. It is more thoroughly capitalist, obviously enough, because all of the communist states, which during the Cold War accounted for about a third of the world's population, have become capitalist. Both there and in other areas outside the highly developed core, world market forces and up-to-date consumer goods have penetrated much more pervasively into daily life than was the case thirty years ago. But even in the wealthy countries, the market now mediates an ever-wider range of social relations. Much of what has been called the "decommodification" of life initiated by Keynesian welfare states in the capitalist core during the Golden Age has been reversed by means of privatization, deregulation, the rollbacks of welfare programs and benefits, and the subjection of government institutions themselves to market logics.[55] Moreover, in these countries, the massive entry of women into the labor market since 1970 means not only that a higher proportion of women's labor is now commodified, but also that many of the services previously performed by women in the home (such as child care, cleaning, and meal preparation) are now purchased on the market.

The increasing dominance of market forces has, among other things, subjected our lives to strikingly increased volatility. For example, income volatility, that is, the likelihood of wide swings in personal income from year to year, has increased markedly in the United States.[56] Secure careers are becoming a rarity in an era of relentless outsourcing, corporate downsizing, takeovers, and technological change. Workers can expect not only to change employers but also to experience shifts into entirely new lines of work – not to mention periods of unemployment, relocation, part-time work, or self-employment. In the United States, the risks faced by workers have grown especially rapidly as major corporations have scaled back or eliminated their once quite generous health insurance and pension programs.[57] At the same time, workers are now enjoined to be entrepreneurial – to constantly acquire up-to-date skills and to be ever ready for new opportunities. Meanwhile, the explosion of consumer credit, one facet of the neoliberal financialization of social relations, has subtly incited virtually everyone to become a small-scale financial entrepreneur in consumption activities. Faced with multiple offers of credit cards, the chance to consolidate the debt on one's overextended cards, the opportunity to refinance mortgages, and the knowledge that home equity can be converted into cash to buy desirable consumer goods or to launch a small business, but that the funds may be needed later to pay for one's child's education or one's own

---

[55] On decommodification, see Esping-Andersen (1990).
[56] Hacker (2006: 2).
[57] Hacker (2006).

retirement – these opportunities and their concomitant risks are now readily available to the mass of the population in the advanced capitalist countries.

Managing this entire range of expanded opportunity and risk, both at work and as a consumer, strains the capacities of all but the best-educated and most alert citizens. In the United States, at least, it appears that this market-oriented, entrepreneurial society has improved the lot of the most highly educated and generally advantaged portions of the population. But most of the population lacks the skills to manage this complexity effectively and has instead experienced an intensification of the wear and tear of daily life.[58] One consequence, in the United States, has been a measurable increase in the troubles experienced by all categories of the population over the past decade – except for those at the very top of the resource spectrum.[59] This general pattern probably holds, with infinite local variations, on a world scale. The marketization of more and more areas of daily life creates opportunities for those with the resources to master the neoliberal world's growing complexity and volatility. But for those with fewer resources, volatility is more a source of anxieties and troubles than of opportunity – and is consequently a potentially significant threat to population health.

In most of the advanced OECD countries, this volatility is compounded by changes in gender roles that have placed considerable strain on families. In these societies, the feminist movements of the late 1960s and 1970s succeeded in massively redefining the relations between the sexes. Women have entered the workforce in mounting numbers and have gained ever more prominent roles in the professions, business, and politics. But among working people, women's entry into the labor force has mainly compensated for stagnating or falling male wages: most of the modest increase in family incomes over the past thirty years has been a consequence of the rise of two wage-earner families. (This cushioning of declining wages, it must be said, has probably served as an important prop to the political viability of neoliberalism.) But families with two wage earners are stretched thin when it comes to caring for children and the aged. The difficulty of care-giving is compounded in Catholic countries by a massive decline since the 1970s in the number of nuns, who undertook an enormous amount of unpaid care work under the previous gender regime.[60] (The decline in the number of nuns is, of course, another consequence of the redefinition of gender roles.) The new regime of greater gender equality has also resulted in considerably higher rates of divorce and

---

[58] On wear and tear, see Hall and Taylor (Chapter 3, this volume).

[59] See the report of a National Opinion Research Corporation study (Smith 2005), which reports that the incidence of a whole range of life difficulties – health problems, work troubles, financial troubles, family troubles – have increased in the United States from 1991 to 2004, but that this incidence has risen most for the poor and uneducated. The only group for whom life difficulties have actually declined is those holding postgraduate degrees. For a roughly parallel finding, see also McLanahan (2004).

[60] Berman, Iannaccone, and Ragussa (2007).

higher rates of out-of-wedlock births – in part because women have sufficient independence to get out of bad marriages or to avoid them altogether. But the rise of divorce and single motherhood and the difficulties of caring for children and the old have significantly magnified the risks already raining down on families as a result of increased economic volatility and receding welfare benefits. These family difficulties can be countered by state provision of generous benefits for child care and elder care (as in Scandinavia and France). But in most of Europe as well as in Japan and Korea, women have adapted mainly by limiting the size of their families, which are now far below the demographic replacement level. The United States is only spared this demographic deficit because Hispanic immigrants there have very high birth rates.

One of the most widely remarked features of the contemporary neoliberal economic world has been globalization – that is, the increasing transnational circulation of people, capital, goods, and cultural forms. Globalization certainly cannot be regarded as a direct consequence of neoliberalism, since the technological innovations on which contemporary globalization has been based – instantaneous worldwide electronic connectivity, the containerization of cargo, and relatively cheap airfares – would surely have resulted in a sharp increase in global intercourse whatever political economic paradigm had been adopted in the wake of the crisis of the 1970s. One can say, however, that globalization in the contemporary world has taken a predominantly neoliberal form. An emphasis on the inevitability and desirability of globalization has been a key feature of neoliberal discourse, and enhancing economic globalization has been a major goal of key neoliberal policy initiatives – for example, the freeing up of international markets in goods, capital, and financial services and the imposition of worldwide intellectual property standards. One of the most significant effects of globalization has been the reorganization of production within firms to take advantage of low labor costs in so-called emerging markets. This practice has helped to bid down labor costs in the wealthy nations and also to undermine labor unions. In this respect there has been a convergence between neoliberal policy, which from the beginning has attacked labor unions, and the economic effects of falling trade barriers and cheap transportation and communications.

Meanwhile, globalization has had manifold effects on the textures of daily life. The enhancement of global economic flows has increased the volatility built into contemporary economic life – because market changes in one part of the world are now felt with ever-greater sensitivity the world over. Meanwhile, elevated levels of migration have made more and more countries multicultural – in terms of daily experience if not in terms of governmental policy. The same inexpensive airfare that has made migration easier has also turned all corners of the world into tourist destinations and has made tourism one of the world's biggest industries. Globalization has made both cultural difference and cultural hybridization an increasingly palpable feature of modern capitalist culture, both in the wealthy countries of the OECD and in the Global South.

Globalization, by increasing the opportunities for those with internationally valuable skills and bidding down the costs of more routine labor, has contributed importantly to another distinctive feature of the neoliberal present: rising levels of income inequality. This tendency has been much disputed – different scholars, basing their arguments on different statistical calculations, have come to sharply contrasting conclusions. As I read the literature, it is indisputable that the mean per capita incomes of nation states have continued to diverge in recent years – as they have for most of the period since World War II. But this result holds only if the nation states are not weighted for population. When they are so weighted, the recent growth in mean per capita income of the demographically huge economies of China and India more than cancels out the relative declines that have taken place in many other developing countries. What is more specific to the neoliberal era – the period since about 1980 – has been rising inequality *within* nation-states. As I read the evidence, quite a few countries have experienced sharply rising inequality, including such very large countries as China, India, the United States, the United Kingdom, and Russia. In most of the remaining countries, inequality has risen only moderately. In only a very few cases has inequality been constant or declined. Across most of the globe, the balance has shifted against individuals, communities, classes, and states that have little to offer except their labor and in favor of those with more substantial resources, whether education, connections, or capital. The shares of very wealthy individuals – the top 5 percent, top 1 percent, top 0.1 percent, or top 0.01 or 0.001 percent – have grown particularly rapidly.[61]

These income trends also suggest the possible emergence of a new global spatial structure – one significantly at odds with that of the past century or two. Immanuel Wallerstein, writing at the end of the long postwar boom, famously distinguished between core, semiperipheral, and peripheral states in the capitalist world-system.[62] Two things are notable about this conceptualization. First, nation-states are taken to be the self-evident units of the world economy. Second, the peripheral areas are assumed to be involved in extensive, if highly exploitative, trading relations with the core; the core could not exist without the periphery. In the current globalized neoliberal world economy, it is not clear that either of these assumptions applies. Both subnational and supranational entities increasingly challenge the economic sovereignty of nation states.[63] Meanwhile, many areas of the globe, containing hundreds of millions of people, are essentially irrelevant to the core of the economy. This would seem to be true, for example, of much of the Chinese interior, most of the vast Gangetic plain of India, the non-oil-producing areas of the Middle East, the Andean highlands of South America, and most of sub-Saharan

---

[61] See, for example, Firebaugh (1999); Sala-i-Martin (2002); Milanovic (2002). For a particularly lucid account and weighing of the debate, see Wade (2004).
[62] Wallerstein (1974).
[63] R. Brenner (2004).

Africa. It also seems that distinctions between core and periphery are now located as much within as between countries. The upper-middle classes of Johannesburg, Bangalore, Kuala Lumpur, Sao Paulo, or Shanghai, who are deeply involved in global production and capital flows, probably belong in the core, while the chronically unemployed minority populations of Los Angeles, the Parisian banlieux, Bradford, or the South Side of Chicago should probably be classified as belonging to the new economically expendable capitalist periphery. Although this is perhaps more a nightmare projection of current trends than a reality, it sometimes seems that we may be witnessing the emergence of a new spatial configuration of capitalism in which states function as much to protect the wealthy from the poor of their own country as to redistribute income and guarantee full employment within nation-states.[64]

PROSPECTS FOR POPULATION HEALTH IN A NEOLIBERAL WORLD

Full-blown neoliberalism clearly has a number of features that are not conducive to maximizing population health. It tends to increase income inequality, which has consistently been shown to depress overall levels of population health. Neoliberal policies have also increased income volatility and have increased people's likelihood of experiencing serious personal, health, and financial troubles. In doing so, it has increased the wear and tear of daily life, and hence vulnerability to disease of all kinds. Finally, because it endeavors to shift responsibility for dealing with personal troubles onto individuals and their families, neoliberalism decreases the publicly available resources that could enable people experiencing such problems as pay cuts, job loss, major illness, or family breakup to cope satisfactorily with the challenges they face. In all these ways, neoliberalism is distinctly harmful to health.

At the same time, it is certainly not true that the adoption of a neoliberal political economic paradigm has caused an actual decline in world health standards. One reason for this is that the introduction of a neoliberal economic architecture has sustained world economic growth and, as has been stated frequently in this volume, rising wealth tends to improve health. Hence the negative effects of neoliberal policies on health have probably been at least partially counterbalanced by whatever economic growth these policies have fostered.[65] But more importantly, it is also clear that advances in medicine during these years would have increased life expectancy whatever political economic paradigm had been in the ascendant. The overall effect

---

[64] See Davis (1990; 2006); Wacquant (1999; 2004).

[65] There is in fact no direct evidence that the introduction of neoliberal reforms has increased world economic growth. Indeed, growth in the world economy was about 3 percent a year from 1960 to 1973 but has fluctuated with no apparent trend around a mean of barely 1 percent a year ever since 1974. But it is arguable that without neoliberal reforms the world economy would have grown less rapidly or might even have entered into a long-term depression. See World Commission on Globalization (2004: 36).

of neoliberalism on health outcomes has not been to cause health to decline, but to depress the extent of the improvement. It should be remembered, however, that this has meant the loss of millions of healthy lives every year across the globe.

If it were possible to introduce policies assuring steady economic growth while producing greater income equality and reducing the troubles that arise from generalized volatility, this would significantly improve the health of the world's population. But as long as the neoliberal political economic paradigm remains hegemonic, some policies known to be extremely beneficial to health are highly unlikely to be instituted – just as systematic sanitary reforms could not be instituted in Victorian Britain even though their beneficial effects were well understood. For example, Communist Party governments in Cuba (in the 1960s) and the Indian State of Kerala (in the late 1950s and the 1960s) instituted fundamental social reforms that greatly reduced inequality and improved education and health care. In both cases, the result was a spectacular and sustained rise in life expectancies. Indeed, both Kerala and Cuba today have life expectancies essentially equal to those in the United States, even though their per capita incomes are only a fraction of American incomes. Replicating the Keralan and Cuban reforms (which included vast redistributions of property) could rapidly improve the health of people in the poorer countries of the globe. But it is clear that instituting this particular set of health-enhancing policies would be absolutely unthinkable in the neoliberal present.

But if radical reforms of this sort are currently unthinkable, this does not imply that no reforms are possible. Shifts from one political economic paradigm to another are usually catalyzed by major political or economic crises. The world economic crisis underway at the time this volume goes to press could well become just such an occasion. The crash of world financial markets and the steep economic downturn certainly has shaken faith in deregulation and kindled a new appreciation of Keynesian economics. It is of course impossible to know whether the current crisis portends a major shift in political economic thinking and in social imaginaries – or merely a course correction within the present paradigm. But policy circles had been abuzz with critiques of unbridled neoliberalism even before the current crisis. Jane Jenson points out that since the late 1990s, policy intellectuals have become increasingly concerned about the rise in poverty that has resulted from strict application of neoliberal policies, in both the developed and developing worlds. The consequence has been a range of proposals to overcome these effects. Among these are various initiatives in early childhood education and "conditional cash transfers" – transfers to poor families that are conditional on school attendance and health visits. Programs of this sort, characterized as "social investment" in children, continue to be premised on key assumptions of the neoliberal political economic paradigm: the superiority of investment, with its promise of future growth, over income support in the present; the emphasis on incentives rather than guarantees; the attempt to build up individual responsibility rather than reliable social provision; and most fundamentally, a preference, at least rhetorically, for markets over state allocation of resources.[66] Jacob Hacker moves beyond a rhetoric of social investment, arguing that markets and individual responsibility need to be supplemented by the principle of social insurance – that in a society beset by rising systemic risk, risks must be pooled across the population as a whole. Here Hacker recasts the still-living legacy of the welfare state in a more market-friendly idiom, speaking of insurance against risk, which preserves human and social capital, rather than a principle of welfare or solidarity.[67]

The basic assumptions of the neoliberal political economic paradigm currently are deeply entrenched in both the logic of institutions and the rhetoric of politics and policy. Many aspects of neoliberalism and its accompanying social imaginary are likely to survive even if the current economic crisis leads to a major rethinking of policy. But attempting to stretch the social imaginary in directions more conducive to the promotion of population health now seems distinctly possible. It is, in any case, important to gain a critical perspective on the assumptions of the present and to think creatively about more health-friendly forms of social and economic organization that may be possible in the future. This book is intended as a contribution to such critical and creative thinking.

---

[66] Jenson (2008). The economic development community's romance with microfinance or the current vogue for carbon trading in environmental circles are additional examples of reforms cast in market rhetoric.

[67] Hacker (2006).

Bibliography

6, Perri. 1997. "Social Exclusion: Time to be Optimistic." *Demos Collection*, 12: 3–9.

Acemoglou, Daron, and James A. Robinson. 2006. *Economic Origins of Dictatorship and Democracy: Economic and Political Origins*. New York: Cambridge University Press.

Acemoglu, Daron, Simon Johnson, and James A. Robinson. 2001. "The Colonial Origins of Comparative Development: An Empirical Investigation." *American Economic Review* 91: 1369–1401.

Acemoglu, Daron, Simon Johnson, and James A. Robinson. 2003. "An African Success Story: Botswana." In *In Search of Prosperity: Analytical Narratives on Economic Growth*, edited by Dani Rodrik. Princeton, NJ: Princeton University Press.

Acemoglu, Daron, Simon Johnson, and James A. Robinson, 2005. "Institutions as Fundamental Determinants of Long-Run Growth." In *Handbook of Economic Growth, Volume 1A*, edited by Philippe Aghion and Steven Durlauf. Amsterdam: Elsevier.

Acheson, Donald. 1998. *Inequalities in Health: Report of an Independent Inquiry*. London: HMSO.

Addison, Tony, and Giovanni Andrea Cornia. 2001. "Income Distribution Policies for Faster Poverty Reduction." In *United Nations WIDER discussion paper no. 2001/93*. Helsinki, Finland: UNU-WIDER.

Adler, Daniel S., Guy Bar-Oz, Anna Belfer-Cohen, and Ofer Bar-Yosef. 2006. "Ahead of the Game: Middle and Upper Paleolithic Hunting Behaviors in the Southern Caucasus." *Current Anthropology* 47 (1): 89–118.

Adler, Nancy E., and Katherine Newman. 2002. "Socioeconomic Disparities in Health: Pathways and Policies." *Health Affairs* 21 (2): 60–76.

Adler, Nancy E., and Joan Ostroye. 1999. Socioeconomic Status and Health: What We Know and What We Don't. *Annals of the New York Academy of Sciences* 896: 3–15.

Agha, Sohail, Thankian Kusanthan, Kim Longfield, Megan Klein, and John Berman. 2002. *Reasons for Non-use of Condoms in Eight Countries in Sub-Saharan Africa*. Washington, DC: Population Services International.

Aglietta, Michel. 1979. *A Theory of Capitalist Regulation: The US Experience*. London: New Left Books.

Alesina, Alberto, and Edward Glaeser. 2004. *Fighting Poverty in the US and Europe: A World of Difference*. Oxford: Oxford University Press.

Alesina, Alberto, Reza Baqir, and William Easterly. 2001. "Public Goods and Ethnic Divisions." NBER working paper 6009. Cambridge, MA: NBER.

Allan, Graham. 1990. "Class Variation in Friendship Patterns." *British Journal of Sociology* 41: 389–92.

Allen, Susan, Jareen Meinzen-Derra, Michele Kautzmana, Isaac Zulud, Stanley Traske, Ulgen Fidelia, Rosemary Musondag, Francis Kasolod, Feng Gaoe, and Alan Haworth. 2003. "Sexual Behavior of HIV Discordant Couples after HIV Counseling and Testing." *AIDS* 17 (5): 733–40.

Allen, Tim. 2004. "Introduction: Why Don't HIV/AIDS Policies Work?" *Journal of International Development* 16 (8): 1123–7.

Allen, Tim. 2006. "AIDS and Evidence: Interrogating Some Ugandan Myths." *Journal of Biosocial Science* 38: 7–28.

Allen, Tim, and Suzette Heald. 2004. "HIV/AIDS Policy in Africa: What Has Worked in Uganda and What Has Failed in Botswana?" *Journal of International Development* 16: 1141–54.

Almedom, Astier M. 2005. "Social Capital and Mental Health: An Interdisciplinary Review of Primary Evidence." *Social Science and Medicine* 61 (5): 943–64.

Altman, Dennis. 1994. *Power and Community: Organizational and Cultural Responses to AIDS*. London: Taylor & Francis.

Anderson, Benedict. 1991. *Imagined Communities: Reflections on the Origin and Spread of Nationalism*. New York and London: Verso.

Anderson, Gerard, and Peter Sotir Hussey. 2001. "Comparing Health System Performance in OECD Countries." *Health Affairs* 20 (3): 219–32.

Aptheker, Herbert. 1992. *Anti-Racism in U.S. History: The First Two Hundred Years*. Westport, CT: Greenwood Press.

Archer, Margaret S. 2000. *Being Human: The Problem of Agency*. New York: Cambridge University Press.

Arnold, R.M. 1964. The New Problem of Large Scale Employability. *The American Journal of Economics and Sociology* 23 (4): 337–50.

Arrighi, Giovanni. 1994. *The Long Twentieth Century: Money, Power, and the Origins of Our Times*. London: Verso.

Arrow, Kenneth Joseph. 1963 [1951]. *Social Choice and Individual Values*. New Haven, CT: Yale University Press.

Ashforth, Adam. 2005. *Witchcraft, Violence, and Democracy in South Africa*. Chicago: University of Chicago Press.

Ashmore, Richard D., Kay Deaux, and Tracy McLaughlin-Volpe. 2004. "An Organizing Framework for Collective Identity: Articulation and Significance of Multidimensionality." *Psychological Bulletin* 130 (1): 80–114.

Atkinson, Michael, and William D. Coleman. 1989. *The State, Business and Industrial Change in Canada*. Toronto: University of Toronto Press.

Authier, Alain. 1992. "La Lutte Contre la Mortalité Infantile au Québec de 1900 à 1970." Paper presented at Hannah Institute for the History of Medicine. Université de Montréal.

Baccaro, Lucio, and Konstantinos Papadakis. 2005. "*The Downside of Deliberative Public Administration*." Ms. ILO, Geneva. [November]: 36–45.

Baillargeon, Denyse. 2004. *Un Québec en Mal d'Enfants: La Médicalisation de la Maternité, 1910–1970*. Montréal: Les Éditions du remue-ménage.

Baldwin, Peter. 1999. *Contagion and the State in Europe, 1830–1930*. Cambridge: Cambridge University Press.

Baldwin, Peter. 2005. *Disease and Democracy: The Industrialized World Faces AIDS*. Berkeley: University of California Press.

Bangura, Yusuf, and Rodolfo Stavenhagen. 2005. *Racism and Public Policy*. New York: Palgrave Macmillan.

Banks, James, Michael Marmot, Zoe Oldfield, James P. Smith. 2006. "Disease and Disadvantage in the United States and England," *Journal of the American Medical Association* 295(17): 2037–45.

Banting, Keith, Richard Johnston, Will Kymlicka, and Stuart Soroka. 2006. "Do Multiculturalism Policies Erode the Welfare State? An Empirical Analysis." In *Multiculturalism and the Welfare State: Recognition and Redistribution in Contemporary Democracies*, edited by Keith Banting and Will Kymlicka. Oxford: Oxford University Press, 49–91.

Bardhan, Pranab K. 2005. *Scarcity, Conflicts, and Cooperation: Essays in the Political and Institutional Economics of Development*. Cambridge, MA: MIT Press.

Barnett, Tony, and Alan Whiteside. 2002. *AIDS in the Twenty-First Century: Disease and Globalization*. New York: Palgrave Macmillan.

Baron, Ruben M., and David A. Kenny. 1986. "The Moderator Mediator Variable Distinction in Social Psychological Research." *Journal of Personality and Social Psychology* 51:1173–82.

Barr, Christina S., Timothy K. Newman, Michele L. Becker, Clarissa C. Parker, Maribeth Champoux, David Goldman, Stephen J. Suomi, and J. Dee Higley. 2003. "The Utility of the Non-human Primate Model for Studying Gene by Environment Interactions in Behavioral Research." *Genes, Brain, and Behavior* 2 (6): 336–40.

Barr, Christina S., Timothy K. Newman, Stephen Lindell, Courtney Shannon, Maribeth Champoux, Klaus Peter Lesch, Stephen J. Suomi, David Goldman, and J. Dee Higley. 2004. "Interaction Between Serotonin Transporter Gene Variation and Rearing Condition in Alcohol Preference and Consumption in Female Primates." *General Psychiatry* 61 (11): 1146–52.

Barrett, Martyn. 2005. Children's Understanding of, and Feelings about, Countries and National Groups. In *Children's Understanding of Society*, edited by Martyn Barrett and Eithne Buchanan-Barrow. Hove: Psychology Press.

Barry, Brian. 2001. *Culture and Equality: An Egalitarian Critique of Multiculturalism*. Cambridge, UK: Polity Press.

Bartley, Mel. 2005. "Job Insecurity and Its Effect on Health." *Journal of Epidemiology and Community Health* 59: 718–19.

Bartley, Mel, ed. 2006. *Capabilities and Resilience: Beating the Odds*. London: Department of Epidemiology and Public Health, University College.

Bartley, Mel, Ingrid Schoon, Richard Mitchell, and David Blane. Forthcoming. "Resilience as an Asset for Healthy Development." In *Health Assets and the Social Determinants of Health*, edited by Enzo Ziglio and Anthony Morgan. Venice, Italy: World Heath Organization European Office for Investment for Health and Development.

Bates, Robert H. 2008. *When Things Fell Apart: State Failure in Late-Century Africa*. New York: Cambridge University Press.

Bateson, Patrick. 2002. "The Corpse of a Wearisome Debate." *Science* 297 (27): 2212–2213.

Beaujot, Roderic, and Jianye Liu. 2002. "Children, Social Assistance and Outcomes: Cross National Comparisons." Luxembourg Income Study working paper 304, June. Luxembourg: Luxembourg Income Study.

Beckfield, Jason. 2004. "Does Income Inequality Harm Health? New Cross-National Evidence." *Journal of Health and Social Behavior* 45(3): 231–48.

Beer, Samuel H. 1957. "The Representation of Interests in British Government: Historical Background." *American Political Science Review* 51 (3): 613–50.

Bell, Daniel. 1999 [1973]. *The Coming of Post-Industrial Society: A Venture in Social Forecasting.* New York: Basic Books.

Bennett, Allyson J., Klaus P. Lesch, Armin Heils, Jeffrey C. Long, Joseph G. Lorenz, Susan E. Shoaf, Maribeth Champoux, Stephen J. Suomi, Markku V. Linnoila, and J. Dee Higley. 2002. "Early Experience and Serotonin Transporter Gene Variation Interact to Influence Primate CNS Function." *Molecular Psychiatry* 7: 118–22.

Berkman, Alan, Jonathan Garcia, Miguel Muñoz-Laboy, Vera Paiva, and Richard Parker. 2005. "A Critical Analysis of the Brazilian Response to HIV/AIDS: Lessons Learned for Controlling and Mitigating the Epidemic in Developing Countries." *American Journal of Public Health* 95 (7): 1162–72.

Berkman, Lisa F. 1995. "The Role of Social Relations in Health Promotion." *Psychosomatic Medicine* 57 (3): 245–54.

Berkman, Lisa F., and Ichiro Kawachi, eds. 2000. *Social Epidemiology.* New York: Oxford University Press.

Berkman, Lisa F., and S. Leonard Syme. 1979. "Social Networks, Host Resistance, and Mortality: A Nine-year Follow-up of Alameda County Residents." *American Journal of Epidemiology* 109 (2): 186–204.

Berkman, Lisa F., Thomas Glass, Ian Brissette, and Teresa E. Seeman. 2000. "From Social Integration to Health: Durkheim in the New Millennium." *Social Science and Medicine* 51: 843–57.

Berman, Eli, Lawrence R. Iannaccone, and Giuseppe Ragusa. 2007. "From Empty Pews to Empty Cradles: Fertility Decline among European Catholics." Department of Economics working paper. San Diego: University of California.

Berman, Sheri. 1998. *The Social Democratic Moment.* Cambridge, MA: Harvard University Press.

Berque, Jacques. 1964. *Dépossession du Monde.* Paris: Éditions du Seuil.

Berry, John, Jean Phinney, David Sam, and Paul Vedder. 2006. "Immigrant Youth: Acculturation, Identity and Adaptation." *Applied Psychology: An International Review* 55 (3): 303–32.

Bickerstaff, Jovonne. 2008. *"Noir et Français: Everyday Anti-racism and Challenging the Racialization of French Identity."* Paper presented at the Culture and Social Analysis Workshop, Department of Sociology, Harvard University, Cambridge, MA.

Blair, Tony. 1998. *The Third Way: New Politics for the New Century.* London: Fabian Society.

Blakely, T., J. Atkinson and D. O'Dea. 2003. "No Association of Income Inequality with Adult Mortality within New Zealand: A Multi-level Study of 1.4 Million 25–64 year olds." *Journal of Epidemiology and Community Health* 57 (4): 279–84.

Blane, David. 1999. "The Life Course, the Social Gradient, and Health." In *Social Determinants of Health*, edited by Michael Marmot and Richard Wilkinson. Oxford: Oxford University Press.

Bluebond-Langner, Myra. 2003. Proposal for "Choiceless Choices: Decision Making for Children with Cancer When Cure Is Not Likely." Rutgers University, Camden, NJ: Center for Children and Childhood Studies.

Boli, John, and George M. Thomas. 1997. "The World Polity Under Construction: A Century of International Non-Governmental Organizing." *American Sociological Review* 62 (April): 171–90.

Boli, John, and George M. Thomas. 1999. *Constructing World Culture: International Nongovernmental Organizations since 1875*. Stanford, CA: Stanford University Press.

Boltanski, Luc, and Laurent Thévenot. 1991. *De la Justification. Les economies de la grandeur*. Paris: Gallimard.

Boltanski, Luc, and Laurent Thévenot. 1999. "The Sociology of Critical Capacity." *European Journal of Social Theory* 2 (3): 359–77.

Boltho, Andrea. 2003. "What's Wrong with Europe?" *New Left Review* 22 (July–August): 5–26.

Bonham, Vence L., Sherrill L. Sellers, and Harold W. Neighbors. 2004. "John Henryism and Self-Reported Physical Health among High–Socioeconomic Status African American Men." *American Journal of Public Health* 94 (5): 737–8.

Boone, Catherine, and Jake Batsell. 2001. "Politics and AIDS in Africa: Research Agendas in Political Science and International Relations." *Africa Today* 48 (2): 3–33.

Booth, John A., and Patricia Bayer Richard. 2001. "Civil Society and Political Context in Central America." In *Beyond Tocqueville: Civil Society and the Social Capital Debate in Comparative Perspective*, edited by Bob Edwards and Michael W. Foley. Hanover, NH: University Press of New England: 43–54.

Boozer, Michael, Gustav Ranis, Frances Stewart, and Tavneet Suri. 2003. "Paths to Success: The Relationship Between Human Development and Economic Growth." Economic Growth Center discussion paper 874. New Haven, CT: Yale University.

Borrell, Luisa N., Catrina I. Kiefe, David R. Williams, Ana V. Diez-Roux, and Penny Gordon-Larsen. 2006. "Self-reported Health, Perceived Racial Discrimination, and Skin Color in African Americans in the CARDIA Study." *Social Science and Medicine* 63 (6): 1415–27.

Bouchard, Gérard. 1986. "La Dynamique Communautaire et l'évolution des Sociétés Rurales Québécoises aux 19e et 20e Siècles. Construction d'un Modèle." *Revue d'histoire de l'Amérique française* 40 (1): 51–71.

Bouchard, Gérard. 1998. "Economic Inequalities in Saguenay Society, 1879–1949: A Descriptive Analysis." *The Canadian Historical Review* 79 (4): 660–90.

Bouchard, Gérard. 2000. *Genèse des Nations et Cultures du Nouveau Monde. Essai d'histoire Comparée*. Montréal: Boréal.

Bouchard, Gérard. 2003a. *Les Deux Chanoines. Contradiction et Ambivalence dans la Pensée de Lionel Groulx*. Montréal: Boréal.

Bouchard, Gérard. 2003b. *Raison et Contradiction. Le Mythe au Secours de la Pensée*. Québec: Éditions Nota bene/Cefan.

Bouchard, Gérard. 2003c. "Une Crise de la Conscience Historique. Anciens et Nouveaux Mythes Fondateurs Dans l'imaginaire Québécois." In *Les Idées Mènent le Québec*, edited by Stéphane Kelly. Québec: Les Presses de l'Université Laval.

Bouchard, Gérard. 2004. *La Pensée Impuissante: Échecs et Mythes Nationaux Canadiens-Français (1850–1960)*. Montréal: Boréal.

Bouchard, Gérard. 2005. "Figures and Myths of America's Blueprint for a Pragmatic Analysis." In *Consensual Disagreement: Canada and the Americas*, edited by Patrick Imbert. Ottawa: University of Ottawa.

Bouchard, Gérard, and Jeannette Larouche. 1989. "Nouvelle Mesure de l'Alphabétisation à l'Aide de la Reconstitution Automatique des Familles." *Histoire Sociale/Social History* XXII (43): 91–119.

Bouchard, Gérard, and Régis Thibeault. 1995. "Origines Géographiques et Sociales du Personnel Religieux Dans la Région du Saguenay (1882–1947)." *Histoire Sociale/Social History* XXVIII (55): 137–57.

Bouchard, Gérard, Raymond Roy, and Pierre Jacques. 1988. "La Composition des Communautés de Religieuses au Saguenay (1882–1947)." *La Société Canadienne d'Histoire de l'Église Catholique, Sessions d'étude* (55): 87–117.

Bourbeau, Robert, and Mélanie Smuga. 2003. "La Baisse de la Mortalité: Les Bénéfices de la Médecine et du Développement." In *La Démographie Québécoise: Enjeux du XXIe Siècle*, edited by Victor Piché and Céline Le Bourdais. Montréal: Les Presses de l'Université de Montréal.

Bourdieu, Pierre. 1977. *Outline of a Theory of Practice*, translated by R. Nice. Cambridge: Cambridge University Press.

Bourdieu, Pierre. 1983. "The Forms of Capital." In *Handbook of Theory and Research for the Sociology of Education*, edited by John G. Richardson. New York: Greenwood.

Bourdieu, Pierre. 1984. *Distinction: A Social Critique of the Judgement of Taste*, translated by R. Nice. London: Routledge.

Bourdieu, Pierre. 1992. "The Practice of Reflexive Sociology (The Paris Workshop)." In *An Invitation to Reflexive Sociology*, edited by Pierre Bourdieu and Loic Wacquant. Chicago: University of Chicago Press.

Bourdieu, Pierre, and Loic Wacquant. 1992. *An Invitation to Reflexive Sociology*, edited by Pierre Bourdieu and Loic Wacquant. Chicago: University of Chicago Press.

Bouthillette, Jean. 1972. *Le Canadien Français et Son Double*. Montréal: L'Hexagone.

Bowman, P. J., and C. Howard. 1985. "Race-Related Socialization, Motivation, and Academic Achievement: a Study of Black Youths in Three-Generation Families." *Journal of the American Academy of Child Psychiatry* 24 (2): 134–41.

Boyce, W. Thomas. In press. "Biology and Context: Symphonic Causation and the Distribution of Childhood Morbidities." In *Nature and Nurture in Early Child Development*, edited by Daniel P. Keating. New York: Cambridge University Press.

Boyce, W. Thomas, and Bruce J. Ellis. 2005. "Biological Sensitivity to Context: I. An Evolutionary-Developmental Theory of the Origins and Functions of Stress Reactivity." *Development and Psychopathology* 17: 271–301.

Boyce, W. Thomas, and Daniel P. Keating. 2004. "Should We Intervene to Improve Childhood Circumstances?" In *A Life Course Approach to Chronic Disease Epidemiology*, edited by Yoav Ben-Shlomo and Diana Kuh. Oxford: Oxford University Press.

Boyer, Robert. 1986. *La théorie de la Regulation: Une Analyse Critique*. Paris: La Découverte.

Brady, Henry E., and David Collier, eds. 2002. *Rethinking Social Inquiry: Diverse Tools, Shared Standards*. New York: Rowman & Littlefield.

Brenner, Neil. 2004. *New State Spaces: Urban Governance and the Rescaling of Statehood*. Oxford and New York: Oxford University Press.

Brenner, Robert. 2002. *The Boom and the Bubble: The US in the World Economy*. London: Verso.

Brenner, Robert. 2004. "New Boom or New Bubble?" *New Left Review* 25: 57–100.

Brenner, Robert. 2006. *The Economics of Global Turbulence*. London: Verso.

Brickson, Shelley. 2000. "The Impact of Identity Orientation on Individual and Organizational Outcomes in Demographically Diverse Settings." *Academy of Management Review* 25 (1): 82–101.

Brubaker, Bill. 2000. "The Limits of $100 Million: Epidemic's Complexities Curb Impact of Bristol-Myers's Initiative." *The Washington Post*, December 29, p. A1.

Brunner, Eric J. 1997. "Socioeconomic Determinants of Health: Stress and the Biology of Inequality." *British Medical Journal* 314: 1472–6.

Brunner, Eric J. 2000. "Toward a New Social Biology." In *Social Epidemiology*, edited by Lisa F. Berkman and Ichiro Kawachi. New York: Oxford University Press.

Buvé, Anne, Kizito Bishikwabo-Nsarhazab, and Gladys Mutangadurac. 2002. "The Spread and Effect of HIV-1 Infection in Sub-Saharan Africa." *The Lancet* 359 (9322): 2011–17.

Caldwell, Cleopatra Howard, Marc A. Zimmerman, Debra Hilkene Bernat, Robert M. Sellers, and Paul C. Notaro. 2002. "Racial Identity, Maternal Support, and Psychological Distress among African American Adolescents." *Child Development* 73 (4): 1322–36.

Caldwell, John C. 1999. "Reasons for Limited Sexual Behavioural Change in the Sub-Saharan African AIDS Epidemic, and Possible Future Intervention Strategies." In *Resistances to Behavioural Change to Reduce HIV/AIDS Infection in Predominantly Heterosexual Epidemics in Third World Countries*, edited by John C. Caldwell, Pat Caldwell, John Anarfi, Kofi Awusabo-Asare, James Ntozi, I. O. Orubuloye, Jeff Marck, Wendy Cosford, Rachel Colombo, and Elaine Hollings. Canberra: The Australian National University.

Caldwell, John C., Pat Caldwell, and Pat Quiggin. 1989. "The Social Context of AIDS in Sub-Saharan Africa." *Population and Development Review* 15 (2): 185–234.

Callaghy, Thomas M., Ronald Kassimir, and Robert Latham. 2001. *Intervention and Transnationalism in Africa: Global-Local Networks of Power*. Cambridge: Cambridge University Press.

Campbell, Catherine. 2003. *'Letting Them Die': Why HIV/AIDS Prevention Programmes Fail*. Bloomington and Indianapolis: Indiana University Press.

Campbell, Catherine, Carol Ann Foulis, Sbongile Maimane, and Zweni Siblya. 2005. "'I Have an Evil Child at My House': Stigma and HIV/AIDS Management in a South African Community." *American Journal of Public Health* 95 (5): 808–15.

Campbell, John L. 1998. *Institutional Change and Globalization*. Princeton, NJ: Princeton University Press.

Canvin, K, C. Jones, and M. Whitehead. 2006. *"Avoiding Social Welfare Services in Britain: Causes and Consequences for Health and Well-Being."* Working paper no. 3. Liverpool: University of Liverpool.

Carpenter, Siri. 2002. "What Can Resolve the Paradox of Mental Health Disparities?" *Monitor on Psychology* 33(4).

Carpiano, Richard. 2006. "Toward a Neighborhood Resource-Based Theory of Social Capital for Health: Can Bourdieu and Sociology Help?" *Social Science and Medicine* 62 (1): 165–75.

Carpiano, Richard M., Bruce G. Link, and Jo C. Phelan. 2008. "Social Inequality and Health: Future Directions for the Fundamental Cause Explanation. In *Social Class: How Does it Work?* edited by Annette Lareau and Dalton Conley. New York: Russell Sage Foundation.

Carter, C. Sue. 2003. "Developmental Consequences of Oxytocin." *Physiology &*
Behavior 79 (3): 383–97.

Carter, Prudence. 2005. *Keepin' It Real: School Success Beyond Black and White.*
New York: Oxford University Press.

Case, R. B, A. J. Moss, N. Case, M. McDermott, and S. Eberly. 1992. "Living Alone
After Myocardial Infarction." *Journal of the American Medical Association.* 267
(4): 469–569.

Caspi, Avshalom, Karen Sugden, Terrie E. Moffitt, Alan Taylor, Ian Craig, Hona Lee
Harrington, Joseph McClay, Jonathan Mill, Judy Martin, Anthony Braithwaite,
and Richie Poulton. 2003. "Influence of Life Stress on Depression: Moderation by a
Polymorphism in the 5-HTT Gene." *Science* 301 (5631): 386–9.

Castoriadis, Cornelius. 1987. *The Imaginary Institution of Society.* Cambridge, UK:
Polity Press.

Central Intelligence Agency. 2008. *The 2008 World Factbook.* https://www.cia.gov/
library/publications/the-world-factbook/ [accessed 12/25/2008].

Cereseto, S., and H. Waitzkin. 1986. "Capitalism, Socialism, and the Physical Quality-
of-Life." *International Journal of Health Services* 16: 643–58.

Chabal, Patrick, and Jean-Pascal Daloz. 1999. *Africa Works: Disorder as Political*
Instrument. Bloomington: Indiana University Press.

Champoux, Maribeth, Allyson Bennett, Courtney Shannon, J. Dee Higley, Klaus Peter
Lesch, and Stephen J. Suomi. 2002. "Serotonin Transporter Gene Polymorphism,
Differential Early Rearing, and Behavior in Rhesus Monkey Neonates." *Molecular*
Psychiatry 7: 1058–63.

Chandler, Michael, and Christopher Lalonde. 1998. "Cultural Continuity as a Hedge
Against Suicide in Canada's First Nations." *Journal of Transcultural Psychology* 35
(2): 191–219.

Chandler, Michael J., Christopher E. Lalonde, Bryan W. Sokol, and Daracy Hallett.
2003. "Personal Persistence, Identity Development, and Suicide: A Study of Native
and Non-native North American Adolescents." *Monographs of the Society for*
Research in Child Development 68 (2): vii–130.

Chang, Ha-Joon, and Peter Evans. 2005. "The Role of Institutions in Economic
Change." In *Reimagining Growth: Institutions, Development, and Society,* edited
by Silvana de Paula and Gary Dymski. London and New York: ZED Books.

Chatman, Celina M., Oksana Malanchuk, and Jacqueline S. Eccles. 2001. "Ethnic
Identity Configurations among African American Early Adolescents." Paper pre-
sented at the biennial meeting of the Society for Research on Child Development,
Minneapolis.

Chevalier, Louis. 1973. *Labouring Classes and Dangerous Classes in Paris during the*
First Half of the Nineteenth Century. London: Routledge and Kegan Paul.

Chilisa, B. (2001). "Assessing the Impact of HIV/AIDS on the University of Botswana."
Pula: Botswana Journal of African Studies 15 (2): 196–203.

Chimbiri, Agnes M. 2007. "The Condom Is an 'Intruder' in Marriage: Evidence from
Rural Malawi." *Social Science and Medicine* 64 (5): 1102–15.

Chrousos, George P, Richard McCarty, Karel Pacak, Giovanni Cizza, Esther
Sternbery, Philip W. Gold, and Richard Kvetnansky, eds. 1995. *Stress: Basic*
Mechanisms and Clinical Implications. Annals of the New York Academy of
Sciences 771: 495–90.

Chung, Haejoo, and Carles Muntaner. 2007. "Welfare State Matters: A Typological
Multi-level Analysis of Wealthy Countries." *Health Policy* 80 (2): 328–39.

Clark, Rodney, Norman B. Anderson, Vernessa R. Clark, and David R. Williams. 1999. "Racism as a Stressor for African Americans: A Biopsychosocial Model." *American Psychologist* 54 (10): 805–16.

Cleland, John, and Susan Cotts Watkins. 2006. "The Key Lesson of Family Planning Programmes for HIV/AIDS Control." *AIDS* 20 (1): 1–3.

Coburn, David. 2004. "Beyond the Income Inequality Hypothesis: Class, Neoliberalism, and Health Inequality." *Social Science and Medicine* 58 (1): 41–56.

Cockerham, William C. 2005. "Health Lifestyle Theory and the Convergence of Agency and Structure." *Journal of Health and Social Behavior* 46 (1): 51–67.

Cockerham, William C. 2007. *Social Causes of Health and Disease.* Cambridge, UK: Polity Press.

Cockett, Richard. 1994. *Thinking the Unthinkable: Think-Tanks and the Economic Counter-Revolution, 1931–1983.* London: Harper Collins.

Coe, Christopher L. 1999. "Psychosocial Factors and Psychoneuroimmunology." In *Developmental Health and the Wealth of Nations,* edited by Daniel P. Keating and Clyde Hertzman. New York: The Guilford Press.

Cohen, S., W. J. Doyle, D. P. Skoner, B. S. Rabin, and J. M. Gwaltney Jr. 1997. "Social Ties and Susceptibility to the Common Cold." *Journal of the American Medical Association* 277 (24): 1940–4.

Coleman, James. 1990. *Foundations of Social Theory.* Cambridge, MA: Harvard University Press.

Colgrove, James. 2002. "The McKeown Thesis: A Historical Controversy and Its Enduring Influence." *American Journal of Public Health* 92: 725.

Collins, Randall. 2004. *Interaction Ritual Chains.* Princeton, NJ: Princeton University Press.

Collins, Sean M., Robert A. Karasek, and Kevin Costas. 2005. "Job Strain and Autonomic Indices of Cardiovascular Disease Risk." *American Journal of Industrial Medicine* 48: 182–93.

Condor, Susan. 1996. "Unimagined Community: Social Psychological Issues Concerning English National Identity." In *Changing European Identities,* edited by Glynis M. Breakwell and Evanthia Lyons. London: Butterworth Heinemann.

Cook, Karen, Russell Hardin, and Margaret Levi. 2005. *Cooperation Without Trust?* New York: Russell Sage.

Copp, Terry. 1978. *Classe Ouvrière et Pauvreté : Les Conditions de Vie des Travailleurs Montréalais 1897–1929.* Montréal: Boréal Express.

Copp, Terry. 1982. "The Health of the People: Montréal in the Depression Years." In *Norman Bethune: His Times and His Legacy,* edited by David A. E. Shephard and Andrée Lévesque. Ottawa: The Canadian Public Health Association.

Corin, Ellen. 1994. "The Social and Cultural Matrix of Health and Disease." In *Why Are Some People Healthy and Others Not? The Determinants of Health Populations,* edited by Robert G. Evans, Morris L. Barer, and Theodore R. Marmor. New York: Aldine De Gruyter.

Cornell, Stephen, and Joseph P. Kalt. 1992. "Reloading the Dice: Improving the Chances for Economic Development on American Indian Reservations." In *What Can Tribes Do? Strategies and Institutions in American Indian Economic Development,* edited by Stephen Cornell and Joseph P. Kalt. Los Angeles: American Indian Studies Center, University of California.

Cornell, Stephen, and Joseph P. Kalt. 2000. "Where's the Glue? Institutional and Cultural Foundations of American Indian Economic Development." *Journal of Socio-Economics* 29: 443–70.

Crepaz, Markus. 2006. "'If You Are My Brother, I May Give You a Dime!' Public Opinion on Multiculturalism, Trust and the Welfare State." In *Multiculturalism and the Welfare State: Recognition and Redistribution in Contemporary Democracies*, edited by Keith Banting and Will Kymlicka. Oxford: Oxford University Press.

Crepaz, Markus. 2007. *Trust Without Borders: Immigration, the Welfare State and Identity in Modern Societies*. Ann Arbor: University of Michigan Press.

Crocker, Jennifer, and Katherine M. Knight. 2005. "Contingencies of Self-Worth." *Current Directions in Psychological Science* 14 (4): 200–3.

Crocker, Jennifer, and Brenda Major. 1989. "Social Stigma and Self-Esteem: The Self-Protective Properties of Stigma." *Psychological Review* 96 (4): 608–30.

Crocker, Jennifer, Brenda Major, and Claude Steele. 1998. "Social Stigma." In *Handbook of Social Psychology*, edited by Daniel T. Gilbert, Susan T. Fiske, and Gardner Lindzey. Boston: McGraw-Hill.

Crocker, Jennifer, Riia Luhtanen, Bruce Blaine, and Stephanie Broadnax. 1994. "Collective Self-esteem and Psychological Well-being among White, Black, and Asian College Students." *Personality & Social Psychology Bulletin* 20 (5): 503–13.

Cummins, R. 2000. "Personal Income and Subjective Well Being: A Review." *Journal of Happiness Studies* 1:133–58.

Cuperus, René, Karl Duffek, and Johannes Kandel. 2003. *The Challenge of Diversity: European Social Democracy Facing Migration, Integration and Multiculturalism*. Innsbruck: Studien Verlag.

Cutler, David M., and Adriana Lleras-Muney. 2008. "Education and Health: Evaluating Theories and Evidence." In *Making Americans Healthier: Social and Economic Policy as Health Policy*, edited by Robert F. Schoeni, James S. House, George A. Kaplan, and Harold Pollack. New York: Russell Sage Foundation.

Cutler, David M., Deaton, Angus S., and Lleras-Muney, Adriana. 2006. "The Determinants of Mortality." National Bureau of Economic Research working paper no. W11963.

Cutrona, Carolyn E., and Beth Troutman. 1986. "Social Support, Infant Temperament and Parenting Self-Efficacy: A Mediational Model of Postpartum Depression." *Child Development* 57 (6): 1507–18.

D'Andrade, Roy. 1995. *The Development of Cognitive Anthropology*. Cambridge: Cambridge University Press.

Dalton, Russell J., S. C. Flanagan, Paul A. Beck, and James E. Alt, eds. 1984. "*Electoral Change in Industrial Democracies: Realignment or Dealignment?*" Princeton, NJ: Princeton University Press.

Daniels, Norman, Bruce P. Kennedy, and Ichiro Kawachi. 1999. "Why Justice is Good for Our Health: The Social Determinants of Health Inequalities." *Daedalus* 128 (4): 215–51.

Davey Smith, George. 2003. *Health Inequalities: Lifecourse Approaches*. Bristol, UK: Policy Press.

Davey Smith, George, Carole Hart, David Blane, Charles Gillis, and Victor Hawthorne. 1997. "Lifetime Socioeconomic Positions and Mortality: Prospective Observational Study." *British Medical Journal* 314: 547–52.

Davis, Mike. 1990. *City of Quartz: Excavating the Future in Los Angeles*. London: Verso.

Davis, Mike. 2001. *Late Victorian Holocausts: El Niño Famines and the Making of the Third World*. London and New York: Verso.

Davis, Mike. 2006. *Planet of Slums*. London: Verso.

Day, Richard. 2000. *Multiculturalism and the History of Canadian Diversity*. Toronto: University of Toronto Press.

Deaton, Angus 2002. "Policy Implications of the Gradient of Health and Wealth." *Health Affairs* 21 (2): 13–30.

Deaton, Angus, and Darren Lubotsky. 2003. "Mortality, Inequality and Race in American Cities and States." *Social Science and Medicine* 56(6): 1139–53.

De Cock, Kevin M., Dorothy Mbori-Ngacha, and Elizabeth Marum. 2002. "Shadow on the Continent: Public Health and HIV/AIDS in Africa in the 21st Century." *The Lancet* 360 (9326): 67–72.

Debord, Guy. 1994 [1967]. *The Society of the Spectacle*. New York: Zone Books.

Deleuze, Gilles, and Felix Guattari. 1983. *Anti-Oedipus: Capitalism and Schizophrenia*, translated by Robert Hurley, Mark Seem, and Helen R. Lane. Minneapolis: University of Minnesota Press.

Derrida, Jacques. 1974. *Of Grammatology*, translated by Gayatri Chakravorty Spivak. Baltimore: Johns Hopkins University Press.

de Waal, Alex. 2003. "How Will HIV/AIDS Transform African Governance?" *African Affairs* 102 (406): 1–23.

De Zwart, Frank. 2005. "The Dilemma of Recognition: Administrative Categories and Cultural Diversity." *Theory and Society* 34: 137–69.

Dickerson, Sally S., and Margaret E. Kemeny. 2004. "Acute Stressors and Cortisol Responses: A Theoretical Integration and Synthesis of Laboratory Research." *Psychological Bulletin* 130 (3): 355–91.

Diener, Ed. 1984. "Subjective Well Being." *Psychological Bulletin* 95: 542–75.

Diener, Ed, and Richard E. Lucas. 2000. "Explaining Differences in Societal Levels of Happiness: Relative Standards, Need Fulfillment, Culture, and Evaluation Theory." *Journal of Happiness Studies* 1: 41–78.

DiMaggio, Paul. 1997. "Culture and Cognition." *Annual Review of Sociology* 23: 263–87.

Dobbin, Frank. 1994a. "Cultural Models of Organization: The Social Construction of Rational Organizing Principles." In *The Sociology of Culture: Emerging Theoretical Perspectives*, edited by Diana Crane. Oxford: Basil Blackwell.

Dobbin, Frank. 1994b. *Forging Industrial Policy: The United States, Britain and France in the Railway Age*. Cambridge: Cambridge University Press.

Dobbin, Frank. 2004. "How Institutions Create Ideas: Notions of Public and Private Efficiency from Early French and American Railroading." *L'Année de la Régulation* 8: 15–50.

Donald, Merlin. 2001. *A Mind So Rare: The Evolution of Human Consciousness*. New York: Norton.

Doran, Michael. 2002. "The Pragmatic Fanaticism of al Qaeda: An Anatomy of Extremism in Middle Eastern Politics." *Political Science Quarterly* 117 (2): 177–90.

Dosi, Giovanni, and David Teece, eds. 1998. *Technology, Innovation and Competitiveness*. Oxford: Oxford University Press.

Dowd, Jennifer B. and Noreen Goldman. 2006. "Do Biomarkers of Stress Mediate the Relation between Socioeconomic Status and Health?" *Journal of Epidemiology and Community Health* 60 (7): 633–9.

Dowsett, Gary W. 1999. "Understanding Cultures of Sexuality: Lessons Learned from HIV/AIDS Education and Behaviour Change among Gay Men in Australia." In *Resistances to Behavioural Change to Reduce HIV/AIDS Infection in Predominantly Heterosexual Epidemics in Third World Countries*, edited by John C. Caldwell, Pat Caldwell, John Anarfi, Kofi Awusabo-Asare, James Ntozi, I. O. Orubuloye, Jeff Marck, Wendy Cosford, Rachel Colombo, and Elaine Hollings. Canberra: The Australian National University.

Dressler, William W. 1991. *Stress and Adaptation in the Context of Culture: Depression in a Southern Black Society*. Albany: State University of New York Press.

Dressler, William W., Kathryn S. Ochs, and Clarence C. Gravlee. 2005. "Race and Ethnicity in Public Health Research: Models to Explain Health Disparities." *Annual Review of Anthropology* 34: 231–52.

Duménil, Gérard, and Dominique Lévy. 2004a. *Capital Resurgent: Roots of the Neoliberal Revolution*, translated by Derek Jeffers. Cambridge, MA: Harvard University Press.

Duménil, Gérard, and Dominique Lévy. 2004b. "Neoliberal Income Trends: Wealth, Class and Ownership in the USA." *New Left Review* 30: 105–33.

Dunbar, Robin I. 1996. *Grooming, Gossip and the Evolution of Language*. Cambridge, MA: Harvard University Press.

Dunbar, Robin I. 2004. *The Human Story*. London: Faber.

Dunn, James R., Bill Burgess, and Nancy A. Ross. 2005. "Income Distribution, Public Services Expenditures, and All Cause Mortality in US States." *Journal of Epidemiology and Community Health* 59 (9): 768–74.

Dunn, James R., Katherine L. Frohlich, Nancy Ross, Lori J. Curtis, and Claudia Sanmartin. 2006. "Role of Geography in Inequalities in Health and Human Development." In *Healthier Societies: From Analysis to Action*, edited by Jody Heymann, Clyde Hertzman, Morris L. Barer, and Robert G. Evans. New York: Oxford University Press.

Durbach, Nadja. 2000. "'They Might As Well Brand Us': Working-Class Resistance to Compulsory Vaccination in Victorian England." *Social History of Medicine* 13: 1.

Durbach, Nadja. 2005. *Bodily Matters. The Anti-Vaccination Movement in England, 1953–1907*. Durham, NC: Duke University Press.

Durham, Deborah, and Frederick Klaits. 2002. "Funerals and the Public Space of Sentiment in Botswana." *Journal of Southern African Studies* 28 (4): 773–91.

Durkheim, Emile. 1951. *Suicide*. New York: Free Press.

Easterly, William. 2001a. "Can Institutions Resolve Ethnic Conflict?" *Economic Development and Cultural Change* 49 (4): 687–706.

Easterly, William. 2001b. *The Elusive Quest for Growth: Economists' Adventures and Misadventures in the Tropics*. Cambridge, MA: MIT Press.

Easterly, William, and R. Levine. 1997. "Africa's Growth Tragedy: Policies and Ethnic Divisions." *Quarterly Journal of Economics* 112: 1203–50.

Easterly, William, and R. Levine. 2003. "Tropics, Germs, and Crops: How Endowments Influence Economic Development." *Journal of Monetary Economics* 50: 3–39.

Eaton, David. 2004. "Understanding AIDS in Public Lives." In *HIV & AIDS in Africa: Beyond Epidemiology*, edited by Ezekiel Kalipeni, Susan Craddock, Joseph Oppong, and Jayati Ghosh. Malden, MA: Blackwell Publishers.

Eberstadt, Nick. 1981. "The Health Care Crisis in the USSR." *The New York Review of Books* 28 (2): 23–31.

Edwards, Bob, Michael W. Foley, and Mario Diani, eds. 2001. *Beyond Tocqueville: Civil Society and the Social Capital Debate in Comparative Perspective.* Hanover, NH: University Press of New England.

Eley, Geoff. 2002. *Forging Democracy: The History of the Left in Europe.* Oxford: Oxford University Press.

Ellis, Bruce J., Marilyn J. Essex, and W. Thomas Boyce. 2005. "Biological Sensitivity to Context: II. Empirical Explorations of an Evolutionary-Developmental Theory." *Development and Psychopathology* 17: 303–28.

Elmer, N. 2001. *Self-Esteem: The Costs and Benefits of Low Self-Worth.* New York: Joseph Rowntree Foundation.

Emerson, Michael, and Christian Smith. 2000. *Divided by Faith: Evangelical Religion and the Problem of Race in America.* New York: Oxford University Press.

Emirbayer, Mustafa, and Jeff Goodwin. 1994. "Network Analysis, Culture, and the Problem of Agency." *American Journal of Sociology.* 99 (6): 1411–54.

Englebert, Pierre. 2000. *State Legitimacy and Development in Africa.* Boulder, CO: Lynne Rienner Publishers.

Epstein, Helen. 2001. "AIDS: The Lessons of Uganda." *The New York Review of Books* 48 (11): 18–23.

Epstein, Helen. 2007. *The Invisible Cure: Africa, the West, and the Fight Against AIDS.* New York: Farrar, Straus and Giroux.

Epstein, Steven. 1996. *Impure Science: AIDS, Activism, and the Politics of Knowledge.* Berkeley: University of California Press.

Erickson, Bonnie H. 1996. "Culture, Class and Connections." *American Journal of Sociology* 102 (1): 217–51.

Erickson, Bonnie H. 2001. "Good Networks and Good Jobs: The Value of Social Capital to Employers and Employees." In Social Capital: Theory and Research, edited by Nan Lin, Karen S. Cook, and Ronald S. Burt. New York: Aldine de Gruyter.

Erickson, Bonnie H. 2002. *"Knowing Men and Women."* Working paper, Department of Sociology, University of Toronto.

Erikson, Kai T. 1976. *Everything in Its Path: Destruction of Community in the Buffalo Creek Flood.* New York: Simon and Schuster.

Escobar, Arturo. 1995. *Encountering Development: The Making and Unmaking of the Third World.* Princeton, NJ: Princeton University Press.

Espeland, Wendy N., and Mitchell L. Stevens. 1998. "Commensuration as a Social Process." *Annual Review of Sociology* 24: 313–43.

Esping-Andersen, Gøsta. 1990. *The Three Worlds of Welfare Capitalism.* Princeton, NJ: Princeton University Press.

Esping-Andersen, Gøsta. 1999. *Social Foundations of Postindustrial Economies.* Oxford: Oxford University Press.

Essed, Philomena. 1991. *Understanding Everyday Racism: An Interdisciplinary Theory.* London: Sage Publications.

Essex, Marilyn. J., W. Thomas Boyce, Lauren H. Goldstein, Jeffrey M. Armstrong, Helen C. Kraemer, and David J. Kupfer. 2002. "The Confluence of Mental, Physical, Social, and Academic Difficulties in Middle Childhood: II. Developing the MacArthur Health & Behavior Questionnaire." *Journal of the American Academy of Child and Adolescent Psychiatry* 41: 588–603.

Esteva, Gustavo. 1992. "Development." In *The Development Dictionary: A Guide to Knowledge as Power,* edited by Wolfgang Sachs. London: Zed Books.

Estevez-Abe, Margarita, Torben Iversen, and David Soskice. 2001. "Social Protection and the Formation of Skills: A Reinterpretation of the Welfare State." In *Varieties of Capitalism: The Institutional Foundations of Comparative Advantage*, edited by Peter Hall and David Soskice. New York: Oxford University Press.

Evans, Alun. 2001. "Benjamin Guy Babington: Founding President of the London Epidemiological Society." *International Journal of Epidemiology* 30: 226–30.

Evans, Peter B. 1992. "The State as Problem and Solution: Predation, Embedded Autonomy and Adjustment." In *The Politics of Economic Adjustment: International Constraints, Distributive Politics, and the State*, edited by Stephan Haggard and Robert R. Kaufman. Princeton, NJ: Princeton University Press.

Evans, Peter B. 1995. *Embedded Autonomy: States and Industrial Transformation*. Princeton, NJ: Princeton University Press.

Evans, Peter B. 1997a. "Eclipse of the State? Reflections on Stateness in an Era of Globalization." *World Politics* 50 (1): 62–87.

Evans, Peter B. 1997b. "State-Society Synergy: Government Action and Social Capital in Development." *Research Series* 94. Berkeley, CA: UC Berkeley International and Area Studies Publications. [Also published as a special section of *World Development* 24 (6): 1033–1132. June 1996.]

Evans, Peter B. 2002. "Collective Capabilities, Culture, and Amartya Sen's Development as Freedom." *Studies in Comparative International Development* 37: 54–60.

Evans, Peter B. 2003. "El Hibridismo Como Estrategia Administrativa: Combinando la Capacidad Burocrática con los Señales de Mercado y la Democracia Deliberativa," ["Hybridity as an Administrative Strategy: Combining Bureaucratic Capacity with Market Signals and Deliberative Democracy"] *Revista del CLAD: Reforma y Democracia* 25 (February): 7–33.

Evans, Peter B. 2004. "Development as Institutional Change: The Pitfalls of Mono-cropping and the Potentials of Deliberation." *Studies in Comparative International Development* 38: 30–53.

Evans, Peter B. 2005. "Challenges of the 'Institutional Turn': Interdisciplinary Opportunities in Development Theory." In *The Economic Sociology of Capitalist Institutions*, edited by Victor Nee and Richard Swedberg. Princeton, NJ: Princeton University Press.

Evans, Peter B. 2007. "Extending the 'Institutional' Turn: Property, Politics and Development Trajectories." In *Institutions for Economic Development: Theory, History, and Contemporary Experiences*, edited by Ha-Joon Chang. Helsinki: UNU-WIDER (World Institute for Development Economics Research). [Also available as WIDER research paper no. 2006/113.]

Evans, Richard J. 1988. "Epidemics and Revolutions: Cholera in Nineteenth Century Europe." *Past and Present* 120: 123–46.

Evans, Robert, Morris Barer, and Theodore Marmor. 1994. *Why Are Some People Healthy and Others Not: The Determinants of Health of Populations*. New York: Aldine de Gruyter.

Eyler, John M. 2001. "The Changing Assessments of John Snow's and William Farr's Cholera Studies." *Social and Preventive Medicine* 46 (4): 225–32.

Faist, Thomas. 1995. "Ethnicization and the Racialization of Welfare-State Politics in Germany and the USA." *Ethnic and Racial Studies* 18 (2): 219–50.

Fanon, Frantz. 1961. *Les Damnés de la Terre*. Paris: François Maspero.

Farmer, Melissa M., and Kenneth F. Ferraro. 2005. "Are Racial Disparities in Health Conditional on Socioeconomic Status?" *Social Science and Medicine* 60 (1): 191–204.

Farmer, Paul. 1992. *AIDS and Accusation: Haiti and the Geography of Blame.* Berkeley: University of California Press.

Farmer, Paul. 2005. *Pathologies of Power: Health, Human Rights and the New War on the Poor.* Berkeley: University of California Press.

Febo, Marcelo, Michael Numan, and Craig F. Ferris. 2005. "Functional Magnetic Resonance Imaging Shows Oxytocin Activates Brain Regions Associated with Mother-pup Bonding during Suckling." *Journal of Neuroscience* 25 (50): 11637–44.

Feliciano, Cynthia. 2005. "Does Selective Migration Matter? Explaining Ethnic Disparities in Educational Attainment among Immigrants' Children." *International Migration Review.* 39 (4): 841–71.

Ferguson, James. 1994. *The Anti-Politics Machine: Development, Depoliticization, and Bureaucratic Power in Lesotho.* Minneapolis: University of Minnesota Press.

Ferguson, James, and Akhil Gupta. 2002. "Spatializing States: Toward an Ethnography of Neoliberal Governmentality." *American Ethnologist* 29 (4): 981–1002.

Ferretti, Lucia. 1992. *Entre Voisins. La Société Paroissiale en Milieu Urbain: Saint-Pierre-Apôtre de Montréal: 1848–1930.* Montréal: Boréal.

Field, Mark. G. 1986. "Soviet Infant Mortality: A Mystery Story." In *Advances in International Maternal and Child Care,* edited by D.B. Jelliffe and E.F.P. Jelliffe. Oxford: Clarendon Press.

Firebaugh, Glenn. 1999. "Empirics of World Income Inequality." *American Journal of Sociology* 104 (6): 597–630.

Fiscella, Kevin, and Peter Franks. 2000. "Quality, Outcomes, and Satisfaction. Individual Income, Income Inequality, Health, and Mortality: What Are the Relationships?" *Health Services Research* 35 (1): 307–15.

Fisher, William F. 1997. "Doing Good: The Politics and Antipolitics of NGO Practices." *Annual Review of Anthropology* 26: 439–64.

Foucault, Michel. 1979. *Discipline and Punish: The Birth of the Prison,* translated by Allan Sheridan. New York: Vintage.

Foucault, Michel. 1988. "The Political Technology of Individuals." In *Technologies of the Self: A Seminar with Michel Foucault,* edited by Luther H. Martin, Huck Gutman, and Patrick H. Hutton. Amherst: University of Massachusetts Press.

Fourcade-Gourchinas, Marion, and Sarah L. Babb. 2002. "The Rebirth of the Liberal Creed: Paths to Neoliberalism in Four Countries." *American Journal of Sociology* 108: 533–79.

Fournier, Daniel. 1983. "Consanguinité et Sociabilité Dans la Zone de Montréal au Début du Siècle." *Recherches Sociographiques* XXIV (3): 307–23.

Fournier, Daniel. 1989. "Pourquoi la Revanche des Berceaux? L'hypothèse de la Sociabilité." *Recherches Sociographiques* XXX (2): 171–98.

Fox, Nathan A., Heather A. Henderson, Peter J. Marshall, Kate E. Nichols, and Melissa M. Ghera. 2004. "Behavioral Inhibition: Linking Biology and Behavior within a Developmental Framework." *Annual Review of Psychology* 56: 235–62.

Frank, David John, and John W. Meyer. 2002. "The Profusion of Individual Roles and Identities in the Post-War Period." *Sociological Theory* 20 (1): 86–105.

Franke, Richard W., and Barbara H. Chasin. 1989. *Kerala: Radical Reform as Development in an Indian State.* San Francisco: The Institute for Food and Development Policy.

Fraser, Nancy. 1998. "Social Justice in the Age of Identity Politics: Redistribution, Recognition and Participation." *The Tanner Lectures on Human Values* 19. Salt Lake City: University of Utah Press, 1–67.

Fraser, Nancy. 2000. "Rethinking Recognition." *New Left Review* 3: 107–20.

Freeman, Gary. 1986. "Migration and the Political Economy of the Welfare State." *Annals of the American Academy of Political and Social Science* 485: 51–63.

Freeman, Jo. 2004. *At Berkeley in the '60s: The Education of an Activist.* Bloomington: Indiana University Press.

Friedman, Milton. 1962. *Capitalism and Freedom,* with the assistance of Rose D. Friedman. Chicago: University of Chicago Press.

Freitag, Markus. 2003. "Beyond Tocqueville: The Origins of Social Capital in Switzerland." *European Sociological Review* 19 (2): 217–32.

Frohlich, Katherine L., Ellen Corin, and Louise Potvin. 2001. "A Theoretical Proposal for the Relationship between Context and Disease." *Sociology of Health and Illness* 23: 776–97.

Frohlich, Katherine L., Louise Potvin, Patrick Chabot, and Ellen Corin. 2002. "A Theoretical and Empirical Analysis of Context: Neighbourhoods, Smoking and Youth." *Social Science and Medicine* 54 (9): 1401–17.

Gans, Herbert. 1999. "The Possibility of a New Racial Hierarchy in the Twenty-First Century United States." In *The Cultural Territories of Race: Black and White Boundaries,* edited by Michèle Lamont. Chicago: University of Chicago Press and New York: Russell Sage Foundation.

Garigue, Philippe. 1971. "Le Système de Parenté en Milieu Urbain Canadien-Français." In *La Société Canadienne-Française,* edited by Marcel Rioux and Yves Martin. Montréal: Hurtubise HMH.

Garrett, Laurie. 2000. "Allies of AIDS: Among Warring Factions in Congo, Disease Is Mutating." *Newsday,* July 9, 2000. Long Island, NY.

Garrett, Laurie. 2000. "Bourgeois Physiology." In *Betrayal of Trust: The Collapse of Global Public Health,* edited by Laurie Garrett. New York: Hyperion.

Gatens, Moira. 2004. "Can Human Rights Accommodate Women's Rights? Towards an Embodied Account of Social Norms, Social Meaning, and Cultural Change." *Contemporary Political Theory* 3 (3): 275–99.

Gaumer, Benoît, and Alain Authier. 1996. "Différenciations Spatiales et Ethniques de la Mortalité Infantile : Québec 1885–1971." *Annales de Démographie Historique* 84: 269–91.

Gauvreau, Joseph. 1914. "La Goutte de Lait." *L'École Sociale Populaire* (29): 1–32.

Geertz, Clifford. 1973. *The Interpretation of Cultures.* New York: Basic Books.

Geoffroy, Marie-Claude, Sylvana M. Côté, Sophie Parent, and Jean Richard Séguin. 2006. "Daycare Attendance, Stress, and Mental Health." *The Canadian Journal of Psychiatry / La Revue canadienne de psychiatrie* 51 (9): 607–15.

George, Alexander, and Andrew Bennett. 2004. *Case Studies and Theory Development in the Social Sciences.* Cambridge, MA: MIT Press.

Giddens, Anthony, 1975. *Class Structure of the Advanced Societies.* New York: Harper and Row.

Giddens, Anthony. 1976. *New Rules of Sociological Method: A Positive Critique of Interpretative Sociologies.* London: Hutchinson.

Giddens, Anthony. 1991. *Modernity and Self-Identity: Self and Society in the Late Modern Age.* Stanford, CA: Stanford University Press.

Giddens, Anthony. 1998. *The Third Way: The Renewal of Social Democracy.* Cambridge, UK: Polity Press.

Giedd, Jay N. 2008. "The Teen Brain: Insights from Neuroimaging." *Journal of Adolescent Health* 42: 335–42.

Giedd, Jay N., Schmitt, James Eric, and Michael C. Neale. 2007. "Structural Brain Magnetic Resonance Imaging of Pediatric Twins." *Human Brain Mapping* 28 (6): 474–81.

Gitlin, Todd. 1995. *The Twilight of Common Dreams: Why America Is Wracked by Culture Wars.* New York: Metropolitan Books.

Glatzer, Miguel. 2008. "Fostering Civil Society: The Portuguese Welfare State and the Development of a Non-Profit Sector." In *Portugal's Democracy: Thirty Years after the Transition* edited by Michael Baum. Lanham, MD: Lexington Books.

Goffman, Erving. 1963. *Stigma: Notes on the Management of Spoiled Identity.* Englewood Cliffs, NJ: Prentice-Hall.

Golden, Miriam. 1993. "The Dynamics of Trade Unionism and National Economic Performance." *American Political Science Review* 87 (2): 439–54.

Goldman, Lawrence. 1986. "The Social Science Association, 1857–86: A Context for Mid-Victorian Liberalism." *English Historical Review* 101 (398): 95–134.

Goldthorpe, John A. 1987. *Social Mobility and Class Structure in Modern Britain, 2nd ed.* Oxford: Oxford University Press.

Goldthorpe, John A., Frank Beckhofer, and David Lockwood. 1969. *The Affluent Worker in the Class Structure.* Cambridge: Cambridge University Press.

Goodhart, David. 2004. "Too Diverse?" *Prospect*, February 2004, pp. 30–7.

Goodman, Elizabeth, Nancy E. Adler, Ichiro Kawachi, A. Lindsay Frazier, Bin Huang, and Graham A. Colditz. 2001. "Adolescents' Perceptions of Social Status: Development and Evaluation of a New Indicator." *Pediatrics* 108 (2): e31.

Gotlib, Ian H., and Blair Wheaton, eds. 1997. *Stress and Adversity over the Life Course Trajectories and Turning Points.* Cambridge: Cambridge University Press.

Gottlieb, Gilbert, and Michael T. Willoughby. 2006. "Probabilistic Epigenesis of Psychopathology." In *Developmental Psychopathology*, edited by Dante Cicchetti and Donald Cohen. Hoboken, NJ: John Wiley and Sons.

Granovetter, Mark S. 1973. "The Strength of Weak Ties." *American Journal of Sociology* 78: 1360–80.

Granovetter, Mark. 1974. *Getting a Job.* Cambridge, MA: Harvard University Press.

Graubard, Stephen. 1964. *A New Europe?* Boston: Houghton Mifflin.

Green, Edward C. 2003. *Rethinking AIDS Prevention: Learning from Successes in Developing Countries.* Westport, CT: Praeger.

Greenstein, Theodore N. 2000. "Economic Dependence, Gender, and the Division of Labor in the Home: A Replication and Extension." *Journal of Marriage and Family* 62 (2): 322–35.

Greif, Avner. 2006. *Institutions and the Path to the Modern Economy.* New York: Cambridge University Press.

Grembowski, D., D. Patrick, P. Diehr, M. Durham, S. Beresfors, and E. Kay. 1993. "Self-Efficacy and Health Behavior among Older Adults." *Journal of Health and Social Behavior* 34: 89–104.

Groulx, Adélard. 1943. "La Mortalité Maternelle et la Mortalité Infantile à Montréal." *L'union Médicale du Canada* 72 (4): 1413–17.

Grunwald, Michael. 2002. "A Small Nation's Big Effort Against AIDS: Botswana Spreads Message and Free Drugs, but Old Attitudes Persist." *The Washington Post*, December 2, 2002, p. A1.

Guérard, François. 2001. "L'hygiène Publique et la Mortalité Infantile Dans une Petite Ville: Le Cas de Trois-Rivières, 1895–1939." *Cahiers Québécois de Démographie* 30 (2): 231–59.

Gunnar, Megan R., and Bonny Donzella. 2002. "Social Regulation of the Cortisol Levels in Early Human Development." *Psychoneuroendocrinology* 27 (1–2): 199–220.

Gunnar, Megan R., and Michelle M. Loman. In press. "Early Experience and Stress Regulation in Human Development." In *Nature and Nurture in Early Child Development*, edited by Daniel P. Keating. New York: Cambridge University Press.

Gupta, Akhil, and James Ferguson. 1992. "Space, Identity, and the Politics of Difference." *Cultural Anthropology* 7 (1): 6–24.

Hacker, Jacob. 2006. *The Great Risk Shift: The Assault on American Jobs, Families, Health Care, and Retirement and How You Can Fight Back*. New York: Oxford University Press.

Hagan, John, and Ron Levi. 2004. "Social Skill, the Milosevic Indictment, and the Rebirth of International Criminal Justice." *European Journal of Criminology* 1: 445–75.

Hall, Peter A., ed. 1989. *The Political Power of Economic Ideas. Keynesianism across Nations*. Princeton, NJ: Princeton University Press.

Hall, Peter A. 1993. "Policy Paradigms, Social Learning and the State. The Case of Economic Policy-making in Britain." *Comparative Politics* 23 (3): 275–96.

Hall, Peter A. 1999. "Social Capital in Britain." *British Journal of Political Science*. 29 (3): 417–61.

Hall, Peter A. 2003. "Aligning Ontology and Methodology in Comparative Research." In *Comparative Historical Analysis: New Approaches and Methods*, edited by James Mahoney and Dietrich Rueschemeyer. New York: Cambridge University Press.

Hall, Peter A., and David Soskice. 2001. *Varieties of Capitalism: The Institutional Foundations of Comparative Advantage*. New York: Oxford University Press.

Hall, Peter, and Michèle Lamont. 2006. *Successful Societies: Culture, Institutions, and the Production of Capacities and Health Inequality*. Unpublished paper. Radcliffe Institute for Advanced Studies, Cambridge, MA.

Hall, Peter A., and Rosemary CR Taylor. 1996. "Political Science and the Three New Institutionalisms." *Political Studies* 44 (5): 936–57.

Hall, Peter A., and Kathleen Thelen. 2009. "Institutional Change in Varieties of Capitalism." *Socio-Economic Review* 7(1): 7–34.

Hamlin, Christopher, and Sally Sheard. 1998. "Revolutions in Public Health: 1848, and 1998?" *British Medical Journal* 317 (7158): 587–91.

Hanna, David, and Sherry Olson. 1990. "Paysage Social de Montréal, 1901." In *Atlas Historique du Canada III : Jusqu'au Coeur du XXe siècle, 1891–1961*, edited by Donald Kerr and Deryck W. Holdsworth. Montréal: Les Presses de l'Université de Montréal.

Harris, Jose. 1992. "Political Thought and the Welfare State 1870–1940: An Intellectual Framework for British Social Policy." *Past and Present* 135 (1): 116–41.

Harvey, David. 1990. *The Condition of Postmodernity: An Inquiry into the Origins of Cultural Change*. Cambridge, MA: Blackwell.

Harvey, David. 2005. *A Brief History of Neoliberalism*. Oxford: Oxford University Press.

Haslam, S. Alexander, Anne O'Brien, Jolanda Jetten, Karine Vormedal, and Sally Penna. 2005. "Taking the Strain: Social Identity, Social Support and the Experience of Stress." *British Journal of Social Psychology* 44: 355–70.

Hatch, Stephani L. 2005. "Conceptualizing and Identifying Cumulative Adversity and Protective Resources: Implications for Understanding Health Inequalities." *The Journals of Gerontology Series B: Psychological Sciences and Social Sciences* 60: 130–34.

Hawkley, Louise C., Gary G. Berntson, Christopher G. Engeland, Phillip T. Marucha, Christopher M. Masi, and John T. Cacioppo. 2005. "Stress, Aging, and Resilience: Can Accrued Wear and Tear Be Slowed?" *Canadian Psychology/Psychologie canadienne.* 46 (3): 115–25.

Hayek, Friedrich. 1976 [1944]. *The Road to Serfdom.* Chicago: University of Chicago Press.

Hearst, Norman, and Sanny Chen. 2004. "Condoms for AIDS Prevention in the Developing World: Is It Working?" *Studies in Family Planning* 35 (1): 39–47.

Heirich, Max. 1971. *The Spiral of Conflict: Berkeley, 1964.* New York: Columbia University Press.

Heller, Patrick. 1999. *The Labor of Development: Workers and the Transformation of Capitalism in Kerala, India.* Ithaca, NY: Cornell University Press.

Heller, Patrick. 2005. "Reinventing Public Power in the Age of Globalization: Decentralization and the Transformation of Movement Politics in Kerala." In *Social Movements in India: Poverty, Power, and Politics*, edited by Raka Ray and Mary Katzenstein. Lanham, MD: Rowman and Littlefield.

Helpman, Elhanan. 2004. *The Mystery of Economic Growth.* Cambridge, MA: Harvard University Press.

Henripin, Jacques. 1961. "L'inégalité Sociale Devant la Mort : La Mortinatalité et la Mortalité Infantile à Montréal." *Recherches Sociographiques* 2: 3–34.

Herbst, Jeffrey. 2000. *States and Power in Africa: Comparative Lessons in Authority and Control.* Princeton, NJ: Princeton University Press.

Hero, Rodney E. 1998. *Faces of Inequality: Social Diversity and American Politics.* New York: Oxford University Press.

Hero, Rodney, and Rob Preuhs. 2006. "Multiculturalism and Welfare Policies in the US States: A State-level Comparative Analysis." In *Multiculturalism and the Welfare State: Recognition and Redistribution in Contemporary Democracies*, edited by Keith Banting and Will Kymlicka. Oxford: Oxford University Press.

Herring, Ronald J. 1991. "Contesting the 'Great Transformation': Land and Labor in South India." Unpublished manuscript. Department of Political Science, Cornell University, Ithaca, NY.

Hertzman, Clyde. 1999. "Population Health and Human Development." In *Developmental Health and the Wealth of Nations: Social, Biological, and Educational Dynamics*, edited by Daniel P. Keating and Clyde Hertzman. New York: Guilford Press.

Hertzman, Clyde. 2000. "The Life-Course Contribution to Ethnic Disparities in Health." In *Critical Perspectives on Racial and Ethnic Differences in Health in Late Life*, edited by Norman B. Anderson, Randy A. Bulatao, and Barney Cohen. Washington, DC: National Academies Press.

Hertzman, Clyde. 2001. "Health and Human Society." *American Scientist* 89 (6): 538–45.

Hertzman, Clyde, and Chris Power. 2004. Child Development as a Determinant of Health Across the Life Course. *Current Pediatrics* 14: 438–43.

Hertzman, Clyde, and John Frank. 2006. "Biological Pathways Linking Social Environment, Development, and Health." In *Healthier Societies: From Analysis to*

Action, edited by Jody Heymann, Clyde Hertzman, Morris L. Barer, and Robert G. Evans. New York: Oxford University Press.

Hertzman, Clyde, and Chris Power. 2006. "A Life Course Approach to Health and Human Development." In *Healthier Societies: From Analysis to Action*, edited by Jody Heymann, Clyde Hertzman, Morris L. Barer, and Robert G. Evans. New York: Oxford University Press.

Hertzman, Clyde, Arjumand Siddiqi, and Martin Bohak. 2002. The Population Health Context for Gender, Stress, and Cardiovascular Disease in Central and Eastern Europe. In *Heart Disease: Environment, Stress, and Gender*, edited by Gerdi Weidner, Maria Kopp, and Margareta Kristenson. Amsterdam: IOS Press.

Herzog, Hanna. 2004. "Absent Voices." In *Israelis in Conflict; Hegemonies, Identities and Challenges*, edited by Adriana Kemp, David Newman, Uri Ram, and Oren Yiftachel. Brighton: Sussex Academic Presses.

Heyman, Jody, Clyde Hertzman, Morris L. Barer, and Robert G. Evans, eds. 2006. *Healthier Societies: From Analysis to Action*. New York: Oxford University Press.

Higonnet, Patrice. 1988. *Sister Republics: The Origins of French and American Republicanism*. Cambridge, MA: Harvard University Press.

Hillemeier, Marianne, John Lynch, Sam Harper, and Michele Casper. 2003. "Measuring Contextual Characteristics for Community Health." *Health Services Research* 38 (6): 1645–717.

Hirschman, Albert. 1964. *Exit, Voice, and Loyalty*. Cambridge, MA: Harvard University Press.

Hobsbawm, Eric. 1994. *The Age of Extremes: A History of the World, 1914–1991*. New York: Vintage.

Hobson, Barbara. 2003. *Recognition Struggles and Social Movements: Contested Identities, Agency, and Power*. Cambridge: Cambridge University Press.

Holm, John, and Patrick Molutsi, eds. 1989. *Democracy in Botswana*. Athens: Ohio University Press.

Hooghe, Marc. 2007. "Social Capital and Diversity. Generalized Trust, Social Cohesion and Regimes of Diversity." *Canadian Journal of Political Science* 40: 709–32.

Hoogvelt, Ankie. 2001. *Globalization and the Postcolonial World: The New Political Economy of Development*. 2nd ed. Baltimore: Johns Hopkins University Press.

Horn, Gerdt-Reiner. 2007. *The Spirit of '68: Rebellion in Western Europe and North America, 1956–1976*. Oxford: Oxford University Press.

House, James S. 2001. "Social Isolation Kills, But How and Why?" *Psychosomatic Medicine* 63: 273–4.

House, James, Robert Schoeni, Alan Pollack, and George Kaplan. 2008. *Making Americans Healthier*. New York: Russell Sage.

Howard, Marc. 2003. *The Weakness of Civil Society in Post-Communist Europe*. New York: Cambridge University Press.

Huber, Evelyne, and John Stevens. 2001. *Development and Crisis of the Welfare State: Parties and Policies in Global Markets*. Chicago: University of Chicago Press.

Hunter, Mark. 2002. "The Materiality of Everyday Sex: Thinking Beyond Prostitution." *African Studies* 61 (1): 99–120.

Idler, Ellen L., and Yael Benyamini. 1997. "Self-rated Health and Mortality: A review of Twenty-seven Community Studies." *Journal of Health and Social Behavior* 38 (1): 21–37.

Ignatiev, Noel. 1995. *How the Irish Became White*. New York: Routledge.

Inglehart, Ronald. 1977. *The Silent Revolution: Changing Values and Political Styles among Western Publics*. Princeton, NJ: Princeton University Press.

Inglehart, Ronald. 1999. "Trust, Well-Being and Democracy." In *Democracy and Trust*, edited by Mark Warren. New York: Cambridge University Press.

Iriye, Akira. 2002. *Global Community: The Role of International Organizations in the Making of the Contemporary World*. Berkeley: University of California Press.

Jackson, J.S., T. Brown, D. Williams, M. Torres, S. Sellers, and K. Brown. 1996. "Racism and the Physical and Mental Health Status of African Americans: A Thirteen Year National Panel Study." *Ethnicity and Disease* 6 (1,2): 132–47.

Jackson, Pamela, B., Peggy A. Thoits, and Howard F. Taylor. 1995. "Composition of the Workplace and Psychological Well-Being: The Effects of Tokenism on America's Black Elite." *Social Forces* 74: 543–57.

Jacobstone, Stephane, and Jane Jenson. 2005. *Care Allowances for the Frail Elderly and their Impact on Women Care-Givers*. Canadian Family Network discussion paper.

Jeffreys, Sheila. 1987. *The Sexuality Debates*. London: Routledge.

Jenkins, Richard. 1996. *Social Identity*. New York: Routledge.

Jenson, Jane. 1986. "Gender and Reproduction: Or, Babies and the State," *Studies in Political Economy* 20: 9–46.

Jenson, Jane. 1989. "Paradigms and Political Discourse: Protective Legislation in France and the United States before 1914." *Canadian Journal of Political Science* 22 (2): 235–58.

Jenson, Jane. 2008. "Redesigning Citizenship Regimes after Neoliberalism: Moving Toward Social Investment." *La Rivista delle Politiche Sociali* (1): 13–31.

Jenson, Jane, and Susan Phillips. 1996. "Regime Shift: New Citizenship Practices in Canada." *International Journal of Canadian Studies* 14.

Jenson, Jane, and Susan D. Phillips. 2002. "Redesigning the Canadian Citizenship Regime: Remaking the Institutions of Representation." In *Citizenship, Markets and the State*, edited by Colin Crouch, Klau Eder, and Damian Tambini. London: Oxford University Press.

Jenson, Jane, and Denis Saint-Martin. 2003. "New Routes to Social Cohesion? Citizenship and the Social Investment State." *Canadian Journal of Sociology* 28 (1): 77–99.

Jenson, Jane, and Denis Saint-Martin. 2006. "Building Blocks for a New Social Architecture: The LEGOTM Paradigm of an Active Society." *Policy and Politics* 34 (3): 429–51.

Jepperson, Ronald L. 1991. "Institutions, Institutional Effects and Institutionalization." In *The New Institutionalism in Organizational Analysis*, edited by Walter W. Powell and Paul J. DiMaggio. Chicago: University of Chicago Press.

Johnson, Martin. 2001. "The Impact of Social Diversity and Racial Attitudes on Social Welfare Policy." *State Politics and Policy Quarterly* 1 (1): 27–49.

Johnson-Hanks, Jennifer. 2002. "On the Modernity of Traditional Contraception: Time and the Social Context of Fertility." *Population and Development Review* 28 (2): 229–49.

Jones, Tanya. 2005. "The Treatment Action Campaign: Counter-Hegemonic Mobilization for Health." Unpublished manuscript. Department of Sociology, University of California, Berkeley.

Judge, Ken. 1995. "Income Distribution and Life Expectancy: A Critical Appraisal." *British Medical Journal* 311: 1282–5.

Kaler, Amy. 2003. "'My Girlfriends Could Fill a Yanu-Yanu Bus': Rural Malawian Men's Claims about Their Own Serostatus." *Demographic Research* S1 (11): 349–72.

Kaler, Amy. 2004. "The Moral Lens of Population Control: Condoms and Controversies in Southern Malawi." *Studies in Family Planning* 35 (2): 105–15.

Kalmijn, Matthijs. 1991. "Status Homogamy in the United States." *American Journal of Sociology* 97 (2): 496–523.

Kaplan, George A., Elsie R. Pamuk, John W. Lynch, Richard D. Cohen, and Jennifer L. Balfour. 1996. "Inequality in Income and Mortality in the United States: Analysis of Mortality and Potential Pathways." *British Medical Journal* 312 (7037): 999–1003. Erratum in *BMJ* 312 (7041): 1253.

Kaplan, George A., Nalini Ranjit, and Sarah A. Burgard. 2008. "Lifting Gates, Lengthening Lives: Did Civil Rights Policies Improve the Health of African American Women in the 1960s and 1970s?" In *Making Americans Healthier*, edited by Robert F. Schoeni, James S. House, George A. Kaplan, and Harold Pollack. New York: Russell Sage Foundation.

Kapp, Clare. 2002. "Coalition Aims to Boost Uptake of Antiretroviral Drugs." *The Lancet* 360 (9350): 2051.

Karasek, Robert A., Jr. 1979. "Job Demands, Job Decision Latitude, and Mental Strain: Implications for Job Redesign." *Administrative Science Quarterly* 24 (2): 285–308.

Karlsen, Saffron, and James Y. Nazroo. 2002. "Relation Between Racial Discrimination, Social Class, and Health Among Ethnic Minority Groups." *American Journal of Public Health* 92 (4): 624–31.

Karlstrom, Mikael. 1996. "Imagining Democracy: The Political Culture and Democratisation in Buganda." *Africa* 66 (4): 485–506.

Kashkooli, Kevan. 2002. "Gender Inequality and HIV/AIDS in Sub-Saharan Africa." Unpublished paper. Department of Sociology, University of California, Berkeley.

Kassimir, Ronald. 1999. "Reading Museveni: Structure, Agency and Pedagogy in Ugandan Politics." *Canadian Journal of African Studies* 33 (2 & 3): 649–73.

Katznelson, Ira. 2005. *When Affirmative Action Was White: An Untold Story of Racial Inequality in Twentieth-Century America*. New York: Norton.

Kawachi, Ichiro. 2000. "Income Inequality and Health." In *Social Epidemiology*, edited by Lisa Berkman and Ichiro Kawachi. New York: Oxford University Press.

Kawachi, Ichiro, and Bruce P. Kennedy. 1999. "Health and Social Cohesion." In *The Society and Population Health Reader: Income Inequality and Health*, edited by Ichiro Kawachi, Bruce P. Kennedy, and Richard G. Wilkinson. New York: The New Press.

Kawachi, Ichiro, and Bruce P. Kennedy. 2002. *The Health of Nations: Why Inequality Is Harmful to Your Health*. New York: New Press.

Kawachi, Ichiro, Bruce P. Kennedy, Kimberly Lochner, and Deborah Prothrow-Stith. 1997. "Social Capital, Income Inequality and Mortality." *American Journal of Public Health* 87 (9): 1491–8.

Kawachi, Ichiro, Bruce P. Kennedy, and Richard G. Wilkinson, eds. 1999. *The Society and Population Health Reader: Income Inequality and Health*, Vol. I. New York: The New Press.

Kawachi, Ichiro, Bruce P. Kennedy, and Roberta Glass. 1998. "Social Capital and Self-Rated Health: A Contextual Analysis." *American Journal of Public Health* 89 (8): 1187–93.

Keating, Daniel P. 1990. "Charting Pathways to the Development of Expertise." *Educational Psychologist* 25: 243–67.

Keating, Daniel P. 1998. "Human Development in the Learning Society." In *International Handbook of Educational Change*, edited by Andrew Hargreaves, Ann Lieberman, Michael Fullan, and David Hopkins. Dordrecht: Kluwer.

Keating, Daniel P. 2001. "Definition and Selection of Competencies from a Human Development Perspective." In *Additional DeSeCo Expert Opinions*. Paris: Organisation for Economic Co-operation and Development.

Keating, Daniel P. 2004. "Cognitive and Brain Development." In *Handbook of Adolescent Psychology*, edited by Richard Lerner and Laurence Steinberg. New York: Wiley & Sons.

Keating, Daniel P. In press a. *Nature and Nurture in Early Child Development*. New York: Cambridge University Press.

Keating, Daniel P. In press b. "Society and Early Child Development." In *Nature and Nurture in Early Child Development*, edited by Daniel P. Keating. New York: Cambridge University Press.

Keating, Daniel P., and Clyde Hertzman. 1999a. "Modernity's Paradox." In *Developmental Health and the Wealth of Nations: Social, Biological, and Educational Dynamics*, edited by Daniel P. Keating and Clyde Hertzman. New York: Guilford.

Keating, Daniel P., and Clyde Hertzman. 1999b. *Developmental Health and the Wealth of Nations: Social, Biological, and Educational Dynamics*. New York: Guilford Press.

Keating, Daniel P., and Fiona K. Miller. 2000. "The Dynamics of Emotional Development: Models, Metaphors, and Methods." In *Emotion, Development, and Self-Organization: Dynamic Systems Approaches to Emotional Development*, edited by Marc D. Lewis and Sally M. Grantham-McGregor. New York: Cambridge University Press.

Keating, Daniel P., and Sharon Z. Simonton. 2008. "Developmental Health Effects of Human Development Policies." In *Making Americans Healthier*, edited by James House, Robert Schoeni, Alan Pollack, and George Kaplan. New York: Russell Sage.

Keating, Norah, Jennifer Swindle, and Deborah Foster. 2005. "The Role of Social Capital in Aging Well." In *Social Capital in Action: Thematic Policy Studies*. Ottawa: Policy Research Institute, Government of Canada.

Keck, Margaret, and Kathryn Sikkink. 1998. *Activists Beyond Borders: Transnational Advocacy Networks in International Politics*. Ithaca, NY: Cornell University Press.

Keeler, John T. S. 1987. *The Politics of Neo-Corporatism in France*. New York: Oxford University Press.

Kernerman, Gerald. 2005. *Multicultural Nationalism: Civilizing Difference, Constituting Community*. Vancouver: UBC Press.

Kertzer, David. 1989. *Ritual, Politics and Power*. New Haven, CT: Yale University Press.

Kesler, Christel, and Irene Bloemraad. 2008. "Do Immigrants Hurt Civic and Political Engagement? The Conditional Effects of Immigrant Diversity on Trust, Membership, and Participation across 19 Countries, 1981–2000." Paper presented to the annual meeting of the Canadian Sociological Association. Vancouver, June 2008.

Keys, Ancel. 1980. *Seven Countries: A Multivariate Analysis of Death and Coronary Heart Disease.* Cambridge, MA: Harvard University Press.

Khagram, Sanjeev, James V. Riker, and Kathryn Sikkink. 2002. *Restructuring World Politics: Transnational Social Movements, Networks and Norms.* Minneapolis: University of Minnesota Press.

Kickbusch, Ilona. 2003. "The Contribution of the World Health Organization to a New Public Health and Health Promotion." *American Journal of Public Health* 93 (3): 383–8.

Klein, Lawrence R., and Marshall Pomer. 2001. *The New Russia: Transition Gone Awry.* Stanford: Stanford University Press.

Kleinman, Arthur. 1981. *Patients and Healers in the Context of Culture.* Berkeley: University of California Press.

Klinenberg, Eric. 2002. *Heat Wave.* Chicago: University of Chicago Press.

Klug, Heinz. 2002. "Access to Health Care: Judging Implementation in the Contest of AIDS: Treatment Action Campaign v. Minister of Health." *South African Journal on Human Rights* 18: 114–24.

Klug, Heinz. 2005. "Comment: Access to Essential Medicines – Promoting Human Rights over Free Trade and Intellectual Property Claims." In *International Public Goods and Transfer of Technology Under a Globalized Intellectual Property Regime,* edited by Keith E. Maskus and Jerome H. Reichman. Cambridge: Cambridge University Press.

Kohli, Atul. 2004. *State-directed Development: Political Power and Industrialization in the Global periphery.* Cambridge and New York: Cambridge University Press.

Kohn, Melvin. 1987. "Cross-National Research as an Analytic Strategy." *American Sociological Review* 52 (6): 713–31.

Kohn, Melvin L., Atsushi Naoi, Carrie Scoenbach, Carmi Schooler, and Kazimierz Slomczynski. 1990. "Position in the Class Structure and Psychological Functioning in the United States, Japan and Poland." *American Journal of Sociology* 95 (4): 964–1008.

Kondratieff, Nicolai D. 1935. "The Long Waves in Economic Life." *Review of Economics and Statistics* 17 (6): 105–15.

Korte, S. Mechiel, Jaap M. Koolhaas, John. C. Wingfield, and Bruce. S. McEwen. 2005. "The Darwinian Concept of Stress: Benefits of Allostasis and Costs of Allostatic Load and the Trade-offs in Health and Disease." *Neuroscience and Biobehavioral Reviews* 29 (1): 3–38.

Kraemer, Helena Chmura, Eric Stice, Alan Kazdin, David Offord, and David Kupfer. 2001. "How Do Risk Factors Work Together? Mediators, Moderators, and Independent, Overlapping, and Proxy Risk Factors." *American Journal of Psychiatry* 158 (6): 848–56.

Krieger, Nancy. 1999. "Embodying Inequality: A Review of Concepts, Measures, and Methods for Studying Health Consequences of Discrimination." *International Journal of Health Services* 29 (2): 295–352.

Krieger, Nancy. 2000. "Discrimination and Health." In *Social Epidemiology,* edited by Lisa F. Berkman and Ichiro Kawachi. New York: Oxford University Press.

Krieger, Nancy. 2001. "Theories for Social Epidemiology in the 21st Century: An Ecosocial Persepctive." *International Journal of Epidemiology* 30 (4): 668–77.

Krieger, Nancy. 2003. "Does Racism Harm Health? Did Child Abuse Exist Before 1962? On Explicit Questions, Critical Science, and Current Controversies: An Ecosocial Perspective." *American Journal of Public Health* 93 (2): 194–9.

Krieger, Nancy. 2005. "Embodiment: A Conceptual Glossary for Epidemiology." *Journal of Epidemiology and Community Health*. 59: 350–5.

Krieger, Nancy, D.L. Rowley, A.A. Herman, B. Avery, and M.T. Phillips. 1993. "Racism, Sexism, and Social Class: Implications for Studies of Health, Disease and Well-Being." *American Journal of Preventive Medicine* 9: 82–122.

Kristenson, Margareta. 2006. "Socio-economic Position and Health: the Role of Coping." *Social Inequalities in Health*, edited by Johannes Siegrist and Michael Marmot. Oxford: Oxford University Press.

Kristenson, Margareta, Hege R. Eriksen, Judith K. Sluiter, Dagmar Starke, and Holger Ursin. 2004. "Psychobiological Mechanisms of Socioeconomic Differences in Health." *Social Science and Medicine* 58 (8): 1511–22.

Kruger, Anne O. 1974. "The Political Economy of the Rent-Seeking Society." *American Law and Economics Review* 64: 291–303.

Kubzansky, Laura D., and Ichiro Kawachi. 2000. "Affective States and Health." In *Social Epidemiology*, edited by Lisa F. Berkman and Ichiro Kawachi New York: Oxford University Press.

Kuh, Diana, and Yoav Ben-Shlomo. 1997. *A Life Course Approach to Chronic Disease Epidemiology: Tracing the Origins of Ill Health from Early to Adult Life.* Oxford: Oxford University Press.

Kuh, Diana, and Yoav Ben-Shlomo. 2004. *A Life Course Approach to Chronic Disease Epidemiology.* Oxford: Oxford University Press.

Kumlin, Staffan, and Bo Rothstein. 2005. "Making and Breaking Social Capital: The Impact of Welfare Institutions." *Comparative Political Studies* 38 (4): 339–65.

Kunst, Anton E., and Johan P. Mackenbach. 1994. "International Variation in the Size of Mortality Differences Associated with Occupational Status." *International Journal of Epidemiology* 23 (4): 742–50.

Kymlicka, Will. 2001. *Politics in the Vernacular: Nationalism, Multiculturalism and Citizenship.* Oxford: Oxford University Press.

Kymlicka, Will. 2007. *Multicultural Odysseys.* Oxford: Oxford University Press.

Lamont, Michèle. 1992. *Money, Morals, Manners: The Culture of the French and American Upper-Middle Class.* Chicago: University of Chicago Press.

Lamont, Michèle. 2000. *The Dignity of Working Men: Morality and the Boundaries of Race, Class, and Immigration.* Cambridge, MA: Harvard University Press.

Lamont, Michèle. 2006. "How French and American Workers Define Cultural Membership." In *Inequalities of the World*, edited by Goran Therborn. London: Verso.

Lamont, Michèle, and Sada Aksartova. 2002. "Ordinary Cosmopolitanisms: Strategies for Bridging Racial Boundaries among Working Class Men." *Theory, Culture and Society* 19 (4): 1–25.

Lamont, Michèle, and Christopher Bail. 2005. "Sur les frontières de la reconnaissance. Les catégories internes et externes de l'identité collective." *Revue Européenne des Migrations Internationales* 21 (2): 61–90.

Lamont, Michèle, and Crystal Fleming. 2005. "Everyday Antiracism: Competence and Religion in the Cultural Repertoire of the African American Elite." *W.E. B. DuBois Review* 2 (1): 29–43.

Lamont, Michèle, and Virág Molnár. 2002. "The Study of Boundaries Across the Social Sciences." *Annual Review of Sociology* 28: 167–95.

Lamont, Michèle, and Laurent Thévenot. 2000. *Rethinking Comparative Cultural Sociology: Repertoires of Evaluation in France and the United States*. London: Cambridge University Press.

Lamont, Michèle, and Mario Small. 2008. "Culture Matters: The Role of Culture in Explaining Poverty." In *The Colors of Poverty: Why Racial and Ethnic Disparities Persist*, edited by David Harris and Ann Lin. New York: Russell Sage Foundation, p. 76–102.

Lamont, Michèle, Ann Morning, and Margarita Mooney. 2001. "North African Immigrants Respond to French Racism: Demonstrating Equivalence through Universalism." *Ethnic and Racial Studies* 25 (3): 390–414.

Lamontagne, Maurice, and Jean-Charles Falardeau. 1947. "The Life Cycle of French-Canadian Urban Families." *Canadian Journal of Economics and Political Science* XIII (2): 233–47.

Lancaster, Carol. 2008. *George Bush's Foreign Aid: Transformation or Chaos?* Washington, DC: Center for Global Development.

Le Goff, Jean-Pierre. 1998. *Mai 68, l'héritage impossible*. Paris: La Découverte.

Leigh, Andrew, and Christopher Jencks. July 2006. "Inequality and Mortality: Long-Run Evidence from a Panel of Countries." KSG working paper no. RWP06-032. Available at SSRN: http://ssrn.com/abstract=902381.

Leith, J. Clark. 2005. *Why Botswana Prospered: Behind the Success of Africa's Sole Economically Prosperous Democracy*. Montreal and Kingston, Ontario: McGill-Queen's University Press.

Lena, Hugh F., and Brace London. 1993. "The Political and Economic-Determinants of Health Outcomes: A Cross-National Analysis." *International Journal of Health Services* 23: 585–602.

Levi-Strauss, Claude. 1958. *Anthropologie structurale*. Paris: Librairie Plon.

Lewis, Stephen. 2003. "Notes from UN Press Briefing by Stephen Lewis, Special Envoy for HIV/AIDS in Africa, at Noon, January 8, 2003." New York: United Nations.

Lieberman, Evan S. 2007. "Ethnic Politics, Risk, and Policy-Making: A Cross-National Statistical Analysis of Government Responses to HIV/AIDS." *Comparative Political Studies* 40 (12): 1407–32.

Lin, Nan, Karen S. Cook, and Ronald S. Burt, eds. 2001. *Social Capital: Theory and Research*. New York: Aldine de Gruyter.

Link, Bruce G., and Jo Phelan. 1995. "Social Conditions as Fundamental Causes of Disease." *Journal of Health and Social Behavior* 35: 80–94.

Link, Bruce, and Jo C. Phelan. 1996. "Understanding Sociodemographic Differences in Health – The Role of Fundamental Social Causes." *American Journal of Public Health* 86 (4): 471–2.

Link, Bruce G., and Jo C. Phelan. 2000. "Evaluating the Fundamental Cause Explanation for Social Disparities in Health." In *Handbook of Medical Sociology*, edited by Chloe E. Bird, Peter Conrad, and Allen Fremont. Upper Saddler River, NJ: Prentice Hall.

Link, Bruce G., and Jo C. Phelan. 2001. "Conceptualizing Stigma." *Annual Review of Sociology* 27: 363–85.

Link, Bruce G., and Jo C. Phelan. 2005. "Fundamental Sources of Health Inequalities." In *Policy Challenges in Modern Health Care*, edited by David Mechanic, Lynn B. Rogut, and David C. Colby. Piscataway, NJ: Rutgers University Press.

Linteau, Paul-André. 2000. "Un Débat Historiographique: L'entrée du Québec Dans la Modernité et la Signification de la Révolution Tranquille." In *La Révolution*

Tranquille: 40 Ans Plus Tard: Un Bilan, edited by Yves Bélanger, Robert Comeau, and Céline Métivier. Montréal: VLB Éditeur.

Linteau, Paul-André, René Durocher, and Jean-Claude Robert. 1979. *Histoire du Québec Contemporain: De la Confédération à la Crise (1867–1929)*. Montréal: Boréal.

Linteau, Paul-André, René Durocher, and Jean-Claude Robert. 1986. *Histoire du Québec Contemporain: Le Québec Depuis 1930*. Montréal: Boréal.

Lipietz, Alain. 1987. *Mirages and Miracles: The Crisis in Global Fordism*, translated by David Macey. London: Verso.

Lipset, Seymour Martin, and Gary Marks. 2000. *It Didn't Happen Here: Why Socialism Failed in the United States*. New York: Norton.

Lipsky, Michael. 1980. *Street-level Bureaucracy*. New York: Basic Books.

LiPuma, Edward, and Benjamin Lee. 2004. *Financial Derivatives and the Globalization of Risk*. Durham, NC: Duke University Press.

Lizzeri, Alessandro, and Nicola Persico. 2004. "Why Did the Elites Extend the Suffrage? Democracy and the Scope of Government, with an Application to Britain's 'Age of Reform'." *The Quarterly Journal of Economics* 119 (2): 707–65.

Lock, Margaret, Vinh-Kim Nguyen, and Christina Zarowsky. 2006. "Global and Local Perspectives on Population Health." In *Healthier Societies: From Analysis to Action*, edited by Jody Heymann, Carl Hertzman, Morris Barer, and Robert G. Evans. New York: Oxford University Press.

Loff, Bebe. 2002. "No Agreement Reached in Talks on Access to Cheap Drugs." *The Lancet* 60 (9349): 1951.

Lovallo, William R. 1997. *Stress and Health: Biological and Physiological Introduction*. London: Sage.

Love, James. 2002. "Access to Medicines: Solving the Export Problem under TRIPs." *Bridges Year* 6 (4): 3.

Love, James. 2006. "Drug Development Incentives to Improve Access to Essential Medicines." *Bulletin of the World Health Organization* 84 (5): 371–5.

Low-Beer, Daniel, and Rand Stoneburner. 2004. "Uganda and the Challenge of HIV/AIDS." In *The Political Economy of AIDS in Africa*, edited by Nana K. Poku and Alan Whiteside. Hants, UK: Ashgate.

Luecken, Linda J., and Kathryn. S. Lemery. 2004. "Early Caregiving and Physiological Stress Responses." *Clinical Psychology Review* 24 (2): 171–91.

Luhtanen, Riia, and Jennifer Crocker. 1992. "A Collective Self-esteem Scale: Self-evaluation of One's Social Identity." *Personality and Social Psychology Bulletin* 18 (3) 302–18.

Lukes, Steven. 1975. "Political Ritual and Social Integration." *Sociology* 9 (2): 289–308.

Luttmer, Erzo. 2001. "Group Loyalty and the Taste for Redistribution." *Journal of Political Economy* 109 (3): 500–28.

Lynch, John W., Sam Harper, and George Davey Smith. 2003. "Commentary: Plugging Leaks and Repelling Boarders – Where to Next for the SS Income Inequality?" *International Journal of Epidemiology* 32: 1029–36.

Lynch, John W., George A. Kaplan, and Sarah J. Shema. 1997. "Cumulative Impact of Sustained Economic Hardship on Physical, Cognitive, Psychological, and Social Functioning." *New England Journal of Medicine* 337 (26): 1889–95.

Lynch, John W., George D. Smith, Sam Harper, Marianne Hillemeier, Nancy Ross, George A. Kaplan, and Michael Wolfson. 2004. "Is Income Inequality a

Determinant of Population Health? Part 1. A Systematic Review." *The Milbank Quarterly* 82: 1–77.

Mackenbach, Johan P. 2002. "Income Inequality and Population Health: Evidence Favouring a Negative Correlation between Income Inequality and Life Expectancy Has Disappeared." *British Medical Journal* 324: 1–2.

MacKinnon, David P., Chondra M. Lockwood, Jeanne M. Hoffman, Stephen G. West, and Virgil Sheets. 2002. "A Comparison of Methods to Test Mediation and Other Intervening Variable Effects." *Psychological Methods* 7 (1): 83–104.

MacLeod, Jay. 1987. *Ain't No Making It*. Boulder, CO: Westview.

Major, Brenda, and Laurie T. O'Brien. 2005. "The Psychology of Stigma." *Annual Review of Psychology* 56: 393–421.

Mamdani, Mahmood. 1996. *Citizen and Subject: Contemporary Africa and the Legacy of Late Colonialism*. Princeton, NJ: Princeton University Press.

Mandell, Ernst. 1980. *Long Waves of Capitalist Development*. New York: Cambridge University Press.

Mansbridge, Jane. 1999. "'You're Too Independent!': How Gender, Race, and Class Make Many Feminisms." In *The Cultural Territories of Race: Black and White Boundaries*, edited by Michèle Lamont. Chicago: University of Chicago Press.

Mansbridge, Jane, and Katherine Flaster. 2007. "The Cultural Politics of Everyday Discourse: The Case of 'Male Chauvinist.'" *Critical Sociology* 33: 627–60.

Marc, Alexandre. 2005. "Cultural Diversity and Service Delivery: Where Do We Stand?" Paper prepared for presentation to the World Bank Conference on "New Frontiers of Social Policy." Arusha, Tanzania (December 12–15, 2005).

March, James G., and Johan P. Olsen. 1989. *Rediscovering Institutions. The Organizational Basis of Politics*. New York: Free Press.

Marcuse, Herbert. 1991 [1964]. *One Dimensional Man: Studies in the Ideology of Advanced Industrial Society*. 2nd edition with a new Introduction by Douglas Kellner. Boston: Beacon Press.

Marmot, Michael G. 2004. *The Status Syndrome: How Social Standing Affects Our Health and Longevity*. New York: Times Books.

Marmot, Michael G., and Michael E.J. Wadsworth. 1997. "Fetal and Early Childhood Environment. Long Term Health Implications." *British Medical Bulletin* 53 (1).

Marmot, Michael, H. Bosma, H. Hemingway, E. Brunnere and S. Stansfeld. 1997. "Contribution of Job Control and Other Risk Factors to Social Variations in Coronary Heart Disease Incidence." *Lancet* 350: 235–9.

Marmot, Michael G., George Davey Smith, Stephen Stansfeld, Chandra Patel, Fiona North, Jenny Head, Ian White, Eric Brunner, and Amanda Feeney. 1991. "Health Inequalities among British Civil Servants: The Whitehall II Study." *Lancet* 337 (8754): 1387–93.

Marmot, Michael G., Carol D. Ryff, Larry L. Bumpass, Martin Shipley, and Nadine F. Marks. 1997. "Social Inequalities in Health: Next Questions and Converging Evidence." *Social Science and Medicine* 44 (6): 901–10.

Marshall, T.H. 1965[1949]. "Citizenship and Social Class." In *Class, Citizenship and Social Development*, edited by T.H. Marshall. New York: Anchor.

McAdam, Doug. 1982. *Political Process and the Development of Black Insurgency, 1930–1970*. Chicago: University of Chicago Press.

McAdam, Doug. 1988. *Freedom Summer*. New York and Oxford: Oxford University Press.

McAdam, Douglas, J.D. McCarthy, and Mayer N. Zald. 1996. *Comparative Perspectives on Social Movements*. New York: Cambridge University Press.

McAdam, Douglas, Sidney Tarrow, and Charles Tilly. 2001. *Dynamics of Contention*. New York: Cambridge University Press.

McDermott, Monica, and Frank L. Samson. 2005. "White Racial and Ethnic Identity in the United States." *Annual Review of Sociology* 31 (1): 245–61.

McEwen, Bruce S. 1998. "Protective and Damaging Effects of Stress Mediators." *New England Journal of Medicine* 338: 171–9.

McEwen, Bruce S. 2003. "Early Life Influence on Life-Long Patterns of Behavior and Health." *Mental Retardation and Developmental Disabilities Research Review* 9: 149–54.

McEwen, Bruce S. 2005. "Stressed or Stressed Out: What Is the Difference?" *Journal of Psychiatry Neuroscience* 30 (5): 315–18.

McIntyre, Sally. 1997. "The Black Report and Beyond. What Are the Issues?" *Social Science and Medicine* 44 (6): 723–45.

McKeown, Thomas. 1965. *Medicine in Modern Society*. London: Allen & Unwin.

McKeown, Thomas. 1976. *The Role of Medicine: Dream, Mirage, or Nemesis?* Oxford: Blackwell.

McKeown, Thomas. 1988. *The Origins of Human Disease*. Oxford: Blackwell.

McKeown, Thomas, and R.G. Brown. 1955. "Medical Evidence Related to English Population Changes in the Eighteenth Century." *Population Studies* 9 (2): 119–41.

McKeown, Thomas, R.G. Brown, and R.G. Record. 1972. "Interpretation of Modern Rise of Population in Europe." *Population Studies* 26 (3): 345–82.

McKeown, Thomas, R.G. Record, and R.D. Turner. 1975. "Interpretation of Decline of Mortality in England and Wales During 20th Century." *Population Studies* 29 (3): 391–422.

McLanahan, Sara. 2004. "Diverging Destinies: How Are Children Faring under the Second Demographic Transition?" *Demography* 41 (4): 607–27.

McLeod, Kari S. 2000. "Our Sense of Snow: The Myth of John Snow in Medical Geography." *Social Science and Medicine* 50 (7): 923–35.

McMichael, Philip. 2005. "Globalization." In *The Handbook of Political Sociology: States, Civil Societies, and Globalization*, edited by Thomas Janoski, Robert Alford, Alexander Hicks, and Mildred A. Schwartz. New York: Cambridge University Press.

Meaney, Michael J. 2001. "Maternal Care, Gene Expression, and the Transmission of Individual Differences in Stress Reactivity across Generations." *Annual Review of Neuroscience* 24: 1161–92.

Meldrum, Julian. 2002. "Scaling Up Antiretroviral Therapy: Learning from Botswana." *HA TIP, NAM Publications electronic newsletter (aidsmap.com)* #8.

Memmi, Albert. 1963. *Portrait du Colonisé*. Montréal: Éditions du Bas-Canada.

Mencher, Joan. 1980. "The Lessons and Non-lessons of Kerala." *Economic and Political Weekly* 15 (41–3): 1781–802.

Mercier, Michael E., and Christopher G. Boone. 2002. "Infant Mortality in Ottawa, Canada, 1901: Assessing Cultural, Economic and Environmental Factors." *Journal of Historical Geography* 28 (4): 486–507.

Mettler, Suzanne. 2002. "Bringing the State Back in to Civic Engagement: Policy Feedback Effects of the G.I. Bill for World War II Veterans." *American Political Science Review* 96: 351–65.

Meyer, John W. 1999. "The Changing Cultural Content of the Nation State: A World Society Perspective." In *State/Culture: State Formation after the Cultural Turn*, edited by George Steinmetz. Ithaca, NY: Cornell University Press.

Meyer, John W., John Boli, George M. Thomas, and Francisco O. Ramirez. 1997. "World Society and the Nation State." *American Journal of Sociology* 103 (1): 144–81.

Miguel, Edward. 2004. "Tribe or Nation? Nation-building and Public Goods in Kenya and Tanzania." *World Politics* 56 (3): 327–62.

Miguel, Edward, and Mary Kay Gugarty. 2005. "Ethnic Diversity, Social Sanctions, and Public Goods in Kenya." *Journal of Public Economics* 89 (11–12): 2325–68.

Milanovic, Branko. 2002. "The Ricardian Vice: Why Sala-i-Martin's Calculations Are Wrong." Typescript, Development Research Group, World Bank. November 2002. Available at SSRN: http://ssrn.com/abstract=403020.

Miles, Matthew B., and Michael Huberman. 1994. *Qualitative Data Analysis: An Expanded Sourcebook*. Thousand Oaks, CA: Sage Publications.

Miller, David. 1995. *On Nationality*. Oxford: Oxford University Press.

Miller, David. 2000. *Citizenship and National Identity*. Cambridge: Polity Press.

Miller, Peggy J., Heidi Fung, and Judith Mintz. 1996. "Self-Construction Through Narrative Practices: A Chinese and American Comparison of Early Socialization." *Ethos* 24 (2): 237–80.

Millward, Robert, and Sally Sheard. 1995. "The Urban Fiscal Problem, 1970–1914: Government Expenditures and Finance in England and Wales." *Economic History Review* 48 (3): 501–35.

Mishra, Vinod, Simona Bignami-Van Assche, Robert Greener, Martin Vaessen, Rathavuth Hong, Peter D. Ghys, J. Ties Boerma, Ari Van Assche, Shane Khan, and Shea Rutstein. 2007. "HIV Infection Does Not Disproportionately Affect the Poorer in Sub-Saharan Africa." *AIDS* 21 (suppl. 7): S17–S28.

Mokyr, Joel. 1983. *Why Ireland Starved: A Quantitative and Analytical History of the Irish Economy, 1800–1850*. London and Boston: Allen & Unwin.

Motseta, Sello. 2003. "Government Fight Against AIDS Sees Results in Botswana." *Associated Press*, May 6, 2003.

Murray, Michael. 2000. "Social Capital Formation and Healthy Communities: Insights from the Colorado Health Communities Initiative." *Community Development Journal* 35 (2): 99–108.

Navarro, Vincente, Carles Muntaner, Carme Borrell, Joan Benach, Agueda Quiroga, Maica Rodríguez-Sanz, Núria Vergés, and M. Isabel Pasarín. 2006. "Politics and Health Outcomes." *Lancet* 368 (9540): 1033–7.

Neighbors, H. W., and Jackson, J. S. 1996. *Mental Health in Black America*. Thousand Oaks, CA: Sage Publications.

Neighbors, Harold W., James S. Jackson, Clifford Broman, and Estina Thompson. 1996. "Racism and the Mental Health of African-Americans: The Role of Self and System Blame." *Ethnicity and Disease* 6: 167–75.

Nettle, Daniel. 2000. "Linguistic Fragmentation and the Wealth of Nations," *Economic Development and Cultural Change* 48 (2): 335–48.

Nguyen, Vinh-Kim, and Karine Peschard. 2003. "Anthropology, Inequality, and Disease: A Review." *Annual Review of Anthropology* 32: 447–74.

Noh, S., M. Beiser, V. Kaspar, F. Hou, and J. Rummens. 1999. "Perceived Racial Discrimination, Depression, and Coping: A Study of Southeast Asian Refugees in Canada." *Journal of Health and Social Behavior* 40 (3): 193–207.

North, Douglass. 1981. *Structure and Change in Economic History.* New York: Norton.

North, Douglass. 1990. *Institutions, Institutional Change, and Economic Performance.* Cambridge: Cambridge University Press.

North, Douglass. 1997 [1993]. "Economic Performance through Time." In *Nobel Lectures, Economics 1991–1995,* edited by T. Persson. Singapore: World Scientific Publishing Company.

Novick, Peter. 1999. *The Holocaust in American Life.* New York: Houghton Mifflin.

Nussbaum, Martha. 2001. *Women and Human Development: The Capabilities Approach.* Cambridge: Cambridge University Press.

Nyago, Kintu. 2003. "How to Use Bush's Cash." *The Monitor,* Kampala, Uganda, July 15, 2003.

Ó Gráda, Cormac. 1988. *Ireland before and after the Famine: Explorations in Economic History, 1800–1925.* New York: St. Martin's Press.

O'Rourke, Dara. 2002. "Community-Driven Regulation: Towards an Improved Model of Environmental Regulation in Vietnam." In *Livable Cities: The Politics of Urban Livelihood and Sustainability,* edited by Peter Evans. Berkeley: University of California Press.

O'Rourke, Dara. 2004. *Community-Driven Regulation: Balancing Development and the Environment in Vietnam.* Cambridge, MA: MIT Press.

Oakley, Ann, and Lynda Rajan. 1991. "Social Class and Social Support: The Same or Different?" *Sociology* 25: 31–59.

Obbo, Christine. 1995. "Gender, Age and Class: Discourses on HIV Transmission and Control in Uganda." In *Culture and Sexual Risk: Anthropological Perspectives on AIDS,* edited by Hanten Brummelhuis and Gilbert Herdt. Amsterdam: Gordon and Breach Publishers.

Offe, Claus. 1999. "How Can We Trust Our Fellow Citizens?" In *Democracy and Trust,* edited by Mark E. Warren. New York: Cambridge University Press.

Offe, Claus. 2006. "Social Protection in a Supranational Context: European Integration and the Fates of the "European Social Model." In *Globalization and Egalitarian Redistribution,* edited by Pranab Bardhan, Samuel Bowles, and Michael Wallerstein. New York: Sage.

Okware, Sam, Alex Opio, Joshua Musinguzi, and Paul Waibale. 2001. "Fighting HIV/ AIDS: Is Success Possible?" *Bulletin of the World Health Organization* 79 (12): 1113–20.

Ollivier, Michèle. 2000. "Too Much Money Off Other People's Backs." Status in Late Modern Societies. *Canadian Journal of Sociology* 25(4): 441–70.

Olson, Mancur. 1965. *The Logic of Collective Action: Public Goods and the Theory of Groups.* Cambridge, MA: Harvard University Press.

Olson, Sherry, and Patricia Thornton. 2001. "La Croissance Naturelle des Montréalais au XIXe Siècle." *Cahiers Québécois de Démographie* 30 (2): 191–230.

Osler, Merete, Eva Prescott, Morten Gronbaek, Ulla Christensen, Pernille Due, and Gerda Engholm. 2002. "Income Inequality, Individual Income and Mortality in Danish Adults: Analysis of Pooled Data from Two Cohort Studies." *British Medical Journal* 324 (7328): 13–16.

Oyserman, Daphna, and Hazel R. Markus. 1990. "Possible Selves and Delinquency." *Journal of Personality and Social Psychology* 59 (1): 112–25.

Oyserman, Daphna, and Janet K. Swim. 2001. "Social Stigma: An Insider's View." *Journal of Social Issues* 57 (1): 1–14.

Oyserman, Daphna, Deborah Bybee, and Kathy Terry. 2006. "Possible Selves and Academic Outcomes: How and When Possible Selves Impel Action," *Journal of Personality and Social Psychology* 91 (1): 188–204.

Oyserman, Daphna, H. M. Coon, and M. Kemelmeier. 2002. "Rethinking the Individualism and Collectivism: Evaluation of Theoretical Assumptions and Meta-Analyses." *Psychological Bulletin* 128: 3–73.

Oyserman, D., M. Kemmelmeier, S. Fryberg H. Brosh, and T. Hart-Johnson. 2003. "Racial-Ethnic Self-Schemas." *Social Psychology Quarterly* 66: 333–47.

Padgett, John F. 1993. "Robust Action and the Rise of the Medici: 1400–1434." *American Sociological Review* 98 (6): 1259–319.

Papillon, Martin, and Luc Turgeon. 2003. "Nationalism's Third Way? Comparing the Emergence of Citizenship Regimes in Quebec and Scotland." In *The Conditions of Diversity in Multinational Democracies*, edited by Alain-G. Gagnon, Montserrat Guibernau, and François Rocher. Montreal: IRPP.

Parekh, Bhikhu. 2004. "Redistribution or Recognition? A Misguided Debate." In *Ethnicity, Nationalism and Minority Rights*, edited by Stephen May. Cambridge: Cambridge University Press.

Parsons, Neil. 1998. *King Khama, Emperor Joe, and the Great White Queen: Victorian Britain through African Eyes.* Chicago: University of Chicago Press.

Pattillo, Mary. 2005. "Black Middle-Class Neighborhoods." *Annual Review of Sociology* 31: 305–29.

Pearce, Nick. 2004. "Diversity versus Solidarity: A New Progressive Dilemma." *Renewal: A Journal of Labour Politics* 12 (3).

Pearlin, L.I.. and C. Schooler. 1978. "The Structure of Coping." *Journal of Health and Social Behavior* 19: 2–21.

Pedersen, Susan. 2005. "Anti-Condescensionism." *London Review of Books,* 1 September 2005. On-line edition, http://www.lrb.co.uk/v27/n17/pede01_.html.

Phillipson, Chris, Graham Allan, and David H.J. Morgan, eds. 2004. *Social Networks and Social Exclusion: Sociological and Policy Perspectives.* London: Ashgate.

Pierson, Paul. 1994. *Dismantling the Welfare State: Reagan, Thatcher, and the Politics of Retrenchment.* Cambridge: Cambridge University Press.

Pierson, Paul. 2003. "Big, Slow-moving, and ... Invisible: Macrosocial Processes in the Study of Comparative Politics." In *Comparative Historical Analysis in the Social Sciences*, edited by James Mahoney and Dietrich Reuschemeyer. Cambridge: Cambridge University Press.

Pierson, Paul. 2004. *Politics in Time: History, Institutions, and Social Analysis.* Princeton, NJ: Princeton University Press.

Pihl, Robert O., and Chawki Benkelfat. 2005. "Neuromodulators in the Development and Expression of Inhibition and Aggression." In *Developmental Origins of Aggression*, edited by Richard E. Tremblay, Willard W. Hartup, and John Archer. New York: The Guilford Press.

Pinel, Elizabeth C. 1999. "Stigma Consciousness: The Psychological Legacy of Social Stereotypes." *Journal of Personality and Social Psychology* 76 (1): 114–28.

Pinker, Stephen. 2002. *The Blank Slate: The Modern Denial of Human Nature.* New York: Viking.

Plotnick, Robert, and Richard Winters. 1985. "A Politico-economic Theory of Income Redistribution." *American Political Science Review* 79 (2): 458–73.

Poku, Nana K., Alan Whiteside, and Bjorg Sandkjaer. 2007. *AIDS and Governance.* Hamphsire, England, and Burlington, VT: Ashgate Publishing.

Policy Research Institute. 2005. *Social Capital as a Public Policy Tool: Project Report.* Government of Canada.

Polletta, Francesca. 2002. *Freedom Is an Endless Meeting: Democracy in American Social Movements.* Chicago: The University of Chicago Press.

Polletta, Francesca, and James M. Jasper. 2001. "Collective Identity and Social Movements." *Annual Review of Sociology* 27: 283–305.

Porter, Dorothy. 1999. *Health, Civilization and the State: A History of Public Health from Ancient to Modern Times.* London: Routledge.

Porter, John. 1965. *The Vertical Mosaic: An Analysis of Social Class and Power in Canada.* Toronto: University of Toronto Press.

Potts, Malcom, Daniel T. Halperin, Douglas Kirby, Ann Swidler, Elliot Marseille, Jeffrey D. Klausner, Norman Hearst, Richard G. Wamai, James G. Kahn, and Julia Walsh. 2008. "Reassessing HIV Prevention." *Science* 320 (5877): 749–50.

Potvin, Maryse. 1999. "Les Dérapages Racistes à l'égard du Québec au Canada Anglais Depuis 1995." *Politique et Sociétés* 18 (2): 101–32.

Power, Chris, and Clyde Hertzman. 1997. "Social and Biological Pathways Linking Early Life and Adult Disease." *British Medical Bulletin* 53 (1): 210–21.

Power, Chris, Orly Manor, and John Fox. 1991. *Health and Class: The Early Years.* London: Chapman & Hall.

Pritchett, Lance, and Lawrence H. Summers. 1996. "Wealthier Is Healthier." *Journal of Human Resources* 31 (4): 841–68.

Putnam, Robert D. 1993. *Making Democracy Work: Civic Traditions in Modern Italy*, with Robert Leonardi, and Raffaella Y. Nanetti. Princeton, NJ: Princeton University Press.

Putnam, Robert D. 2000. *Bowling Alone: The Collapse and Revival of American Community.* New York: Simon and Schuster.

Putnam, Robert. 2007. "E Pluribus Unum? Diversity and Community in the 21st Century." *Scandinavian Political Studies* 30 (2): 137–74.

Putzel, James. 2004. "The Politics of Action on AIDS: A Case Study of Uganda." *Public Administration and Development* 24 (1): 19–30.

Pyszczynski, Tom, Jeff Greenberg, Sheldon Solomon, and Jamie Arndt. 2004. "Why Do People Need Self-Esteem? A Theoretical and Empirical Review." *Psychological Bulletin* 130 (3): 435–88.

Ramiah, Ilavenil, and Michael R. Reich. 2005. "Public-Private Partnerships and Antiretroviral Drugs for HIV/AIDS: Lessons from Botswana." *Health Affairs* 24 (2): 545–51.

Reich, Robert B. 1992. *The Work of Nations: Preparing Ourselves for Twenty-First-Century Capitalism.* New York: Vintage Books.

Reidpath, Daniel.D., Kit Y. Chan, Sandra M. Gifford, and Pascale Allotey. 2005. "'He Hath the French Pox': Stigma, Social Value, and Social Exclusion." *Sociology of Health and Illness* 27 (4): 448–67.

Resource Flows Project. 2004. "Financial Resource Flows for Population – Activities in 2002 – Summary." United Nations Population Fund (UNFPA), Joint United Nations Programme on HIV/AIDS (UNAIDS), and Netherlands Interdisciplinary Demographic Institute (NIDI).

Rice, Andrew. 2006. "Made Man." *New Republic* 234 (7): 12–14.

Rilling, James K. 2006. "Human and Nonhuman Primate Brains: Are They Allometrically Scaled Versions of the Same Design?" *Evolutionary Anthropology* 15 (2): 65–77.

Robinson, Solveig. 2006. "Review of Bodily Matters. The Anti-Vaccination Movement in England, 1853–1907." *Perspectives in Biology and Medicine* 49 (3): 471–3.

Rodgers, Gregory B. 1979. "Income and Inequality as Determinants of Mortality: An International Cross-section Analysis." *Population Studies* 3 (2): 343–51.

Rodgers, Gregory B. 2002. "Income and Inequality as Determinants of Mortality: An International Cross-section Analysis. 1979." *International Journal of Epidemiology* 31 (3): 533–8.

Rodrik, Dani. 1999. "Institutions for High-Quality Growth: What Are They and How to Acquire Them." Paper presented at IMF conference on Second-Generation Reforms. Washington, DC (November 8–9, 1999).

Rodrik, Dani. 2002. "Feasible Globalizations." Unpublished paper. Harvard University, Cambridge, MA.

Rodrik, Dani, Arvind Subramanian, and Francesco Trebbi. 2004. "Institutions Rule: The Primacy of Institutions over Geography and Integration in Economic Development." *Journal of Economic Growth* 9 (2): 131–65.

Rohrer, Tim. 2001. "Pragmatism, Ideology and Embodiment: William James and the Philosophical Foundations of Cognitive Linguistics." In *Language and Ideology: Cognitive Theoretical Approaches*, edited by Ersa Sandriklogou and René Dirven. Amsterdam: John Benjamins.

Rorty, Richard. 2000. "Is 'Cultural Recognition' a Useful Concept for Leftist Politics?" *Critical Horizons* 1 (1): 7–20.

Rose, Geoffrey. 1992. *The Strategy of Preventive Medicine*. Oxford: Oxford University Press.

Rose, Richard. 1995. "Russia as an Hour-glass Society: A Constitution without Citizens," *East European Constitutional Review* 14 (3): 34–42.

Rosenberg, Tina. 2001. "Look at Brazil." *New York Times Magazine*, January 28, 2001, p. 30.

Ross, Kristin. 2002. *May '68 and Its Afterlives*. Chicago: University of Chicago Press.

Ross, Nancy A., Danny Dorling, James R. Dunn, Goran Henriksson, John Glover, John Lynch, and Gunilla Weitoft. 2005. "Metropolitan Income Inequality and Working-age Mortality: A Cross-sectional Analysis Using Comparable Data from Five Counties." *Journal of Urban Health* 82 (1): 101–10.

Ross, Nancy A., Michael C. Wolfson, James R. Dunn, Jean-Marie Berthelot, George A. Kaplan, and John W. Lynch. 2000. "Relation between Income Inequality and Mortality in Canada and in the United States: Cross-sectional Assessment Using Census Data and Vital Statistics." *British Medical Journal* 320 (7239): 898–902.

Ross, Nancy A., Michael Wolfson, George A. Kaplan, James R. Dunn, John Lynch, and Claudia Sanmartin. 2006. "Income Inequality as a Determinant of Health." In *Healthier Societies: From Analysis to Action*, edited by Jody Heymann, Clyde Hertzman, Morris L. Barer, and Robert G. Evans. New York: Oxford University Press.

Rothstein, Bo. 2003. "Social Capital, Economic Growth and Quality of Government: The Causal Mechanism." *New Political Economy* 8(1): 49–71.

Rothstein, Bo. 2005. *Social Traps and the Problem of Trust*. New York: Cambridge University Press.

Rothstein, Bo, and Dietlind Stolle. 2005. "How Political Institutions Create and Destroy Social Capital: An Institutional Theory of Generalized Trust". Paper presented at the meeting of the Successful Societies Program, Canadian Institute for Advanced Research, Vancouver (January 20–22, 2005).

Rothstein, Bo and Eric M. Uslaner. 2004. "All for All: Equality and Social Trust". Center for European Studies working paper no. 117. Cambridge, MA: Harvard University.

Rubenstein, W. D. 1983. "The End of 'Old Corruption' in Britain 1780–1860." *Past and Present* 101 (1): 55–86.

Rudin, Ronald. 1997. *Making History in Twentieth-Century Québec.* Toronto: University of Toronto Press.

Runciman, W. G. 1964. *Relative Deprivation and Social Justice.* Harmondsworth: Penguin.

Sachs, Jeffrey D., and Andrew M. Warner. 2001. "Natural Resources and Economic Development: The Curse of Natural Resources." *European Economic Review* 45 (4–6): 827–38.

Sala-i-Martin, Xavier. 2002. "The World Distribution of Income (Estimated from Individual Country Distributions)." National Bureau of Economic Research working paper 8933. Cambridge, MA: National Bureau of Economic Research.

Salter, Frank Kemp. 2004. *Welfare, Ethnicity and Altruism: New Findings and Evolutionary Theory.* London: Frank Cass.

Sampson, Robert J., Stephen W. Raudenbush, and Felton Earls. 1997. "Neighborhoods and Violent Crime: A Multilevel Study of Collective Efficacy." *Science* 277 (5328): 918–24. doi: 10.1126/science.277.5328.918.

Sampson, Robert J., Jeffrey D. Morenoff, and Thomas Gannon-Rowley. 2002. "Assessing Neighborhood Effects: Social Processes and New Directions in Research." *Annual Review of Sociology* 28: 443–78.

Sapolsky, Robert M. 2005. "The Influence of Social Hierarchy on Primate Health." *Science* 308 (5722): 648–52.

Sapolsky, R. M., and L. J. Share. 1994. "Rank-Related Differences in Cardiovascular Function among Wild Baboons: Role of Sensitivity to Glucocorticoids." *American Journal of Primateology* 32: 261–75.

Sapolksy, R. M., S. C. Alberts, and J. Altmann. 1997. "Hypercortisolism Associated with Social Subordinance or Social Isolation among Wild Baboons." *Archives of General Psychiatry.* 54 (12): 1137–43.

Sargent, Judy T., Jennifer Crocker, and Riia K. Luhtanen. 2006. "Contingencies of Self-worth and Depressive Symptoms in College Students." *Journal of Social and Clinical Psychology* 25 (6): 628–46.

Sayer, Andrew. 2005. *The Moral Significance of Class.* New York: Cambridge University Press.

Schelling, Thomas. 1978. *Micromotives and Macrobehavior.* New York: Norton.

Schlinger, Henry D. 2002. "Not So Fast, Mr. Pinker: A Behaviorist Looks at the Blank Slate. A Review of Steven Pinker's The Blank Slate: The Modern Denial of Human Nature." *Behavior and Social Issues* 12 (1): 75–79.

Schnittker, Jason. 2004. "Education and the Changing Shape of the Income Gradient in Health." *Journal of Health and Social Behavior* 45 (3): 286–305.

Schnittker, Jason, and Jane D. McLeod. 2005. "The Social Psychology of Health Disparaties." *Annual Review of Sociology* 31: 75–103.

Schoon, Ingrid. 2006. *Risk and Reslience: Adaptations in Changing Times.* Cambridge: Cambridge University Press.

Schor, Juliet. 1991. *The Overworked American: The Unexpected Decline of Leisure.* New York: Basic Books.

Schudson, Michael. 1989. "How Culture Works." *Theory and Society* 18: 153–80.

Scott, James. 1990. *Domination and the Arts of Resistance: Hidden Transcripts*. New Haven, CT: Yale University Press.

Schweder, Richard, Martha L. Minow, and Hazel Markus. 2002. *Engaging in Cultural Differences*. New York: Russell Sage Foundation.

Selle, Per. 1999. "The Transformation of the Voluntary Sector in Norway: A Decline in Social Capital?" In *Social Capital and European Democracy*, edited by Jan W. Van Deth, Marco Maraffi, Kenneth Newton, and Paul F. Whiteley. London: Routledge.

Sellers, Robert M., Tabbye M. Chavous, and Deanna Y. Cooke. 2003. "Racial Ideology and Racial Centrality as Predictors of African American College Students' Academic Performance." *Journal of Black Psychology* 24 (1): 8–27.

Seloilwe, E., A. Jack, K. Letshabo, K. Bainame, D. Veskov, M. Mokoto, M. Kobue, and R. Muzila. 2001. "HIV/AIDS at the University of Botswana: Behavioural and Prevention Issues." *Pula: Botswana Journal of African Studies* 15 (2): 204–10.

Sen, Amartya. 1981. *Poverty and Famines: An Essay on Entitlement and Deprivation*. Oxford: Oxford University Press.

Sen, Amartya. 1983. "Poor, Relatively Speaking." *Oxford Economic Papers*. 35 (2): 153–69.

Sen, Amartya. 1999. *Development as Freedom*. New York: Alfred A. Knopf.

Setel, Philip. 1999. *A Plague of Paradoxes: AIDS, Culture and Demography in Northern Tanzania*. Chicago: University of Chicago Press.

Sewell, William H., Jr. 2005. *Logics of History: Social Theory and Social Transformation*. Chicago: University of Chicago Press.

Sewell, William H., Jr. 2008. "The Temporalities of Capitalism." *Socio-Economic Review* 6 (3): 517–37.

Sharma, Aradhana. 2006. "Crossbreeding Institutions, Breeding Struggle: Women's Empowerment, Neoliberal Governmentality, and State (re)Formation in India." *Cultural Anthropology* 21 (1): 60–95.

Shea, John J. 2003. "Neandertals, Competition, and the Origin of Modern Human Behavior in the Levant." *Evolutionary Anthropology* 12: 173–87.

Shelton, James D., Michael M. Cassell, and Jacob Adetunji. 2005. "Is Poverty or Wealth at the Root of HIV?" *Lancet* 366 (9491): 1057–8.

Sherry, David F. 2006. "Neuroecology." *Annual Review of Psychology* 57 (1): 167–97.

Shibuya, Kenji, Hideki Hashimoto, and Eiji Yano. 2002. "Individual Income, Income Distribution, and Self Rated Health in Japan: Cross-sectional Analysis of Nationally Representative Sample." *British Medical Journal* 324 (7328): 16–19.

Shih, Margaret, Todd Pittinsky, and Nalini Ambady. 2002. "Stereotype Susceptibility: Identity Salience and Shifts in Quantitative Performance," *Psychological Science* 10 (1): 80–3.

Shively, C. A., and T. B. Clarkson. 1994. "Social Status and Coronary Artery Atherosclerosis in Female Monkeys." *Arteriosclerosis and Thrombosis* 14: 721–6.

Shively, C. A., K. Laer-Laird, and R. F. Anton. 1997. "Behavior and Physiology of Social Stress and Depression in Female Cynomolgus Monkeys." *Biological Psychiatry* 41: 871–82.

Sidanius, Jim, Felicia Pratto, Colette van Laar, and Shana Levin. 2004. "Social Dominance Theory: Its Agenda and Method." *Political Psychology* 25 (6): 845–80.

Sieber, S. 1974. "Toward a Theory of Role Accumulation," *American Sociological Review* 39: 567–78.

Silbey, Susan S., and Patricia Ewick. 2003. "Narrating Social Structure: Stories of Resistance to Legal Authority." *American Journal of Sociology* 108 (6): 1328–72.

Silverman, Bertram, and Murry Yanowitch. 2000. *New Rich, New Poor, New Russia: Winners and Losers on the Russian Road to Capitalism*, expanded edition. Armonk, NY: M. E. Sharpe.

Singh, Gopal K., and Mohammad Siahpush. 2002. Increasing Inequalities in All-cause and Cardiovascular Mortality among US Adults Aged 25–64 Years by Area Socioeconomic Status, 1969–1998. *International Journal of Epidemiology* 31 (3): 600–13.

Singh-Manoux, A., M. G. Marmot, and N. E. Adler. 2005. "Does Subjective Social Status Predict Health and Change in Health Status Better than Objective Status?" *Psychosomatic Medicine* 67: 855–61.

Skeggs, Beverley. 1997. *Formations of Class and Gender: Becoming Respectable.* Thousand Oaks, CA: Sage.

Skocpol, Theda, and Morris P. Fiornia, eds. 1999. *Civic Engagement in American Life.* Washington, DC: Brookings Institution.

Small, Mario. 2004. *Villa Victoria: The Transformation of Social Capital in a Boston Barrio.* Chicago: University of Chicago Press.

Smedley, Brian D., S. Leonard Syme, and Committee on Capitalizing on Social Science, and Behavioral Research to Improve the Public's Health. 2001. "Promoting Health: Intervention Strategies from Social and Behavioral Research." *American Journal of Health Promotions* 15 (3): 149–66.

Smeeding, Timothy M., and Katherine Ross. 1999. "Social Protection for the Poor in the Developed World: The Evidence from LIS." Luxembourg Income Study working paper 204. Luxembourg: Luxembourg Income Study.

Smelser, Neil, and Richard Swedberg. 1994. *Handbook of Economic Sociology.* Princeton, NJ: Princeton University Press.

Smith, Kristen P., and Nicholas A. Christakis. 2008. "Health and Social Networks," *Annual Review of Sociology* 24: 405–29.

Smith, Robert C., and Richard Seltzer. 1992. *Race, Class, and Culture: A Study in Afro-American Mass Opinion.* New York: State University of New York Press.

Smith, Steven R., and Michael Lipsky. 1993. *Nonprofits for Hire: The Welfare State in the Age of Contracting.* Cambridge, MA: Harvard University Press.

Smith, Tom W. 2005. *Troubles in America: A Study of Negative Life Events Across Time and Sub-groups.* Chicago: National Opinion Research Center.

Snibbe, Alana Conner, and Hazel Rose Markus. 2005. "You Can't Always Get What You Want: Educational Attainment, Agency, and Choice." *Journal of Personality and Social Psychology* 88 (4): 703–20.

Snow, David A., Sarah A. Soule, and Hanspeter Kriesi, eds. 2004. *The Blackwell Companion to Social Movements.* Malden, MA: Blackwell Publishing.

Son Hing, Leanne S., Winnie Li, and Mark P. Zanna. 2002. "Inducing Hypocrisy to Reduce Prejudicial Responses among Aversive Racists." *Journal of Experimental Social Psychology.* 38: 71–8.

Sontag, Susan. 1978. *Illness as Metaphor.* New York: Farrar, Straus and Giroux.

Soroka, Stuart, Keith Banting, and Richard Johnston. 2006. "Immigration and Redistribution in the Global Era." In *Globalization and Social Redistribution*, edited by Pranab Bardham, Samuel Bowles, and Michael Wallerstein. Princeton, NJ: Princeton University Press.

Soroka, Stuart, Richard Johnston, and Keith Banting. 2004. "Ethnicity, Trust and the Welfare State." In *Cultural Diversity versus Economic Solidarity*, edited by Philippe Van Parijs. Brussels: Editions De Boeck Université.

Soss, Joe. 1999. "Lessons of Welfare: Policy Design, Political Learning and Political Action." *American Political Science Review* 93: 363–80.

Soss, Joe. 2008. "Making Clients and Citizens: Welfare Policy as a Source of Status, Belief, and Action." In *Deserving and Entitled: Social Constructions and Public Policy*, edited by Anne Schneider and Helen Ingram. New York: State University of New York Press.

Soss, Joe, Sanford Schram, and Richard Fording. 2003. *Race and the Politics of Welfare Reform*. Ann Arbor: University of Michigan Press.

Soss, Joe, Sanford Schram, Thomas Vartanian, and Erin O'Brien. 2001. "Setting the Terms of Relief: Explaining State Policy Choices in the Devolution Revolution." *American Journal of Political Science* 45 (2): 378–95.

Soysal, Yasemin Nuhoglu. 1994. *Limits of Citizenship: Migrants and Postnational Membership in Europe*. Chicago: University of Chicago Press.

Statistics Canada and Organization for Economic Cooperation, and Development. 1995. *Literacy, Economy and Society*. Paris: OECD.

Steele, Claude M. 1988. "The Psychology of Self-Affirmation: Sustaining the Integrity of the Self." *Advances in Experimental Social Psychology, Vol. 21: Social Psychological Studies of the Self: Perspectives and Programs*. San Diego: Academic Press.

Steele, Claude M. 1999. "Thin Ice: 'Stereotype Threat' and Black College Students." *The Atlantic Monthly* 284 (2): 44–7; 50–4.

Steele, Claude M., and Joshua Aronson. 1998. "Stereotype Threat and the Test Performance of Academically Successful African Americans." In *The Black-White Test Score Gap*, edited by Christopher Jencks and Meredith Phillips. Washington, DC: The Brookings Institution Press.

Steele, Claude, and Jennifer Crocker. 1998. "Social Stigma." In *Handbook of Social Psychology*, edited by Daniel T. Gilbert, Susan. T. Fiske, and Gardener Lindzey. Boston: McGraw-Hill.

Steensland, Brian. 2006. "Cultural Categories and the American Welfare State: the Case of the Guaranteed Income Policy." *American Journal of Sociology* 111 (5): 1273–326.

Steinberg, Lawrence, Ronald Dahl, Daniel P. Keating, David Kupfer, Anne Masten, and Daniel Pine. 2006. "Adolescent Psychopathology." In *Handbook of Developmental Psychopathology*. New York: Wiley & Sons.

Steinmetz, George. 2005. *The Politics of Method in the Human Sciences: Positivism and Its Epistemological Others*. Durham, NC: Duke University Press.

Stephens, John. 1979. *The Transformation from Capitalism to Socialism*. Urbana: University of Illinois Press.

Stewart, Frances, and Severine Deneulin. 2002. "Amartya Sen's Contribution to Development Thinking." *Studies in Comparative International Development* 37 (2): 61–70.

Stiglitz, Joseph E. 2002. *Globalization and Its Discontents*. New York: Norton.

Stolle, Dietlind and Marc Hooghe, eds. 2003. *Generating Social Capital: Civil Society and Institutions in Comparative Perspective*. New York: Palgrave Macmillan.

Stolley, Paul, Thomas LaViest, and Nancy Krieger. 2004. "A Debate on Race, Racism, Health, and Epidemiology." In *Political and Economic Determinants of Population Health and Well-Being: Controversies and Developments*, edited by Vincente Navarro and Carles Muntaner. Amityville, NY: Baywood Publishing.

Stone, Lawrence. 1972. *Causes of the English Revolution* New York: Harper.

Stoneburner, Rand, and Daniel Low-Beer. 2004. "Population-level HIV Declines and Behavioral Risk Avoidance in Uganda." *Science* 304 (5671): 714–18.

Subramanian, S. V., Daniel Kim, and Ichiro Kawachi. 2002. "Social Trust and Self-rated Health in US Communities: A Multi-level Analysis." *Journal of Urban Health* 79 (Suppl. 1): S21–S34.

Suomi, Stephen J. 1999. "Developmental Trajectories, Early Experiences, and Community Consequences." In *Developmental Health and the Wealth of Nations*, edited by Daniel P. Keating and Clyde Hertzman. New York: The Guilford Press.

Suomi, Stephen J. 2000. "A Biobehavioral Perspective on Development Psychopathology." In *Handbook of Developmental Psychopathology, 2nd ed.*, edited by Arnold Sameroff, Michael Lewis, and Suzanne Miller. New York: Kluwer Academic/Plenum Publishers.

Susser, Mervyn. 2000. "Editorial: The Technological Paradox of Health Inequality, and a Probe with a Practical Tool." *Journal of Epidemiology and Community Health* 54 (12): 882–3.

Svensson, Lennart, and Casten Von Otter. 2002. "Strategies for Regional Regeneration: Learning from the Bergslagen Regional Research Center." *Economic and Industrial Democracy* 23 (2): 421–39.

Swank, Duane. 2002. *Global Capital, Political Institutions, and Policy Change in Developed Welfare States.* Cambridge: Cambridge University Press.

Swidler, Ann. 1986. "Culture in Action: Symbols and Strategies." *American Sociological Review* 51 (2): 273–86.

Swidler, Ann, and Susan Cotts Watkins. 2007. "Ties of Dependence: AIDS and Transactional Sex in Rural Malawi." *Studies in Family Planning* 38 (3): 147–62.

Synergy Project. 2002a. *What Happened in Uganda? Declining HIV Prevalence, Behavior Change, and the National Response.* Washington, DC: Synergy project with support from the Office of HIV/AIDS, Bureau of Global Health, U.S. Agency for International Development.

Synergy Project. 2002b. "Country Summaries, HIV/AIDS in Uganda: A USAID Brief." TvT Associates under The Synergy Project, www.synergyaids.com/documents/Uganda_brief_rev_1a.pdf (July).

Szanton Sarah L., Jessica M. Gill, and Jerilyn K. Allen. 2005. "Allostatic Load: A Mechanism of Socioeconomic Health Disparities?" *Biological Research for Nursing* 7 (1): 7–15.

Szreter, Simon. 1997. "Economic Growth, Disruption, Deprivation, Disease, and Death: On the Importance of the Politics of Public Health for Development." *Population and Development Review* 23 (4): 693–728.

Szreter, Simon. 1999. "Rapid Economic Growth and 'The Four Ds' of Disruption, Deprivation, Disease and Death: Public Health Lessons from Nineteenth Century Britain for Twenty-first-century China?' *Tropical Medicine and International Health* 4 (2): 146–52.

Szreter, Simon. 2002. "Re-thinking McKeown: The Relationship Between Public Health and Social Change." *American Journal of Public Health* 92 (5): 722–5.

Sztompka, Piotr. 1999. *Trust: A Sociological Theory.* New York: Cambridge University Press.

Tajfel, Henry 1981. "Social Stereotypes and Social Groups." In *Intergroup Behaviour*, edited by John C. Turner and Howard Giles. Oxford: Blackwell.

Tanner, Andrea. 1999. "Scarlatina and Sewer Smells: Metropolitan Public Health Records 1855–1920." *Hygiea Internationalis* 1 (1): 37–48.

Tarrow, Sidney. 1989. *Democracy and Disorder: Protest and Politics in Italy, 1965–1975*. New York: Oxford University Press.

Tarrow, Sidney. 1996. "Making Social Science Work Across Time and Space: A Reflection on Robert Putnam's Making Democracy Work." *American Political Science Review* 90 (2): 389–97.

Tarrow, Sidney. 2005. *The New Transnational Activism*. Cambridge: Cambridge University Press.

Tavory, Iddo, and Ann Swidler. 2009. "Condom Semiotics: Meaning and Condom Use in Rural Malawi." *American Sociological Review* 74 (2): 171–89.

Taylor, Charles. 1993. *Multiculturalism and the Politics of Recognition*. Princeton, NJ: Princeton University Press.

Taylor, Charles. 1994. *Reconciling the Solitudes: Essays on Canadian Federalism and Nationalism*, edited by Guy Laforest. Montreal: McGill-Queen's University Press.

Taylor, Charles. 2002. "Modern Social Imaginaries" *Public Culture* 14 (1): 91–124.

Taylor, Miles. 1992. "John Bull and the Iconography of Public Opinion in England c. 1712–1929." *Past and Present* 134: 93–128.

Taylor, Rosemary CR. 1982. "The Politics of Prevention." *Social Policy* (13) 1: 32–41.

Taylor, Rosemary CR. 2004. "What's Culture Got To Do With It? Public Health and 'Foreign Bodies'." Paper presented to the Institute for Advanced Study (Wissenschaftskolleg), Berlin (June).

Taylor, Shelley E., Rena L. Repetti, and Teresa Seeman. 1999. "What Is an Unhealthy Environment and How Does It Get under the Skin." In *The Society and Population Health Reader: Income Inequality and Health*, edited by Ichiro Kawachi, Bruce P. Kennedy, and Richard G. Wilkinson. New York: The New Press. pp. 351–78.

Taylor-Gooby, Peter. 2005. "Is the Future American? Or, Can Left Politics Preserve European Welfare States from Erosion through Growing 'Racial' Diversity?" *Journal of Social Policy* 34 (4): 661–72.

Tendler, Judith. 1997. *Good Government in the Tropics*. Baltimore: Johns Hopkins University Press.

Tendler, Judith, and Sara Freedheim. 1994. "Trust in a Rent-seeking World: Health and Government Transformed in Northeast Brazil." *World Development* 22 (12): 1771–91.

Tétreault, Martin. 1991. *L'état de santé des Montréalais: 1880–1914*. Montréal: Regroupement des chercheurs-chercheures en histoire des travailleurs-travailleuses du Québec.

Tharamangalam, Joseph. 1998. "The Perils of Development without Economic Growth: The Development Debacle of Kerala, India." *Bulletin of Concerned Asian Scholars* 30: 23–34.

Thelen, Kathleen. 2004. *How Institutions Evolve: The Political Economy of Skills in Germany, Britain, the United States and Japan*. New York: Cambridge University Press.

Thelen, Kathleen, and Sven Steimo. 1992. "Introduction." In *Structuring Politics: Historical Institutionalism in Comparative Perspective*, edited by Sven Steinmo, Kathleen Thelen, and Frank Longstreth. Cambridge: Cambridge University Press.

Thoits, P. 1983. "Multiple Identities and Psychological Well-Being: A Reformulation of the Social Isolation Hypothesis." *American Sociological Review* 48: 174–87.

Thompson, E.P. 1971. "The Moral Economy of the English Crowd in the Eighteenth Century," *Past and Present* 50: 76–136.

Thornton, Patricia A., and Sherry Olson. 1991. "Family Contexts of Fertility and Infant Survival in Nineteenth-Century Montréal." *Journal of Family History* 16 (4): 401–17.

Thornton, Patricia A., and Sherry Olson. 2001. "A Deadly Discrimination among Montréal Infants, 1860–1900." *Continuity and Change* 16 (1): 95–135.

Tilly, Charles. 1984. *Big Structures, Large Processes, Huge Comparisons.* New York: Russell Sage Foundation.

Todd, Jennifer. 2006. *Identity, Identity Change and Group Boundaries in Northern Ireland.* Unpublished manuscript. UCD Geary Institute: Dublin.

Torpe, Lars. 2003. "Social Capital in Denmark: A Deviant Case?" *Scandinavian Political Studies* 26 (1): 27–48.

Tremblay, Marc-Adélard, and Gérald Fortin. 1964. *Les comportements économiques de la famille salariée du Québec: une étude des conditions de vie, des besoins et des aspirations de la famille canadienne-française d'aujourd'hui.* Québec: Les Presses de l'Université Laval.

Trostle, James. A., and Johannes Sommerfeld. 1996. "Medical Anthropology and Epidemiology." *Annual Review of Anthropology* 25: 253–74.

Tully, James. 2000. "Struggles over Recognition and Distribution." *Constellations* 7 (4): 469–82.

Turmel, A., and L. Hamelin. 1995. "La grande faucheuse d'enfants : la mortalité infantile depuis le tournant du siècle." *Revue canadienne de sociologie et d'anthropologie* 32 (4): 439–63.

Twenge, J. M., and Crocker, J. 2002. "Race and Self-Esteem: Meta-Analyses Comparing Whites, Blacks, Hispanics, Asians, and American Indians and Comment on Gray-Little and Hafdahl." *Psychological Bulletin* 128: 371–408.

Tyler, Tom R., and Steven Blader. 2000. *Cooperation in Groups: Procedural Justice, Social Identity and Behavioral Engagement.* London: Psychology Press.

UNAIDS (Joint United Nations Programme on HIV/AIDS). 2002. *Epidemiological Fact Sheets on HIV/AIDS and Sexually Transmitted Infections: 2002 Update Uganda.* Geneva: United Nations/UNICEF/World Health Organization.

UNAIDS (Joint United Nations Programme on HIV/AIDS). 2005. *AIDS in Africa: Three Scenarios to 2025.* Geneva: UNAIDS.

UNAIDS (Joint United Nations Programme on HIV/AIDS). 2006. *2006 Report on the Global AIDS Epidemic.* Geneva: UNAIDS.

UNAIDS (Joint United Nations Programme on HIV/AIDS). 2007. *AIDS Epidemic Update: December 2007.* Geneva: UNAIDS.

UNAIDS/WHO. 2002. *AIDS Epidemic Update, December 2002.* Geneva: Joint United Nations Programme on HIV/AIDS (UNAIDS) and World Health Organization (WHO).

UNAIDS/WHO. 2005. *AIDS Epidemic Update: December 2005.* Geneva: Joint United Nations Programme on HIV/AIDS (UNAIDS) and World Health Organization (WHO).

UNICEF. 1999. "Women in Transition." In *The MONEE Project Regional Monitoring Report. No. 6.* Florence, Italy: ICDC.

United Nations Development Program (UNDP). 2004. *Human Development Report 2004: Cultural Liberty in Today's Diverse World.* New York: UNDP and Oxford University Press.

U.S. Agency for International Development (USAID). 2002. *What Happened in Uganda? Declining HIV Prevalence, Behavior Change, and the National Response.* Washington, DC: USAID.

Uslaner, Eric M. 2003. "Trust, Democracy and Governance: Can Government Policies Influence Generalized Trust?" In *Generating Social Capital*, edited by Dietlind Stolle and Marc Hooghe. New York: Palgrave Macmillan.

Vagero, Denny, and Robert Erikson. 1997. "Socioeconomic Inequalities in Morbidity and Mortality in Western Europe." *Lancet* 350 (9076): 516–18.

Vagero, Denny, and Olle Lundberg. 1989. "Health Inequalities in Britain and Sweden." *Lancet* 2 (8653): 35–36.

Valle, Carla. 2003. "Political Catholicism in Post-War Italy: How Social Organizations Respond to Political Change." Ph.D. Dissertation, Department of Government, Harvard University.

Vallières, Pierre. 1969. *Nègres Blancs d'Amérique: Aautobiographie Précoce d'un Terroriste Québécois*. Montréal: Parti pris.

Van Cott, Donna Lee. 2006. "Multiculturalism versus Neoliberalism in Latin America." In *Multiculturalism and the Welfare State*, edited by Keith Banting and Will Kymlicka. Oxford: Oxford University Press.

Van Parijs, Philippe. 2004. "Cultural Diversity Against Economic Solidarity?" In *Cultural Diversity versus Economic Solidarity*, edited by Philippe Van Parijs. Brussels: Deboeck Université Press.

Veenstra, Gerry. 2005. "Social Space, Social Class and Bourdieu: Health Inequalities in British Columbia, Canada." *Health and Place* 13 (1): 14–31.

Wacquant, Loic. 1999. *Les Prisons de la Misère*. Paris: Raisons d'Agir.

Wacquant, Loic. 2004. Punir les Pauvres: *Le Nouveau Gouvernement de l'Insecurité Social*. Marseille: Agone.

Wade, Robert Hunter. 2004. "Is Globalization Reducing Poverty and Inequality?" *World Development* 32 (4): 567–89.

Wagstaff, Adam, Pierella Paci, and Eddy van Doorslaer. 1991. "On the Measurement of Inequalities in Health." *Social Science and Medicine* 33 (5): 545–57.

Walkowitz, Judith. 1980. *Prostitution and Victorian Society*. Cambridge: Cambridge University Press.

Wallerstein, Immanuel. 1974. *The Modern World-System I: Capitalist Agriculture and the Origins of the European World-Economy in the Sixteenth Century*. New York: Academic Press.

Wallerstein, Immanuel. 1980. *The Modern World-System II: Mercantilism and the Consolidation of the European World-Economy, 1600–1750*. San Diego: Academic Press.

Wallerstein, Immanuel. 1989. *The Modern World System III: The Second Era of Great Expansion of the Capitalist World-Economy, 1730–1840s*. San Diego: Academic Press.

Wallerstein, Nina. 2002. "Empowerment to Reduce Health Disparities." *Scandinavian Journal of Public Health* 30 (2): 72–7.

Wallis, J., and B. Dollery. 2002. "Social Capital and Local Government Capacity." *Australian Journal of Public Administration* 61 (3): 76–85.

Warren, Mark, ed. 1999. *Democracy and Trust*. New York: Cambridge University Press.

Warren, Mark. 2001. "Power and Conflict in Social Capital." In *Beyond Tocqueville: Civil Society and the Social Capital Debate in Comparative Perspective*, edited by Bob Edwards, Michael W. Foley, and Mario Diani. Hanover, NH: University Press of New England.

Watkins, Susan Cotts. 2004. "Navigating the AIDS Epidemic in Rural Malawi." *Population and Development Review* 30 (4): 673–705.

Weaver, Anne H. 2005. "Reciprocal Evolution of the Cerebellum and Neocortex in Fossil Humans." *Proceedings of the National Academy of Sciences* 102 (10): 3576–80.

Weber, Eugen. 1976. *Peasants into Frenchmen: The Modernization of Rural France, 1871–1914.* Stanford, CA: Stanford University Press.

Weber, Max. 1978. *Economy and Society, Vols. 1 and 2.* Berkeley: University of California Press.

Weil, David N. 2005. "Accounting for the Effect of Health on Economic Growth." National Bureau of Economic Research working paper 11455. Cambridge, MA: NBER.

Wheaton, Blair, and Philippa Clarke. 2003. "Space Meets Time: Integrating Temporal and Contextual Influences on Mental Health in Early Adulthood." *American Sociological Review.* 68 (5): 680–706.

Whiteside, Alan, Robert Mattes, Samantha Willan, and Ryann Manning. 2002. "Examining HIV/AIDS in Southern Africa through the Eyes of Ordinary Southern Africans." Rondebosch, South Africa: Centre for Social Science Research, Democracy in Africa Unit, University of Capetown.

Wilkinson, Richard G. 1986. "Income and Mortality." In *Class and Health: Research and Longitudinal Data,* edited by Richardson Wilkinson. London: Tavistock.

Wilkinson, Richard G. 1996. *Unhealthy Societies. The Afflictions of Inequality.* New York: Routledge.

Wilkinson, Richard. 1997. "Health Inequalities: Relative or Absolute Standards?" *British Medical Journal* 314: 591–5.

Wilkinson, Richard G. 1998. "Letter to the Editor." *Social Science and Medicine* 47 (3): 411–12.

Wilkinson, Richard G. 1999. "Health Hierarchy and Social Anxiety." *Annals of the New York Academy of Sciences* 896 (1): 48–63.

Wilkinson, Richard G. 2001. *Mind the Gap: Hierarchies, Health and Human Evolution.* New Haven, CT: Yale University Press.

Wilkinson, Richard G. 2005. *The Impact of Inequality: How to Make Sick Societies Healthier.* New York: Free Press.

Wilkinson, Richard G., and Kate E. Pickett. 2006. "Income Inequality and Population Health: A Review and Explanation of the Evidence." *Social Science and Medicine.* 62 (7): April. Available from "Articles in Press" at http://www.sciencedirect.com/science/journal/02779536.

Williams, David R. 1997. "Race and Health: Basic Questions, Emerging Directions." *Annals of Epidemiology* 7: 322–33.

Williams, David R. 1999. "Race, Socioeconomic Status, and Health. The Added Effects of Racism and Discrimination." *Annals of the New York Academy of Sciences.* 896: 173–88.

Williams, David R. 2005. "Patterns and Causes of Disparities in Health." In *Policy Challenges in Modern Health Care,* edited by David Mechanic, Lynn B. Rogut, and David C. Colby. Piscataway, NJ: Rutgers University Press.

Williams, D.R., and M. Harris-Reid. 1999. "Race and Mental Health: Emerging Patterns and Promising Approaches." In *A Handbook for the Study of Mental Health: Social Contexts, Theories, and Systems,* edited by Allan V. Horwitz and Teresa L. Scheid. New York: Cambridge University Press.

Williams, David R., Harold W. Neighbors, and James S. Jackson. 2003. "Racial/Ethnic Discrimination and Health: Findings from Community Studies." *American Journal of Public Health* 93 (2): 200–8.

Williams, Raymond. 1977. *Marxism and Literature*. Oxford: Oxford University Press.

Williamson, Oliver. 1985. *The Economic Institutions of Capitalism*. New York: Free Press.

Willis, Paul. 1977. *Learning to Labour: How Working Class Kids Get Working Class Jobs*. Farnborough, Hants, UK: Saxon House.

Willms, J. Douglas. 1999. "The Effects of Families, Schools, and Communities." In *Developmental Health and the Wealth of Nations: Social, Biological, and Educational Dynamics*, edited by Daniel P. Keating and Clyde Hertzman. New York: Guilford Press.

Wilson, Edward O. 1998. *Consilience: The Unity of Knowledge*. New York: Knopf.

Wimmer, Andreas. 2008. "The Making and Unmaking of Ethnic Boundaries: A Multilevel Process Theory." *American Journal of Sociology* 113 (4): 970–1022.

Wolf, Joan. 2004. *Harnessing the Holocaust: The Politics of Memory in France*. Stanford, CA: Stanford University Press.

Wolfe, Alan, and Jyette Klausen. 1997. "Identity Politics and the Welfare State." *Social Philosophy and Policy* 14 (2): 213–55.

Wolfe, Alan, and Jyette Klausen. 2000. "Other Peoples." *Prospect* (Dec.): 28–33.

Wong, Carol A., Jacquelynne S. Eccles, and Arnold Sameroff. 2003. "The Influence of Ethnic Discrimination and Ethnic Identification on African American Adolescents' School and Socioemotional Adjustment." *Journal of Personality* 71 (6): 1197–232.

World Bank. 1993. *World Development Report 1993. Investing in Health*. Oxford: Oxford University Press, p. 34.

World Bank, Agriculture and Environment Operations Division. 1997. *Vietnam: Economic Sector Report on Industrial Pollution Prevention*. Washington, DC: World Bank.

World Bank. 2002. *Education and HIV/AIDS: A Window of Hope*. Washington, DC: The International Bank for Reconstruction and Development/The World Bank.

World Commission on Globalization. 2004. *A Fair Globalization: Creating Opportunities for All*. Geneva: The International Labour Office.

Worthman, Carol M., and Jennifer Kuzara. 2005. "Life History and the Early Origins of Health Differentials." *American Journal of Human Biology* 17 (1): 95–112.

Wuthnow, Robert. 2002. "United States: Bridging the Privileged and the Marginalized." In *Democracies in Flux*, edited by Robert D. Putnam. New York: Oxford University Press.

Yang, Dali L. 1996. *Calamity and Reform in China: State, Society, and Institutional Change since the Great Leap Famine*. Stanford, CA: Stanford University Press.

Yang, Lawrence H., and Pamela Collins. 2004. "Measuring Mental Illness Stigma." *Schizophrenia Bulletin* 30 (3): 511–41.

Yang, Lawrence H., Arthur Kleinman, Bruce G. Link, Jo C. Phelan, Sing Lee, and Byron Good. 2007. "Culture and Stigma: Adding Moral Experience to Stigma Theory." *Social Science and Medicine* 62: 1524–35.

Yashar, Deborah. 1999. "Democracy, Indigenous Movements, and the Postliberal Challenge in Latin America," *World Politics* 52 (1): 76–104.

Zambon, Alessio, Will Boyce, Ester Cois, Candace Currie, Patrizia Lemma, Paola Dalmasso, Alberto Borraccino, and Franco Cavallo. 2006. "Do Welfare Regimes

Mediate the Effect of Socioeconomic Position on Health in Adolescence? A Cross-National Comparison in Europe, North America, and Israel." *International Journal of Health Services* 36 (2): 309–29.

Zartman, I. William. 1995. *Collapsed States: The Disintegration and Restoration of Legitimate Authority.* Boulder, CO: Lynne Rienner Publishers.

Ziff, Edward, and Israel Rosenfield. 2006. "Evolving Evolution." *New York Review of Books* 53 (8).

Zuberi, Dan M. 2001. *Transfers Matter Most.* Luxembourg Income Study working paper 271: Luxemburg: LIS.

Zuberi, Dan M. 2006. *Differences That Matter: Social Policy and the Working Poor in the United States and Canada.* Ithaca, NY: Cornell University Press.

Zubrzycki, Geneviève. 2006. *Auschwitz with, or without the Cross? Nationalism and Religion in Post-communist Poland.* Chicago: University of Chicago Press.

Zurn, Christopher. 2004. "Group Balkanization or Societal Homogenization: Is There a Dilemma between Recognition and Distribution Struggles?" *Public Affairs Quarterly* 18 (2): 159–86.

Index

ABC campaign, 135, 137
abstinence, 137
access, 54, 203, 226
achievement, 163
Ackernecht, Erwin, 203, 204
Adler, Nancy, 63
administrative capacity, 119, 204
affluence, 255, 262. *See also* wealth
Africa, 3, 128, 131, 233, 261, 263, 279.
    See also Botswana; Uganda
African Comprehensive HIV/AIDS
    Partnership (ACHAP), 136, 138
African National Congress (ANC), 121
African-Americans, 160, 236, 245
    and coping strategies, 78
    and group identification, 156
    anti-racism among, 158–9, 160
Age of Reform, 213–17, 224
agency, 33, 105, 119, 153, 174, 270
AIDS, 128, 131, 133, 147. *See also* HIV
    and cultural frameworks, 16, 96
    leadership against, 134–5
    and moral identity, 149
    prevention programs, 15, 144
    responses to, 3, 128, 131, 132–4, 139,
        147–8
    in South Africa, 121
    stigma of, 142–6
    summary of issue, 128–32
    Treatment Action Campaign, 121
AIDS Commission, 137
AIDS Information Centre, 141

AIDS/STD Unit (Botswana), 136, 143,
    144
Alesina, Alberto, 232, 239, 245
Allen, Tim, 141, 142, 144
allostasis, 57, 74
allostatic overload, 57, 74, 76
Altman, Dennis, 148
Anderson, Benedict, 12
anger, 5, 6, 10, 85
antibiotics, 26
anti-development, 106, 107
anti-vaccination movement, 213, 222
anxiety, 5, 6, 10, 84, 85, 93. *See also* stress
archemyth, 189
associational life, 7, 8, 17, 89, 99, 100,
    228, 247
autonomy, 8, 79, 80, 93, 139, 154, 157,
    170, 222, 262

Baccaro, Lucio, 121, 122
balance, 85
Baldwin, Peter, 130, 203, 204, 211, 225
Baltic countries, 35, 36
Banting, Keith, 241
Beckfield, Jason, 114, 115
behavior, 54, 56
Bell, Daniel, 264
belonging, 202, 244. *See also* connection
Berkman, Lisa, 170
biculturalism, 164
Bill and Melinda Gates Foundation, 136
biological embedding, 33, 47, 63, 68–9

biological pathways, 5, 43–4, 152
biological systems, 58–60
Black Nationalism, 266
Black Power, 266
Blair, Tony, 276
Bluebond-Langner, Myra, 149
Boards of Guardians, 215
bodily integrity, 222, 224
bonding, 78, 228
Booth, John, 99
Bosanquet, Helen, 220
Botswana, 134, 138, 139
    compared with Uganda, 102, 132, 133
    cultural frames and AIDS in, 16
    institutions and culture in, 124, 138–9,
        140–1, 142
    and NGOs, 137, 138
    public health approach of, 134, 137
    reasons for failure with AIDS, 128,
        146–7
    response to AIDS in, 3, 15, 121, 123,
        133–4, 135, 136
    and stigma against AIDS, 143–4
boundaries, 89, 95, 102, 114, 155, 233,
        249, 250
    class, 167
    and collective imaginaries, 12
    group, 156, 157, 168
    racial, 245
    of responsibility, 206
    social, 13
    and social organizations, 10
    symbolic, 7, 11, 157, 167
    and webs of meaning, 11
boundary work, 13, 158
boundedness, 37
Bourdieu, Pierre, 166
Boyce, W. Thomas, 62
brain, 59, 79
Brazil, 120
Brenner, Robert, 259
Bristol-Myers Squibb, 136
Butler, Josephine, 223

Campbell, Catherine, 97, 147
Canada,
    compared with United States, 44–5,
        47–8
    income inequality in, 31

multicultural policies in, 18, 251–2
    public attitudes in, 246–7
capabilities, 59, 60, 80–1, 84, 85, 109
    and associational life, 90
    collective, 131
    and collective imaginaries, 92
    of communities, 95–7, 102
    and cultural frameworks, 13, 124
    expansion of, 109
    and life challenges, 85, 86, 89
    personal, 6–7, 14, 15, 85, 91, 130
    and social recognition, 13
    and status, 93
capability approach, 104, 105, 107–9,
        113, 123, 124–5
capacity, 122
capital accumulation, 106
capitalism, 21. *See also* neoliberalism
    and population health, 255–6
    shifting paradigms of, 254–6
    state-centric paradigm of, 256–62
capitalist world-system, 284
capitalist/socialist divide, 110
Carter, Prudence, 164
Castoriadis, Cornelius, 12, 174
Catholic Church, 123, 179, 183, 196
Ceará, Brazil, 120, 124
Center for Policy Studies, 273
Cereseto, S., 110
Chadwick, Edwin, 209, 210, 211, 215,
        216
Chamberlain, Joseph, 219
Chambers, Julius, 159
Charity Organization Society, 220
child care, 46
childhood, 62–3
children, 212
cholera, 208, 209, 211, 218
Cité libre, 183
citizenship, 44, 101, 130, 202, 203,
        206, 212, 213, 224, 266. *See also*
        citizenship regime
    British norms of, 224
    concept of, 100–1
    cultural, 13
    and inclusion/exclusion, 205
    narrative of, in England, 213
    and the poor, 215
    and public health, 30, 202, 205

transnational, 130
citizenship regime, 17, 18, 204, 205–7,
  211, 215, 224
  changes in, 218–19
  and non-citizens, 221
  and role of public vs. private
    provision, 209
  and the sanitary idea, 207–25
civic gospel, 220
Civil Rights movement, 265
civil society, 32
class, 7, 167, 236, 255
cleanliness, 225
Clinton, Bill, 276, 277
collective action, 8, 9, 84, 85, 89, 91,
  116, 124, 126, 155
collective identity, 13, 144
collective imaginary, 90–2, 94, 95, 96,
  119, 120, 124, 184, 190, 193, 206,
  232, 245
  as articulation of reason and
    myth, 171–5
  and capacity for mobilizaton, 96
  and citizenship regime, 17
  cost of, 102
  of Czech Republic, 20
  defined, 12, 170, 174
  French Canadian, 186–90
  and health, 14
  impact of, on social life, 197
  importance of, 198
  and multiculturalism, 229, 253
  and social relations, 91
  and status, 101
  suppleness of, 18
  and the welfare state, 229
collective narratives, 7, 10, 12, 14, 17,
  102, 119, 120, 124, 146
  and population health, 14
  and webs of meaning, 11
collective representations, 18
collective solidarities, 134
commercial interest, 204
communicative strategy, 122
Communist Party, 118, 119, 122, 123,
  125, 257, 260, 261, 263
communities, 23, 61
  capabilities of, 95–7, 102
Community-Driven Regulation (CDR), 122

comparative perspective, 34–7. *See also*
  Canada; United States
competence, 11, 61, 78, 80, 118, 121,
  129, 133, 141, 159, 160
competition, 86
condoms, 135, 137, 144, 147, 148, 149
Condor, Susan, 154
connectedness. *See* social connectedness
consciousness, 79–80
consumption, 160
contagion, 207, 209
Contagious Diseases Acts, 222–4
control, sense of, 58, 74–7
cooperation, 85, 93
coping, 153, 171
Cornell, Stephen, 10, 132, 139
corroding effect, 235, 237, 248, 249, 252
cortisol, 58, 74, 75, 77
credit, 281
Crepaz, Markus, 240, 243
critical period effects, 63, 70
Crocker, Jennifer, 165
crowding out, 235, 236, 237, 248
Cuba, 286
cultural capital, 164
cultural citizenship, 151, 155
cultural diversity. *See* multiculturalism
cultural frameworks, 7, 12, 15, 19, 83,
  87, 88, 96, 101, 254, 256
  and comparative studies, 19
  and institutions, 5, 14–15
  and mobilization, 10
  and policy making, 17
  and policy regimes, 15
cultural match, 132, 139
cultural misrecognition, 236
cultural models, 155, 160
cultural repertoires, 1, 18, 152, 153, 155,
  161, 163, 164, 165, 167, 197
  changes in, 262–72
cultural schemas, 152
cultural scripts, 253
cultural structures, 2, 4, 73, 155, 167
cumulative effect, 34
Czech Republic, 3, 20, 48–50

daycare, 86
decolonization, 179, 188, 263
decommodification, 281

deindustrialization, 272, 275
democracy, 109, 117, 140, 141
Deneulin, Séverine, 109
depression, 5, 6
deprivation, 8, 10, 93, 94, 104, 105, 154
destigmatization strategies, 13, 152, 154,
    155–8, 161, 198, 228, 250
  of African-American elites, 159–60
  of African-American marketing
    executives, 160
  comparison of, 167
  impact on mental health, 162–5
  of North African immigrants, 161
  results of, 168
determinism, 63, 68–70
development, 106
  institutional approach, 73–4
development theory, 104, 106, 107,
    109, 126
developmental mediators, 68, 71–2
developmental pathways, 63, 72
developmental systems, 58–60
developmentalist state, 261, 262
dikgotla, 138
discrimination, 13, 64, 152, 160. *See also*
    racism
  and agency, 153
  and AIDS, 147
  and mental health, 162–5
  and social recognition, 13
  and stress, 75
disease-prevention, 129
distribution
  of health, 7, 12, 23
  of resources, 4, 7
  of status, 12
distrust, 227
diversity, 228–31, 248, 253
Dodson, Betty Lou, 160
Dona Bochang, Vietnam, 123, 125
Dowd, Jennifer B., 75
Dowsett, Gary, 148
Dunn, James R., 2, 30
Duplessis, Maurice, 183
Durbach, Nadja, 222
Durham Report (1839), 190
Durkheim, Emile, 25, 43,
    87, 91
duties, 206

Eastern Europe, 260, 279
Eberstadt, Nick, 92
economic disparities, 60
economic marginalization, 236
education, 53, 62, 112, 113, 144
  about AIDS, 136
  access to, 86
  as destigmatization strategy, 160
  among French Canadians, 180
  and inequality, 115
efficacy, 95, 150. *See also* self-efficacy
egalitarianism, 267
embodiment, 33, 47, 68, 139
England. *See* United Kingdom
environmental determinism, 69
epidemiology of daily life, 33
epigenesis, 70
Epstein, Helen, 96
Erikson, Kai, 92
Esping-Anderson, Gøsta, 45
Estonia, 35
ethnicity, 53, 54, 61, 101, 179, 232, 244,
    245, 246, 249, 250
  and population health, 226–7
  and social boundaries, 11
  and social solidarity, 265
  and support for social programs, 246
ethnocentrism, 227, 232
Europe, 28, 31, 251, 258, 262,
    277, 278
Evans, Peter, 96
evo/devo, 70
evolution, 70
exclusion, 152, 205, 229
experience, 34

Fabianism, 220
Family Welfare Educators, 136
famine, 110, 116–18, 123, 263
Farmer, Paul, 97
Farr, William, 209, 217, 218
Finland, 35, 36
fluoxetine, 59, 77
Fordism, 258, 267
Foucault, Michel, 130
fragmentary thought, 187
France, 161, 202, 265
Fraser, Nancy, 236
Freeman, Gary, 233

French Canadians, 179, 180, 188, 190
  economic status of, 180
  and education, 180
  life expectancy among, 192
  stereotypes about, 190
Friedman, Milton, 273
frustration, 43, 84, 85

Gabon, 110, 111
gas and water socialism, 219
gay community, 128, 148
gender, 61, 265
gender gap, 45. *See also* life expectancy
gene-environment interaction, 77
General Board of Health (UK), 210
genetic determinism, 69
genetics, 70, 226, 244
geoepidemiological location, 204
germ theory, 222
Giovani, Nikki, 159
Gitlin, Todd, 235
Glaeser, Edward, 232
Global South, , 104–6, 107, 109, 117,
  118, 126, 261, 278, 279
globalization, 275, 283–5
Goffman, Erving, 144
Goldman, Maureen, 75
Gottlieb, Gilbert, 70
governance, 206, 207, 209, 214,
  215, 216
  changes in, 218–19
gradient effect, 27, 28, 56, 58, 61,
  63, 71
gradients. *See* health gradient
Grande Noirceur, 180, 183, 190
Great Darkness, 180
Green, Edward C., 147
Groulx, Lionel, 187, 189
group identification, 156, 157, 165
growth theory, 104, 109, 113, 124,
  125, 126

habitus, 33, 47, 68, 92
Hacker, Jacob, 273, 287
Hall, Peter, 36, 258
happiness, 24
Hayek, Friedrich, 273
Heald, Suzette, 142
health agents, 120

health gradient, 4, 34, 54. *See also* social
  gradient
  characteristics of, 27–9
  cross-national variations in, 90
  and emotional factors, 152
  explanations for, 83–4
  frameworks for, 154–5
  and socioeconomic status, 26–33
health/wealth effect, 53
heart disease, 26, 28
heterogeneity/redistribution trade-off,
  230, 231–3, 240, 244–8
Hirschman, Albert, 157
HIV, 3, 129, 133, 135, 147, 149. *See also*
  AIDS
  infection rates, 16, 96, 128, 134
Hobsbawm, Eric, 257, 262
hotel workers, 47–8
house inspections, 213
Human Development Index, 108,
  109, 112
hygiene, public, 204
hypothalamic-pituitary-adrenocortical
  (HPA) system, 5, 152

identity, 59, 73, 75, 79, 148, 149, 155,
  170, 175, 189, 248. *See also* social
  identity
  black cultural, 160
  in Canada, 251
  and the citizenship regime, 206
  collective, 64, 80, 155
  and collective imaginaries, 198
  development of, 79
  group, 14, 163, 164
  moral, 132
  national, 189
  and neo-nationalism, 184
  racial, 163
identity politics, 226, 229
immigrants, 47
immigrants and immigration, 102,
  230, 233
  in Canada, 251–2
  cultural repertoires of, 161
  and multicultural policies, 241–2
  opposition to, 231
  and social solidarity, 18
  and social spending, 18, 238–9, 240

inclusion, 205, 221
income distribution, 31, 44, 49, 50, 52, 54, 56, 86, 94, 95, 210
income inequality, 7, 8, 30, 31, 32, 44, 50, 61, 66, 113, 133, 284, 285
    and health outcomes, 31, 202, 203
    in poor countries, 114
    and population health, 113–16
    and the social gradient, 54
    and social spending, 43
    and status, 94
income volatility, 281, 285
income, national, 4, 15, 23, 50, 111, 112
indigenous peoples, 239, 242
individual relations, 32
inequality, 29, 43, 152, 255. *See also* income inequality
infant determinism, 69
infant mortality, 191, 192, 195
infectious diseases, 28
Inglehart, Ronald, 99, 265
injustice, 155, 248
Institute for Economic Affairs, 273
institutions, 14, 108, 124–26
    and citizenship regimes, 18
    and culture in Botswana, 138
    in Czech Republic, 50
    evolution of, 50
    importance of, 50–1, 52
    public, 124
    reliance on, in Russia, 49–50
    role of, 14–15
    social, 29
integrative paradigm, 169
intellectuals, 198
International Monetary Fund (IMF), 278, 279

Jackson, James, 78
Japan, 258, 260, 262
Jenkins, Richard, 156
Jenson, Jane, 105, 286
John Bull, 214, 219
John Henryism, 164
John Q. Public, 267
Joseph, James, 159, 160

Kalt, Joseph, 10, 132, 139
Karlström, Mikael, 139, 140

Kawachi, Ichiro, 44
Kenya, 102, 142, 145
Kerala, India, 15, 110, 117–20, 121, 123, 124, 125, 126, 286
Kesler, Christel, 247
kgotla system, 140
Khama, Ian, 140
Khama, Seretse, 139, 140
Klausen, Jyette, 235
Klinenberg, Eric, 96
Kraemer, Helena Chmura, 66
Krieger, Nancy, 154, 162
Kruger, Ann, 279
Kumlin, Staffan, 99
Kuzara, Jennifer, 57
Kymlicka, Will, 101

labor unions, 47, 268, 272
Ladies' National Association for the Repeal of the Contagious Diseases Act, 223
Lamont, Michèle, 148
latent effects, 20, 34, 63
Latin America, 261
Latvia, 35
leadership, 134–5
Lena, Hugh F., 110
Lévesque, René, 183
Lewis, Stephen, 142
L-HPA, 74, 75, 76, 79
liberation, 264
life challenges, 6, 7, 11, 84, 85
life expectancy, 25, 109
    in Baltic countries, 35–6
    in Canada, 3, 38, 42
    as core capability, 109
    in Czech Republic, 3, 48
    and education, 112
    in Europe, 278
    in Finland, 35–6
    and GDP per capita, 31
    and health care spending, 26
    and income, 35–6
    and income inequality, 61
    in Kerala, 118
    male vs. female, 38, 45–6, 61
    in nineteenth-century Britain, 207
    in Quebec, 192
    and race, 61

role of medication in, 26
in Russia, 3, 48
in the United States, 3, 38, 42, 278
of women, 3
Link, Bruce G., 55, 56, 83, 254
Linteau, Paul Andre, 185
literacy, 180
Lithuania, 35
living standards, 105
local biologies, 47, 48
Local Councils (Uganda), 141–2, 146
London Epidemiological Society, 221
London, Brace, 111
longitudinal perspective, 23
Luxembourg Income Study, 29

Mackenbach, Johan P., 113
Marc, Alexandre, 252
markets, 51, 125, 260, 281–3
Marmot, Michael G., 95, 154
Marx, Karl, 87, 231
Masire, Ketumile, 135
material resources, 4, 7, 83, 97, 101
McEwen, Bruce, 74, 76
McKeown thesis, 105
McKeown, Thomas, 26, 105
mediator model, , 66–8, 71, 73, 75, 78
medical insurance, 47
membership, 206
Merck Foundation, 134, 136
merit, 202
meta-narratives, 197
Meyer, John, 130
miasma, 209, 216
microeconomics, 271
migrant stock, 238
Miguel, Edward, 102
Miller, David, 249
Milner, Thirman, 159
minorities, 53, 239, 242, 266
misdiagnosis effect, 235–6, 237, 248
mobility, population, 211
mobilization, 10, 96, 114, 119, 121, 122,
    123, 124, 125, 131, 148, 213
    and AIDS, 128, 137, 144–6, 147, 148,
    150
    and AIDS prevention, 132
    in Botswana, 138
    in Kerala, 118

and the "sanitary idea," 207
social, 15
and social organizations, 10
in Uganda, 141
modernist thesis, 181–2, 183–4, 185,
    190, 199
modernity's paradox, 203
modernization theory, 269, 270
Mogae, Festus, 135, 140
Moi, Daniel arap, 142
monetarism, 273, 274
monotonic effects, 53
Montréal, 180, 181, 182, 190, 192, 196
moral character, 165
moral economy, 91
moral identity, 149
moral order, 91, 148, 155
moral universalism, 161
morality, 158
morbidity, 78
Morpeth, 210
mortality, 25, 26, 31, 38, 110, 192
multicultural policies, 101, 234–8, 241–4,
    248–52
    merits of, 252
    and nationhood, 18
    and social spending, 18
multiculturalism, 159, 230, 234, 247,
    251, 266. *See also* multicultural
    policies
    and identity politics, 229
    and nation-building, 251
    and the welfare state, 252
Municipal Corporations Act of 1835, 214
Municipal Reform Act of 1835, 217
municipal socialism, 219
Museveni, Yoweri, 134, 135, 139, 141,
    142, 146
myths, 14, 92, 153, 163, 174, 189, 190,
    198
    and collective imaginary, 173–4
    contradictory, 188
    definition of, 173–4
    French Canadian, 184, 186–90, 186–93

narratives, 174
narratives, cultural, 178–85
National Association for the Repeal of
    the Contagious Diseases Act, 223

National Association of People Living
    with AIDS (NAPWA), 121
national identity, 229, 232, 235, 245,
    248, 249, 253. *See also* nationhood
national pride, 250
National Resistance Movement
    (Uganda), 135, 139, 141, 146
nation-building, 251
nationhood, 18, 229–30, 235, 253
nature vs. nurture, 69
neighborhood, 61
neoliberalism, 106, 205, 255, 273
    and population health, 287
    characteristics of, 280–5
    rise of, 272–80
neo-quarantinism, 211, 213
neuroscience, 59
Nevers, Edmond de, 187
New Poor Law (1834), 215
New Russia Barometer, 49
Newman, Katherine, 63
nongovernment organizations (NGOs),
    121, 128, 131, 133, 137, 138, 140,
    141, 142, 146, 149
North Africans, 161
North America, 262
North, Douglass, 108
Norton, Eleanor Holmes, 159, 160
Novick, Peter, 266
Nussbaum, Martha, 109

O'Rourke, Dara, 110, 122, 123, 125
obesity, 76, 95, 201
occupation, 53
Old Corruption, 214, 216
ontological security, 10
Organization for Economic Cooperation
    and Development (OECD), 28, 29,
    84, 238
Ottawa, 191
outcome inequalities, 66
oxytocin, 78
Oyserman, Daphna, 10

paleoanthropology, 59
Papadakis, Konstantinos, 121, 122
pathway effect, 34
pathway effects, 62, 63, 70
personality, 85

Phelan, Jo, 53, 55, 56, 83, 154, 254
Pickett, Kate, 113
Pierson, Paul, 20, 36
Pinker, Stephen, 69
Piot, Peter, 129
policy making,
    and social connectedness, 98–100
    and social hierarchy, 100–1
    as social resource creation, 83, 97–8
    and social resources, 16–18, 103
political narratives, 202
political rights, 86, 213, 214, 218, 221,
    224
politics, 203–5, 205–7
pollution, 33, 122, 123, 125
Poor Law Guardians, 212, 214, 222
Porter, Dorothy, 203, 210, 215
postmodernism, 251, 270
poststructuralism, 270
poverty, 29–30, 34, 110–6, 132, 215
Pritchett, Lance, 110
private provision, 255
property rights, 14, 15, 108, 125, 126,
    132
prophylactic strategies, 204
prosperity, 39–40, 50
prostitutes, 222
protection, chains of, 63
provision of services, 86
Prozac, 59, 77
psychosocial factors, 19, 33,
    64–5, 75
public health, 201, 202, 203–5
Public Health Act (1848), 209–10, 212,
    213, 217
Public Health Act (1872), 217
Public Health Act (1875), 217
Public Health Agency of Canada, 201
public provision, 23, 31, 38, 42, 43, 44,
    51, 52, 209, 255
Putnam, Robert, 23, 88, 90, 98, 99,
    227, 232

quarantines, 204, 209, 211,
    212, 223
Quebec, 190–7
Quebec Indians, 176–8
Québécois, 180, 184, 189. *See also*
    French Canadians

Quiet Revolution, 180, 183, 184, 185,
    189, 193, 197

race, 53, 54, 61, 101, 232, 236
    and population health, 226–7
    and social hierarchy, 227
    and social solidarity, 265
racial profiling, 101
racism, 152, 156, 227. *See also*
    discrimination
radicalism, 265
rape, 132
rational choice movement, 271
rationality, 175
Reagan, Ronald, 272, 274
reason, 172–3, 174, 175, 187
reciprocity, 88, 89
recognition politics, 226, 234
recognition/redistribution trade-off,
    240–4, 248–9
redistribution, 18, 41, 42, 44, 50, 52, 86,
    230, 232, 233, 238, 243, 251
    based on personhood, 248–9
    of income, 38
    inter-ethnic, 232
    of status, 101
    and political participation, 219
    politics of, 234
    social, 246
redistribution, income, 86
reflective consciousness, 6, 59, 79, 85
Reform Act of 1832, 214
religion, 158, 268–9
rent seeking, 279
resentment, 5, 10, 84, 268
resilience, 6, 8, 20, 62, 85, 89, 90, 91,
    130, 131, 153, 155, 162, 164, 190
Resistance Councils, 140
resources, distribution of, 30, 86
respect, 101
responsibility, 285
responsibility mix, 206, 207, 209, 213,
    215, 216, 218, 224
Révolution tranquille, 180
rhetoric, political, 101
Richard, Patricia Bayer, 99
rights, 206
risk accumulation, 63
Rosenberg, Tina, 129

Rothstein, Bo, 99
Rubin, Robert, 276
Runciman, W. G., 94
Russia, 3, 48–50, 193, 279

Saguenay region (Quebec), 191, 193
Sampson, Robert, 9
sanitarian interventions, 204
Sanitarians, 204, 207, 209, 215, 217,
    218, 219, 220
    opposition to, 220–4
sanitary idea, 205, 207, 209, 211, 213,
    216, 222
    and citizenship regime, 213–17
    partial implementation of, 207–13
    support for, 218–20
Sapolsky, Robert, 56, 57, 74, 76
Seattle, Washington, 47
security, 44, 47, 170, 255
selective serotonin re-uptake inhibitors
    (SSRI), 59
self-concept, 163
self-efficacy, 11, 14, 93, 162, 163, 164
self-esteem, 2, 13, 85, 93, 95, 153, 157,
    162, 163, 165
self-interest, 149
self-mastery, 164
self-worth, 154
Sen, Amartya, 6, 15, 59, 85, 107, 108,
    109, 110, 116, 117,
    124, 130
Senegal, 132
sensitive period effects, 63, 70
serotonergic system, 58, 77, 79
Setel, Philip, 96
Severe Acute Respiratory Syndrome
    (SARS), 201
sewers, 209, 211, 218
sexual coercion, 132
sexuality, 265
Shock Therapy, 279
Simon, John, 212
Skocpol, Theda, 99
Small, Mario, 164
smallpox, 208, 212, 222
Smith, George Davey, 166
smoking, 26
social capital, 8, 43, 51, 56, 64, 73, 88–9,
    227, 232, 246, 247

(*cont.*)
  and policy making, 98–100
  and social relations, 9
social categorization, 156
social class differentiation, 113
social cohesion, 18, 32, 56, 64, 88, 91
social collectivism, 220
social connectedness, 77–8, 87–8,
    88–9, 98–100, 227. *See also* social
    resources
social connection, 58
social disparities, 55, 60–1, 71–2, 72–3.
    See also status
social drift, 25
social epidemiology, 4, 9, 20, 34, 44, 54,
    82, 152, 154, 166, 203
social factors, 20–1
social factors, 19, 21, 23–6, 29–33, 83–5
social gospel, 219–20
social gradient. *See also* gradient effect
  causes of, 54–5
  conceptual framework of, 65–71
  definition of, 54
  outcomes of, 56–7
  patterns of, 60–3
  psychosocial factors of, 64–5
  social and developmental mediators
      of, 71–4
  strength of, across populations, 55
  systemic explanation of, 56–7
social hierarchy, 4, 17, 27, 32, 76, 87,
    93–5, 100–1, 114, 227, 228
social history, 171
social identity, 156
social imaginaries, 174, 175, 205, 262,
    267, 271, 277. *See also* collective
    imaginary
social inclusion, 151, 156
social inequality, 43–4
social infrastructure, 38
social investment, 286
social isolation, 91, 144, 227. *See also*
    stigma
social knowledge, 202, 203, 207,
    221, 224
social marginality, 203
social mediators, 68
social mobilization, 121, 135
social network analysis, 271

social networks, 7, 20, 43, 48, 73, 83,
    88, 89, 100, 102, 149,
    227, 228
  and collective mobilization, 96
  and health, 8, 89–90
  and logistical support, 9
  and policy delivery, 17
social organization, 16, 57, 96
social participation, 170. *See* connection
social partitioning, 54
social policy, 55
social polity, 64
social position, 55. *See also* status
social recognition, 11, 13–14, 93,
    101, 151
social relations, 4, 8, 9, 87–8, 103. *See
    also* social networks
social resources, 7, 9, 17, 20, 82, 83,
    103, 227
  access to, 7
  and cultural frameworks, 17
  distribution of, 94, 100
  and government, 84
  need to conserve, 22
  and policy making, 97–8
  and relationships, 88
  and social relations, 19
Social Science Association, 216, 223
social solidarity, 18, 102, 128, 144, 145,
    149, 205
social spending, 18, 30, 43, 238–9, 246,
    277
social structures, 51
social transformation, 119
social trust, 32, 44, 64, 78, 88, 89, 90,
    98, 99
social welfare policies, 48
societal aggregation levels, 32
societal support, 110, 114, 115,
    116, 123
Society for Women and AIDS in Zambia
    (SWAAZ), 145
socio-cultural/health framework, 169,
    171, 177, 185, 195, 199
socioeconomic environment,
    national, 32
socioeconomic factors, 33
socioeconomic gradient. *See* health
    gradient

socioeconomic status, 27, 28, 30, 61,
    227. *See also* health gradient
  as cause of health differences, 55
  as cause of health gradient, 83
  and health gradient, 4, 7, 83
  and social drift, 25
sociology, 171
solidarity, 132, 150, 165, 202, 230, 244,
    250, 265
  national, 229, 230, 232, 248, 249,
    250, 253
  and race, 245
Soskice, David, 258
South Africa, 96, 120–2, 123. *See also*
    South Africa
South African National AIDS Council
    (SANAC), 121
spending, 38, 40–1, 56. *See also* social
    spending
standard-form relationship, 27
state, role of, 216
status, 42, 43, 48, 55, 56, 87, 88, 93,
    101, 120, 153, 164, 242, 272, 273
  and capabilities, 93
  and collective imaginary, 101
  and education, 62
  effects of, on well-being, 32–3
  and genetic determinism, 69
  and health, 10–1
  and L-HPA functioning, 75
  and material circumstances, 32
  monotonic effect of, on health, 53
  multidimensionality of, 94
  psychosocial consequences of, 64
  redistribution of, 101
  and resilience, 155
  and social gradient, 55
  and social hierarchy, 227
  and social networks, 90
  and social organizations, 10
  and social recognition, 93
  and social resources, 20
  sources of, 94
  and stereotypes, 94
  and stigma, 153
status hierarchies, 8, 12, 65, 93
  and collective imaginaries, 12
  cross-national differences in, 95
  and social recognition, 13

Steensland, Brian, 198
stereotypes, 10, 12, 95, 151, 155, 189,
    249
Stewart, Frances, 109
stigma, 64, 80, 144
  and AIDS, 142–6, 147
  and racism, 152
  and status, 153
  and stress, 75
stigmatization, 227
stress, 62, 84, 255. *See also* wear
    and tear
  and biological pathways, 43
  as cause of illness, 84
  contributors to, 33
  identifying extent of, 84–5
  and social networks, 90
  and trade-offs, 76
stress model, 65
stress reactivity, 65
stress response system, 58, 63, 65, 68,
    74–7, 78, 79
structural adjustment, 279
students, 264
substate national groups, 242
Summers, Lawrence, 110
surveillance, 212, 222–4
survival thesis, 178–80, 183, 185, 190,
    193, 196, 199
Sweden, 45, 102, 275
sympathetic-adrenal-medullary (SAM)
    system, 5, 75
synthesis paradigm, 169
system, 56

Tajfel, Henry, 154
Tanzania, 97, 102, 145
Taylor, Charles, 175, 205
Taylor-Gooby, Peter, 239
Tendler, Judith, 110
Thatcher, Margaret, 272, 273,
    274
The AIDS Support Organisation (TASO),
    141, 146
therapy programs, 177
threshold effects, 54
tradition, 163
transfer payments, 30
travel, 211

Treatment Action Campaign (TAC), 121,
    122, 123
Trois-Rivières, 191
Trudeau, P. E., 183
trust, 88, 99, 232, 237,
    246–7
tuberculosis, 26

Uganda, 16, 96, 102, 128, 133, 135, 142
    compared with Botswana, 132
    cultural frames and AIDS in, 16
    institutions and culture in, 139–40,
        141–2
    leadership in, 134
    and NGOs, 137, 140, 141
    public health approach of, 137
    reasons for success with AIDS, 146–7
    response to AIDS in, 3, 15, 134
    and stigma against AIDS, 142–3
Ul-Haq, Mahbub, 108
unemployment, 100, 268
United Kingdom, 202
    citizenship regime and sanitary
        idea in, 207–25
    and gradient effect, 28
    income inequality in, 31
    and neoliberalism, 274
    quarantine policy in, 211–12
    sanitarian movement in, 207
    social capital in, 98
    social networks in, 100
    status hierarchy in, 95
United Nations, 108, 115, 127
United States
    and capitalist political economy, 256–7
    compared with Canada, 44–5, 47–8
    healthcare spending in, 4
    income inequality in, 31
    and neoliberalism, 274
    poverty rates in, 29
    race and ethnicity in, 233
    social capital in, 98–9
    workers in, 281
universities, 264, 265
University of Chicago, 273

Vaccination Act (1853), 212, 213, 221
Vaccination Act (1871), 218

Vaccination Officers, 221
vaccines and vaccinations, 26, 129, 209,
    212–13
Van Cott, Donna Lee, 237
Vancouver, British Columbia, 47–8
vasopressin, 78
venereal disease, 208, 223
victimhood, 267
Vietnam, 110, 111, 122, 125
Villermé, Louis René, 202
Volker, Paul, 274
voluntary associations, 98

Waitzkin, H., 110
Wallerstein, Immanuel, 284
Washington Consensus, 106, 277
water supply, 209, 210, 211, 218
wealth, 31, 32, 33, 38, 53, 56, 61,
    133, 285
    effect of, on population health, 33
wear and tear, 6, 46, 74, 84, 85, 93, 227,
    255, 282, 285
Webb, Beatrice and Sidney, 220
Weber, Max, 9, 12, 87, 93
webs of meaning, 11
welfare state, 228–31, 233, 240, 252,
    262, 276
well-being, 2, 24
Whitehall study, 26, 27
whites, 245
Wilkinson, Richard G., 32, 113,
    114, 154
Williams, Raymond, 271
Willoughby, Michael T., 70
Wolfe, Alan, 235
women, 46, 281, 282
women's movement, 46, 268
workers, 158–9
workplace issues, 23, 46, 75, 93
World Bank, 107
worth, 12
Worthman, Carol, 57
Wuthnow, Robert, 99

yellow fever, 209

Zambia, 112, 133, 145
Zimbabwe, 133, 145